File Manager Toolbar

Icon	Function
	Connect to network drive
	Disconnect from network drive
	Share your directory
	Stop sharing your directory
	View files by name only
	View file details
	Sort files by name
	Sort files by type
	Sort files by size
	Sort files by date

Networking with Windows™ for Workgroups

Cheryl Currid & Company

SYBEX®

San Francisco • Paris • Düsseldorf • Soest

Acquisitions Editor: Dianne King
Developmental Editor: David Kolodney
Editor: Brenda Kienan
Technical Editor: Dan Tauber
Assistant Editor: Abby Azrael
Book Designer: Diane Ellerbe
(Based on a design by: Helen Bruno)
Technical Artist: Diane Ellerbe
Desktop Publishing Specialists: Diane Ellerbe, Diane Bolin, Dianne Davison
Proofreaders: Dianne Davison, Dorothy Wolf, Diane Bolin
Indexer: Paul Kish
Cover Designer: Archer Design
Cover Photographer: Richard Miller

SYBEX is a registered trademark of SYBEX Inc.

TRADEMARKS: SYBEX has attempted throughout this book to distinguish proprietary trademarks from descriptive terms by following the capitalization style used by the manufacturer.

SYBEX is not affiliated with any manufacturer.

Every effort has been made to supply complete and accurate information. However, SYBEX assumes no responsibility for its use, nor for any infringement of the intellectual property rights of third parties which would result from such use.

Copyright© 1993 SYBEX Inc., 2021 Challenger Drive, Alameda, CA 94501. World rights reserved. No part of this publication may be stored in a retrieval system, transmitted, or reproduced in any way, including but not limited to photocopy, photograph, magnetic or other record, without the prior agreement and written permission of the publisher.

Library of Congress Card Number: 92-62326
ISBN: 0-7821-1228-5

Manufactured in the United States of America
10 9 8 7 6 5 4 3 2 1

To Ray, Tray, and Justin.
Thanks again.
- C.C.

Acknowledgments

Every book project turns out to be a team effort. This one brought together an especially energetic team. We pushed for a very aggressive timetable and drafted some willing (and not so willing) members to meet the commitment.

Thanks must first go to the Sybex team who, with a great spirit of cooperation, undertook this project. Our editor, Brenda Kienan, worked tirelessly to blend a chorus of voices that sometimes strayed out of key. Our technical reviewer, Dan Tauber, kept us in check, reminding us about details. We owe a great deal of thanks to acquisitions editor Dianne King for her lightning action in getting this book project from a crazy idea to a real concept to reality, and, of course, to managing editor Barbara Gordon for being so flexible about our design.

We'd also like to thank Tanya van Dam and Erin Carney of Microsoft for planting and sowing the seeds for this book. It turned out to be a great project, no matter how unrealistic our deadlines seemed at first.

We sincerely appreciate the efforts of Hedy Baker and John Sweney of Compaq Computer for help in securing a loaner printer. The Pagemarq printer performed flawlessly through over 8,000 pages of drafts and rewrites. Mike Clark will probably be surprised that this book ever made it to press, and we thank him for his initial support when we had another networking idea in mind. (Gee, Mike, we know this isn't about LAN Manager — but we're close.) Thanks also to Pam Miller of Aldus for helping out with PageMaker. It was a delight to set up this book.

We are very indebted to Ed Tittle, who was an inspiration to us all and who helped bring together some of the participants for this book. For all the midnight reading and proofing, we appreciate the efforts of the

Currid & Company team of Dianne Davison, Diane Goulding, Dorothy Wolf, Tony Croes, and Michael and Diane Ellerbe. Diane Ellerbe's work on design, layout, and typesetting helped bring the words to life.

One more word of thanks should go to the talented development team at Microsoft — without them we wouldn't have had anything to write about. Windows for Workgroups works! It's solid, stable, and even fun. Keep 'em coming.

CONTENTS AT A GLANCE

Introduction		**xxi**

CHAPTERS

1	Introducing Workgroup Computing	1
2	Networking Workgroups: How the Technology Works	11
3	Installing Windows for Workgroups	35
4	Test Driving Shared Files and Printers	55
5	Setting Up and Using Workgroup E-Mail	89
6	Setting Up and Using Schedule+	113
7	Getting More Productive with Windows for Workgroups Utilities	139
8	Security and the Workgroup	169
9	Administrative Chores for the Network	179
10	Sample Workgroup Configurations	201
11	Advanced Topics: Custom Setup and Tuning	221
12	Advanced Topics: Windows for Workgroups on a Novell LAN	251
13	Troubleshooting	267
14	Changing Habits, Working Smart	281

APPENDICES

A	Installing and Testing the Network Hardware	299
B	A Summary of Windows for Workgroups Programs, Menus, and Commands	321
C	The Workgroup Connection	357
D	Sample Configuration Files	367
	Glossary of Terms	385
	Index	421

Contents

Introduction   xxi

1 Introducing Workgroup Computing   1

The Adventure Begins   2
    Technology's Move   4
Working in Groups   4
Workgroup Computing   6
    Benefits of Technology   6
Computer Literacy on the Rise   7

2 Networking Workgroups: How the Technology Works   11

Networks and Planning   13
Networking Software   14
Getting Acquainted with Peer-to-Peer Networks   15
Selecting a Topology   17
    Linear-Bus   18

Star-Shaped 19
Architecture 20
ArcNet 20
Ethernet 22
Token Ring Networks 26
Selecting the Right Topology for You 28
Network Shopping List 28
Moving Along 33

3 Installing Windows for Workgroups 35

Planning Your Windows for Workgroups Network 37
Planning the Workgroup 37
Naming Users and Resources 38
Defining the Network Physical Layout 39
Cabling 40
Making an Inventory of the Existing Systems 40
Installing Windows for Workgroups 42
Express Setup 43
Defining Passwords 51

4 Test Driving Shared Files and Printers 55

Brushing Up on Windows Basics 57
The Basic Elements of Windows 57
Pointing and Clicking with the Mouse 59
Choosing and Selecting 60

  Minimizing and Maximizing Windows 61

  Controlling Window Size and Positioning 62

  Getting Help 64

  Starting Applications 65

Basic Sharing with Windows for Workgroups 66

Sharing Files and Directories: Using File Manager 66

  Organizing and Naming Shared Directories 67

  Sharing the Directory 69

  Gaining Access to Files on Other Computers 71

  Viewing Lists of Files 74

Printing on the Network 75

  Sharing Your Printer 75

  Printing to Another's Printer 77

  Connecting to Shared Printers 77

  Controlling Printers 79

Sharing Documents: Using the ClipBook 81

  Connecting to Another ClipBook 82

  Sharing Your ClipBook 84

  ClipBook Features 85

5 Setting Up and Using Workgroup E-Mail 89

Introducing E-Mail 91

  How E-Mail Works 91

  Establishing E-Mail Roles 92

Setting Up Windows for Workgroups E-Mail 93

Choosing a Postoffice Computer   93
Creating the Postoffice   95
Ongoing E-Mail Administration   102
For E-Mail Users: Using Mail for the First Time   103
Mail's Special Visual Cues and Icons   106
Basic Mail Functions   106
E-Mail Etiquette   111

6 Setting Up and Using Schedule+   113

What You Can Do with Schedule+   115
Getting to Know Schedule+   116
Scheduling Made Easy with Appts   116
Getting an Overview with Planner   117
Keeping Track of Your "To Do" List with Tasks   118
Getting Back to Today   119
Using Schedule+   119
Logging Out   120
How Schedule+ Works with Mail   120
Sharing Your Schedule+ Information with Others   120
Scheduling Appointments   122
Scheduling Meetings   126
Responding to a Meeting Appointment   128
Working with an Assistant   129
Viewing Multiple Calendars   129
Working with Resources   130

Tasks   131

Printing   133

Working Offline   134

Creating Archives   135

Using Archives   136

7 Getting More Productive with Windows for Workgroups Utilities   139

Utilities That Come with Windows for Workgroups   140

Clock   141

Cardfile   142

Calculator   148

Chat   150

Write   152

Character Map   154

Paintbrush   155

Notepad   157

Recorder   158

Utilities from the Resource Kit   160

Graphics Viewer   160

Top Desk   161

Document Management with Windows for Workgroups   162

Object Linking and Embedding   163

Shareware and Freeware Utilities   166

What Is Shareware?   166

8 Security and the Workgroup 169

Who Is Responsible for Security? 171
How Windows for Workgroups Security Works 172
    How Logon Security Works 172
    Basic Password Concepts 172
    Sharing Directories and Security 174
    Deciding Who Should Have How Much Access 174
    What to Do When You Forget Your Password 177

9 Administrative Chores for the Network 179

Protecting Data by Backing Up Files 181
Defragmenting for Increased Performance 191
Providing Training and Support 192
Maintaining Configuration Information on Your Network 194
Protecting against Computer Viruses 195
Managing the Mail System's Disk Space 197

10 Sample Workgroup Configurations 201

Guidelines for Organizing Your Groups 203
Guidelines for Allocating Network Resources 208
Sample Networks 211
    A Simple Three-Person Workgroup 211
    A Seven-System Workgroup 214
    Attaching to a Novell NetWare Network 216

11 Advanced Topics: Custom Setup and Tuning 221

Customizing Your Workspace   222
    Changing the Look of Your Workspace   223
    Other Desktop Features   231
    More Features You Can Customize   233

Customizing Your Work Environment   235
    Organizing Program Groups   235
    The Startup Group   235
    Run Minimized   236
    Running Your DOS Applications in Windows   237

Tuning for Better Performance   241
    Random Access Memory   241
    Memory-Resident Programs   242
    Program Tuning Issues   242
    Looking at Virtual Memory and Swap Files   245
    Disk Usage Issues   247

12 Advanced Topics: Windows for Workgroups on a Novell LAN 251

Potential Conflicts   253
    Drive Mappings   253
    Printer Sharing   258

Complementary Features   259
    Using NetWare Security   259

Placing the Postoffice on a Novell Server   259
Software Installation   261
Printer Sharing   263
Memory Considerations   264
Workstation Memory   264
Server Memory   265

13 Troubleshooting   267

General Troubleshooting Guidelines   268
Troubleshooting Basic Problems   272
Printer Won't Work   275
Application Software Doesn't Install Correctly   275
Contacting Microsoft   277

14 Changing Habits, Working Smart   281

Commandments for Change   283

The First Commandment of Change:
Thou Shalt Not Compute Alone   284

The Second Commandment of Change:
Place Thy PC on Thy Desk   284

The Third Commandment of Change:
Thou Shalt Not Keep a Paper Calendar   285

The Fourth Commandment of Change:
Thou Shalt Stuff Thy Calculator in a Drawer   285

The Fifth Commandment of Change:
Thou Shalt Give Up Thy Notepaper   285

The Sixth Commandment of Change:
Thou Shalt Stop Using Handwritten "To Do" Lists   286

The Seventh Commandment of Change:
Remove Thy Rolodex   286

The Eighth Commandment of Change:
Thou Shalt Remember to Multitask   287

The Ninth Commandment of Change:
Thou Shalt Use No More White Boards   289

The Tenth Commandment of Change:
Thou Shalt Not Recreate the Wheel   289

Procedures to Facilitate Workgroup Computing   290

    The Postoffice PC   290

    PCs with Printers Attached   290

    Load Mail and Schedule+ at Startup   291

    File-Naming Conventions   291

Tips to Simplify Your Use of Windows for Workgroups   296

    Minimize, Don't Close   296

    Keep Your Icons Handy   296

    Keep Mail and Schedule+ Loaded and Minimized   296

Putting It All Together   297

APPENDICES

A Installing and Testing the Network Hardware   299

Choosing a Bus   300

Selecting Your Network Interface Card   301

Hardware Installation Task List   302

Gather the Necessary Equipment   302

Installing the Network Cabling   304

Installing the Network Interface Card   305

Connecting to the Network   315

Testing the Network   318

Install the Network Software   319

B A Summary of Windows for Workgroups Programs, Menus, and Commands   321

Where the Keys Are   323

Windows for Workgroups System Keys   325

Keys You Can Use within Menus   331

Keys You Can Use within Dialog Boxes   332

Editing Keys and Where You Can Use Them   335

Keys to Move the Cursor Around   337

Keyboard Shortcuts for Windows for Workgroups Programs   338

   Program Manager   338

   File Manager   339

   Directory Tree Box   340

   File List Box   341

   Drive Box   342

   Control Panel   343

   ClipBook Viewer   345

   Windows for Workgroups Setup   345

   PIF File Editor   345

       PIF File Editor   345
       Mail   345
       Schedule+   346
       Write   348
       Paintbrush   349
       Terminal   350
       Notepad   350
       Recorder   350
       Cardfile   351
       Character Map   351
       Media Player   351
       Sound Recorder   352
       Clock   352
       Chat   352
       WinMeter   352
       NetWatcher   353
       Minesweeper   353
       Solitaire   353
       Hearts   353

C   The Workgroup Connection   357

    Installing Workgroup Connection   359
    Starting Workgroup Connection   364
    Using Mail with Workgroup Connection   366

D Sample Configuration Files 367

The CONFIG.SYS File 369

The AUTOEXEC.BAT File 372

The WIN.INI File 373

The SYSTEM.INI File 380

Advice About Changing Configuations 383

Glossary of Terms 385

Index 421

Introduction

Microsoft's Windows for Workgroups is going to change the world — or at least the way the world thinks about networking. Within the blink of an eye, the twist of a screwdriver, and the start of SETUP, people around the globe are going to get connected. The change will start with the workgroup — the local collection of people and PCs — and then spread out. At its center, we expect to see Windows for Workgroups providing powerful options to share information, files, printers, and other resources.

The Structure of This Book

We have divided this book into fourteen chapters, four appendices, and a glossary. Each chapter can stand on its own as a reference, but if you are new to networking and new to the Windows environment, we suggest you start at the beginning and end at the end.

Chapter 1 sets the stage for Workgroup Computing, defining the concept and discussing its virtues. Chapter 2 talks about networking technology and what you'll need to consider when you put in a network for the first time. Chapter 2 is supplemented by Appendix A, which is provided in case you have to install your own hardware, cabling, and networking gear.

Chapter 3 takes you step by step through the software installation of Windows for Workgroups. It shows you the screens and prompts, and helps you through your setup. Chapter 4 shows you how to take Windows for Workgroups for a test drive, concentrating on the sharing of your files, printers, and documents.

Chapters 5 and 6 introduce you to two of the most exciting features of Windows for Workgroups — the built-in electronic mail system (Mail) and the electronic appointment book (Schedule+). With these applications, you'll have a chance to recapture a lot of productivity — especially if *everyone* in your workgroup begins to use these features.

Chapter 7 expands on other productivity tools — here we'll discuss more of the built-in features of Windows for Workgroups.

Chapter 8 turns to security. Networks are only as secure as you make them. This chapter presents the ins and outs of the Windows for Workgroups security features — passwords and sharing options.

Chapter 9 sets up administrative chores for the network. While you'll undoubtedly find Windows for Workgroups a low-maintenance network, that doesn't mean it's a "no-maintenance" network. In this chapter we'll map out routine tasks for keeping things going.

Chapter 10 unveils a few sample workgroup configurations for you to think about. Because Windows for Workgroups is so flexible, we thought we'd give you some food for thought when it comes to putting your network configuration together.

Chapters 11 through 13 open doors to advanced topics. We'll move to our more technical discussions of setting up custom environments and how to tune your system for better performance, with plenty of little tips, tricks, and special techniques to get better performance from Windows for Workgroups. We'll also discuss how to work with Windows for Workgroups on a Novell LAN.

Chapter 14 closes the book with a nontechnical but oh-so-important topic: changing your habits. Both individuals and workgroups will get the most out of Windows for Workgroups when they begin to shed their time-honored but time-wasting habits. Be sure to tune in for Currid & Company's Ten Commandments for beneficial computerization.

Finally, we've included several appendices:

- ▲ for a guide through hardware installation, turn to Appendix A;
- ▲ for a concise reference and summary of commands, turn to Appendix B;
- ▲ for help in installing the Workstation Connection for DOS-only computers, turn to Appendix C; and
- ▲ for sample configuration files, turn to Appendix D.

We've also included a glossary of all the buzz words you're likely to hear when talking about Windows for Workgroups.

We think Windows for Workgroups is a great product. For those who master its finer points, there are great connections ahead.

CHAPTER 1

Introducing Workgroup Computing

CHAPTER 1

FEATURING:
- **Working in Groups**
- **Workgroup Computing**
- **Computer Literacy on the Rise**

The adventure begins . . .

8:00 Monday morning. Craig Gilbert arrives at his office, flips on his PC, and walks down the hall to grab a cup of coffee. As he returns, a familiar bell coming from his computer signals an important message. He taps a mouse button and gazes at the computer monitor. "Big day ahead," he says to himself. "Two important meetings, a review of the Mega Manufacturing proposal, and a project list that's due later this week. Better get George, Sue, and Linda involved."

Craig notices electronic mail waiting for him. He clicks on the e-mail symbol and sees more good news. Harry, the company president, was working over the weekend and dumped a dozen "to do" notes on the system for Craig. Craig really begins to feel the heat. He already had a full day ahead, now his in box overflows with chores delegated from a newly computer-literate boss.

Repositioning his mouse and keyboard, Craig takes a deep breath and springs into action. He splits up Harry's requests and forwards them to his team members. He sends Don the distribution check requests, Sam the sales forecast, Mike the manufacturing questions, and Fred the finance inquiry. He marks the requests "Urgent!" You can almost hear the sound waves as Don, Sam, Mike, and Fred click open their morning mail within a few minutes.

Then Craig turns to his own schedule, looking for time to get together with Sue and George. He checks their calendars electronically, finds a convenient meeting time and place, then marks their calendars.

10:00. Information comes back from Don, Sam, Mike, and Fred. Craig attaches their responses to his note to Harry, and with the stroke of a mouse, sends back the answers to Harry's questions.

Leaving for the meeting at Mega Manufacturing with his blood pressure dropping to normal, Craig has had a big morning, but was able to maneuver through his activities (both those he had planned, and those Harry had planned for him) without a hitch.

By now you might be thinking that Craig is a cousin of George Jetson. He's not. Craig is a 1990s worker who has harnessed the power of desktop computing and networks. He doesn't have to be a space-age rocket scientist or a computer guru, he just needs to use a few good tools and get connected to his colleagues. Craig isn't using any high priced custom coded strategic business weapon software, either. All the tools that Craig uses are low-cost, off-the-shelf, and available today.

People in business today don't work in isolation — they work with others. More and more jobs are becoming interdependent, fast acting, and information driven, and those trends are likely to continue. People are challenged to find ways to do newly defined jobs — and do them faster, better, and more efficiently each year. Moreover, they have discovered that the need to collaborate and share information isn't just a convenience, but a necessity.

Technology's Move

Radical changes in information technology have occurred in the past decade. The power of processor technology — the brains behind computers — has been doubling every year or two. Because of this, computers have been transformed from highly specialized devices to broadly useful machines anyone can use. Once computers cost millions of dollars and required special climate-controlled rooms — now they are reasonably priced and can sit on your desk or be packed in a briefcase.

What's more, computer use was limited to specially trained engineers who had to optimize each instruction to conserve very expensive resources. They communicated in strange "languages" and counted in unusual number systems.

According to a recent article in Harvard Business Review, one million instructions per second (MIP) of computer power cost $250,000 in 1980. By 1985 that unit had dropped to $25,000 and by 1990 it had plunged to $2,500. Some industry observers believe MIPs will cost less than $500 by 1994 or 1995.

The 1980s and 1990s have also ushered in easy-to-use software like Microsoft Windows, a graphical user interface (GUI) that makes computing as easy as clicking on on-screen pictures. With just a little orientation, nearly anyone can now become computer literate. New software packages are making computers almost as easy to use as a toaster. (Well, almost.)

Working in Groups

Business and technology changes have given rise to the era of *workgroup* computing. Your workgroup is the collection of people you interact with to get your job done — usually people who are in close proximity to you. They may work in your department, down the hall, or across the way in another building. Sometimes, however, members of your workgroup aren't housed in the same location you are. They may be in another city, state, or country. While it might take a little ingenuity and the combination of a variety of technologies, everyone can be connected together today, with low cost off-the-shelf products.

Workgroups change. You might find yourself in a completely different workgroup today than you were in a year ago. You may work in a large organization that is shifting from a functional structure, divided into accounting, marketing, and sales, to a process team structure, in which a group of people are responsible for handling everything that has to do with a customer order.

How a workgroup works together depends on the company's culture — how formally or informally they behave. Larger groups often need more formal lines of communication and interaction. This can sometimes bog things down, because it takes many people and a set of formal procedures to get things done.

For example, we know of a case where the status report of an information services department in a Fortune 100 company takes two full-time professional people a full month to collect, compile, and produce, with contributing efforts from another six people. Then several secretaries take several days to arrange a meeting for more than five additional people. Everyone's calendar has to be checked, coordinated, and rechecked for possible conflicts, and a conference room has to be booked. The process is agonizingly tedious.

Smaller workgroups are easier to manage, but tend to consist of individuals with file drawers full of separately maintained banks of information. Sometimes if you need something from someone else's bank, it may as well have been locked in a vault than in the guy next door's office.

So what's the answer for large and small workgroups? It's workgroup computing.

Workgroup Computing

Connecting the computers of workgroup members connects the people, too. With a solid computing platform, members of the group can share information, meeting dates, and messages, quickly and easily without a lot of administrative down time.

Workgroup computing takes more than simply hooking wires to the backs of personal computers and installing a network. To be effective, workgroup computing requires specially designed software that makes it easy for people to share information. That software is sometimes called *groupware* because it facilitates group work, through features such as:

- ▲ Electronic mail,
- ▲ Personal and group calendars/schedulers,
- ▲ Task or project management aids, and
- ▲ Document or file management.

Windows for Workgroups includes many of the basic features of groupware, and provides a platform on which many groupware applications will appear.

Benefits of Technology

In their recent book, *Technology for Teams*, Susanna Opper and Henry Fersko-Weiss explore the benefits of workgroup computing. The greatest gain, they find, is in time. They ask: "How much time is wasted each year in American businesses by telephone tag? No one knows. Nor is there a line item in your budget for miscommunications or time wasted having the same discussion more than once. There's no accounting method for costing out the inability to find the right piece of paper...." Many fundamental business changes of the last decade — globalization, merger mania, privatization, and the rise of small business — have resulted in basic changes in the way professional office work is done. People increasingly find themselves in the information business.

Introducing Workgroup Computing

According to Peter Drucker in his article "The New Society of Organizations" (Harvard Business Review, September/October 1992), there has been a shift to a knowledge society. Drucker explains, "In this society, knowledge is the primary resource for individuals and for the economy overall. Land, labor, and capital — the economist's traditional factors of production — do not disappear, but they become secondary. They can be obtained, and obtained easily, provided there is specialized knowledge."

For example, few people who go to the local bank ask to see their money piled up in the vault. Instead, they want information about their accounts, such as their current balance, their recent deposits, and which checks have cleared. In the insurance industry, there is no tangible product, but a service — customers want to know how much insurance they have, the cost to them, and how to file their claims. Customers vote with their business dollars for the carriers who provide complete services, lower premiums, and faster claims processing.

Even product-oriented industries are becoming information intensive. In a product-centered organization, only a small percentage of the workers actually touch the product. The rest of the company focuses on selling, distributing, accounting for the money, and figuring out what to do next. In other words, they focus on *information* about the product.

Computer Literacy on the Rise

The changes in the way people work and jobs they do have given rise to a new type of worker — the *computer-literate* corporate citizen. These workers need information to do their jobs, and have become competent in using information tools like personal computers.

Computer literacy is becoming a requirement for many positions, particularly in the service sector, where a recent study has shown that as much as 80% of the jobs now require some degree of computer literacy.

People are expected to be self-sufficient at using tools like word processing software, spreadsheets, and electronic mail to get their jobs done.

It wasn't always that way. Not too many years ago, if a corporate citizen wanted to get a piece of information, he or she had to requisition it from an information services department. It was often a time consuming process.

If you wanted to get a report to a co-worker down the hall, you had to go through hoops to do it. Take, for example, one major company's official 16-step procedure for handling any memo or document — first it was handwritten by an executive; then proofed for spelling and company logos by a secretary; logged in and typed by word processors; reviewed and edited by the secretary; logged in again and corrected by the word processor; then copied for filing, addressed, sent to the mail room, and finally hand delivered — you get the picture. Total elapsed time between drafting and delivery was often three days or more.

This is no joke or exaggeration. The same procedure was followed for everything from a one page memo to a 200 page report — no exceptions. Administrators in each department made sure no one short-circuited the procedures. In fact, when the first personal computers came into this company, there was a major confrontation in trying to stop the business people from handwriting their own memos.

Contrast that with the power of electronic mail, which allows the executive to draft, edit, file a copy, and electronically deliver the document in as little as three minutes, depending on the length of the document.

Considering all the factors, such as labor, materials, and supplies, today's approach costs no more than the old system did.

Whether the worker wants to get information to the guy down the hall or around the globe, information and networking technology like easy-to-use Windows for Workgroups ushers in a new paradigm for business people doing their jobs. People like Craig Gilbert will soon be the rule, not the exception.

CHAPTER 2

NETWORKING WORKGROUPS: HOW THE TECHNOLOGY WORKS

FEATURING:

- → Basic Network Planning
- → Peer-to-Peer Networks
- → Selecting the Right Topology
- → Network Shopping List

If, as a child, you ever connected cups with wire to make a play telephone, you've already installed your first network. To make things work, you stretched wire between the two cups, and created the link. Voilà! It worked.

Connecting your LAN (local area network) doesn't have to be much more complicated than that. LANs connect computers by using three basic components: cables, network hardware, and network software. There are, however, many options for laying out the cables and making the connections work, and sometimes those combinations of cable, hardware, and software can get confusing.

Do you use coaxial cable or twisted pair cables? Should you use ArcNet, Ethernet, or Token Ring topology? Must you buy new PCs? To answer these questions, you will need to select carefully among your options, making sure everything works together.

This chapter introduces you to the basics of LAN technology, which is the foundation for Windows for Workgroups. We'll examine the options, whether you are starting from scratch or already have some of the network in place, and make recommendations for selecting basic pieces that you'll need for your network. First, we'll discuss how networks work. Then we'll introduce the technology components and make some recommendations about what you should buy. Finally, we'll outline the shopping list, giving you a minimum set of products needed to make your network work.

Networks and Planning

If you were planning the plumbing for a new house, you'd have to know where the kitchen and bathrooms were located. You'd sketch the layout of pipes through the walls and ceiling, the special bends and turns you'd have to take, and which fixtures are connected by the pipes. You'd select plastic or copper pipes, depending on your needs, and order all the complementary pieces.

LANs, like household plumbing, must be planned for efficient movement (in this case, of information) throughout the system. To set up a LAN for your workgroup, you need to sketch out where all the offices are located, and choose the appropriate type of cable, network hardware, *topology* (layout), and software.

If you are planning your workgroup network from scratch, we recommend you make your selections in the following order:

1. Network software,
2. Topology,
3. Architecture (peer-to-peer or client-server), and
4. Hardware and cabling.

This approach is almost the reverse of the way you will install the network, but it will ensure that you select compatible pieces.

If you are new to networking and don't have a lot of time to investigate the options, a *starter kit* (a pre-packaged network including adapter cards, cables, and sometimes even the software) will get things up and running quickly.

Many network resellers are also willing to handle the installation of small workgroups for a nominal fee if you buy the hardware and software from them. If you go that route, make sure you watch over the software installation part so you know how your PCs have been set up and you can keep things going after the reseller leaves.

Networking Software

Windows for Workgroups follows the architecture of *peer-to-peer* networking, in which each PC on the network has direct access to the resources (hard disk, printers, some software) of the others without a master computer acting as a traffic cop.

Windows for Workgroups offers just about any feature you could ask for in networking a workgroup. It is the first product to closely incorporate the user-friendly Windows environment into a network operating system. It also offers well-integrated electronic mail, electronic scheduling, and calendars for individuals and groups, and network document management, which allows groups to work on one common document (preventing discrepancies between versions).

Windows for Workgroups can also run simultaneously with traditional server-based network operating systems, such as Novell NetWare or Microsoft LAN Manager.

Easy-to-use, easy-to-set-up, Windows for Workgroups has low administrative requirements, and it works more smoothly with the operating system than other peer-to-peer networks, making it feel to the user as if network capability were part of the computer.

Getting Acquainted with Peer-to-Peer Networks

As mentioned before, Windows for Workgroups makes use of a peer-to-peer networking scheme — each computer on the network can be configured to share peripherals (such as printers), and disk space. There is no need for a dedicated *file server* (master computer) to direct files, communications, or printing tasks through the network.

As a user on a peer-to-peer network, your experience would be like having extra disk drives — your own computer's hard disk is defined as drive C:, and you can also have access to a directory on Harry's hard disk as Drive D:, Sam's as drive E:, and Joe's as drive F:. People in the workgroup can easily share hard disk space and files.

Peer-to-peer networks differ from traditional file-server or client-server based networks in several important ways. Since peer-to-peer networks allow each computer to share its resources, there is no need for an expensive dedicated file server. This allows groups of very small sizes (say, three to ten people) to justify networking. Peer-to-peer networks are also generally easier to set up — it is a simple matter of installing network adapter cards and connecting cables, and then configuring the software. A five- or six-station network can be up and running within a few hours. Administration of peer-to-peer networks is also far simpler than that of other networks, because each user controls access to his or her computer and there is no need for a full-time LAN administrator.

Theoretically, peer-to-peer networks can handle hundreds of connected PCs. Realistically, most are quite a bit smaller, containing fewer than 25 computers. If a peer-to-peer network grows larger, it can be reconfigured to include a dedicated file server.

Is Peer-to-Peer Right for Your Workgroup?

Depending on the size of your workgroup, the location of its members, and the applications you need to do your job, a peer-to-peer network may or may not be the appropriate network platform. Table 2.1 lists criteria for selecting a network operating system.

Table 2.1 Types of Networks

	Peer-to-Peer	**Client-Server**
Workgroup Size	2-25	20-200
Remote Locations	Limited to telephone access.	May include many remote locations.
Applications	Primarily productivity software such as word processing, databases, spreadsheets, graphics, e-mail, scheduling.	Primarily a large database such as an order entry or billing system. Can also include standard productivity software.
Security	Password is satisfactory for most data. Users determine and administer security needs for themselves.	Data is sensitive and requires full authentication of users for each application. Security administrator is required to make changes.

> **NOTE** Remember that, as a peer-to-peer network, Windows for Workgroups can inter-operate with other systems, using the same networking hardware and cables. In fact, during the installation process, Windows for Workgroups will detect the existence of other networks, such as Novell NetWare, and make the appropriate installation adjustment. You can use the peer-to-peer system for your immediate workgroup while still being connected to the corporate network.

Selecting a Topology

Once your network operating system is selected, you need to plan a *topology*, or layout scheme for the network, which will determine the path through which data travels in the network. The most popular options today are linear-bus and star-shaped. A ring topology is also available, but not widely used today. Ring topology networks, where the cable is laid in a circle, are nearly extinct. Although you may hear the word "ring" used to talk about networking, it is mostly used to refer to a protocol standard, such as Token Ring. A *protocol standard* is nothing more than a standard method for data to be sent across the wire. Figure 2.1 illustrates a ring topology.

Figure 2.1

Ring topology

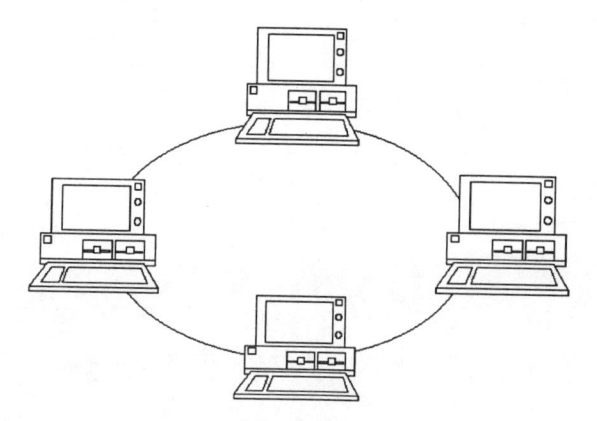

Linear-Bus

In a linear-bus arrangement, a single cable, called the bus or trunk, is installed — usually along a cable path in the ceiling or a wall — and terminated at each end. Every PC is connected to the bus by using short stub cables or a T-style connector. See Figure 2.2 for an example of a linear-bus topology.

Linear-bus topology is low-cost and simple to design. Assuming you can keep track of the primary cable, it is easy to set up additional PCs by simply tapping into and expanding the trunk cable. Since each PC is attached directly to the cable, there is no need to purchase additional hardware such as hubs or wire centers. Another advantage is that you will use less cable than with the star-shaped option.

Unfortunately, any break in the cable can cause the entire network, or a good part of it, to fail. A failure can also be caused by one end or the other losing proper termination. These failures can be difficult to diagnose.

Convenient and inexpensive, a linear-bus topology is appropriate for very small workgroups of between three and ten members.

Figure 2.2

Linear-bus topology

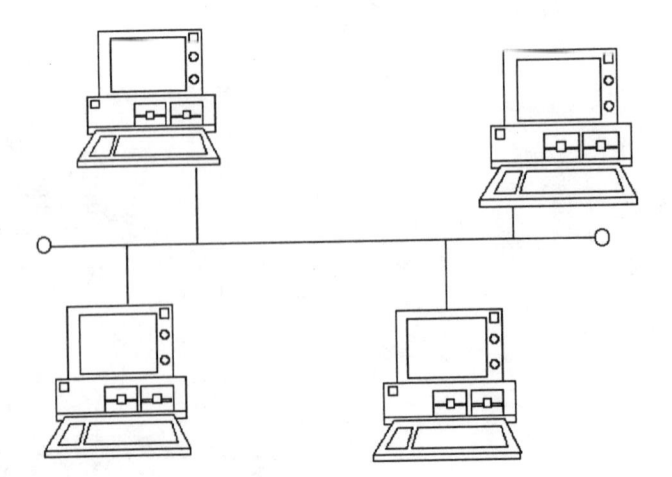

Networking Workgroups: How the Technology Works

Star-Shaped

In a star-shaped arrangement, an individual wire is run from each PC to a central location, where all the wires are connected to a hub device, which completes the electronic connections. This is similar to a telephone system where each phone is connected to a central switchboard. See Figure 2.3 for an example of a star-shaped topology.

Figure 2.3

Star-shaped topology

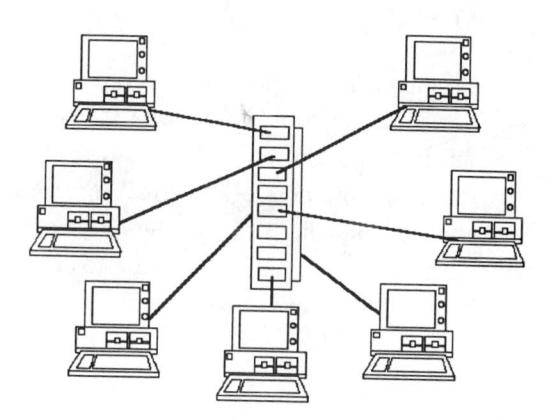

Star-shaped wiring uses more cable, but has several important benefits. Since each PC's cable is unique to that machine, if there is a cable fault, only the PC attached to the broken cable is likely to be affected. The star-shaped topology is also supported by many vendors and communications standards called protocol standards. For example, if you start with a star-shaped LAN cabled with common unshielded twisted pair (telephone type) wiring for Ethernet, then later decide to replace the Ethernet with Token Ring, you won't have to rewire your offices.

Star-shaped topology is easier to manage and administer than linear-bus. Once it is set up, it can be easily documented. Most hubs that connect star-shaped networks contain some form of status lights that help you diagnose both whether a PC is properly connected and problems with network management software, so faults in the system are easier to locate.

The disadvantage of a star-shaped configuration is cost. More cable is needed, as well as a hub to connect all the wires together.

Given the benefits of greater control over cabling network faults, however, it may be well worth the effort to install this type of network.

Architecture

Windows for Workgroups supports three networking architectures (or protocol standards). ArcNet, Ethernet, and Token Ring are the three most popular options on the market today. Particularly if you are planning your network from scratch, it's important to know the differences among them so you can plan expansion beyond the immediate workgroup, and have the option to connect to mini computers, RISC-based servers, or mainframes.

ArcNet

ArcNet topology is a popular choice for networks, especially in small offices that don't need to link to anything else. It is inexpensive and easy to install, and has been widely available since the 1970s.

ArcNet passes information around the network using a *token passing scheme* (where each computer has an individual turn to relay information) at a speed of 2.5 Mbps (mega-bits per second). This is somewhat slower than Ethernet (10 Mbps) or Token Ring (4 or 16 Mbps) networks. When working on a small ArcNet network of five or ten PCs, however, it is doubtful that most people would find the slower speed noticeable.

ArcNet is a very efficient protocol, compensating for its slow speed. It's based on a predictable and orderly token passing scheme, in which messages are attached to a token to be passed along the cabling. This is as if the message got on a train at the station, followed the train's pre-established route, and departed at the destination. The time it took to get from here to there is predictable because only one train is on the track.

Networking Workgroups: How the Technology Works

The process could only be slowed down by adding more stops along the route. In a token passing network adding many more PCs on the network could slow it down, but generally speaking, you won't notice the difference unless you add another 50 or 100 PCs.

To its credit, ArcNet is inexpensive, stable, and robust. Most ArcNet adapter cards cost less than $150 and can be purchased from a wide variety of vendors. ArcNet LANs are relatively slow at 2.5 Mbps, but a faster version that travels at 20 Mbps is available from Datapoint.

ArcNet adheres to a star-shaped topology and requires cable (that is wired back to a central location), a hub, an ArcNet card for each PC, and the appropriate drivers for Windows for Workgroups.

Cable

ArcNet runs on several types of cable:

- ▲ RG-62, a common form of coaxial cable found in many companies that have mainframe IBM 3270 type terminals,
- ▲ Unshielded twisted pair (UTP), and
- ▲ Fiber-optic cable.

ArcNet requires a star-shaped cable configuration with all cable run back to a central location.

Network Interface Cards

An ArcNet adapter card is required for each PC on the network. These adapter cards come from a variety of vendors, such as SMC and Datapoint. Make sure you select the proper type for the cable you have chosen (e.g. coaxial cable, twisted-pair, etc.). ArcNet adapters do not have preset network addresses, so it is important to set up each card individually and not to allow two cards to share the same network address. (See Appendix A for detailed installation information.)

Hubs

An active hub connects cables together and provides the network connection. Hubs are generally sold with 8 or 12 ports, or more. You must have a free port for each PC you plan to put on the network.

Some ArcNet suppliers also support passive hubs that can extend the length or flexibility of the cable. Traditionally, passive hubs have not been reliable.

Making a Choice

ArcNet may be appropriate for very small, self-contained offices. While Windows for Workgroups supports ArcNet LANs, it does not provide full support. For example, because of the way Microsoft implemented the networking software and limitations within the ArcNet protocol standard, you cannot connect to a Novell NetWare LAN and Windows for Workgroups at the same time if you have an ArcNet LAN. There is also little wide area network (WAN) support for ArcNet LANs. This could hamper growth, should the need arise.

If you are starting from scratch, we do not recommend using Windows for Workgroups with ArcNet-based LANs. While ArcNet LANs are low-cost and easy to set up, we feel ArcNet is a fading technology. ArcNet LANs do not have the industry-wide support of Ethernet or Token Ring. If you already have an ArcNet LAN and don't plan to expand to a WAN or connect to a Novell NetWare LAN, then you need not feel your ArcNet LAN has to be replaced. It will function fine in a small environment.

Ethernet

Ethernet is a very fast (10 Mbps) and efficient standard that enjoys wide support for both small and large computers. The most popular networking protocol standard today, Ethernet was invented by Xerox in the mid-

1970s and is defined in the IEEE (Institute of Electrical and Electronics Engineers) standard 802.3. An appropriate choice for small workgroups and large ones that also must connect to mini computers or mainframes, this standard is supported by Digital Equipment Corp., Hewlett-Packard, IBM, Intel, and others.

Ethernet is a *contention-based* protocol standard. Unlike a token passing scheme, all the computers can "talk" at once — an individual PC doesn't have to wait for a token to come by so it can hop on to transmit a message. But it is also possible, since any PC can transmit a message at any time, that messages can collide and be destroyed before reaching their destination. To deal with this, Ethernet LANs use CSMA/CD (carrier sense multiple access/collision detection), a technique that first listens to the wire and determines that it is not being used, then sends the message, and listens again to see if the message got through. If the message collided with another, CSMA/CD waits and resends the message. While this approach sounds less predictable than a token passing scheme, in practice it works quite well over large and small networks alike.

Depending on their configuration, Ethernet LANs can also be very inexpensive. Since Ethernet is available in linear-bus or star-shaped topologies, full installation prices will vary. For a linear-bus configuration, with thin coaxial cable and inexpensive adapter cards, prices can range from $125 to $200 per PC. Star-shaped configurations will cost more, ranging between $200 and $300 per PC, because they require cabling, cards, *and* hubs.

Cable

Depending on its topology, Ethernet runs on several types of cable:

- ▲ Coaxial cable,
- ▲ Twisted pair cable, and
- ▲ Fiber optic cable.

If Ethernet is set up as a linear-bus, coaxial cable is used. Two types of coaxial cable cables are supported by Ethernet. Thin-net (RG-58, 50 ohm) can be used for bus segments less than 304 meters; or thick-net (RG-11, 50 ohm) for bus segments less than 500 meters. For greater distances, transceivers or signal boosters can be placed on the network, allowing a network segment of over 1,000 meters.

Many people now prefer unshielded twisted pair (UTP, or telephone wiring) rather than coaxial cable. UTP wiring must be positioned in a star shape, but it can be installed by any competent telephone installer.

Fiber optic cabling, another option for Ethernet LANs, can support high transmission speeds and long cable runs. While it provides a nice growth path for the future if high speed video, images, or combinations are used, it is overkill for many environments today. Fiber optic cable is more difficult to install and more expensive than coaxial or twisted pair cable. For most small single office workgroups, fiber optic cable is an unnecessary expense.

Care must be taken when installing cable. Perhaps your building maintenance crew will run cables for you. Otherwise, check with a qualified electrician or telephone installer who can work with your specifications. Special contractors who set up networks are also available.

If you do decide to do it yourself, plan carefully, and do some exploratory work first, looking into how much cable you'll need to get around firewalls and across common areas.

Cables should be run through the walls or above the ceiling. It is not a good idea to try to run cables across the floor or under carpeting, as someone tripping over, or stepping on, the loose cable presents a danger both to the person and to the cable.

Your installation will be much cleaner and more reliable if you run the cables through the walls of your office rather than over carpets where they can be kicked or cut. Many office buildings have extra conduit in place for running communication wiring. Some buildings are already wired for twisted-pair or Thin Ethernet cable. Check with your building supervisor before you get started.

For the cable run out of the wall or down from the ceiling to the computer system, you should cover the cable with external plastic conduit. An inexpensive plastic conduit that attaches to the wall with a self-stick adhesive can be purchased at many office supply stores.

Network Interface Cards

An Ethernet interface card is required for each PC you place on the network. Available from a variety of vendors, such as Intel, 3COM, SMC, and others, many newer cards support multiple cable types, but make sure the ones you select will work in your PC (see Appendix A). Each Ethernet card comes with a preset network identification number that makes every PC on the network unique.

Hubs

If you choose an Ethernet linear-bus topology, attach the main network cable directly to the network Inteface card in each PC or make use of a short stub cable on the PC end. A hub is unnecessary.

If you choose an Ethernet twisted pair topology, you will need a hub at the wire center location. Available from a variety of vendors such as SMC, Gateway, and others, hubs are generally sold with eight or more ports. You must have a free port on the hub for each PC on the network.

Making a Choice

Ethernet is appropriate for small or large groups. The Ethernet linear-bus topology is better for smaller groups of less than 20 PCs. Ethernet in a twisted pair topology, while a little more expensive, is a better choice in that it provides fault isolation and better network management capability.

If you are starting from scratch, twisted pair Ethernet might be a good choice because it provides a great deal of flexibility for both small and large networks. Linear-bus-based Ethernet is also a good option, especially if cost is a primary concern. A 10baseT configuration (a star-shaped configuration based on unshielded twisted pair cabling), while it may be slightly more expensive to install, will offer the most flexibility for connecting with other networks.

Token Ring Networks

Token Ring networks were popularized in the mid-1980s when IBM began to support the Token Ring protocol standard. A number of IBM computers, including mini computers and mainframes, have direct connections to Token Ring. This greatly simplifies linking PCs to larger computers.

Today, IEEE 802.5 describes Token Ring. There are two speeds available, 4 mega-bit and 16 mega-bit. A number of third party vendors such as Proteon, Intel, Madge, 3Com, and others sell Token Ring products.

Token Ring, like ArcNet, uses a token passing scheme. It is predictable, orderly, very fast, and has gained wide industry support. Token Ring networks always use a star-shaped topology.

Depending on the configuration, Token Ring LANs are likely to be more expensive than Ethernet or ArcNet. Generally the network interface cards (NIC) cost a little more, and Token Ring requires twisted pair cabling as well as hubs for connections. Depending on configuration, prices may range between $300 and $600 (or more) per PC.

Cable

Token Ring runs only on twisted pair cable — either shielded twisted pair (STP), sometimes called type 1 or type 2; or unshielded twisted pair (UTP), sometimes called type 3. For environments where there may be electromagnetic interference from overhead lights or nearby elevators, STP cable or a special UTP, called type 4 or type 5, is preferred.

Network Interface Cards

Token Ring interface cards, required for each PC on the network, are available from a variety of vendors, such as Proteon, IBM, Intel, Madge, 3COM, and others. Many newer cards support either 4 mega-bit or 16 mega-bit speeds. You must set all cards on the network to the same speed or they won't work.

Hubs

A hub is necessary if you choose Token Ring. There are two types of hubs: *smart* hubs and regular ones. A smart hub has some built-in network management capability. It can detect a problem with a card or cable, and shut itself off. A regular hub, like IBM's multi-station access unit (MSAU) does not have error or fault checking.

Making a Choice

Token Ring is appropriate for large or small networks, and is especially useful when you are connecting your network to IBM host computers, such as AS-400 mini computer models or mainframes, because IBM supports the Token Ring protocol standard more than any other.

If you are starting your network from scratch, and have IBM mini or mainframe equipment to connect to, Token Ring will provide a great deal of flexibility and support. Token Ring networks may cost a few dollars more, but they are extremely reliable and the 16 mega-bit version is very fast.

Selecting the Right Topology for You

Your budget, plans for growth, and connections to other networks all must be considered in choosing topology. You must carefully consider how big or complex your network *might* grow someday. If you might expand beyond a small workgroup, narrow your search between Ethernet and Token Ring. Both are well supported by a large following of vendors, and their specifications are governed by IEEE, which sets standards. It is unlikely that either of these choices will force your network into any kind of a dead end.

Table 2.2 outlines considerations and protocol standards you might choose to meet your needs.

These are guidelines, not hard-and-fast rules. For example, you can connect an Ethernet-based LAN to an IBM mainframe with a little more effort than connecting a Token Ring-based LAN. For specific advice about your exact workgroup connection requirements, consult with a qualified network engineer. You may pay a few dollars for consulting advice, but it could save you from having to change everything later on.

Network Shopping List

Once you have an idea of your networking plans, it is time to make a shopping list, based on the pieces you already have as well as what you'll be needing to complete the connections.

Personal Computers

Check out your existing personal computers. Each computer on the network should be a 386- or 486-based PC — the faster the speed (above 25, 33, or 50 mhz) the better. Windows for Workgroups will run on 286-based computers, but you cannot share files on your computer if you have a 286-class PC. You'll also find Windows and any of the Windows applications to be intolerably slow.

Table 2.2 Choosing a Protocol Standard

Network Condition	ArcNet	Ethernet	Token Ring
Workgroup may have to connect to a DEC, HP, or non-IBM mini computer or mainframe		X	
Workgroup will connect to an IBM mini computer or mainframe			X
Workgroup may connect to a Novell NetWare LAN		X	X
Workgroup may require access to a client-server database	X	X	X
Workgroup will remain small	X	X	X
Network budget is limited to $200 or less per PC	X	X	

Memory

Although Windows for Workgroups only requires 2 MB RAM (random access memory), Windows software will run faster if you have more memory in your computer — 8 MB is recommended.

Hard Disk Space

Ideally, you'll have several computers with over 100 MB hard drives; each PC hard disk should have a *minimum* of 60 MB. Windows and DOS will occupy the first 10 MB or so; then your applications, such as spreadsheets and word processors, will quickly fill up the rest of the space. Keep in mind that most Windows applications consume large amounts of hard disk space — sometimes 15 or 20 MB per application.

Monitors and Graphics Adapters

For maximum productivity, your PC screens should be easy on the eyes. Install good quality monitors and high-end graphics capability. You'll probably want at least standard VGA (640 x 480) resolution, but a super VGA (SVGA) monitor and graphics card giving you at least 800 x 600 resolution will make it easier to get more applications up on the screen at one time. Windows for Workgroups fosters a work environment where you'll be spending a lot of time in front of your PC. Spending a few extra dollars on what you see is worth the money.

Printers

Because printers are easy to share with Windows for Workgroups, you won't have to buy everyone in the office an individual printer. The printers you do buy should be good ones, for example a laser printer that is compatible with the Hewlett Packard LaserJet. If your workgroup prints graphics documents, you might also consider a printer that has a RISC (reduced instruction set computer) processor to speed up graphics printing. For desktop publishing, a PostScript printer would be useful.

Accessories and Desktop Placement

PCs should be placed *on people's desks* — front and center. They won't be used as effectively if they are relegated to a side table, back bar, or credenza. Check out the height of the keyboard. Also, most professionals' and executives' desk surfaces are too high for keyboards to be comfortable. Positioning the PC, monitor, and keyboard in the proper place might require that you purchase special keyboard drawers, monitor lifts, CPU side-mounting brackets, or other equipment. Most office supply stores or computer superstores have an abundant selection of accessories.

Make sure, too, that cables are long enough so the workstation can be moved around.

Networking Software

Windows for Workgroups is available in several packages. The options include:

If you have no hardware or software:
- ▲ Windows for Workgroups Starter Kit
  Contents: Complete set of networking hardware and software to set up two PCs with Thin Ethernet in a bus topology. Includes a network interface card, Ethernet cable, connectors, terminators, and a screwdriver. Also includes an instructional video tape.
- ▲ Windows for Workgroups User Kit
  Contents: Set of network hardware, cable, and software to add one PC to your workgroup.

If you already have Windows 3.1 but no network:
- ▲ Windows for Workgroups Add-on Starter Kit
  Contents: Network hardware (cable, cards, and terminators) and networking software upgrade for existing Windows 3.1. (Same as above starter kit, without Windows 3.1 software.)
- ▲ Windows for Workgroups Add-on User Kit
  Contents: Network hardware and networking software upgrade for existing Windows 3.1. (Same as above.)

If you have no Windows but are networked:
- ▲ Windows for Workgroups
  Contents: Microsoft Windows version 3.1 and the workgroup add-ons. (That is: Mail, Schedule+, built-in file and printer sharing, Network dynamic data exchange-DDE.)

If you already have Windows 3.1 and are networked:
- ▲ Windows for Workgroups Add-on for Windows 3.1
  Contents: Same as above, without Windows 3.1 software.

If you have Windows 3.0 and are networked:
▲ Windows for Workgroups Upgrade for Windows 3.0
Contents: A reduced-price Microsoft Windows version 3.1 and the workgroup add-ons. (That is: Mail, Schedule+, built-in file and printer sharing, Network dynamic data exchange-DDE.)

For non-Windows capable PCs:
▲ Workgroup Connection
Contents: Software that lets DOS-only computers access Windows for Workgroups machines, use shared files and printers, and send and receive electronic mail. Does not allow files on DOS computers to be shared.

For expanding Mail and Schedule+ to larger networks:
▲ Microsoft Mail and Schedule+ Extensions to Windows for Workgroups
Contents: A gateway to other e-mail systems, remote dial-in capabilities to Workgroup Mail, and functions to connect mail and scheduling across multiple workgroups.

Networking Hardware

Each PC on the network must have its own network interface card and cable. If you choose the appropriate starter kit combinations, all the necessary pieces will be in the box. If you have selected a star-shaped topology, you'll also need a hub that is compatible with your network.

Moving Along

If you are installing the network hardware yourself, see Appendix A for specific instructions, listed by protocol standard. We'll walk you through the steps for several popular networking schemes. Once you have installed the hardware, or if you are installing Windows for Workgroups on a pre-existing network, turn directly to Chapter 3, where we'll be taking you through the operating system installation procedure.

CHAPTER 3

INSTALLING WINDOWS FOR WORKGROUPS

CHAPTER 3

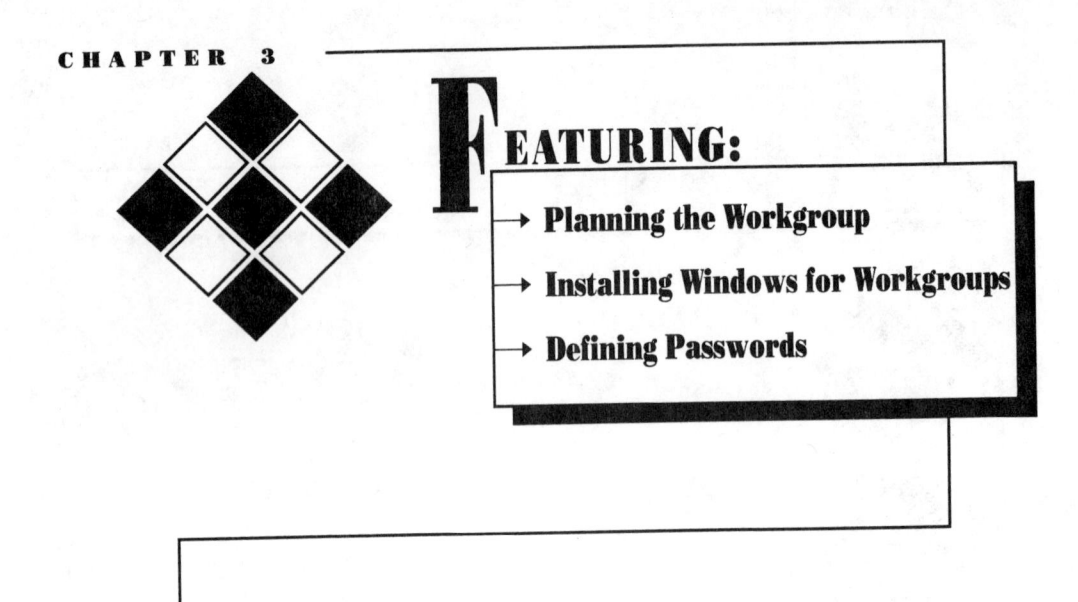

FEATURING:

- Planning the Workgroup
- Installing Windows for Workgroups
- Defining Passwords

There's an old saying, "Heed the 5 P's: proper planning prevents poor performance." Proper planning also creates a successful installation.

A good rule of thumb for setting up computer systems (especially networked ones) is to spend about a third of your time planning for the task. Part of the benefit of Windows for Workgroups lies in its flexibility — that you can implement your system in any number of ways. But without good planning, that flexibility can lead straight to confusion and a poor system.

This chapter will take you through the installation of Windows for Workgroups software, assuming that you have already installed your network cards and cables. (If you have not, please see Appendix A for hardware installation instructions.) We'll start with tips on planning your network, then discuss naming conventions. After that, we'll roll up our sleeves to install and configure Windows for Workgroups.

Planning Your Windows for Workgroups Network

The first step in building a workgroup system is to analyze your needs. Many dollars have been wasted purchasing unworkable or flawed systems. Make sure your network is going to consist of PCs in a DOS/Windows 3.1 operating environment. For networks that include Macs or UNIX-based machines, you'll have to tie into a NetWare network or a LAN Manager network. (Those computers won't be able to use the Windows for Workgroups software directly, but you will be able to exchange files with them.)

Planning the Workgroup

Your workgroup may be pretty constant, like a department or team, but your projects will sometimes cross organizational boundaries. You may belong, for example, to the Sales department, but at the same time be working with people in Marketing on a special project. That Marketing group may include people from Product Development and Finance.

Windows for Workgroups allows that kind of organizational flexibility to be reflected in your computer systems. Members of a workgroup can easily exchange mail, look at the documents they are working on together, and even tie their documents together with shared electronic clipboards.

You should consider the groups in your office to determine who and what should be on the network you are creating. Include as many and as much as your budget will allow. Omitting users or resources from your scheme can lead to "islands of information," undermining the power and effectiveness of the network.

Naming Users and Resources

Networks identify and locate users and resources through their names. If two names are the same, the system cannot determine where to direct a request. It's a good idea to establish a convention for names of various types - a way to keep them unique.

Windows for Workgroups allows user names up to 63 characters long. Computer and workgroup names can be no longer than 15 characters.

We recommend that you establish a naming convention for your computer and workgroup names. You can name the computers with the user's name, but if you have a lot of people moving around your office, you'll have to rename computers often to keep users and computers synchronized. A better approach for large offices is to name the computer after a location, such as Office 201 or Desk 147. Keep in mind that as other people connect to your computer, they will see the computer on the network by the computer name, not the user's name. Therefore, it's important to keep the naming convention easy for people to recognize. If, according to your convention, computer names and user logon names are the same, then 15 characters is the effective length for both, because you only have 15 characters available in the computer name.

Naming workgroups should also be done with great care, especially if you are a part of a larger organization. Your workgroup could be named Marketing, for the marketing department, or Order Fulfillment, for the order processing group. In a small organization, you might simply call the workgroup All Office because everyone in the office is going to be a member of the group.

Again, we advise you choose your naming conventions carefully. Many small LAN installations began using first names, then found themselves some months down the road with six Bobs and twelve Susans. Have some guidelines in place, and don't handle things on a case-by-case basis.

We recommend you name users by their last name (or last name and first initial, or first name and last initial) to avoid potential duplications. When you name printers and other devices, prefix them with a few characters to indicate their location, such as "3EHPLaserIII," for the third-floor, east-corridor HP LASERJET III. If you are already tied to a larger network such as NetWare or LAN Manager, your MIS representatives may have established naming conventions, and you might want to follow those guidelines. A name such as "Randy's Printer" may work, but it isn't much help if you want to know what type of printer that is. Figure 3.1 shows an example of naming a printer.

The *comment* attached to each resource is extra information about the location or capability of a device. With 40 or 50 shared directories in your work group, it will be a real help to have a note describing the directory.

Figure 3.1
Naming shared devices

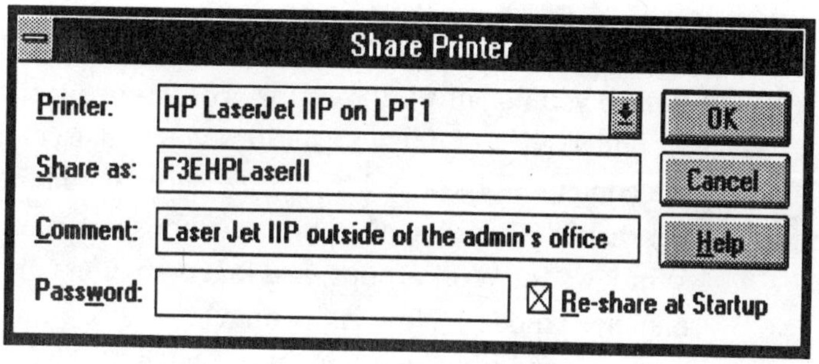

Share Printer	
Printer:	HP LaserJet IIP on LPT1
Share as:	F3EHPLaserII
Comment:	Laser Jet IIP outside of the admin's office
Password:	☒ Re-share at Startup

[OK] [Cancel] [Help]

Defining the Network Physical Layout

If you are already on another network, you won't be concerned about the physical layout of the LAN — it will already be done. If you are setting up a new network, you will want to plan the physical connections carefully. You should obtain, or carefully draw, a floor plan for the area. Indicate the locations of desks and computer tables. You want to place LAN cable connectors nearby.

Don't forget to plan for the printers. Shared network printers are best placed in common areas, as there will be a lot of traffic around the printer when workgroup members pick up their documents. Sharing a printer in a private office could be disruptive to the person who sits in that office.

Cabling

Even if you plan on doing the rest of the work yourself, you'll probably want to contract out the cabling. As mentioned in both Chapter 2 and Appendix A, there are many considerations for laying cable. If you are in a large office, make sure you coordinate this effort with specialists. If you are in a smaller environment, you may want to try your hand at setting up the cabling yourself.

Making an Inventory of the Existing Systems

Before you install Windows for Workgroups, get a notebook and go around to each of the workstations you plan to include and write down the computer type and whether it is already running Windows. (Remember that 286-based workstations cannot share directories or printers under Windows for Workgroups, and that computers must be running in 386-enhanced mode.) Now is the time to shuffle computers around or purchase additional equipment or systems. Also, make sure that there is sufficient free disk space on each computer to install Windows for Workgroups. To run the package, you need:

▲ A computer with an 386SX processor (or higher). Windows for Workgroups will install and run in a limited way on a 286-based computer, but we don't recommend it. You will experience very slow performance and you won't be able to set your computer up for sharing disks or files.

NOTE If you must include 286-based computers on your network, use the Workstation Connection software supplied with Windows for Workgroups. This software will allow non-Windows users access to the network to share other people's directories and access the electronic mail system. They will not, however, be able to share directories on their own disks. See Appendix C for details on using the Workstation Connection.

▲ At least 8 MB of RAM (640 K of conventional and the balance configured as extended memory). While Windows for Workgroups will install and run on a computer configured with less RAM, we advise against it. During our testing and use of Windows for Workgroups, we found performance to be very sluggish on computers configured with less than 8 MB of RAM. In fact, while running everyday office software (such as spreadsheet, word processing, and e-mail), we found that 386-based computers configured with 8 MB of RAM performed better than 486-based computers with 4 MB of RAM.
▲ More than 9.5 MB of free disk space (14.5 MB recommended).
▲ One floppy disk drive (3.5" or 5.25").

Windows for Workgroups has a graphical user interface, so you will need to have a supported graphic monitor to run it. Check the list of compatible hardware in the Windows for Workgroups documentation. Also, each workstation must have a mouse.

Each system must have a network interface card. Some systems may already have network cards in them. Make sure they're compatible with the cable you have chosen, and find out if you need connectivity to another system.

As part of your inventory, run a program which inventories the usage of hardware and software interrupts. Microsoft Diagnostics, which comes with Windows, or the SI utility in Norton Utilities, will list the software and hardware interrupts being used by various options in your system and the base addresses of I/O (input/output) ports. A printed report on this information will be useful when you set up your network cards. Lay the report next to each computer so you can refer to it when the computer is off.

Installing Windows for Workgroups

After installing your network's physical plant, you can begin to install Windows for Workgroups on the individual systems. See Appendix A if your hardware and network are not already installed.

There are really two phases to the SETUP installation program. The DOS phase, which occurs first, checks to see what type of computer, graphic display, mouse, keyboard, language, and network you are running on. You will notice that on the status line it reports that SETUP is "Analyzing running software...." Setup looks at the software you have running in your system and determines if there will be any conflict between SETUP and any of the programs. After copying a minimal set of Windows for Workgroups program files to your system, SETUP brings up the graphical environment and continues the setup process.

To install Windows for Workgroups, place the diskette labeled Disk 1 into one of the diskette drives of your computer. Then type A:SETUP (assuming it's drive A: you're using) and press the ENTER key.

You'll then see a screen that welcomes you to the SETUP program and lets you know that you can quit the program without installing by pressing the F3 key. An explanation of the SETUP program is available by pressing F1.

INSTALLING WINDOWS FOR WORKGROUPS

Follow the directions on the screen and press the ENTER key. You now have a choice — you may press ENTER to do the Express Setup, or press C for the Custom Setup. Microsoft recommends that you perform the Express Setup and allow the SETUP program to automatically configure your system. If you want to preserve your preferences from a previous Windows installation, there is no need to do anything special. The SETUP program retains your preferences for you.

Express Setup

Express Setup will analyze your hardware configuration and install the necessary drivers and entries in the appropriate .INI files. The .INI files will contain information used by Windows for Workgroups to run itself and applications. Express Setup will also modify your CONFIG.SYS and AUTOEXEC.BAT files as needed to run Windows for Workgroups — it will create the necessary entries to load the drivers and the protocols necessary to connect your computer system with others on the network.

NOTE If you do keep your old version of Windows on the hard disk, and want to run Windows for Workgroups as your usual working environment, you must not have any references to the directory for your older version of Windows in your AUTOEXEC.BAT and CONFIG.SYS files.

SETUP will search for a previous version of Windows and will install Windows for Workgroups in the directory that contains the previous version if possible. If not, the directory C:\WINDOWS will be used and you will be asked if you want Windows for Workgroups installed there.

Some Windows experts redirect SETUP to install the operating software in a directory called C:\WIN rather than the default C:\WINDOWS.

They reason that the shorter directory name is easier to find and places less strain on an internal counter in the system called the environment space. Whatever you decide to name the Windows directory, keep it consistent across the workgroup. It's much easier to maintain a network where software is placed in directories named the same. Also, as you add Windows compatible software, each will write a small configuration file to the Windows directory. Your consistent naming convention will be helpful in the long run.

NOTE If your hard disk space is inadequate, SETUP will alert you and give you the option of installing a minimal subset of Windows for Workgroups. You can then add additional functional components as room is available. If you encounter this situation, and if you have a clear idea what functionality you want and which files are required, you might want to back out of the SETUP program by pressing F3, and try again with the Custom Setup. If you are new to Windows, it is still best to stick with Express Setup and allow Windows for Workgroups to do its best for you.

If you do not have a previous copy of Windows installed, the SETUP program will ask you to verify the hardware components of your system. If any of its choices are wrong, you may correct them by selecting them with the arrow keys and pressing ENTER. Once you are satisfied with the setting, select the last option to continue.

The system brings up the Windows graphical user interface, and a dialog box appears. You will be asked to enter your name, a computer name (by which your system will be identified on the network), and the name of a workgroup to which you will belong. You can move through the fields either using the TAB key, or by clicking on the boxed entry area with the mouse. A note to new Windows users — do not press ENTER until you are ready to continue. The ENTER key acts as a mouse-click on the default option, and will signal the program to Continue.

Installing Windows for Workgroups

After filling in the screen, you can review the information. If it all seems correct, press the ENTER key again. The Windows SETUP Program will now install the rest of Windows for Workgroups on your computer system.

You will be led through Printer installation, where you will be asked to locate your printer from a list provided. Select the printer (or printers) that you plan to use. Later, you can share your printer (or access another's printer) through the Print Manager software.

Installing Network Interface Card Drivers

For the network card to function, you must load software *drivers* for the NIC. A driver is a program that controls a device such as a printer, disk drive, or, in this case, access to the network. The device driver uses a set of commands to communicate with the device it controls.

As part of the SETUP process, you are asked to specify which NIC you have in your system. The SETUP program will then install a device driver for that NIC. SETUP first tries to determine the NIC in your machine — if it recognizes the card, it will prompt you. Otherwise, SETUP will ask you to select from a list of network interface cards, as shown in Figure 3.2.

Figure 3.2

Network interface card setup

```
                Install New Network Adapter
Select a Network Adapter to Install:
Unlisted or Updated Network Adapter              OK
3Com EtherLink 16
3Com EtherLink II or IITP (8 or 16-bit)          Cancel
3Com EtherLink III
3Com EtherLink Plus                              Help
3Com EtherLink/MC
3Com TokenLink
Amplicard AC 210/AT
Amplicard AC 210/XT
ARCNET Compatible
Artisoft AE-1
Artisoft AE-2 (MCA) or AE-3 (MCA)
Artisoft AE-2 or AE-3
```

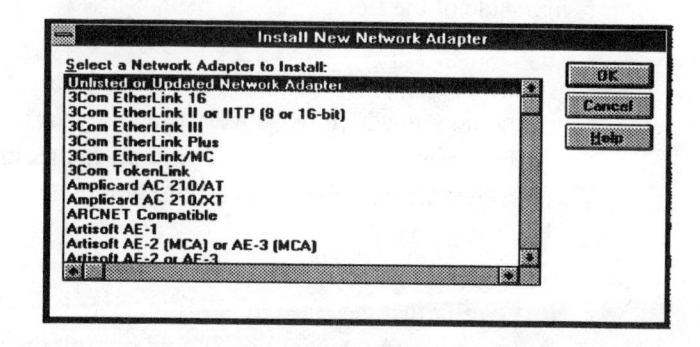

Scroll through the list of supported adapters and select the exact name of your network card. Highlight it and then click on the OK button.

Next you will be asked to verify the interrupt request number (IRQ), Base I/O Port, and Base Memory Address to be used by the driver in communicating with your card. The IRQ number will be highlighted as shown in Figure 3.3. Selecting the adapter you're using from the list, and specifying the configuration of the IRQ and Port, allows SETUP to configure and install a device driver for your NIC. (Depending on what NIC you have installed, you may have to supply information about how your card is set. Make sure you have this information handy.)

Figure 3.3

Configuring your network adapter

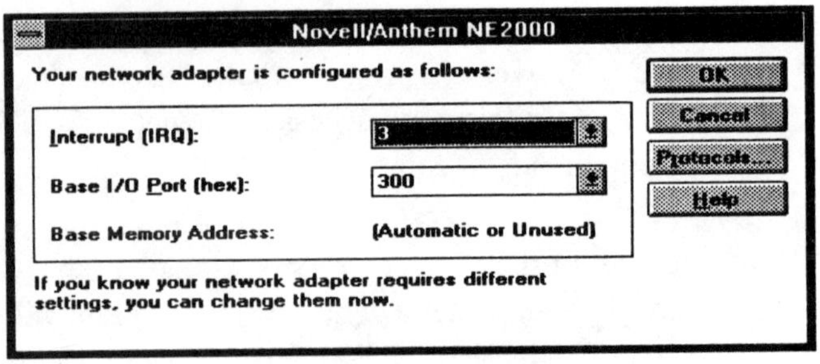

SETUP has shown you a default value for the IRQ number. To get a list of other possible values, click on the downward-pointing arrow on the right side of the field.

When you set up the card and put it into the PC, you collected some information on which IRQs were used by your other devices. You should consult that now and determine whether the IRQ number selected by SETUP matches the IRQ number you selected on the network card. They *must* match.

Next, verify that the Base I/O Port indicated matches the setting you gave the network card. Again, you should consult the notes you made while configuring. To change the I/O Port, use the mouse to point and click on the Up Arrow or Down Arrow to the right of the entry for the I/O Port address. When you do this you will notice that the entry changes. Note that these addresses are in hexadecimal notation, just like the information you captured in the configuration notes.

Figure 3.4

Setting the base I/O port address

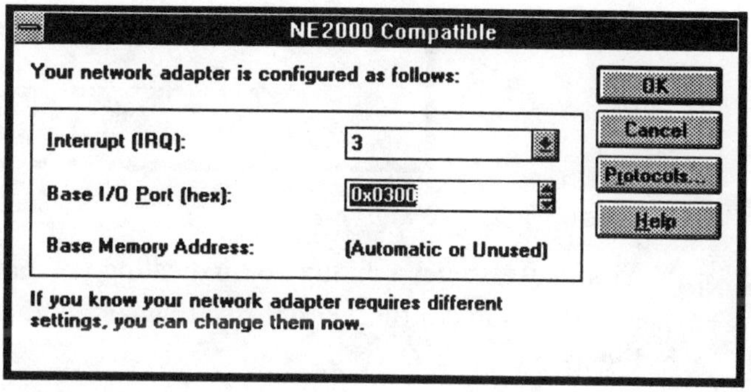

![NE2000 Compatible dialog showing Interrupt (IRQ): 3, Base I/O Port (hex): 0x0300, Base Memory Address: (Automatic or Unused)]

You can select the I/O Port address by moving the mouse pointer to the entry and clicking. You can type in a number; however, it is best to use the arrows to scroll through settings as these are valid choices and you are less likely to make a typing error. Figure 3.4 shows an example of setting the I/O Port address.

Depending on what NIC you are using, your next step may involve setting a Base Memory Address. In most cases the Base Memory Address for the card will either be set automatically or it will not be used. However, in cases where you need to set the size of a block of RAM for the transfer area, you should use the network card vendor's configuration utility.

After you have entered the configuration settings, point and click on the OK button. If the IRQ you have selected is determined by the SETUP program to be in conflict with another adapter, you will get the screen shown in Figure 3.5.

Figure 3.5

Conflicting IRQ number

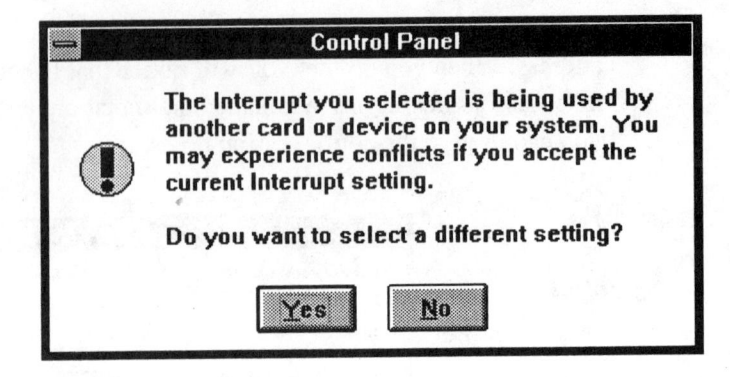

> **Control Panel**
>
> ⚠ The Interrupt you selected is being used by another card or device on your system. You may experience conflicts if you accept the current Interrupt setting.
>
> Do you want to select a different setting?
>
> [Yes]   [No]

You may also get a dialog box indicating you have selected a Base I/O Port that is in conflict with the settings of another device, as shown in Figure 3.6.

If you elect to change the setting of the Base I/O Port, Windows for Workgroups will return you to the Network Adapter dialog box. Check your notes and verify that the settings are correct. If they seem to be, you should go back through the inventory of other devices and see if there are other IRQ and Base I/O Port settings which are not used by another device. Try these settings one at a time until you find a combination that does not result in a conflict.

After you have successfully completed configuration of the network adapter, SETUP will ask you to specify any compatible networks that

Figure 3.6

SETUP detected a conflicting base I/O port

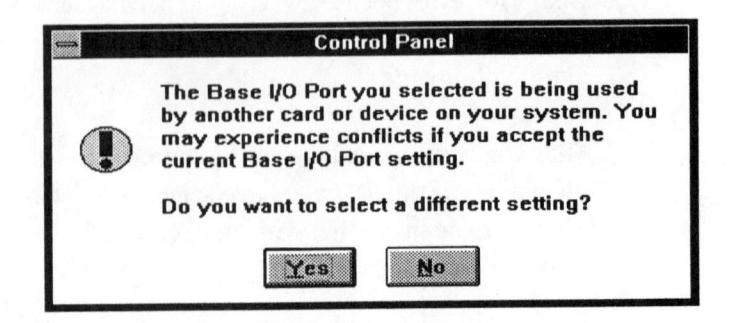

> **Control Panel**
>
> ⚠ The Base I/O Port you selected is being used by another card or device on your system. You may experience conflicts if you accept the current Base I/O Port setting.
>
> Do you want to select a different setting?
>
> [Yes]   [No]

Installing Windows for Workgroups

you want to support from your Windows for Workgroups environment. Upon selection of a particular network, the necessary drivers will be installed.

A dialog box will ask if you want to select a network to add to the "Other Networks in Use List." Here you can tell Windows for Workgroups to add support for any other networks you may be connected to. See Figure 3.7 for your choices of other networks.

Figure 3.7

Network selection

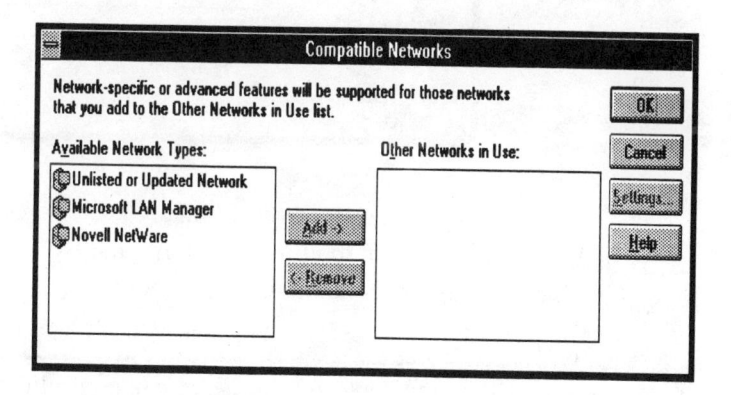

[Compatible Networks dialog box showing Available Network Types: Unlisted or Updated Network, Microsoft LAN Manager, Novell NetWare; with Other Networks in Use list and buttons OK, Cancel, Settings, Help, Add, Remove]

You may be prompted to insert a disk containing the network drivers needed by SETUP to configure your system to support the selected network.

SETUP will also look through your hard disk and create icons in the Program Manager for all of your Windows applications. It's a good idea to allow SETUP to do this. You can easily remove the ones you don't want, or regroup them to your liking, after they are set up. One thing about this automatic setup of applications, though — it sets the default working directory to be the directory where the program files are found. This is not usually what you want, so you'll need to go back and use the Properties option in the Program Manager's File menu to change this after you have finished with the installation as shown in Figure 3.8. If, in a previous installation, you had set up working directories as you wanted them, they will be preserved.

Figure 3.8

Changing the working directory of an application

[Program Item Properties dialog box showing Description: Microsoft Word, Command Line: C:\WINWORD\winword.exe, Working Directory: C:\wfwbook, Shortcut Key: None, Run Minimized unchecked, with OK, Cancel, Browse, Change Icon, and Help buttons]

SETUP also recognizes and sets up many DOS applications, by creating a .PIF file and an icon to allow you to run the DOS application by double-clicking on the icon with your mouse.

> **NOTE** Users who have special needs can control the Windows for Workgroups setup, overriding many of the default values. If, for example, you are installing Windows for Workgroups on a PC with limited disk space and you have some experience with Windows, you might want to go this route. It requires more interaction though, and more time, but you can pick and choose which Windows components you want.
>
> If you are not familiar with Windows and don't have the time to look through all of the documentation to determine what choices to make, you will want to stick with the Express Setup, which does a fine job with ease.

The next dialog box to appear will ask if you want to run the Windows tutorial. If you are new to the Windows environment, we suggest you take some time to run it. If you don't have time, or don't feel you need the tutorial, then you may bypass this option.

You will see a dialog box which gives you the option of restarting your computer so that all of the configuration settings will take effect. You should select this with the mouse and wait while Windows reboots your computer. When you come back up to the DOS prompt, type:

WIN

Windows for Workgroups will come up.

Defining Passwords

When you log on for the first time, you will see the dialog box shown in Figure 3.9. The Logon Name will match the name you gave earlier in the installation process. If you want to use a password to control access to your resources, you should enter one now.

Figure 3.9

Logging on to Windows for Workgroups

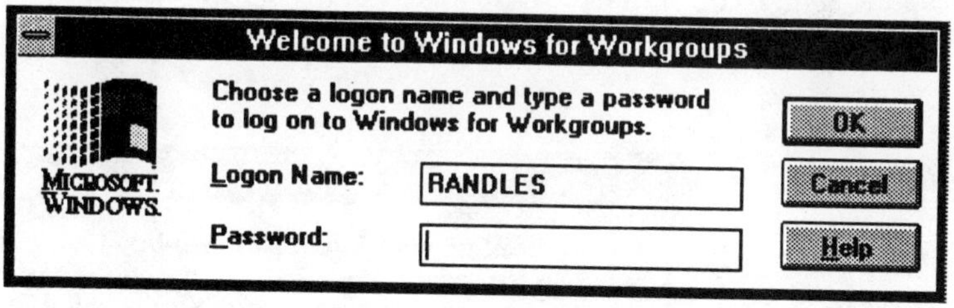

When you begin sharing resources on a network, your system and the systems of your coworkers become more accessible. That is the end you are trying to achieve, but you don't want just anyone to have access to sensitive information you might have stored in your system. Passwords allow Windows for Workgroups to protect your privacy, by verifying the identity of the person connecting.

Each time you log on, the password you supply gives you access to the resources on the network. This is done by verifying your password with a list of passwords for resources. The first time you log on, though, you will not have a password-list file established on your system. You should see a dialog box similar to the one shown in Figure 3.10.

Figure 3.10

Creating the password list file

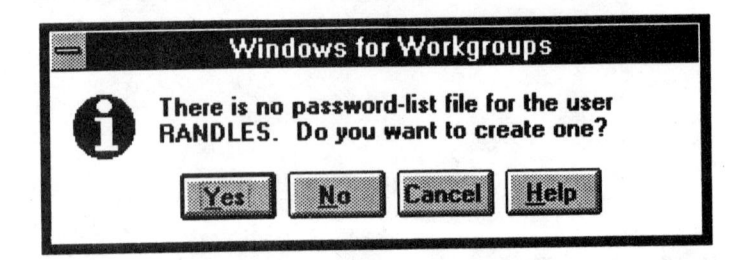

Select Yes and the system will create a password-list file for you, which is protected (through use of your password) from access by other people. You will be asked to retype your password to confirm it and ensure that you have entered it correctly. (Next time you log on, you will have to enter your password only once.) Figure 3.11 illustrates the password confirmation process. Click on OK to confirm your password.

Figure 3.11

Defining your password

Continuing with your first logon session, you should see a screen similar to that shown in Figure 3.12. If you select the option Log on at StartUp,

INSTALLING WINDOWS FOR WORKGROUPS

you'll be prompted for your password and logged on to the network each time you start up Windows for Workgroups.

When you log on, any previous connections you had to shared resources on other computers will be restored. This provides you the same context each time you work.

Figure 3.12

Logon settings

```
┌─────────────────── Logon Settings ───────────────────┐
│ ┌─Logon Status──────────────────────┐    [   OK   ]  │
│ │ Currently logged on as RANDLES    │    [ Cancel ] │
│ │ Default Logon Name:  [RANDLES   ] │    [  Help  ] │
│ │ [ Log Off ]                       │                │
│ └───────────────────────────────────┘                │
│ ┌─On Startup────────────────────────┐                │
│ │ ☐ Log On at Startup               │                │
│ └───────────────────────────────────┘                │
└──────────────────────────────────────────────────────┘
```

It is best to password-protect the resources on even the smallest network. Windows for Workgroups makes using passwords easy. After they are set up for each of the resources and you have a password list, the system will automatically supply your passwords to the network you are connecting to. You will have to supply only your logon password and not the passwords for sharing files.

This chapter took us from a standing start to a fully installed Windows for Workgroups computer. We discussed the planning steps: choosing naming conventions for people and workgroups, taking an inventory of your computers and how they are set up, and preparing for cabling. Then we began the installation process with the Windows for Workgroups SETUP utility, and installed the software on our first computer.

Your next step is to install the software on the other PCs in your workgroup. Then, you'll be ready for a test drive of your network.

CHAPTER 4

TEST DRIVING SHARED FILES AND PRINTERS

CHAPTER 4

Featuring:

- **Brushing Up on Windows Basics**
- **Basic Sharing with Windows for Workgroups**
- **Sharing Files and Directories**

Now, the real adventure begins. The cables are connected, PCs are buttoned up, the software is installed, and everything is ready to roll. It's time to take your bright, shiny new Windows for Workgroups LAN for a test drive.

In this chapter, we'll tour the basic Windows interface, then the three primary sharing utilities built into Windows for Workgroups: File Manager, for sharing your files and directories; Print Manager, for sharing printers; and ClipBook Viewer, for sharing objects, documents, and graphics.

If you are an experienced Windows user, you may already know something about these utilities, but in a stand-alone environment, many people don't spend much time with them (especially Print Manager and the Clipboard, which often work in the background). With Windows for Workgroups, however, you'll find these utilities much more a part of your work day. New functions like File Manager, for example, will become your method of accessing other people's files and sharing your own. With Print Manager, you'll connect to other printers on the network, and with

ClipBook Viewer, you'll be able to share information easily and effectively with other Windows for Workgroups users.

In this chapter, we'll start by providing grounding in the fundamentals for those who are new to Windows. Even if you consider yourself an experienced user, it's a good idea to brush up on some of the basics, just to make sure you know all the tips and tricks. After that, we'll turn our attention to sharing your files and directories. We'll explore how files are organized and created, then focus on using the File Manager for both granting and gaining access to files across the network. Then we turn our attention to printing. Using the Print Manager, we'll see how to share a local printer and connect to printers that other users have shared. Finally, we'll take a quick look at the power of the ClipBook Viewer for sharing documents, graphs, and objects across the network.

Brushing Up on Windows Basics

The Windows interface is more than a pretty face for your computer. There is great visual consistency within Windows applications, and that consistency combined with Windows' intuitive organization is a great asset. As you pass from one Windows application to another, you won't have to learn new commands and re-learn where things are. Once you learn the function for scroll bars, dialog boxes, and sizing buttons, you have mastered the interaction. It's like driving a car — the gas pedal, brakes, and steering wheel are always in the same place, so if you change from a Ford to a Buick, you still know how to drive.

The Basic Elements of Windows

The first window you see when Windows is run is the Program Manager window, as shown in Figure 4.1. The Program Manager is the primary application window from which other applications are launched. It is sometimes called a "shell" — a program that acts as a shell around other applications. Looking at the Program Manager, you can see some of the standard elements of the Windows interface.

Figure 4.1

Annotated Program Manager window

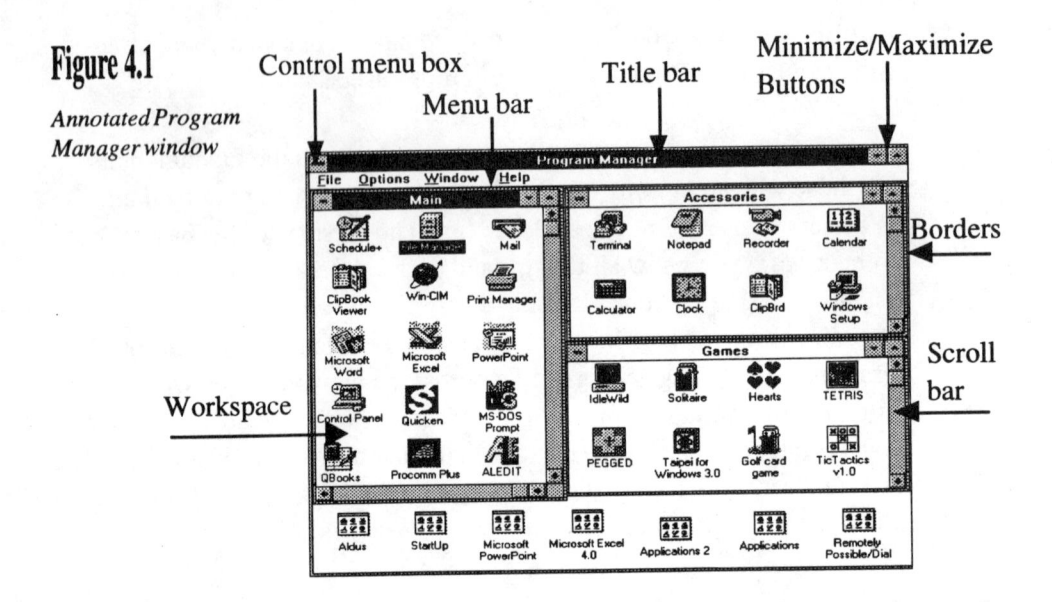

Windows makes a distinction between an *application window* and a *document window*. An *application window* consists of an open and running application. The window includes certain features (explained below) such as the name of the application on a title bar, a control box, sizing buttons, and a menu bar. Within an application window, you may also find a *document window* which holds one or more documents pertaining to the application. A document window does not have a menu bar, but does have a title bar, control-menu box, and sizing buttons.

The basic elements of a window (as illustrated in Figure 4.1) are:

▲ Borders: the edges that mark the boundaries of a given window.
▲ Title bar: an area at the top of the window, containing either the application's name or the name for a function that you are performing within the application. Some applications will also indicate the name of the file on which you are operating.

- ▲ Control-menu box: the box (containing a bold dash) at the far left of the Title bar. Clicking on this button one time presents you with the Control menu that controls this window. Double-clicking on this box closes the application.

- ▲ Minimize/Maximize buttons: two buttons that control the sizing of the window, these are the Minimize (down arrow) and Maximize (up arrow) buttons. Maximized windows do not have a Maximize button. They have a Restore icon that restores the window to its original screen size. We'll discuss their use later in this section.

- ▲ Menu bar: contains menus presenting the available commands for an application. Menu bars will vary a little between applications, but most will include the File, Window, and Help menus.

- ▲ Scroll bars: when there is too much text or too many icons to be displayed within a window, Windows automatically adds one or more scroll bars to the right or bottom edge of the screen. By placing the mouse pointer on the arrows or boxes in the scroll bars and holding down the left mouse button, you can maneuver around inside the work area.

- ▲ Workspace: the area below the Menu bar and within the bounds of the window's borders is called the workspace, desktop, or work area.

Pointing and Clicking with the Mouse

You can control Windows through keyboard commands or by using a mouse to point and click on icons or menu selections. Most people prefer the convenience of using a mouse.

A good way to learn how to use the mouse is through the Windows Tutorial that comes standard with the software. Press and hold the ALT key and then press the H key to run the Tutorial. The Help menu on the Program Manager's Menu bar will appear, as shown in Figure 4.2. Now type W and the Tutorial program will begin. Follow the directions on the screen and you will be on your way to becoming a skilled mouse expert. If you find yourself having problems at first, don't give up. Using a mouse is like riding a bicycle — you can be a little wobbly at first, but soon it becomes a very natural action. The Tutorial also covers the basics of using a Windows environment. If you are new to Windows, it is a good idea to run through this tutorial at least once.

Figure 4.2

Selecting the Windows Tutorial

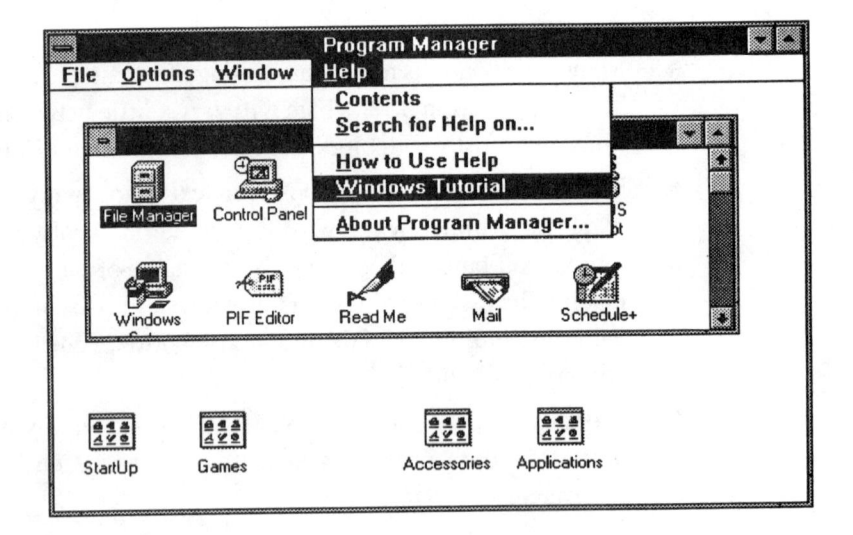

Choosing and Selecting

Windows makes a distinction between *choosing* and *selecting*. *Selecting* an icon, option, or line of text from a list highlights it and establishes it as the object for a subsequent action. Selecting does not cause any action to occur. When you *choose* an option or icon, you execute it and cause something to happen. Choosing requires an action to occur.

Selecting is done by clicking once on an object somewhere in the window. An object can be an item from a list, a button, or an icon.

TEST DRIVING SHARED FILES AND PRINTERS

In Windows, you'll often have to select an item or items from a list (for example, from a list of files or names). To select a single item, you point to that item on screen and click the mouse button.

To select multiple items from a list (several continuous files, for example) select the first item, then press and hold down the SHIFT key. Move the mouse pointer to the last item you want to select and click the left mouse again. All items between the first item you clicked on and the last will be selected.

To select multiple items that aren't together, press and hold down the CTRL key, and then click on each item you want to include. Each of the items you have selected is highlighted.

When you *choose* a menu option or icon, you execute it, causing an action to occur. For example, you may choose from a menu an option that opens a window, brings up a dialog box, or causes some other operation to be performed. Choosing is done by selecting an object and pressing the ENTER key, or by pointing at the item on screen and double-clicking (that is, clicking twice rapidly on the left mouse button). You can also choose multiple actions by selecting a number of options within a dialog box and then selecting the OK or CONTINUE button in the dialog box.

Minimizing and Maximizing Windows

Since you are likely to be working with more than one application at a time, Windows gives you opportunities to customize your screen. Each application window has Minimize and Maximize buttons.

Maximizing

Windows automatically sizes an application window to fit on your screen. It does this based on its knowledge of the other applications that are currently open and their sizes. Most application windows will open in a window that is smaller than the full screen. Most users find working in an application more convenient when it appears full screen. Windows provides a convenient way to size applications to full screen with minimal effort. You can simply click on the Maximize button (the up-arrow button to the far right of the Title bar) to make the application cover the full screen.

Minimizing

After you have the window Maximized, you may want to move it out of the way temporarily to gain access to another application or perform another task. Click on the Minimize button to reduce the application window to an icon. The program will still be running, it's just smaller and out of the way. Some people call this iconizing a program. Double-clicking on the icon will bring the window back to its original size. This feature is very useful when you need to work for a moment with another application, and then get back to your original task.

Restoring

If you want to look at other applications, but don't want to completely reduce the application window to an icon, you can use the Restore button. The Restore button, represented with arrows pointing both up and down, is at the extreme right of the Menu bar. It shows up only when you have Maximized the main window of an application. If the program is Minimized to an icon, you can Restore by selecting the icon and choosing the Restore menu option off the Control-menu, as shown in Figure 4.3.

Controlling Window Size and Positioning

Sometimes you will want to see multiple applications up on the screen. You might need to cut or copy information from a spreadsheet and paste it into a word processing document. Windows makes it easy to do this. But you'll need to know how to use Windows sizing features.

Figure 4.3

The Control menu

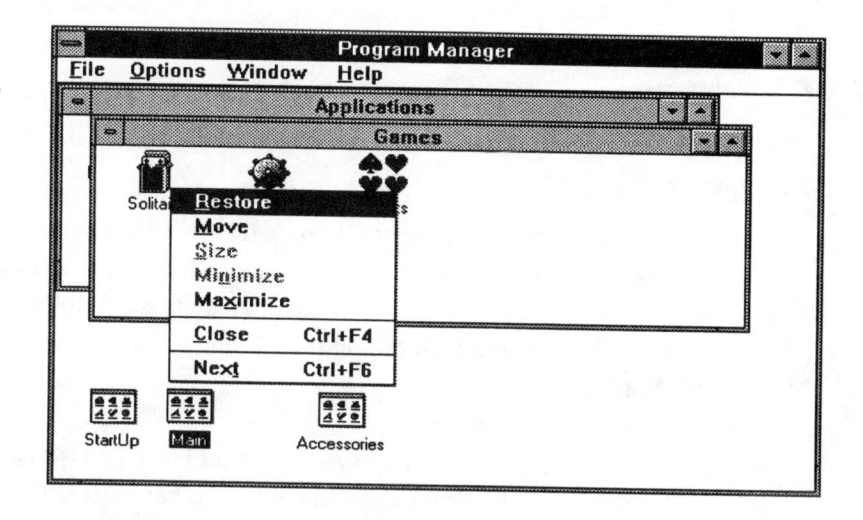

[Figure: Program Manager window showing the Control menu opened on the Games window, with options: Restore, Move, Size, Minimize, Maximize, Close Ctrl+F4, Next Ctrl+F6]

Sizing Windows

You can control an application's size and position on the screen. Move the mouse pointer onto one of the borders of an application window, and the pointer's shape will change to a bidirectional arrow. (You must put the pointer directly on the border to size a window.) When the pointer changes shape, press down the left mouse button, hold it down, and move the mouse. The application window size will follow your mouse movements, getting smaller or larger as you wish. To speed things up, you can grab the application window on a corner (the mouse pointer will turn into a diagonal bidirectional arrow) and size in two directions at once.

Many Windows applications will remember your sizing preferences. When you close an application or exit from Windows, the last size and screen position you indicated in each application window will be saved. Windows utilities like Program Manager and File Manager will remember their positions if Save Settings on Exit on the Options menu is active.

Positioning Windows

To position an application window somewhere else on the screen, move the mouse pointer to the Title bar, then press and hold the left mouse button. This grabs the application window and lets you move it around to different locations.

Getting Help

Windows provides an extensive Help system, which is context-sensitive – it uses internal information to provide help with the window or dialog box you are in and even the task you are trying to accomplish. You can get to the Help system by pressing the F1 key, or by choosing Help from the Menu bar.

To get an overview of the Help system, select How To Use Help from the Help menu on the Program Manager Menu bar. After selecting this option, you will see a window containing text information, as shown in Figure 4.4.

Figure 4.4

How to Use Help screen window

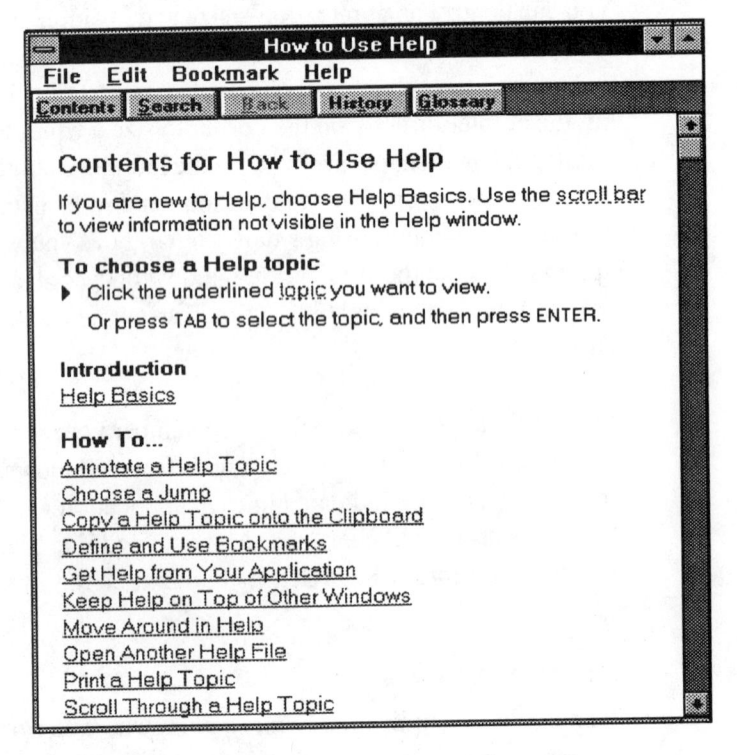

> **NOTE** Some of the words on the Help screens are underlined. That means there is additional information about each of these words if you need it. To access this extra help, click on the word that pertains to your desired topic. More information will appear. You can also use this feature as an electronically indexed manual. Do this by choosing the Search for Help On... option on the Help menu.

Taking a little time to experiment with the Help system will assist you in learning to make Windows a productive environment. As you need to accomplish a given task, you can go straight to the relevant information using the Search capability. This can save hours of browsing through manuals trying to find tidbits of information.

Starting Applications

With the basic elements in hand, let's look at how to start other applications from within Program Manager. When you first installed Windows for Workgroups, it created up to five Program Groups (fewer if you did not install everything). The program groups help you manage applications by organizing sets that go together. For instance, the games that come with Windows for Workgroups are put into a Games program group window. Each group — Main, Accessories, Applications, Startup, and Games — contains icons for each program you can run within that group. In the Main group, you will see icons for File Manager, Control Panel, Print Manager, Mail, Schedule+, and several other programs.

To demonstrate how to start any application from Program Manager, let's open the Main program group window and run File Manager.

1. Open the Main program group window by choosing the icon marked Main. (If the window is already open, you may not need to do this. Instead, bring the Main window to the foreground by clicking its Title bar.)

2. Choose the File Manager icon by double-clicking on it. This will start the File Manager application. The File Manager window displays the directories for your disks, so it needs a lot of screen space. You might want to open up File Manager, use it, and then minimize it, so you can keep it open but out of the way.

So far, everything we've talked about in this chapter has been oriented to the basics of the Windows environment. Both the stand-alone version of Windows and Windows for Workgroups share many traits. But, Windows for Workgroups picks up where the regular version of Windows leaves off – and that is when it comes to sharing.

Basic Sharing with Windows for Workgroups

Sharing information and resources is at the heart of working cooperatively. As mentioned earlier in this chapter, Windows for Workgroups provides several built-in utilities for connecting to or sharing resources (files, printers, or documents). These utilities – File Manager, Print Manager, and the ClipBook Viewer – use option buttons that look like those described in Table 4.1.

In the next sections of this chapter, you will see how sharing, unsharing, connecting, and disconnecting are used in each utility. Since Windows for Workgroups applies these concepts so consistently, once you know how to use one option, the rest are easy.

Sharing Files and Directories: Using File Manager

The File Manager utility provided with Windows for Workgroups allows you to share the files on your hard disk with other users on a network. To do this without a network and special utility, you would have to copy files to a diskette and pass the diskette to your colleagues, and they

Table 4.1 Toolbar buttons for connecting, disconnecting

Icon	Function
	Connects to another person's resource
	Disconnects from another person's resource
	Shares a resource on your computer
	Stops sharing a resource on your computer

would have to copy the files to their computers. If you consider that this must occur each time the file is revised, it is easy to see that a good bit of productivity is lost in the exercise.

When you and your coworkers have access to the same directories, the flow of your work becomes more efficient. For example, when you complete a budget for your project you can simply place it in a shared directory and send e-mail to your manager saying it is there.

Organizing and Naming Shared Directories

Your computer stores its data files and programs in directories. You can have as many directories as you'd like and can arrange them so that some directories are subsets of others. Given that flexibility, it is important to develop and maintain an orderly *directory structure* with meaningful names. Otherwise, it is easy to "lose" files in the computer.

Maintaining some kind of order over files becomes even more important when you are sharing information among members of a workgroup. Files should be grouped according to logical relationships, just as they are in paper filing systems. For example, in well-kept paper systems, we label cabinets with names like Financial Reports, and then have folders for each company we keep reports on.

The directory structure represents a filing system for the documents and programs we keep on our personal computer systems. A disk drive designation (like C:\) or a directory (like C:\WINDOWS) can be thought of as a filing cabinet. Directories, which are represented as file folder icons in Windows, are analogous to drawers in a filing cabinet. Within a directory there can be other subdirectories which can contain more subdirectories, as shown in Figure 4.5.

Figure 4.5

Directory and subdirectory structures

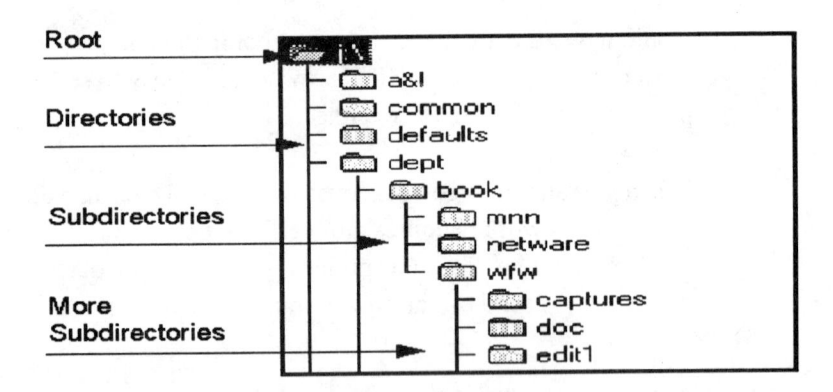

Imagine the directory and subdirectory structure as being similar to a tree. The trunk of the structure is called the "root" and the first entry that branches directly off the root is called a "directory." A directory branching from another directory is called a "subdirectory."

If your PC filing system becomes too complex, it will be a hindrance and not a help, just as a large, poorly organized file system for paper might. If the structure of the PC directory tree is too deep, it becomes difficult to navigate and hides files contained in the next subdirectory level. If the

TEST DRIVING SHARED FILES AND PRINTERS

directory structure is too flat, people will have to scan a lot of directories they are not interested in to find the file they want. You wouldn't put all the files for your company in one set of cabinets, organized alphabetically. Instead, you group documents logically — the marketing statistics together, the payroll records together, and the tax records in another system. The same principles apply to organizing your directory structure.

As a rule, we suggest you keep your directory and subdirectory structures to no more than four levels. This will give you plenty of room for maintaining both simple and complex files.

In naming directories, it is important to make sure that the name conveys something about the category of information contained within. "MYSTUFF" is an example of how not to name a directory. You need to be more specific. The top level of your information might be "RPATTERS" if your name was "Randy Patterson". Within that, you might group things by file type, say "DOC" for all your documents. Or you might want to organize based on projects rather than users' names, and then within the projects by type of file, so that you have a directory called "SLSREPRT," and within that directories for "DOC" and "FINSTATS," for the documents and spreadsheets you are keeping.

Windows for Workgroups allows you to attach a comment to shared directories and printers. The comment can be seen by others when they pull up a list of directories or printers. This is very useful in letting people know more about the contents of a directory than the cryptic eight character directory name DOS will allow. We'll see how to attach comments to directories later in this chapter.

Sharing the Directory

The File Manager lets you set up a directory to be shared with members of your workgroup. The process is very simple and a lot quicker than walking down the hall with a diskette in hand.

To share a directory, first start the File Manager as we demonstrated earlier. The steps in sharing a directory are:

1. From File Manager, select the directory you want to share from the list in the directory window.
2. Choose the Share button from the Toolbar (or choose the Share As option from the Disk menu). The Share Directory dialog box will appear similar to the one shown in Figure 4.6. Note that the Path name is already filled in. If it is incorrect, you can edit the entry in that field.
3. From within the Share Directory dialog box, make sure there is a Share Name filled in. The Share Name is the name by which others will see the directory over the network. If it does not exist, or if you want to change it, you can enter any name into it in this box. Just below the Share Name, make sure the Path section is filled out correctly. The path should point to the directory location on your computer, as shown in Figure 4.6.

Figure 4.6

Sharing a directory

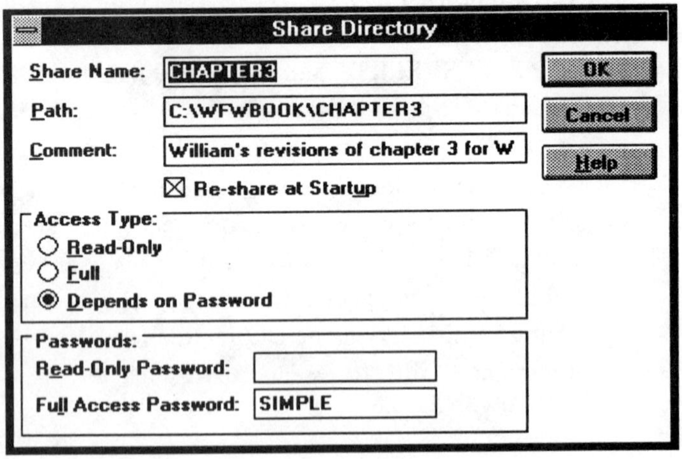

Test Driving Shared Files and Printers

4. Next you should fill in the Comment field. This will give other members of the workgroup information about the directory's contents. (An entry for Comment is optional, but we recommend it.) Just below the Comment field is a check box to Re-share at Startup. Select this check box if you want to share this directory at all times. If the check box is not checked, you will share the directory for this session only. (Next time you start Windows for Workgroups, the directory will not automatically be shared.)

5. Select the Access Type you want by clicking on the appropriate button. Read-Only will allow others to read the files in the directory, but they will be unable to make changes or delete them. Full access lets others add, change, or delete files in the directory. If you select Depends on Password, you can have two separate passwords, one for reading (but not updating or deleting) files; and one for full access to the directory.

6. Click on the OK button and you have shared your first directory. Notice that an icon representing the shared directory is now shown on the list.

Now your coworkers have access to files in this directory. When you finish with a document and want someone else to review it you simply share the directory.

Gaining Access to Files on Other Computers

You can connect to someone else's shared directories easily. When you connect to a shared directory, you create a new drive letter on your computer — each shared directory you connect to will take up one drive letter. For example, on a standard PC, the first shared directory you connect to will be assigned the drive letter D:, the next one will be assigned drive letter E:, and so on. If you run out of drive letters, you can disconnect from a shared directory you are not currently using and use that drive letter.

If a password has been set up for the directory you are attempting to access, you will need to supply that password. To access a shared directory on someone else's computer:

1. Choose the Connect button (or Select Connect Network Drive... from File Manager's Disk menu). This will bring up the Connect Network Drive dialog box.
2. Notice the Drive letter designation. Unless you change it, it will default to the next available letter in alphabetical order.
3. Select the Path from the pick list. First, click on the computer name whose shared directories you wish to see, and you'll be presented with a list of the Shared Directories. (The window will appear similar to that shown in Figure 4.7.) Choose the directory you want to use.

Figure 4.7

Connecting to a network directory

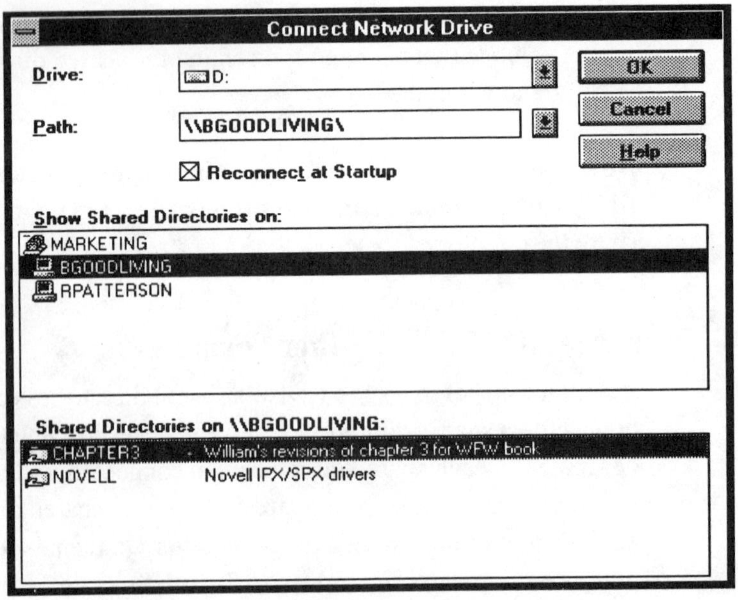

4. After you have selected the directory you want to share, click on the OK button in the upper right corner of the dialog box.

Test Driving Shared Files and Printers

5. If the other person password-protected the directory, an Enter Network Password dialog box will appear. You must enter the correct password to gain access to the directory. Note the Save this Password in Your Password List check box on the lower left of the dialog box. Choosing this option causes the system to keep track of this password in the future, so that when you connect to this directory, the system will automatically supply the password. As shown in Figure 4.8, enter the password and then click on the OK button.

Figure 4.8

Entering your password

```
┌─────────────── Enter Network Password ───────────────┐
│ You must supply a password to make this connection:  │
│                                                [  OK  ]│
│                                                [Cancel]│
│ Drive Letter:   D:                             [ Help ]│
│ Resource:       \\BGOODLIVING\CHAPTER3                │
│ Password:       [            ]                        │
│ ☒ Save this Password in Your Password List            │
└───────────────────────────────────────────────────────┘
```

You are now connected to the other computer's directory. Note the designation of the Resource, which contains both the computer name and directory path following the drive letter. The files are now accessible in the same manner as any of the other files under File Manager. You can now read, update, and even load programs from the other system's disk.

NOTE Keep in mind that our examples allowed you full access to the shared directory. If the owner of a directory elects to share Read-only privileges, you will not be able to create, update, or delete files.

Viewing Lists of Files

File Manager gives you several options for viewing lists of files. You can see files by their file names or with full details regarding file size, attributes, and creation date and time. Optionally, you can sort the list of files in several ways — alphabetically by name, by extension name or type, by size, or by date. You can change the way files are listed by using one of the view tools from the Toolbar (see Table 4.2), or by selecting one of the sort options from the View menu.

Table 4.2 File Manager tools

Icon	Title	Function
	View Name	Displays all files from a directory only as file name and extension. Includes no details about file size, creation date, or other information.
	View All File Details	Displays all files from a directory with information about file size, the date and time the file was last saved, and the file's attribute information. (Attributes include: r for files marked read-only, a for archive files that have changed since the last backup, h for hidden files, s for system files.)
	Sort by Name	Displays files in alphabetic order according to the file name.
	Sort by Type	Displays files in alphabetical order according to the file extension (the three characters to the right of the period in the file name).
	Sort by Size	Displays files according to size, in descending order.
	Sort by Date	Displays files according to date, with the most recent date first.

Printing on the Network

Many people who set up networks do so for the express purpose of sharing printers. Especially now, when color printers or high quality laser printers can be shared by so many people, it doesn't make sense to buy each person an individual printer. Instead, with Windows for Workgroups' Print Manager, an enhanced utility that lets you give or gain access to any printer on the network, you can share expensive printers and reduce costs.

Sharing Your Printer

First, let's look at the process of sharing a local printer with other workgroup members. This is very similar to sharing directories. First, choose the Print Manager by double-clicking on the Print Manager icon in the Main program group window. The Print Manager window will appear, as illustrated in Figure 4.9.

Figure 4.9

The Print Manager window

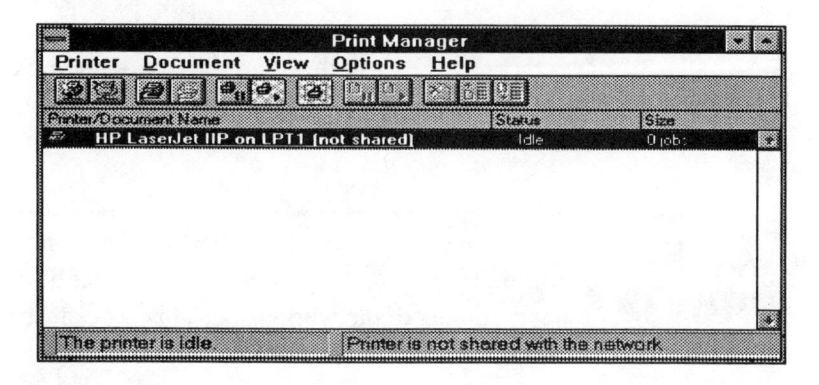

Notice that the printer in our example is designated as Not Shared. The steps to share a printer are:

1. Select the printer you wish to share from the Print Manager window, then choose the share icon (or choose Share Printer As... from the Printer menu) on Print Manager's menu bar.

2. The Share Printer dialog box will appear. To name the printer and type in any comments you have, fill out the information requested. (Our example in Figure 4.10 includes a Comment line saying that we always load company letterhead in this printer.)

Figure 4.10

Share Printer dialog box

Share Printer	
Printer:	HP LaserJet IIP on LPT1
Share as:	HP
Comment:	Printer is always loaded with letterhead
Password:	☒ Re-share at Startup

Buttons: OK, Cancel, Help

If you want, you can attach a password to the printer so that only people who know the password have access to it. Note, too, the Re-share at Startup check box that is selected in our example. This indicates that the printer will be re-shared whenever Windows for Workgroups is started.

3. Next, choose OK and the Share Printer dialog box will close. Now others on the network can print their documents on your shared printer.

NOTE You cannot close the Print Manager application after sharing a printer. If you do, the printer will no longer be available to other members of the workgroup. This is because the Print Manager works as a background task, handling the printing tasks for remote systems that have connected to the printer. You may also notice that your shared printer will not work when you are using full-screen DOS applications. Many DOS applications take full control of your computer and won't let Print Manger work, even in the background. (These applications are said to be running the exclusive mode of DOS.)

Printing to Another's Printer

Printing over the network allows printers to be viewed as a shared resource. This can allow a workgroup or small business to easily cost justify buying a high quality laser printer. Everyone in the workgroup can have access to quality printing at a lower per-person cost than would be accrued if you equipped everyone with a lower quality printer.

When using shared printers, make sure you have the correct print driver installed for each printer you want to connect to. If you haven't done so previously, you should now install all the printer drivers you need. Directions for installing printers were given in Chapter 3 (Installing Windows for Workgroups). If you have installed a print driver and connected it to an LPT port, it will appear in the list of printers in the Print Manager window.

When you use the shared printing ability of Windows for Workgroups you are essentially fooling the system and applications by setting up your system to have more printers than you have connected to your PC. Connecting to a shared printer is then a matter of establishing a link over the network from the printer driver, which thinks it is talking to a local printer port, to the actual printer which is attached to a port on the remote system. Windows for Workgroups manages everything in between, linking up the print drivers on the two systems and managing the data sent to the logical printer on one system to the actual print device on the other.

Connecting to Shared Printers

Windows for Workgroups makes it easy to use another person's printer. To do so, first the printer must be shared by the owner (using the steps we just described). Then, it is a simple matter of connecting to the remote printer.

Here are the steps:

1. To connect to a shared printer choose the connect button from the Toolbar (or the Connect Network Printer... option from the Printer menu on the Print Manager menu bar).
2. The Connect Network Printer dialog box will appear, as shown in Figure 4.11. The workgroups on your network are displayed in a list in the lower portion of the screen.

Figure 4.11

The Connect Network Printer dialog box

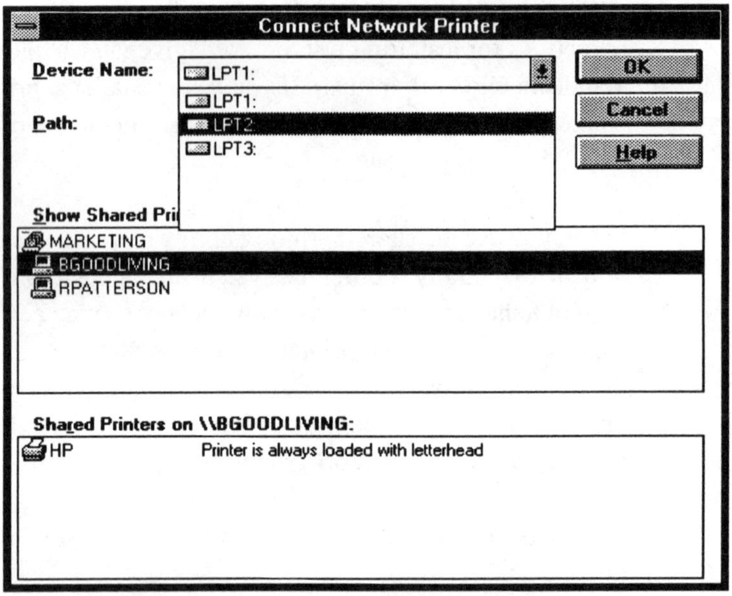

3. Choose the name of the computer with the printer you want. If you don't see the printer you want, just choose another computer system until you do see the printer you want. When you find the right printer, choose it by clicking on the item in the list.
4. Next, you should pick the port to connect the network printer. (This is the same technique we used for accessing files — instead of using drive letters, this time use printer ports to designate the shared resource.) To choose the printer port to attach the shared printer to, click on the down arrow to the right

Test Driving Shared Files and Printers

of the Device Name field. A list of ports will be presented. Simply choose an unused printer port. (If you choose LPT1: and it is in use for a local printer, you will receive a warning message).

5. After choosing the printer port, you can choose the network printer to connect to. Simply select the printer from the list provided. Also note the Reconnect at Startup check box. Just as it happened with the shared file directory, checking this box will cause the system to automatically connect you to the shared printer when Windows for Workgroups is brought up.

6. You are now ready to connect by clicking on the OK button at the upper right-hand of the dialog box. The Print Manager window will appear. The remote printer is ready to be used by your applications just as if it were connected to the LPT2 port of your local system.

Controlling Printers

Sometimes you'll want to print your documents in a special order, or you'll want to start or stop printing a job. Print Manager provides flexibility in starting and stopping print jobs, as well as moving specific jobs up or down in the queue. Table 4.3 shows the Toolbar buttons that let you control the printers.

> **NOTE**
> Keep in mind that you can change documents only in the queue that you created, unless you are the owner of the printer. For example, you can re-order the printing of your own documents on another's printer, but you cannot move your documents to print before those of someone else in the queue. Similarly, you can delete your document from the queue, but not those of other workgroup members.
>
> If, however, you are the printer owner (that is the shared printer is attached to your computer) you can use Print Manager to rearrange or delete *anyone's* print jobs.

Table 4.3 Printer Toolbar

Icon	Title	Function
	Pause Printer	Stops the printer. You must first select the printer you want to stop, then choose the Pause Printer button.
	Resume Printer	Restarts a printer that has been stopped. The printer must be selected, then you can choose the Resume Printer button.
	Set Printer Default	Makes the currently selected printer your default printer. Every print job from every Windows application from now on will be sent to this printer unless otherwise directed.
	Pause Printing Document	Stops the currently selected document from being printed. To use, you must first select a document, then choose the Pause Printing Document button. (You can pause only documents that you sent to a printer, unless you are the printer's owner, in which case you can pause any document.)
	Resume Printing Document	Restarts printing the currently selected document. (You can resume printing only your documents unless you are the printer's owner.)
	Delete Document	Deletes the currently selected document from the queue. (You can delete only the documents that you sent to the printer unless you are the printer's owner.)

Table 4.3 Printer Toolbar (continued)

Icon	Title	Function
	Move Document Down	Moves the currently selected document down in the print queue to be printed later. (You can move only the documents that you control. You cannot move ahead of another.)
	Move Document Up	Moves the currently selected document up in the print queue to print ahead of other documents. (You can move only the documents you control.

Sharing Documents: Using the ClipBook

Perhaps one of the most novel and potentially useful utilities included with Windows for Workgroups is the ClipBook Viewer. This lets you share documents or graphics with anyone on the Windows for Workgroups network. In many ways, the ClipBook Viewer is like an electronic cork board. You can post files, spreadsheets, documents, or other objects onto a page of the ClipBook to share them. (See Chapter 7 for a discussion of how ClipBook can be used for document management on the LAN.)

The ClipBook works similarly to File Manager or Print Manager — allowing you to share some of your resources with others. With ClipBook, however, you can be very selective about what you share. Say, for example, you want to share a particular graph you have created in a spreadsheet program — you can elect to share only the graph, not the whole spreadsheet file.

ClipBook works hand-in-hand with the Clipboard utility of Windows, but there are two primary differences between Clipboard and ClipBook.

First, Clipboard is a *temporary* storage place, used if you cut or copy something in or from a Windows application. It works like this: when you execute a cut or copy command, the contents of what you have selected are temporarily stored on the Clipboard by Windows. As soon as you store something else on the Clipboard, the first set of contents is erased. ClipBook, on the other hand, lets you save your work to a *permanent* page. You can recall that page at any time.

The second difference is ClipBook lets you *share* your work. You can select any of the pages in your ClipBook for sharing with members of your workgroup.

Connecting to Another ClipBook

The steps to access another person's ClipBook are:

1. Start the ClipBook application. From Program Manager, Choose the ClipBook icon located in the Main program group.
2. Choose the Connect button from the ClipBook Toolbar (or choose Connect... from the File menu). This brings up the Select Computer dialog box.
3. Choose the computer that you wish to connect to from the list and click on OK. In our example, Figure 4.12, we have selected the computer named DAVISON. ClipBook will take a few seconds to establish a link. If, when you try to connect to it, the computer is not running Windows for Workgroups, you will receive an error message indicating that a link could not be established.
4. When the link is established, you will see a list of all the shared pages on the other person's ClipBook. It should look like the example shown in Figure 4.13.

Figure 4.12

Connecting to another's ClipBook

Figure 4.13

Shared ClipBook pages on another's computer

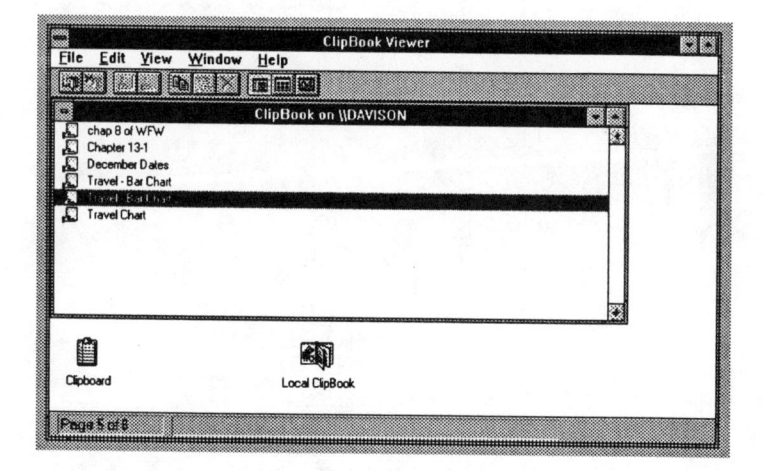

To view or use a page from the ClipBook, simply double-click on it. The contents of the clipped page will be displayed. If you want to use that page, copy it to your Clipboard and paste it into an application. Choose the Copy button from the Toolbar or choose the Copy option from the

Edit menu to copy the contents into your local Clipboard. Then, bring up the application you want to use, and use the Paste option from the Edit menu of the application.

> **NOTE** You can create a link to multiple ClipBooks across the network. If you do, it is a good idea to minimize each of the ClipBooks when you are not using them. This keeps the workspace neater and more organized. See Figure 4.14 for an example of several open ClipBooks on the workspace. Note that you can tell who the ClipBook belongs to.

Figure 4.14

Multiple Open ClipBooks

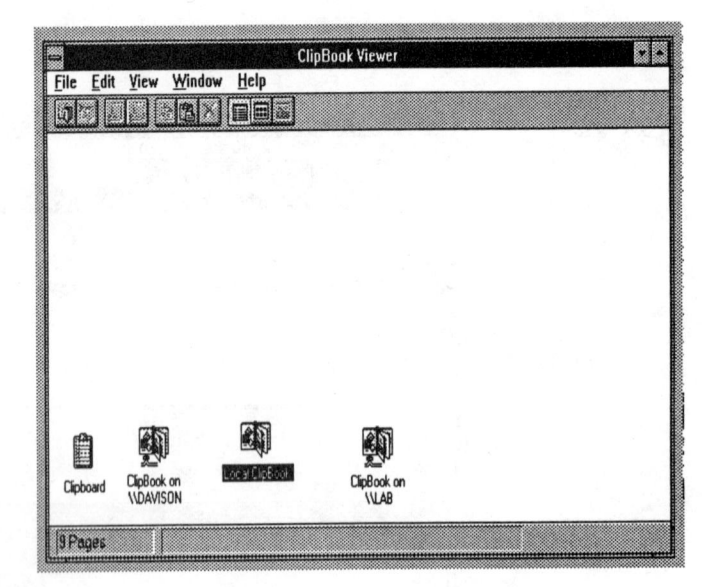

Sharing Your ClipBook

Your own ClipBook is shared on a page-by-page basis. You can elect to share pages in your ClipBook as you create them, or later on.

Test Driving Shared Files and Printers

To share pages from your ClipBook, follow these steps:

1. From an application, such as Excel for Windows, copy or cut something that you want to store in your ClipBook. For example, you may want to save a graph. From Excel, select the graph you want to copy, then choose Copy from the Edit menu.

2. Bring up the ClipBook Viewer. You can do this by minimizing Excel and choosing the ClipBook Viewer from the Main group of the Program Manager. When the ClipBook Viewer is loaded, choose Paste from its Edit menu.

3. The Paste dialog box will appear. Give your ClipBook page a name, and check the correct box to indicate whether you want to share the page or not, as shown in Figure 4.15.

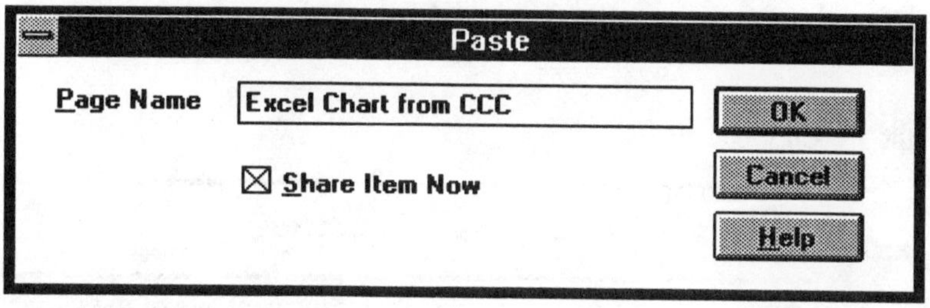

Figure 4.15

The Paste dialog box

4. If you decide to share this page now, the next dialog box will let you set the options for sharing. (See Figure 4.16.) You should complete filling out the options for sharing, access type and passwords (if any) for the ClipBook page. Then press the OK button and your ClipBook page is shared.

At any time, you can stop sharing a page from your ClipBook by selecting it from the list and choosing the Stop Sharing button from the Toolbar (or choosing Stop Sharing from the File menu).

ClipBook Features

The ClipBook provides several tools to make, arrange, and view pages. You can see ClipBook pages as a list, a full screen, or in miniature

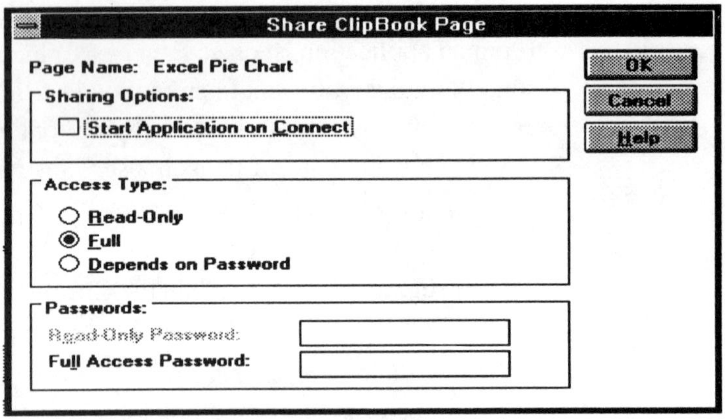

Figure 4.16

Share ClipBook Page

pictures called thumbnails. These tools are available from the Toolbar or through the menus. Table 4.4 lists the Toolbar icons.

Table 4.4 ClipBook Toolbar

Icon	Title	Function
	Paste	Pastes the contents of the current Clipboard into a ClipBook page.
	Delete	Deletes the current page from the ClipBook (if Clipboard is active, this will delete only the contents of the current Clipboard).
	Table of Contents	Displays the contents of the ClipBook as a list, by page name.
	Thumbnails	Displays the contents of the ClipBook as miniature pictures.
	Full Page	Displays the current ClipBook page enlarged to fill as much of the window as possible (size of the window depends on how you have sized the ClipBook on the screen).

In this chapter, we toured the major utilities of Windows for Workgroups, and examined how to share files, printers, and documents. We saw how Windows for Workgroups puts you in control of sharing your resources.

Frankly, we've just touched the surface of what Windows for Workgroups can do. In the chapters that follow, we'll explore other utilities and begin to add more use to our Windows environment. The best is yet to come!

CHAPTER 5

SETTING UP AND USING WORKGROUP E-MAIL

CHAPTER 5

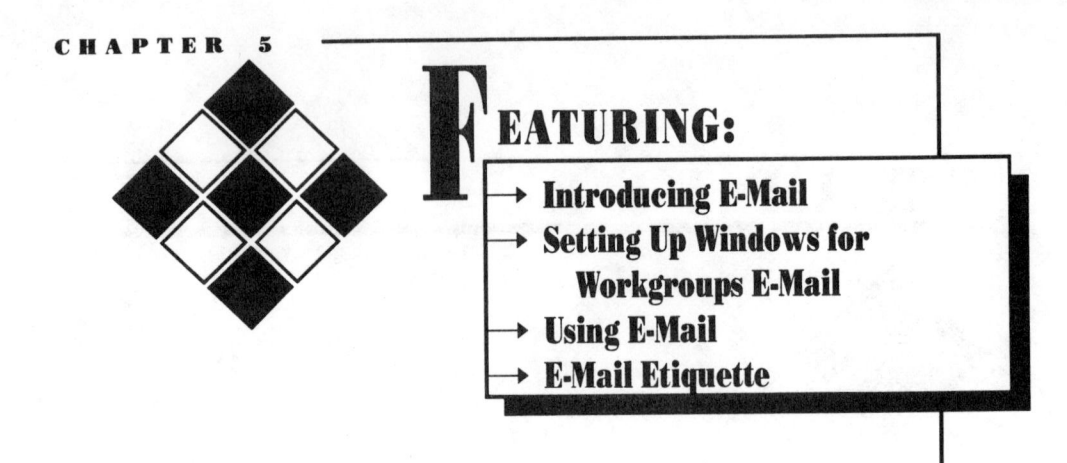

FEATURING:

- **Introducing E-Mail**
- **Setting Up Windows for Workgroups E-Mail**
- **Using E-Mail**
- **E-Mail Etiquette**

For many people, electronic mail (e-mail) turns into one of the most important applications available on a computer. E-mail provides people with a way to communicate, escaping the constraints of time, space, and location. Its business benefits can be so far-reaching that Intel's energetic president, Andy Grove, once quipped that e-mail is a *killer application* because once you've got it you can't live without it. Lots of e-mail advocates agree.

Members of your workgroup can communicate information via e-mail when they need to — and get answers when it is convenient. E-mail puts an end to time-robbing phone tag, and paper-chasing memos that circulate around until, forgotten, they find a final resting place in a file drawer.

To be effective, however, e-mail has to be installed and implemented in a convenient, easy-to-use way. Each workgroup will have to tailor e-mail to their own specific needs.

In this chapter we'll introduce you to the robust e-mail system that comes with Windows for Workgroups. First, we will sketch out some basic e-mail concepts. Then, we'll give you step-by-step instructions for establishing and administering your workgroup. Next, we will turn our attention to using e-mail — how to access Mail for the first time, and the basics of sending, receiving, and filing messages. Finally, we'll give you a head start on e-mail etiquette — how to send and reply to messages in a way that keeps communication flowing, without clogging up your system.

Introducing E-Mail

If you have never used electronic mail before, you are in for a treat. E-mail is easy to learn because it is so much like the regular mail system, but it's faster and takes fewer people to administer.

The e-mail provided with Windows for Workgroups, Mail, supplies important features for sending, receiving, and filing messages. It also includes a comprehensive and accessible help system — you don't have to be an expert or spend a lot of time learning Mail to use it. You can learn as you go.

How E-Mail Works

In most mail systems (electronic or manual), there is a postoffice to store and forward the mail, a mailbox for each person, and a vehicle to deliver mail. In good electronic mail systems, there are extra conveniences, for instance, the ability to attach another file (a spreadsheet, document, or other information) to your message; the option of requiring a return receipt notice; and the possibility of storing your mail in folders, which can be shared with others. And, with a specially equipped multimedia PC, you can add voice annotations to your e-mail.

The most basic services of e-mail are sending, receiving, and forwarding messages, which are often short notes of just a few lines — "bits" of information that you pass among members of the workgroup. For these uses, Mail provides a very easy interface. Almost anyone can begin to use the system without a lot of training.

Many people will want to attach documents such as letters or spreadsheets to their messages, and include objects such as graphs or charts. Some will also want to make use of electronic folders, so they don't have to manually file printed messages and memos anymore.

Establishing E-Mail Roles

Because the computers do most of the work, with e-mail you won't need a fleet of trucks to move the mail, a team of sorters to sort it, a mail carrier to deliver it, or clerks to file it after it's read.

To establish a successful e-mail system, you do need to define roles for a mail *administrator* and a group of mail *users*.

You will need a mail *administrator* to setup the system and periodically perform maintenance chores. For most workgroups (under 50 people), this is not a difficult or time-consuming task. Mail setup can usually be accomplished in less than an hour and administration shouldn't take more than an hour or two a week. The e-mail administrator will:

- ▲ Create the Postoffice,
- ▲ Assign Postoffice password,
- ▲ Add/Change/Delete mailboxes and users,
- ▲ Monitor disk space on the Postoffice computer,
- ▲ Back up files on the Postoffice computer,
- ▲ Maintain Mail system files, and
- ▲ Troubleshoot problems.

People must *use* an e-mail system in order to get any benefit from it. This is a key point. Some individuals and groups may have to make adjustments in their organizational culture to get the full benefits of e-mail.

SETTING UP AND USING WORKGROUP E-MAIL

E-mail users will have to:

▲ Check into the mail system frequently,
▲ Delete unnecessary messages,
▲ Reply promptly to messages, and
▲ Adjust their personal habits to accommodate e-mail's advantages.

Setting Up Windows for Workgroups E-Mail

There are three basic steps for setting up Windows for Workgroups Mail. They are:

1. Choosing a Postoffice computer,
2. Setting up the Workgroup Postoffice, and
3. Setting up mailboxes for each member of your workgroup.

Choosing a Postoffice Computer

You must select a computer in the workgroup to be your Postoffice. Unless you specify differently, Windows for Workgroups will install a special subdirectory below the Windows directory and will call it \WGPO, which stands for *Workgroup Postoffice*. This subdirectory (and subdirectories below it) will house the master mail files and information about everyone's mailbox.

Almost any computer on the network will be able to run the mail software and act as postoffice, but you should select one that has a lot of free disk space, is never turned off (turning off the computer closes down the postoffice), and has a fast processor (for example, a 486-class computer). On the computer you establish as the postoffice, you will need to allow:

▲ 360 K of free disk space per Postoffice,
▲ 16 K and 1 MB of free disk space per User Mailbox

> **NOTE** Keep in mind that some users will not use more than 100 K of disk space for their mailboxes, while others will use much more. 1 MB per user is a safe number to start with if your workgroup is unfamiliar with e-mail. If your e-mail users are experienced, or if they expect eventually to link into other e-mail systems, you should start 2 MB per user. This disk space requirement is for postoffice data only, and is over and above the amount you'll need for software, other applications, and data files from other applications.

Table 5.1 suggests the amount of free disk space you'll need for a postoffice, comparing the amount of disk space that might be needed by new users to that needed by more experienced users.

Table 5.1 Disk space needed for the Postoffice

Users	New to E-Mail	Experienced
5	5.5 MB	11 MB
10	11	22
15	16	32
20	22	43
40	43	84

SETTING UP AND USING WORKGROUP E-MAIL

95

Creating the Postoffice

Once you identify the computer that will act as Postoffice, it's time to create mail service for your workgroup. This is part of the role of mail administrator.

In the Main group of the Windows for Workgroups Program Manager, double-click (click twice rapidly) on the Mail icon to start the mail system.

When you are prompted to select or create a new Workgroup Postoffice, choose: Create a new Workgroup Postoffice, as shown in Figure 5.1.

Figure 5.1

Starting up a new Workgroup Postoffice

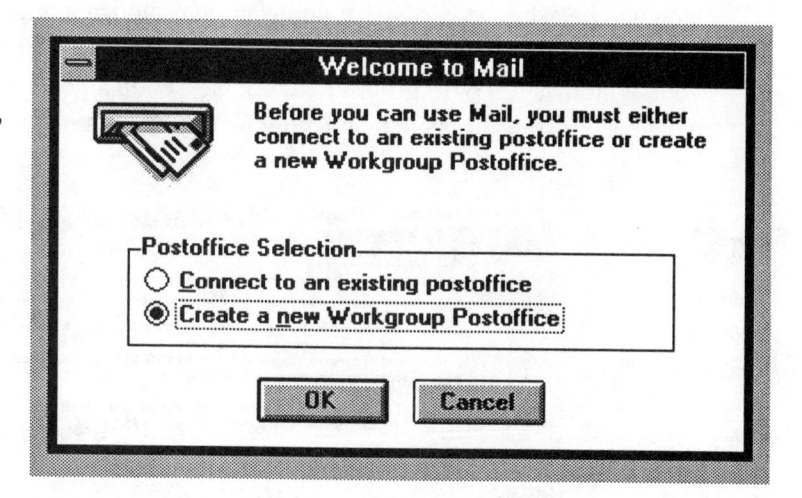

[Welcome to Mail dialog box: "Before you can use Mail, you must either connect to an existing postoffice or create a new Workgroup Postoffice." Postoffice Selection: ○ Connect to an existing postoffice / ⦿ Create a new Workgroup Postoffice. OK / Cancel buttons.]

NOTE If you don't get this exact dialog box, someone may have already established a Mail file, or tried to run Mail, on this particular PC. Check the \WINDOWS directory for a file called MSMAIL.INI. If the file exists, delete it, then try running Mail again.

The next screen will prompt you with a warning that only one Workgroup Postoffice should exist within a workgroup. Be careful to heed this warning, because there is currently no inter-workgroup communication with Windows for Workgroups.

> **NOTE** All the members of your workgroup must belong to the same postoffice or they will not be able to exchange mail with each other. For example, if Joe and Jack are in different workgroups but the same postoffice, they can communicate via Mail, whereas if Joe and Jack are in different postoffices, they cannot communicate via Mail.

You will be asked to verify that you want to establish a brand new Postoffice, as shown in Figure 5.2. Since this is the first time anyone in your Windows for Workgroups network has set up a postoffice, simply acknowledge this message by clicking on the Yes button.

Figure 5.2

Warning message

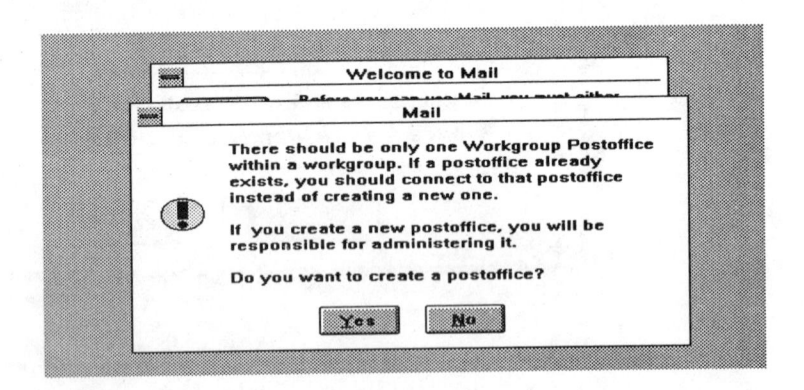

The next prompt, shown in Figure 5.3, will ask you where you wish to create your Workgroup Postoffice (WGPO) directory. You have the

Setting Up and Using Workgroup E-Mail

option of placing the postoffice files on the local drive of the computer you are working on, or on any of the network drives to which you have security access. This includes drives on non-Windows for Workgroups computers, such as Novell NetWare servers or Microsoft's LAN Manager servers. It is important to make a careful selection now, but if you change your mind later, there are utilities provided with Windows for Workgroups to move the postoffice to another computer.

Figure 5.3

Creating a Workgroup Postoffice

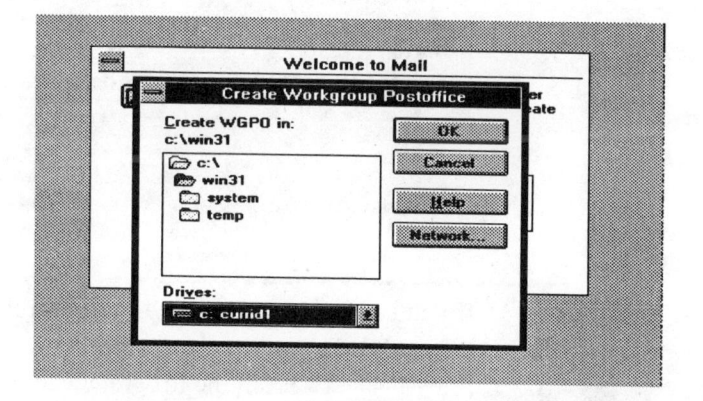

Now that you have created the mail system and a postoffice, it's time to set up yourself as the administrator, and then the postoffice users. The installation program will prompt you with a window for entering in your Administrator Account Details, as shown in Figure 5.4.

Next, the installation program will prompt you with confirmation of where the Workgroup Postoffice files were created. It will also remind you to share the directory with the other members of the workgroup. See Figure 5.5.

Figure 5.4

Administrator Account Details dialog box

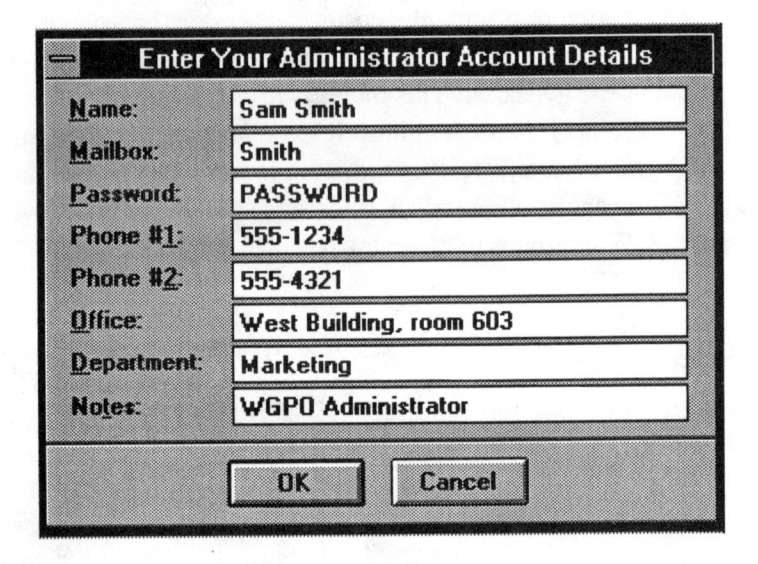

Enter Your Administrator Account Details	
Name:	Sam Smith
Mailbox:	Smith
Password:	PASSWORD
Phone #1:	555-1234
Phone #2:	555-4321
Office:	West Building, room 603
Department:	Marketing
Notes:	WGPO Administrator

[OK] [Cancel]

NOTE

If you have chosen to place the workgroup files on a local PC hard disk, you should share it now. You can do this with File Manager. From the Program Manager, click on the File Manager icon, then select the button for sharing drives. We suggest you share this drive with full access and no password protection to make it easier for users to connect to the Postoffice.

Figure 5.5

Confirmation of Postoffice directory

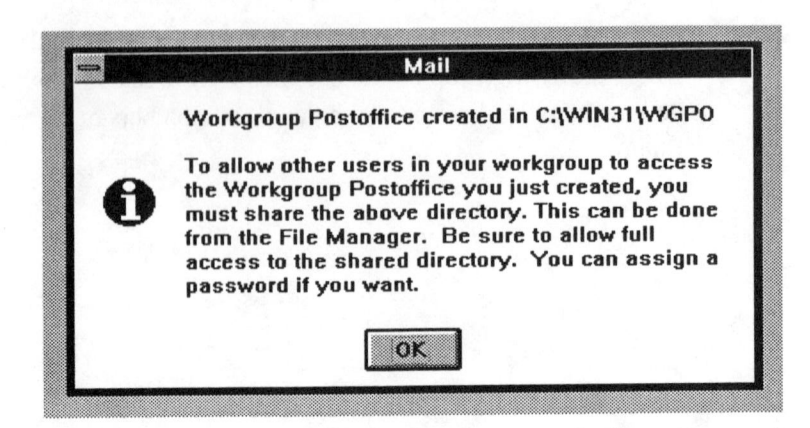

Mail

Workgroup Postoffice created in C:\WIN31\WGPO

To allow other users in your workgroup to access the Workgroup Postoffice you just created, you must share the above directory. This can be done from the File Manager. Be sure to allow full access to the shared directory. You can assign a password if you want.

[OK]

SETTING UP AND USING WORKGROUP E-MAIL

If you have selected another PC's hard disk connected by Windows for Workgroups as the directory for the WGPO, no further action is necessary, because the directory is already shared. If you have selected a NetWare or LAN Manager server for the mail files, make sure the appropriate security is assigned so that each user has read and write access to the WGPO directory and the subdirectories the WGPO creates.

Click on the OK button to confirm everything has been set up correctly. At this time, Mail will begin a session for you. You will be prompted with the first mail screen.

As the Postoffice administrator, you can now begin to set up other people on the system. To do this, choose the Postoffice Manager... option from the Mail menu, as shown in Figure 5.6.

Figure 5.6

Choosing Postoffice Manager

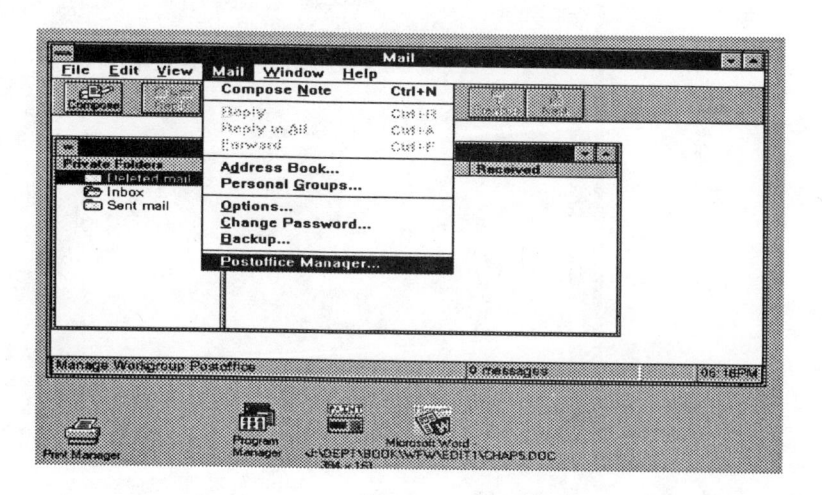

> **NOTE:** As the postoffice administrator, you are the only one who has access to the Postoffice Manager... menu option. This option will not show up on the menus of regular users.

After you choose the Postoffice Manager... option, the next screen you'll see shows the people in your workgroup who are registered with the mail system. Since this is a new system, the only name you will see is your own. Of course, as your system grows, everyone assigned to the Mail system will have an entry here.

The Postoffice Manager window (as shown in Figure 5.7) gives you a number of options for working with your own mail information, or that of other users. There are six buttons on the right side of the window:

Figure 5.7

The Postoffice Manager window

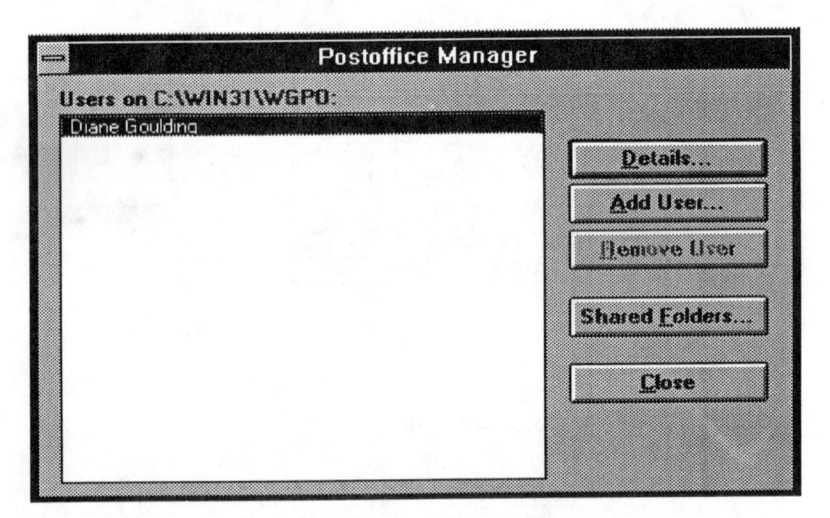

Details...	Lets you view and edit user information
Add User...	Lets you add a new user
Remove User	Lets you delete a new user
Shared Folders...	Lets you compress disk space taken by folders
Close	Closes the Postoffice manager window
Help	Provides help administering the postoffice

By selecting your name and pressing the Details... button on the right side of the screen, you can complete the important information needed about yourself.

As the mail administrator, you should first fill out the information requested, then assign a password to your record. (If you followed our installation instructions, you've already filled out the information details, as shown in Figure 5.4. earlier in this chapter.)

> **NOTE** Be careful to assign a password that you can easily remember. A mail administrator's password cannot be recovered if you forget it. If you lose or forget the password, you will have to recreate the entire postoffice.

Establishing Naming Conventions for People and Mailboxes

Mail distinguishes users by their mailbox name, which must be unique for every user. It sorts the mail list (or directory) by the first characters of the name that is entered in the Name field. Before you add the first user, you should establish conventions for making user names and mailbox names unique. Many administrators of small workgroups fall into the trap of using everyone's first name as their e-mail and mailbox name. We suggest that you don't. Some first names are so common that you are likely to have duplicates in a group as small as five or six people. Also, Mail alphabetizes the list by the first characters in the line, so you will need to enter names as: *Lastname, Firstname* in order for your mail list to show up in alphabetical order by the user's last name.

Adding New Users

You have the option of setting up all your workgroup users, or letting them add themselves, or some combination of both. We suggest that the postoffice administrator set up each user, so consistent naming standards can be established.

Depending on how computer literate the system users are, it may be acceptable for them to add themselves. If you decide to have users administer themselves, be sure to give them specific directions about where the Postoffice is located, naming conventions, and passwords.

To add users, you must have the following information for everyone:

Name:	Up to 30 characters
Mailbox:	Up to ten alphanumeric characters (must be unique)
Password:	Up to eight characters (default is "password")

Other information that is not required but will help users identify each other (particularly if your system someday grows large), includes:

Phone #1:	Up to 32 characters (usually used for office phone number)
Phone #2:	Up to 32 characters (usually used for FAX number)
Office:	Up to 32 characters
Department:	Up to 32 characters
Notes:	Up to 128 characters

To add new users to the system, return to the Postoffice Manager screen and click on the Add User button on the right side of the window.

Ongoing E-Mail Administration

Once the mail system is set up and users are added, there are a few ongoing maintenance tasks that you'll have to perform, specifically:

adding, deleting, and changing user information; managing disk space on the WGPO; administering (compressing the space in) shared folders; fixing corrupted files; helping users when they forget their passwords; possibly changing the name of the workgroup or moving the postoffice if it runs out of disk space; and general troubleshooting.

These are not time-consuming chores. Most workgroup mail administration can be done in less than an hour per week. If you move the mailbox to another computer, however, plan on spending several hours to move all the postoffice files.

For E-Mail Users: Using Mail for the First Time

As a Mail system user, you will have to tell the system a little about yourself and your workgroup the first time you check into the mail system. The mail system needs to know:

- ▲ Whether you are connecting to an existing postoffice or setting up a new one,
- ▲ What computer and directory your postoffice files reside on, and,
- ▲ Whether you already have an account established at the postoffice.

Mail will record your information in a file so you won't have to answer setup questions again. Be sure that you are prepared to answer these questions, so your file will be created correctly. If you do not answer the questions correctly, on subsequent attempts to access the mail system, you may not be able to do so. If this happens, call your mail administrator. (You or your mail administrator may have to delete the MSMAIL.INI file in your Windows directory and start over.)

To start up Mail for the first time, click on the Mail icon, located in the Main Group of the Program Manager. When the mail system starts, it will ask if you wish to connect to an existing system or start a new one. Click on Connect to an existing postoffice, as shown in Figure 5.8.

Figure 5.8

Connecting to an existing postoffice

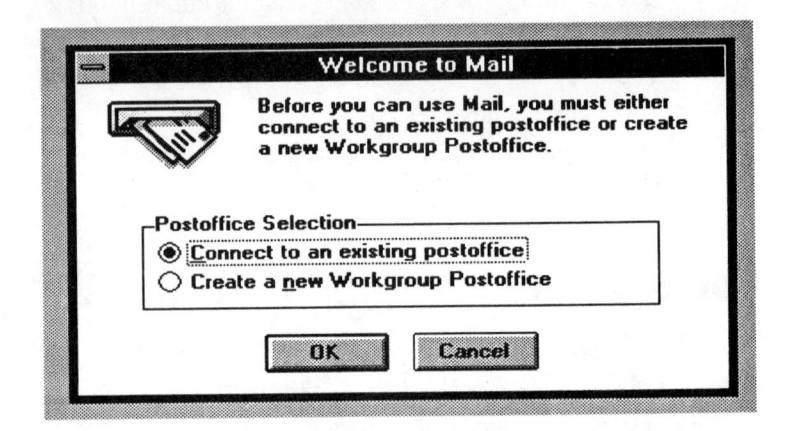

You will then be prompted to locate the postoffice files. (Your mail administrator should have given you the computer and directory names for you to correctly fill in the information on this screen.) Figure 5.9 shows a sample of a filled-in screen. In our case, the Workgroup Postoffice was located in the WGPO directory on the computer named Lab.

Mail will then ask if you already have an account set up on the postoffice you specified. If your mail administrator has preset your information, simply click on the Yes button. You will need to supply your mail account name and password. Keep in mind that, depending on how the mail administrator set up the record, this may be a different name than your user name or computer name. If you are unsure, check with your mail administrator. If your mail administrator did not preset your information, click on the No button and be prepared to answer some more questions about yourself. You will need to supply your Name, Mailbox, and Password. You can supply other information as shown in Figure 5.10. Check with your mail administrator to see if there are any established conventions for your name, such as "last name first."

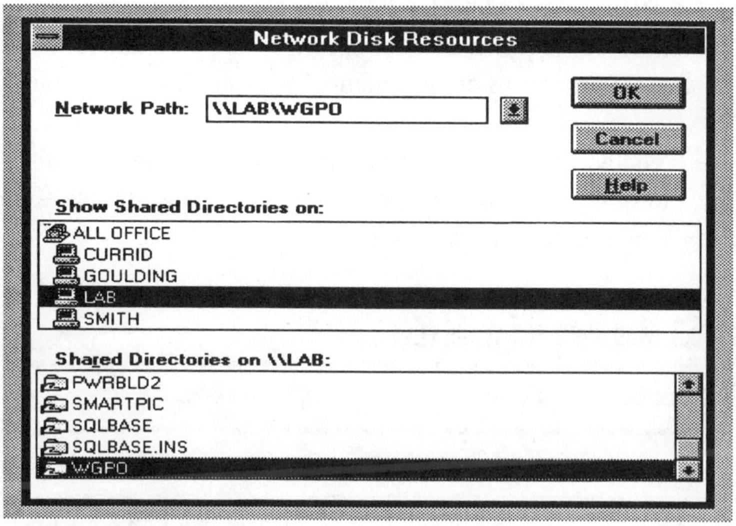

Setting Up and Using Workgroup E-Mail

Figure 5.9

Locating the network disk resources for an existing postoffice

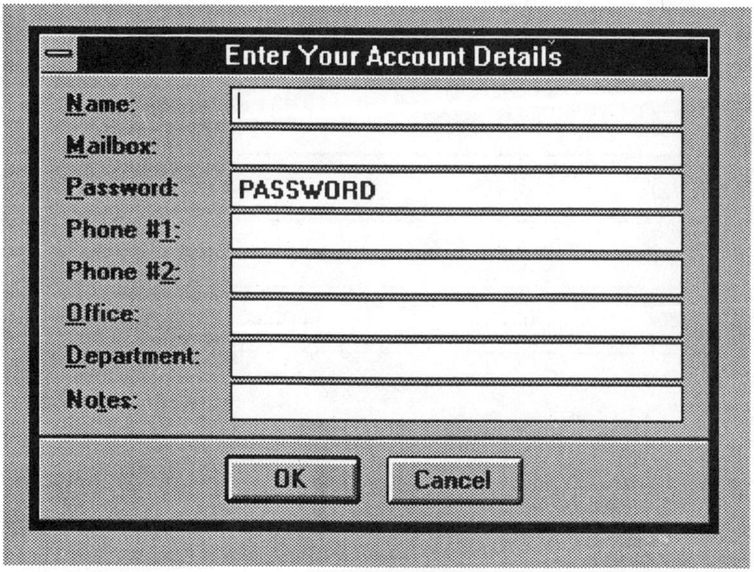

Figure 5.10

E-Mail account window

Mail's Special Visual Cues and Icons

Mail introduces a number of new visual cues and icons to the Windows for Workgroups environment. These are listed in Table 5.2.

You will find that these visual cues, icons, and symbols are a great way to spot priority mail, new messages versus messages already read, and messages with files attached.

Table 5.2 Mail icons and visual cues

Icon	Title	Function
✉	Closed Envelope	for unread mail
✉	Open Envelope	for mail that you have read
📎	Paperclip	for mail with an attachment
!	Red!	for high priority mail
↓	Down arrow	for low priority mail
📁	Folders	for places to file mail
📥	In box	a place where your new mail comes in
📤	Out box	a place where you store outgoing mail

Basic Mail Functions

E-mail systems are the electronic equivalent of the way we handled paper mail. There are in boxes, out boxes, addresses, messages, and folders. Your incoming paper mail has always arrived in your in box and stayed there until you read it and took action, discarding it or filing it into a folder. Most likely, your folders were arranged by subject, but

Setting Up and Using Workgroup E-Mail

they could also have been arranged by date or by some other convention. E-mail sets up a similar environment, but one in which each step of the process takes place on the computer, with no paper involved.

To use an e-mail system effectively, you should know how to send a message, how to receive and read a message, and how to reply to a message. You'll probably also want to know how to forward messages, file them into folders, and delete them.

Sending a Message

To send a Mail message, you follow three steps: address the message, enter the text, and click on the Send button. You can also choose to attach files, request options such as a return receipt, or include special priority notices with your messages.

To send a message, start at the main Mail screen. (See Figure 5.11.) Click on the Compose button — the left button on the tool bar.

Figure 5.11

Mail screen with Toolbar

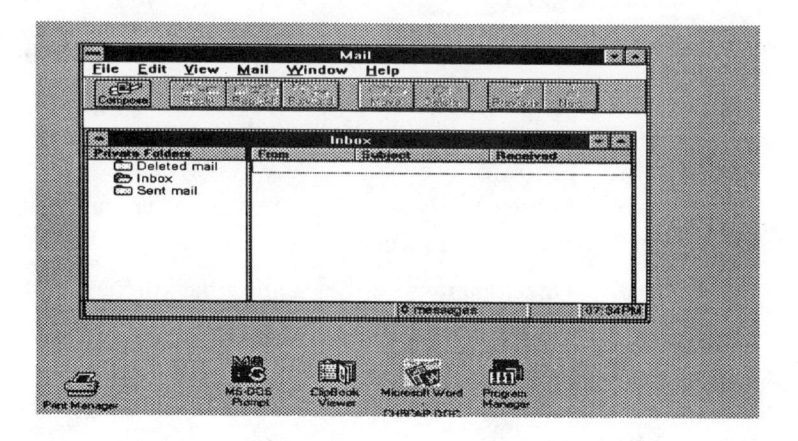

The Send Note window will appear next as shown in Figure 5.12. This window is used to create and send your message. It contains fields to fill out for the standard message header:

Figure 5.12

The Send Note window

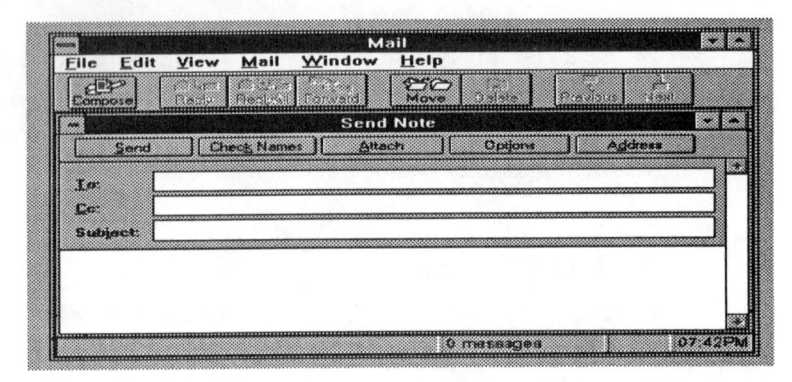

To: (The addressee)
Cc: (Courtesy copy addressees)
Subject: (The main subject of the memo)

There is no FROM: field, because Mail automatically fills in your name.

Five option buttons are available in the Send Note window. These buttons control the message that you are working on, but not subsequent messages. The option buttons include:

▲ **Send** actually sends the message once you have completed addressing and composing the message.

▲ **Check Names** verifies names that you have already typed into the To: and Cc: fields. If the names are found in Mail's directory they will be underlined. (Note: this button does not work unless names have already been entered into the To: or Cc: fields.)

▲ **Attach** lets you attach a file to your message. Any spreadsheet or word processed document can be attached. Other types of attachments and objects can also be placed here.

▲ **Options** allows you to set the priority of the mail message (high, normal, or low), and, if you wish, request a return receipt.

▲ **Address** accesses an address book listing people to whom you can send mail.

> **NOTE**
> If you choose to attach a file or embed an object into your message, be sure you know in which subdirectory it is located. The Attach window will let you browse the subdirectories of any local or network drive to select the attached file. Remember that files are attached to messages in their native state — not necessarily as text. For example, if you send an Excel spreadsheet file, the person on the other end will have to have access to Excel (or a utility that reads Excel files) before he or she can see the file.

Receiving a Message

Messages that are addressed to you will come to your in box. If you are running the Mail system when a message arrives, your cursor will quickly flash as an icon that looks like an envelope and you will hear a short beep, signaling you that new mail has arrived. A mailbox icon with a letter in it will also appear on the status bar.

To pick up your message, simply select it from the main Mail screen in box folder. A list of messages (both opened and unopened) will appear, along with information about who sent the message, the subject, and the date and time the message was sent.

To select and read your message, use the mouse to point and click at the message. To accomplish this same purpose, you may instead use your cursor keys to highlight the message on the list and press the ENTER key to read it.

If you have a number of messages waiting for your attention, you can choose to view and sort through them in several ways. This is handy when your mailbox is overflowing. You can sort by sender name, priority, date, or subject. To use the message sorting feature, simply choose View from the main Mail screen and click on the type of sort you wish to use.

Replying to a Message

Once you have selected and opened a message, you can reply to it, if you like. Actually, you can answer a message at any time — it is not necessary to reply upon receipt.

To answer a message, choose one of the Reply buttons from the Toolbar. If you choose the Reply button, your response will be addressed automatically to the sender (but not to anyone on the Courtesy copy list). If you choose the Reply All button, your response will be addressed automatically to both the sender and the people the sender has listed in the Courtesy copy list on the message.

Mail will automatically send back a copy of the original message with the reply you created.

Forwarding a Message

Messages can be forwarded to anyone on the Mail address list. To forward a message, open it and select the Forward button (which is next to the Reply button) on the Toolbar. You can enter comments to be included with the original message.

Filing Messages into Folders

Mail allows you to set up both private folders and public folders for storing your messages. As their names suggest, private folders are for your personal use, while public folders are intended to be shared among members of your workgroup.

Each Mail user starts out with three private folders: his or her in box, deleted mail, and sent mail. You can add additional folders by choosing New Folder from the File menu.

To store a message in a folder, you can either drag the message from the message list to the folder list, or you can click on the Move button on the Toolbar.

Deleting Messages and Folders

If you do not wish to save a message, you can easily delete it by highlighting it on the Message list and clicking on the Delete button located on the right side of the Toolbar.

E-Mail Etiquette

Regular users of e-mail tend to develop their own set of customs. Many e-mail messages take on a much less formal tone than traditional business correspondence. The main purpose is to get a thought across, so messages are often very short. E-mail users also often write in short-hand expressions, or acronyms, for example:

BTW	means By The Way,
FWIW	means For What It's Worth,
FYI	means For Your Information,
IMHO	means In My Humble Opinion,
IOW	means In Other Words.

and for Grin (meaning you are making a joke), they often use glyphs, such as:

\<g\>
:-)
%^)

The quick pace of interaction in e-mail seems to inspire creative ways to communicate effectively.

In this chapter we opened the door for you to begin using Mail, the e-mail provided with Windows for Workgroups. We installed and set up a workgroup postoffice, then walked through the steps of getting, sending, receiving, and filing mail. Now it's your turn to spend some time with Mail. Send a few test messages to members of your workgroup. You'll find it is an easy process. If you do need help, Mail comes with an excellent on-line Help system that can be accessed from the Main menus.

In the next chapter, we'll explore Mail's counterpart, Schedule+, which will help you and your workgroup manage time and appointments.

CHAPTER 6

SETTING UP AND USING SCHEDULE+

CHAPTER 6

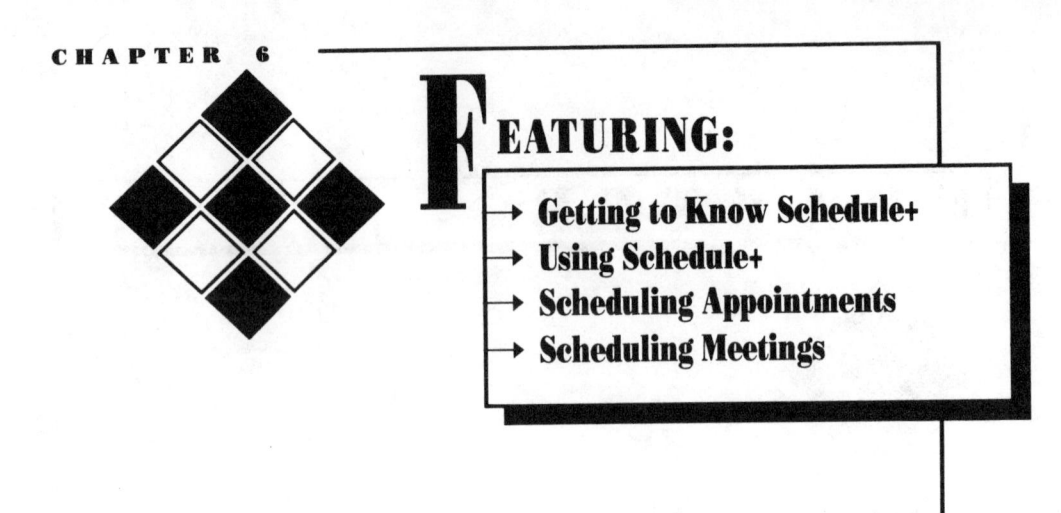

FEATURING:

- **Getting to Know Schedule+**
- **Using Schedule+**
- **Scheduling Appointments**
- **Scheduling Meetings**

Like e-mail, a computer-assisted appointment book can become an indispensable tool for today's workgroup member. Manual appointment systems take too much time, are inefficient, and frequently cause people to resort to keeping multiple calendars. How many times have you seen a busy executive with a leather-bound calendar on his desk, and a secretary with an almost identical copy? Everything is fine until the phone starts ringing and the schedule starts changing. Before you know it, the calendars get out of sync and nobody is sure what to do, where to go, or when to go do it.

The problem gets worse with busy workgroups. Getting together for team meetings, or bringing in new team members can turn into a major ordeal to coordinate.

Do electronic scheduling programs really make things easier? After all, there have been scheduling programs available on computers for a number of years. It hasn't seemed to help that much.

The problem with "first generation" computer calendar programs was that they were oriented to the personal user on unconnected computers.

This simply doesn't add much value to an office environment where people work together.

The solution starts with software that is designed for people to share information. That's exactly what the Schedule+ program of Windows for Workgroups does.

This chapter is divided into two parts. The first part outlines what Schedule+ is capable of doing — we'll introduce you to its rich features and functions. Then we'll take you on a hands-on tour of starting up the scheduling system. We'll show you how to schedule your appointments, make notes for each day, and work with groups, the planner, and the Task list. Finally, we'll give you tips and techniques to help you make Schedule+ a productive tool.

What You Can Do with Schedule+

Schedule+ serves three primary functions, all centered around managing and maintaining your projects and your day-to-day work. The program's functions include:

Appointments	Maintaining your calendar
Planner	Scheduling meetings or group events
Tasks	Keeping track of your "to do" list

Schedule+ can go where you do. You can work with Schedule+ on your desktop computer or export its files to another computer, even a notebook or pocket-style computer. This is a great convenience for busy professionals who work both in and out of an office.

Schedule+ is also specifically designed to work with your workgroup. It interacts closely with the Mail system, so Mail system users can share schedules and access copies of schedule information.

You can grant different levels of access to different members of your organization, providing security for your shared schedules. For example, you can allow some people to make your appointments for you; permit others to just view your appointments; allow still others to just see whether you are busy at certain times, but not your activities; and prevent others from seeing anything at all.

You can also use the program to schedule use of common resources, such as conference rooms, AV equipment, or computers.

Getting to Know Schedule+

The primary Schedule+ functions are easily accessible from the program's main window, where Schedule+ uses the graphical metaphor of an appointment book. Inside the book, on the left, are several tabs labeled Tasks, Planner, Appts, and Today. Clicking the mouse on any of these tabs will take you to the corresponding page for tasks, planner, and appointments.

You can also access the individual pages by holding down the ALT key and pressing the underlined letter for the tab you wish to choose — T for Tasks, P for Planner, and so on. If you select the tab marked Today, your appointment book will revert back to the appointment page of the current date, no matter where you started.

Within each primary function area is a host of features to help you manage even the busiest workdays.

Scheduling Made Easy with Appts

To keep your appointments in order electronically, use the scheduling section of Schedule+. Click on the Appts tab to the left of the main Schedule+ window, and you'll see one day displayed at a time, with a notebook-like schedule for the business hours of the day, the calendar for

Setting Up and Using Schedule+

the current month, and a notepad for extra bits of information. The day and date appear at the top of the screen. (See Figure 6.1.)

Figure 6.1

The main Schedule+ opening window

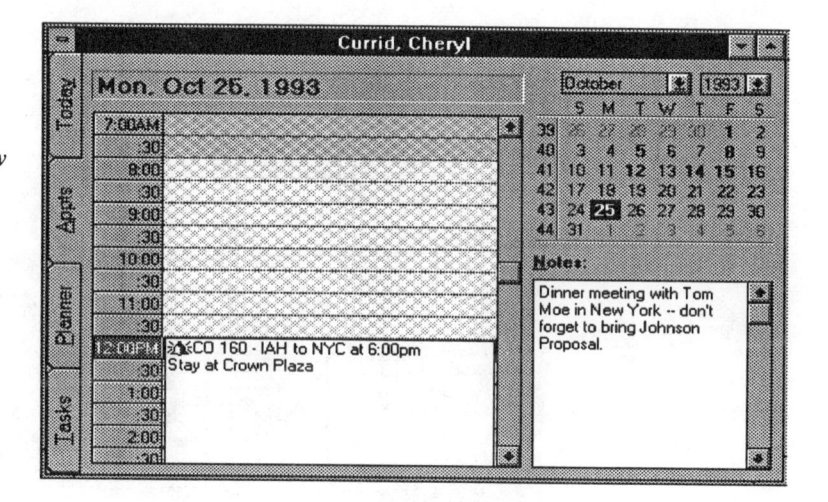

You can schedule appointments or block time for meetings or other work as you need to, and indicate whether the appointment is confirmed or tentative. You can attach notes for each day, then search the notes later to refresh your memory about the planned event.

You can keep up your own calendar, as well as those of other members of your workgroup, depending on your individual needs. To switch to another person's calendar, choose Open Other's Appt Book from the File menu.

Getting an Overview with Planner

The Planner displays a bird's-eye view of scheduled activities. It can also be used to plan meeting times with others, and to get a quick view of individual and group availability. The Planner works in concert with the Mail postoffice directory list, so you can choose who will attend your meeting.

The Planner window, shown in Figure 6.2, lists the current day and next group of days with times that are scheduled highlighted with vertical bars. The number of days displayed depends upon the size of the viewing window.

Figure 6.2

The Planner window

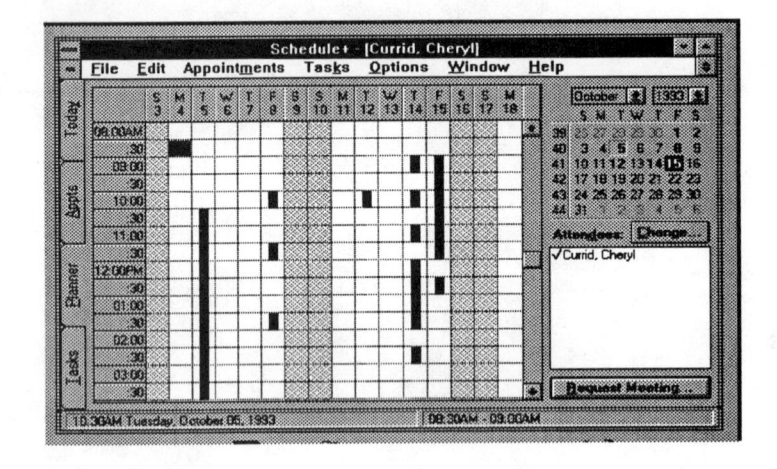

If you double-click on any time period of any day, Planner will automatically take you to the appointment calendar for more detailed information about the time period.

Planner also displays a calendar for the current month and a list of the scheduled attendees for the appointment on the right side of the window.

Keeping Track of Your "To Do" List with Tasks

The Tasks function lets you maintain a "to do" list within Schedule+. You can categorize your tasks by projects and display your Task list within each project. Schedule+ also lets you set up recurring tasks, for example, preparing the monthly status report. If you want, you can set up an alarm to remind you that the task is going to be due soon. You also have complete control over sharing your tasks, including the option to make them public or private.

Setting Up and Using Schedule+

119

Visual cues help you track items on the Task list, as shown in Figure 6.3. For example, overdue tasks are displayed on the screen in red. Recurring tasks, tasks marked with reminders, and private tasks, are all marked with appropriate icons on the Task list. You can sort your Task list by priority, due date, or description. And, as an extra reminder, you can even add a task to your appointment calendar.

Figure 6.3

The Task list

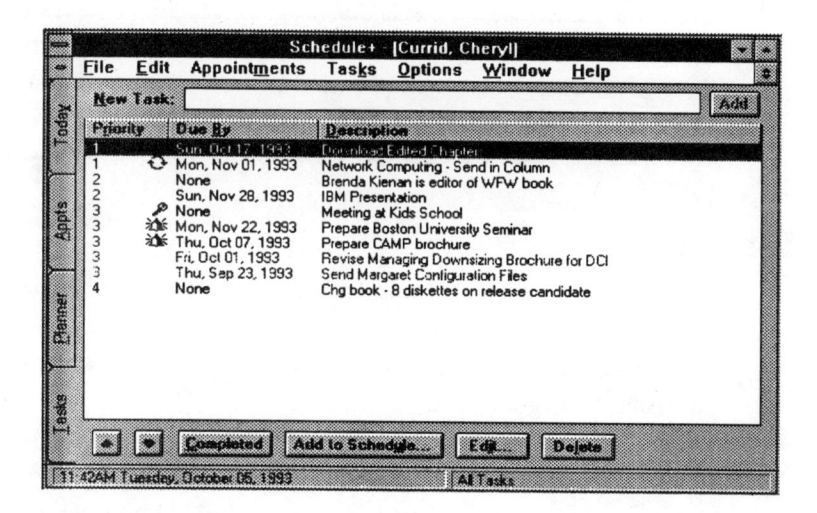

Getting Back to Today

The top tab on the Schedule+ screen is Today, which simply takes you back to the appointment window for the current day. Today is handy when you are working on advanced planning or your Task list and you need to get back to the current day momentarily.

Using Schedule+

If you installed Windows for Workgroups using the default setup, the Schedule+ icon was placed in Main group of the Program Manager. To start the program, locate the Schedule+ icon and double-click on it. (See Figure 6.4)

Figure 6.4

The Schedule+ icon.

If you are not logged into the Mail application, you will be prompted to give the system your Mail password.

> **NOTE** Schedule+ works with the Mail system and therefore uses the same password. If Mail is loaded, you will not be prompted to give your password.

Logging Out

You can log out of Schedule+ at any time by either choosing Exit or Exit and Sign Out. Exit removes the program icon, but still keeps you connected so that alarms will go off when necessary and mail and messages can get to you.

Exit and Sign Out removes the program entirely and prevents alarms or messages from reaching you. If you are logged into the mail system, Exit and Sign Out will also close Mail.

How Schedule+ Works with Mail

Schedule+ and Mail work cooperatively in the Windows for Workgroups environment. They share the postoffice directory list of names, and they share the same users' passwords. You can add or remove people from your personal Mail list directory from Schedule+.

Sharing Your Schedule+ Information with Others

When you first start using Schedule+, plan to spend a few minutes setting up the way you want your appointment book to be shared with

SETTING UP AND USING SCHEDULE+

co-workers. That way your colleagues can set up meetings and check your availability without having to disturb you.

To share your appointment book information, choose Set Access Privileges... from the Options menu at the top of the Schedule+ screen.

The next window will present a series of privileges options, providing security levels for your appointment book that range from No access to Full access, or the ability to create, change, and delete information. (See Table 6.1) To establish a set of standard security privileges, set up a Default User. (The program will apply the default privileges to everyone except those people you specify as having different privileges.)

Table 6.1 Security for Access Privileges

Access Privilege	Capabilities
None	No access to your appointment book.
View Free/Busy Times	Only sees that time slots are marked busy or not busy.
Read Appointments & Tasks	Can read appointments or tasks (except those marked private), but cannot change or delete them.
Create Appointments & Tasks	Can read and create new appointments or tasks (except those marked private), but cannot change or delete them.
Modify Appointments & Tasks	Can read, create, modify, or delete appointments or tasks (except those marked private).
Assistant	Same as above, except can send and receive messages on your behalf. (Still prevented from seeing activities marked private.)

For maximum flexibility, we suggest that you set up your default user with privileges to Create Appointments & Tasks. For maximum security, you might want to set it up for Read Appointments and Tasks. That way, only a few people will be able to schedule your day. Everyone else can view your schedule and request appointments.

Next, you can assign privileges to individual members of your workgroup. Choose the Add... button from the Set Access Privileges window. A list of your postoffice's members will be displayed. Select the person you wish to add by highlighting his or her name with a mouse-click. Assign privileges by selecting one of the options, and then choose the OK button.

It's a good idea to set someone up as your Schedule+ assistant. An assistant has maximum security capability and can act on your behalf if you aren't there. An assistant can also send and receive messages on your behalf, and can create, modify, and delete your appointments or tasks.

NOTE Schedule+ allows you to select only one assistant at a time. You can, however, change your assistant by selecting a new security access privilege from the Set Access Privileges window. Therefore, if you remove your current assistant, you can make someone else your assistant.

Scheduling Appointments

The easiest way to schedule an appointment is to select the date of the appointment and enter the information on the screen next to the appropriate time slot.

To set an appointment, locate the page for the date. A good way to do this is to click on the Today tab, then choose the appointment date by clicking on the list box arrow next to the month. This list box is located on the right side of the appointment page, just above the calendar. If you want to choose a month for the appointment that is not the current month, choose one by clicking on it with the mouse. See Figure 6.5.

Figure 6.5

Choosing a month for an appointment

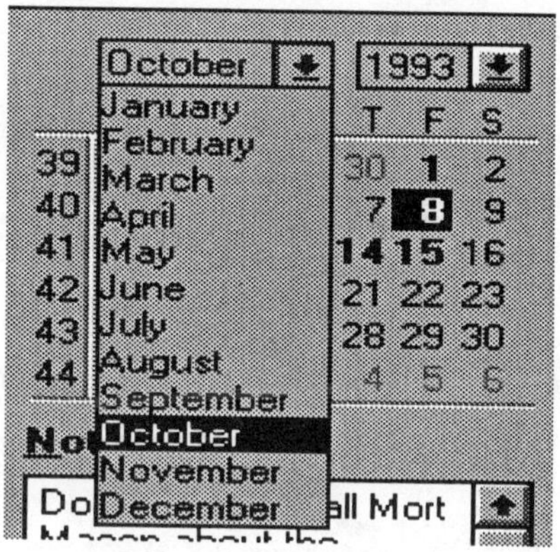

Next, move the mouse down to the days of the month and click on the appropriate date for the appointment. Notice that the date is now displayed as a highlighted color on the calendar and that the date is also displayed at the top of the appointment book.

Move the mouse to the appropriate time on the appointment book, click once, and enter the appointment information. If your appointment will span more than one time slot or if you need to change the appointment time, you can use the mouse to drag the appointment over multiple time periods. Place your mouse cursor on one of the horizontal lines above (or below) the appointment, and when the cursor turns into a double arrow, drag that line to the correct time. When you are done, return to the current day by clicking on the Today tab.

Alternatively, you can enter more specific information about your appointment by double-clicking on the appointment time. This brings up the Appointment window, as shown in Figure 6.6. Here you have the option of changing the appointment time, marking the appointment tentative, setting a reminder message for the appointment, marking it as private, or inviting other people to attend.

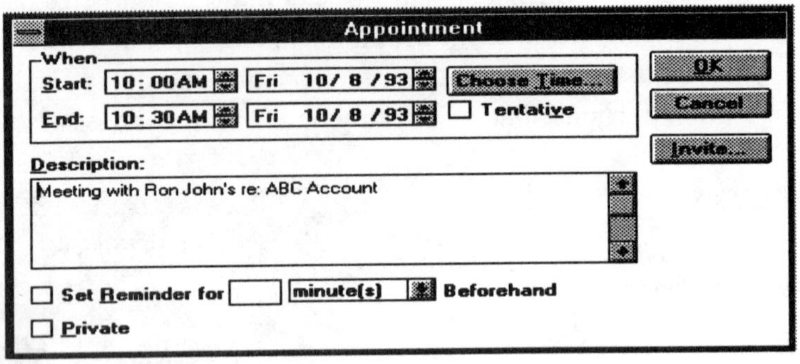

Figure 6.6

The Appointment window

As explained in Table 6.2, the appointment options give you an opportunity to customize the way Schedule+ treats the appointment. You get more flexibility than in a paper system.

Table 6.2 Appointment options

Option	Result
Choose Time	Allows meeting attendees to visually select the time.
Tentative	Marks the appointment "tentative" (gray) in your book.
Invite	Invites people on your postoffice list to the meeting, as you specify. (If you have privileges, you can also view their appointment books using the Choose Time... button after you have selected them.)
Set Reminder for	Sends you or your designated assistant a reminder prior to the meeting.
Private	Marks the appointment private. You can see details; those with privileges to view your calendar will see that your time is blocked, but not what you are doing.

Setting Up and Using Schedule+

Another way to schedule appointments is to choose New Appointment from the Appointments menu of the Schedule+ menu screen. That brings you directly to the Appointment window.

You can also schedule recurring appointments on your calendar. To do so, pull down the Appointments menu. Choose New Recurring Appt... . This brings up the Recurring Appointment dialog box, as shown in Figure 6.7. You can select when the appointment begins and ends, enter a description of the appointment, and set a reminder on this screen.

Figure 6.7

Recurring Appointment dialog box.

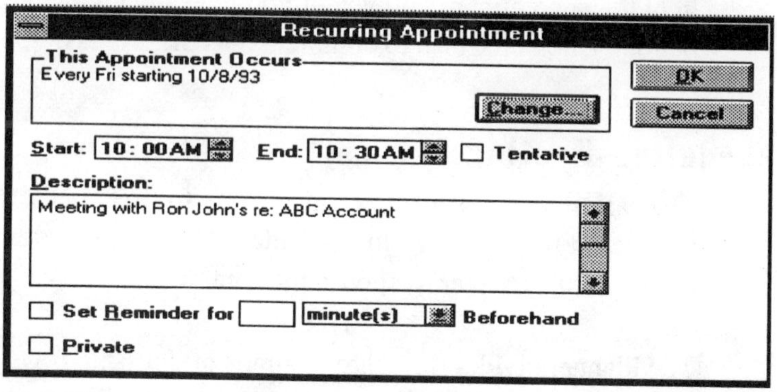

The default period for the appointment is weekly. To change the default appointment settings, click on the button marked Change. Select the frequency of the appointment (daily, weekly, biweekly, monthly, yearly). On the basis of frequency, Schedule+ presents a dialog box with more details about the occurrence. See the example in Figure 6.8.

Set the duration for regularly scheduling the appointment by specifying the starting date and ending date. If you prefer, you can schedule the appointment indefinitely by marking the box for "No End Date." Click on OK to save your recurrence settings. To update your schedule with the recurring appointment, click on OK. The appointment will be identified on your schedule with a special icon.

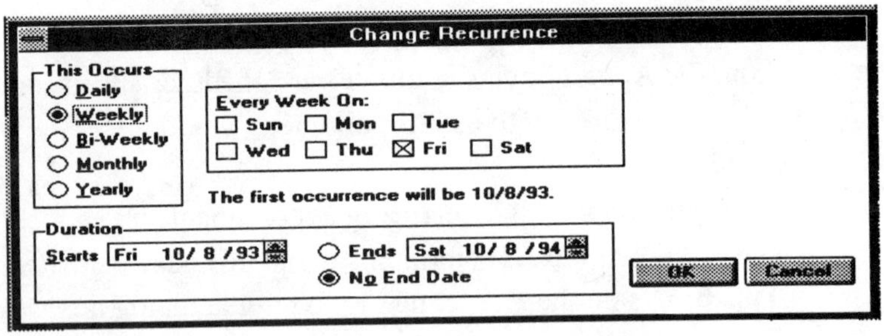

Figure 6.8

Changing the frequency of a recurring appointment

To remove a recurring appointment from your calendar, access the Appointments menu. Choose the Edit Recurring Appts...option. Highlight the appointment you want to remove and click on the Delete button. Click on Close to complete the edit process.

Scheduling Meetings

The easiest way to schedule a meeting is to first click on the Planner tab, then select the date from the calendar. Use the procedures outlined earlier in this chapter to choose the date.

The Planner divides time into columns of days and rows of time periods. It will display as many days as possible, within the size of the window, starting with Sunday of the week you've chosen. To the right of the screen, underneath the calendar is an Attendees box (see Figure 6.9). For now, only your name will appear in that box.

Your personal activities will be highlighted, showing the time that you have blocked for them. If you move the mouse over any of the time periods and click once, the Planner will verify whether you are busy then or not. If you are not busy, there will be a check mark beside your name in the Attendees box.

If you have appointments for this time slot that are marked as tentative, they will not show up on the Planner. If you are busy with a confirmed appointment, a red X will appear beside your name.

Setting Up and Using Schedule+

To add other people to your meeting, choose the Change... button on the right side of the window, above the Attendees box. Select the attendees from the postoffice list. As you make your selections, notice that their names are being added to the attendees list at the bottom of the screen. The names are underlined, which confirms that the postoffice has an e-mail address for them. If you are unsure of a name on the list, you can select the Details button in the middle of the window to get more information about the person.

Figure 6.9

The Planning window

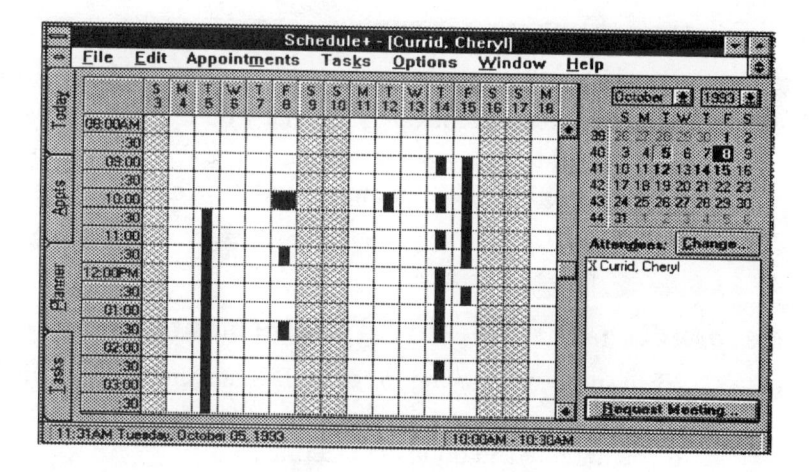

When you have finished, select OK on the bottom of the Select Attendees window. You will return to the Planner window and your meeting participants will be listed in the Attendees box. Their schedules, in a different color than yours, will appear on the time and date grid. Times when two or more people are unavailable will be noted with cross-hatched bars. If you click once on these overlapping time periods, an X will appear in the Attendees box next to the names of the people who are unavailable.

At this point, you can search manually for a good meeting time, or ask Schedule+ to help out. Press CRTL-A, or choose Auto-Pick from the Appointments menu. Schedule+ will find the first time that's open in all the appointment books you've specified.

> **NOTE** Auto-Pick searches forward in time from wherever the cursor is located. For example, if the cursor is located at 2:00 on Wednesday, and a free time slot exists for everyone at both 1:00 Wednesday and 1:00 Thursday, Auto-Pick will suggest only 1:00 Thursday.

After you establish the date and time of a meeting, the next step is to notify attendees. Depending on what security privileges you have to the schedules of others, you may either update their calendars immediately with the meeting information, or send them all a meeting message, or both.

Responding to a Meeting Appointment

When someone is trying to schedule a meeting request with you, he or she schedules a meeting and sends a message inviting you. Then it is up to you to reply and book the meeting.

You will be notified that someone is trying to schedule a meeting with you by an entry in the messages window of Schedule+. If you have a designated assistant, he or she also will be notified. When you receive the meeting notice, you have four options. As shown in Table 6.3, you can accept the meeting request, decline, book it as a tentative meeting or view your schedule.

Table 6.3 Responses to meeting requests

Response	Effect
Accept	Places meeting on your appointment book, sends you a message confirming successful scheduling, and lets you personalize a reply.
Decline	Sends back a message declining your attendance, and lets you personalize the response.
Tentative	Tentatively marks your appointment book with the meeting, and sends back a message.
View Schedule	No action; simply lets you view your schedule for the meeting day.

Working with an Assistant

As mentioned earlier in this chapter, Schedule+ lets you designate one person as your assistant. An assistant has maximum security privileges and can work with everything in your appointment book except appointments and tasks that you marked private. An assistant will also receive and respond to meeting requests.

Viewing Multiple Calendars

Sometimes it's helpful to have instant access to the schedules of certain workgroup members. Schedule+ allows you to load more than one person's calendar at a time and to keep them on your screen.

To do this, choose Open Other's Appt Book from the File menu. Select the name of the person from the list provided and click on the OK button. Notice that all appointment books — yours and those of others — look alike.

NOTE: The appointment book owner's name is displayed on the Title bar of the Appointment window. Be sure to check whether you're looking at your own book or someone else's. If you keep multiple appointment books on screen, it's a good idea to minimize everyone's book but your own. To do this, click on the Minimize button at the upper-right corner of the individual appointment book's screen. That appointment book becomes an icon at the bottom of the screen, with the person's name displayed below it.

Working with Resources

A resource account allows scheduling of shared devices or assets — conference rooms, portable computers, or other devices for which people need to schedule use.

To set up a resource account, you must first add it to the postoffice. The postoffice administrator must set up a mailbox for the resource, in the same manner as was used to set up a mailbox for a workgroup member. Then, someone (either the mail administrator or a user who knows the resource's password) must sign in to Schedule+ using the mailbox name and password of the resource.

Next, security privileges must be set for others to use the resource. This involves three steps: first, the mailbox account must be flagged as a resource account; second, default access privileges must be set; and third, someone should be named as assistant to the resource. (The third step is optional, but recommended, so that a member of the workgroup will be notified when the resource is being used, and can make a judgment in case of conflict.)

Tasks

Schedule+ can also work as your personal project manager. In the Tasks section of the appointment book (see Figure 6.10), you can create both projects and tasks within those projects to remind you of your work assignments.

You can access the Task list at any time by clicking the Tasks tab on your Schedule+ screen. A window displays a list of your tasks, and gives you the options to add new tasks to the list or your appointment book, mark tasks completed, and edit or delete the listing of a task.

Figure 6.10

Task window

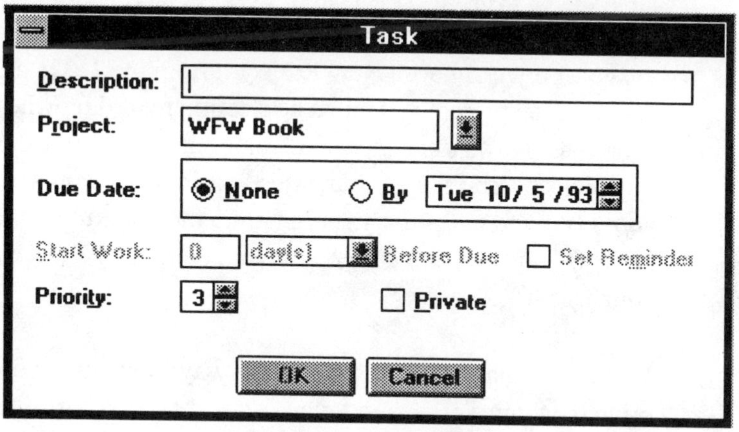

To add a task quickly, click in the New Task text box and enter a one-line task description. When you are finished, press the ENTER key. Your task automatically will be assigned a priority, a project (if you have defined projects) and a due date (of "none" by default). It will also be placed in the Task list and highlighted.

You can include more information about the task if you double-click on the highlighted task or press the ENTER key again. This opens the Task window, which contains seven options for modifying the task information. You can edit or change its description, assign it to a project, specify a due date, choose a time to start work on the project, assign the task a priority, mark it private so only you can see the task, set up an automatic reminder message, or any combination of these choices.

When you are finished modifying the task information, you can click on the OK button to return to the Task list.

Alternatively you can use the CTRL-T key sequence or choose New Task... Tasks from the menu to immediately bring up the Task window.

As previously mentioned, Schedule+ lets you associate your tasks with an assigned project. This is helpful if you are working on a number of projects and have many tasks that relate to each of the projects. To create a project, choose New Project... from the Tasks menu. Fill in a name for the project and make a selection regarding whether this project is private. Now, whenever you create a new task, you can assign it to this project. You'll appreciate this feature when you want to sort through your tasks and make the Task list more meaningful. Remember, private projects and tasks can be seen by you, but not by everyone with access to your schedule.

You can display the Task list several ways, depending on how you sort it. From the main Tasks menu, you can sort tasks by priority, due date, or description. You can also view the tasks within each project, or as one Task list.

In addition to setting up one-time-only tasks, you can set up recurring tasks, by choosing New Recurring Task... from the Tasks menu. Recurring tasks appear on your Task list on a daily, weekly, biweekly, monthly, or yearly basis, as you select. You can also select on which day of the week the task should occur and the duration for scheduling the task on that day. If you have to submit a report every Monday for the next two months, you should choose a weekly task, to be run on

SETTING UP AND USING SCHEDULE+

Monday, starting today and ending two months from now. Schedule+ places a recurring task icon to the left of the item on the Task list.

> **NOTE** Tasks do not appear on your appointment schedule unless you flag them. To do this, highlight the task from the Task list and click on the Add to Schedule... button on the bottom of the Tasks window. You will be prompted to choose a time for the task. When you have finished, the task will appear as a scheduled appointment in your appointment book as well as on the Task list.

Printing

Even though there are many optional ways to view your schedule and task information on the screen, there will be times when you'll want to print a hardcopy report. Schedule+ includes flexible printing options (see Figure 6.11). You can print at any time by choosing Print from the File menu, or by using the CTRL-P key sequence to bring up the printing window.

You should first select the view that you want to print. The options are: Daily View, Weekly View, Monthly View, Text View, and Tasks. The Print window will verify to which printer your reports will be sent, and give you the option to select a date range (this option is available for all views except Tasks). You can also select print quality and paper format.

> **NOTE** If you want the smallest print available for your schedule, choose Pocket from the paper format option on the Print menu. This produces the most compact version of your schedule.

Figure 6.11

The Print window

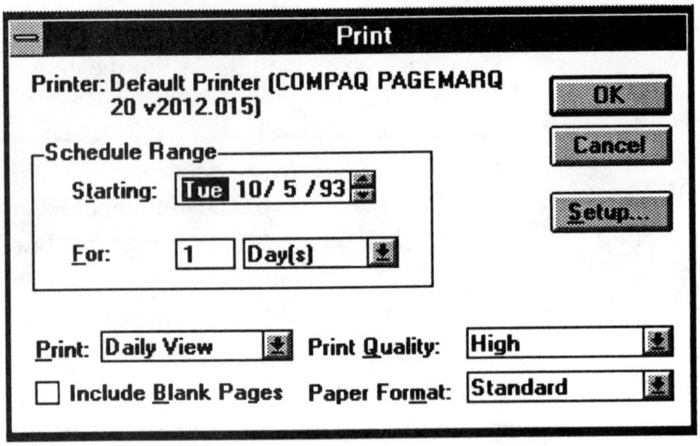

Working Offline

You can work with Schedule+ even when you are not connected to your network or LAN. For example, you might want to take your Schedule+ files traveling — you can load your schedule files on a laptop or notebook computer. You can take text versions of your appointments, or, if your computer is capable of running Windows, you can load Schedule+ in your Windows 3.1 directory.

Or, if you want to take schedule files home with you and keep a copy on your home computer, you can do so. There may also be times when you cannot make a connection to your network postoffice, but still need to update your schedule information. For these occasions, Schedule+ allows you to maintain most of your information by working *offline* (when you are not connected to the network). During offline sessions you can still schedule your personal appointments, add tasks to your Task list, and review your planner.

However, there are a few things you can't do when working offline. You cannot open another person's appointment book, create a group meeting, send or resend messages, or set access privileges.

NOTE If you do update your scheduled activities, or create or change appointments offline, be sure to make the appropriate changes on your primary, network-connected, desktop PC. This can be done easily by exporting your updated files from your offline session, then importing them into your regular PC. This step is not necessary if you were working offline *on* your primary PC. In that case, the software will automatically update its files when the postoffice connection is reestablished.

To export your appointments, choose Export Appointments from the File menu of Schedule+. Then follow the dialog boxes to select a range of dates and file name for your appointments.

Creating Archives

Over time, your Schedule+ files can become full of information that you don't need to access on an immediate basis. There is a housekeeping function that will let you store these records in another file and let you see them again if you need to. The process is called creating archives (or backup copies) of your appointment and meeting information.

A good practice is to create your archives every quarter and store information that is more than six months old. That means that if you start archiving in September, you save records that are dated March and before. Of course, if you are a very active user of Schedule+ and you find yourself exporting your schedule to other computers often, you may want to archive more frequently.

To create an archive file, choose Create Archive from the File menu. You will then be prompted to give an archive date. All information on and before the date you select will be moved to the archive file.

The next prompt will ask you to assign a directory and give your archive a file name. Schedule+ defaults to storing the file in your Windows directory using your Mail login name and an extension of .ARC. For example, if your Windows directory is C:\WINDOWS and your mail login name is SMITH, then your archive file will be saved as C:\WINDOWS\SMITH.ARC.

Of course you have the option of saving the file to any directory on your local computer or network drive you wish. You can also rename the file to any legal DOS file name you like (DOS allows you an eight-character name and a three-character extension of your choice, separated by a period).

We recommend that you create a file name scheme that will make it easy to remember the dates of your archives. The ideal scheme might be four letters describing you, and four digits describing the time period of the archive. For example, if your Mail login name is SMITH and you are archiving records for the first quarter 1993, you could name your file SMTHQ193.ARC.

NOTE Only appointment book information (including any notes for the day) is saved in archive files. Your Task list is not archived with the file.

Using Archives

Schedule+ will let you open and view your archived files, but it does not put the records in your current schedule, nor does it let you edit any of the archived records. You can't change history. If you need to look up information in your archived files, you can retrieve the records through a simple process.

To view your archived files, choose Open Archive... from the File menu. Then select from the list of archived files the one you want to see. If you don't see the correct archived file, make sure you are viewing the directory where you saved the archived file(s). When you have found the correct file, highlight it and click on the OK button.

Schedule+ will open an archive window that looks very much like your regular appointment window, except that there are no tabs for Task Planner Appts and Today. You can select dates to view from the archive appointment book. When you are finished viewing the archive, double-click on the Control menu box to close the archive. (Remember, if you have changed anything on the archive appointment book, it will not be saved.)

In this chapter we introduced the basics of Schedule+. As a key component of Windows for Workgroups, Schedule+ offers the workgroup member a valuable tool for organizing and sharing information. This program is easy to use, consistent, and well integrated with the mail system. By just changing a few habits, you and your workgroup will improve productivity with Schedule+.

CHAPTER 7

GETTING MORE PRODUCTIVE WITH WINDOWS FOR WORKGROUPS UTILITIES

CHAPTER 7

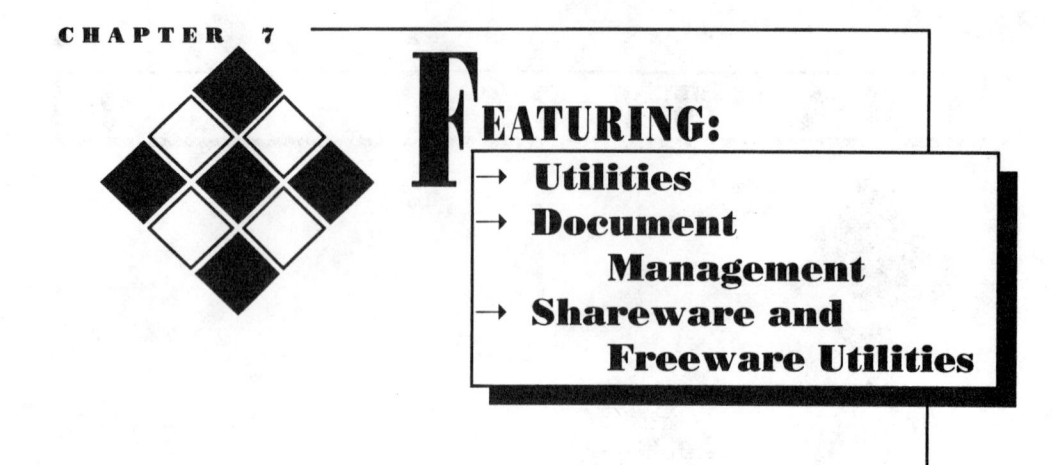

FEATURING:
- Utilities
- Document Management
- Shareware and Freeware Utilities

In previous chapters, we explored Mail and Schedule+, two programs that come with Windows for Workgroups and help you manage your time and work more effectively. Programs like these are called utilities because that's exactly what they are: useful tools designed to assist you in everyday tasks. Let's look at some of the other utilities the Windows world provides you. Some of these programs come with Windows for Workgroups, some are available separately from Microsoft, and some are sold by other vendors. Each can help you organize telephone numbers, dial out through your modem, watch system usage, view graphics files, and more, without having to leave the Windows for Workgroups environment. In this chapter, we'll look at some of our favorites and discuss what they can do for you.

Utilities That Come with Windows for Workgroups

When you buy Windows for Workgroups, it comes with several utilities, including a drawing program, a simple word processor, and a number of organizing tools. Some of these are surprisingly powerful, and once you know what they offer, you may find them to be extremely useful. Most include far more options than we have room to discuss here, so we will try to give you an overview of what they can do, and then we encourage you to explore. By reading the online help and trying different menu selections, you will discover many more features of the individual utilities. Unless you have moved them, the utilities will appear in the Accessories program group. Just after installing, this group looks like the window in Figure 7.1.

Figure 7.1

The Accessories group window

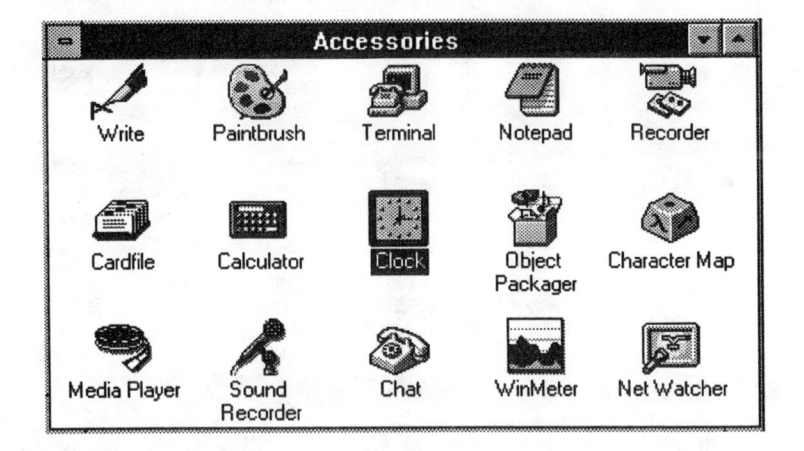

Clock

The Clock is a simple little program that does just what you'd expect: it displays a clock on your screen. You can set it up to display the clock in either analog or digital mode — that is, either with a dial or a number face. (In the dial, or analog mode, it has a working second hand.) When the Clock utility is running minimized (as an icon on your desktop), the icon still displays the current time. If you place the Clock utility in your Startup group and use the Run Minimized option, it will start up as an icon every time you start Windows for Workgroups, giving you a constant on-screen reference. Figure 7.2 illustrates part of a desktop with an iconized clock running.

Figure 7.2

Running the Clock as an icon

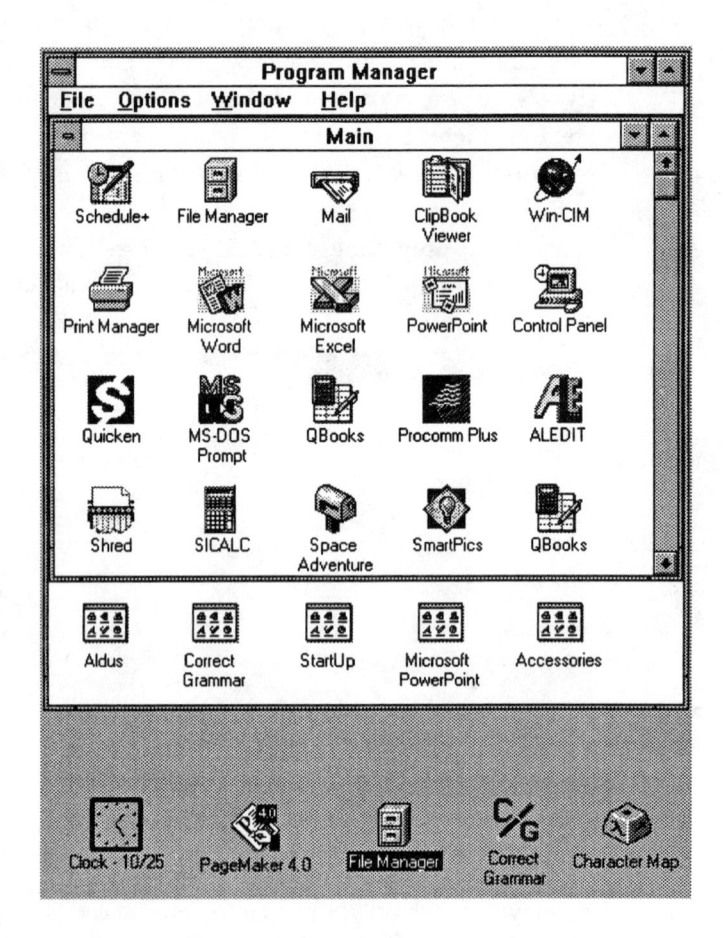

For more information about placing applications in your Startup group or running them minimized, see Chapter 11, Custom Setup and Tuning.

Cardfile

Cardfile is useful if you need to store a number of similarly structured pieces of information, like Rolodex-type cards or recipes. You could type this information into a word processing or text file, but it would be hard to work with. Using Cardfile, you can store several kinds of information on each card and then sort the cards, search through them, scroll through them, delete one without affecting the others, and save them.

Creating Cards

When you start Cardfile, it presents you with a blank card. The card has an index line across the top and space below for text, and the cursor is sitting in the text area.

Text

Click in the text area of the card, and the I-beam cursor will appear — you type in lines of text up to 39 characters long, and you can include up to 11 lines on a card. This text entry follows the usual conventions for text entry throughout Windows for Workgroups.

Index

If you wish, you can add an index line to the card. Many of Cardfile's helpful features, like sorting and searching, use the index line, so it's a good idea to include one if you have more than a few cards in your file. Index lines may be as long as 39 characters. To add an index to the current card, type F6 or double-click in the index area.

New Cards

To create a new card, select Add on the Card menu, or press the F7 key. Cardfile will save the contents of the current card and present you with another blank one. Cardfile stores each new card, sorted alphabetically, within the list of cards. The list is circular, which means that when you get to the end of the list and move to the next card, Cardfile will bring up the first card in the list.

Another way to create a new card is to copy an existing one, which you'll find useful when you're looking for a card that is similar to one you already have. To copy a card, select the original, then select Duplicate on the Card menu. A new card comes up containing the same information as the original, ready for you to change.

Viewing Your Cards

You can choose to display information from your cards either in a list with just the index lines showing, or as cards, which show the index line and text area of the first card and the index lines of all the other cards. Figures 7.3 and 7.4 illustrate these two views of card lists.

Figure 7.3

Viewing your cards

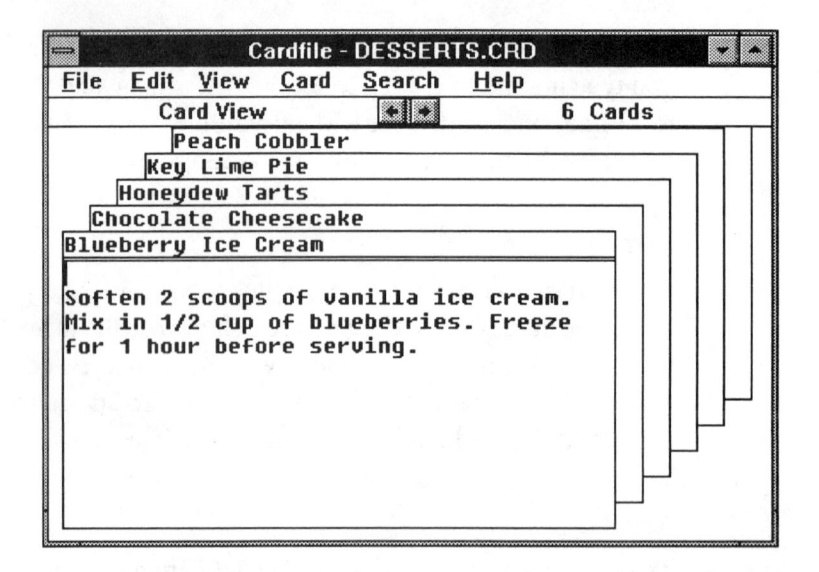

Figure 7.4

Viewing the index lines of your cards

Searching through the Cards

You can search through either the text or the index lines of your cards. To search for something in the text, you must be using Card display from the View menu. Select Go To from the Search menu (or press F4), and enter the text string you want to find. To find the next instance of the same string, press F3, or select Find Next from the Search menu. To search for a particular index, select Go To from the Search menu and enter a word or part of a word from the index you want to find. Cardfile will bring that card to the front if you're in Card view, or will move the selection line to that index if you are in List view.

Embedding Pictures and Sound into Your Cards

You can embed objects, drawings, charts, and even sound into your cards, just as you might in any other document, but you can only have one object embedded in each card. If an object is too big for the card, Cardfile will scale it down before putting it into the card. To embed a picture, for example, select Picture from the Edit menu, to tell Cardfile that you are working now with drawings instead of text. Then select Insert Object from the Edit menu. A window pops up with a list of the available types of objects. Select an object type, and Cardfile starts the utility that creates that type of object — such as drawings (created with Paintbrush, discussed below), graphs, and Word Art, a feature of Microsoft Word, which is text to which you can apply a number of special effects, as shown in Figure 7.5. (If you have Word for Windows installed, Word Art is directly accessible from Cardfile by choosing MS Word Art from Insert Object... of Cardfile's Edit menu.)

When you finish the picture, select Update from the File menu and Cardfile will store the picture in your current card. Now whenever you want to edit the picture, just select Picture from the Edit menu, then double-click on the picture on the card. Cardfile will start the application you used to create the picture you can make your changes. To embed other types of objects, and then follow the same procedure we described for embedding a picture. You can also open a File Manager Window next to your Cardfile window, drag any file from File Manager, and drop it into a card. The file will then show up as an object in Cardfile. This object can be a sound, graph, chart, or text.

Figure 7.5

Embedding Word Art in a card

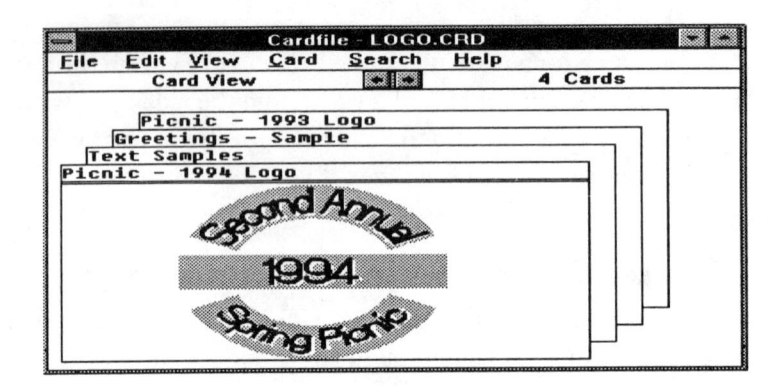

This is just a short introduction to the enormous number of ways you can use and update objects in cards and other documents. As you try various features of the menus and explore the online help, you will learn many more.

Dialing a Telephone Number from a Card

With Cardfile, you can dial telephone numbers listed on your cards electronically with your PC rather than having to dial from your telephone's keypad. If you can store a lot of numbers in the speed dial list of your telephone, you may not have much use for this feature, but it is handy for seldom-used numbers, and it ensures that you won't misdial (as long as the number on the card is correct). You need a modem and a telephone attached to your computer. Just bring up the correct card, select the telephone number and then either tap the F5 key or select Autodial from the Card menu, as shown in Figure 7.6.

Figure 7.6

Dialing from a card in Cardfile

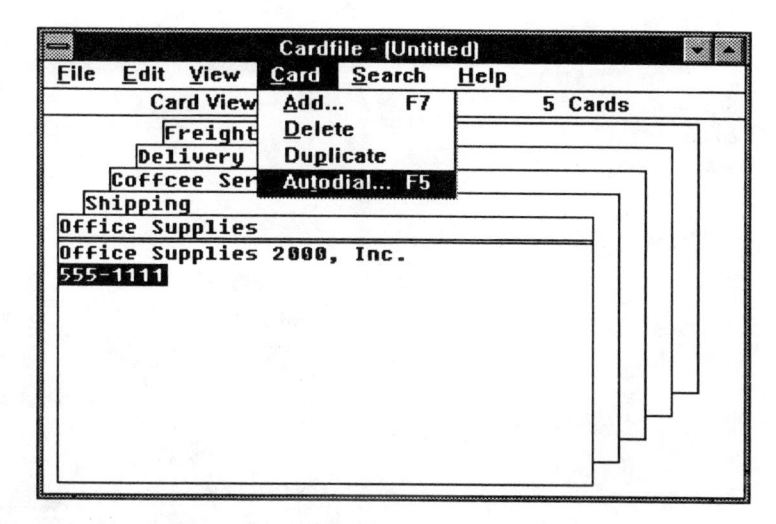

```
┌─────────────────── Cardfile - [Untitled] ───────────────┬─┬─┐
│ File   Edit   View   Card   Search   Help               │ │ │
│              Card View   Add...      F7      5 Cards    │ │ │
│         ┌─Freight──────┤ Delete                         │ │ │
│         │Delivery      │ Duplicate                      │ │ │
│         │Coffcee Ser   │ Autodial... F5                 │ │ │
│     ┌───Shipping──────────────────────────────┐         │ │ │
│ ┌───Office Supplies─────────────────────────┐ │         │ │ │
│ │ Office Supplies 2000, Inc.                │ │         │ │ │
│ │ 555-1111                                  │ │         │ │ │
│ │                                           │ │         │ │ │
│ │                                           │ │         │ │ │
│ │                                           │ │         │ │ │
│ │                                           │ │         │ │ │
│ │                                           │ │         │ │ │
│ └───────────────────────────────────────────┘ │         │ │ │
└───────────────────────────────────────────────┴─────────┴─┴─┘
```

> **NOTE**
>
> Cardfile will use the first number on the card as the telephone number if you don't select one. In the example in Figure 7.6, for instance, it would dial 2000 if 555-1111 were not selected. Because of this, you might want to enter the information on your cards so that the telephone number is always the first number on each card.

Now Cardfile brings up a window to show you the number it's going to dial. If you click on the Setup button you can set the configuration of your modem, as Figure 7.7 shows. In Setup you can select Tone or Pulse dialing, the port to which your modem is attached, and the baud rate of the modem. Autodial also allows you to dial a prefix before the telephone number (for instance, you could dial 9 to get an outside line).

If your modem has a speaker, you will be able to hear the dialing process: dial tone, dialing the digits, ringing, and answering. As soon as Autodial has started the call a box pops up instructing you to pick up your telephone receiver. When you do, you'll hear this process through the telephone instead. Complete your call as usual.

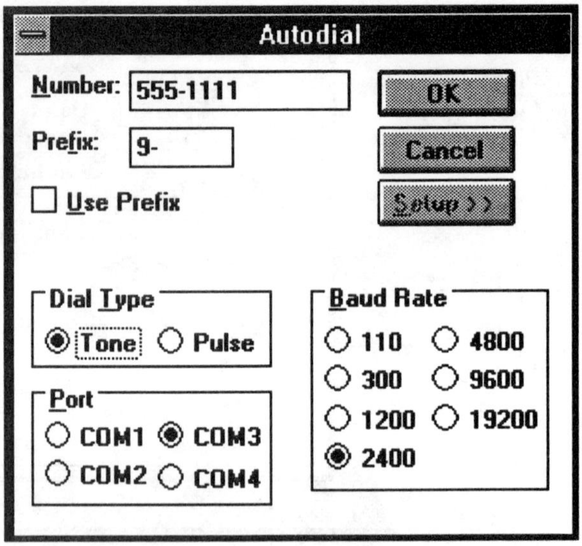

Figure 7.7

Setting the configuration of your modem

Printing Cards

When you print your cards on a laser printer, Cardfile actually draws each card and the text or drawings within it, and gets about four cards onto a sheet of paper. This is not very efficient. If you print your cards to a text printer (such as a dot-matrix printer), on the other hand, it won't print your drawings but it will fit as much information as possible on each page.

Calculator

The Calculator that comes with Windows for Workgroups has several advantages over standard desk calculators. Some of the most notable features are that it lets you enter larger numbers than most calculators, provides a set of advanced scientific functions, lets you store intermediate calculations in its four-function memory, and has a backspace key. Not only that, but it's right there in the Accessories group, always ready to use. Calculator offers far too many functions for us to describe here, but it probably does whatever you want it to do. In this section we will overview the highlights; you can get more detailed information by viewing the online Help system.

Standard View

When you start Calculator for the first time, it comes up in Standard mode, as shown in Figure 7.8.

In this mode, you can enter numbers, add, subtract, multiply, and divide; and perform square roots, inverses, and percentages. There is a four-function memory; the box near the upper right contains an 'M' when you have something stored in the memory. You can clear the memory with the MC key, store the current value in the memory with MS, and add the current value to the memory with the M+ key. The MR key stands for Memory Recall. This key places the memorized number in the current window, without changing the contents of the memory. If the number you enter is too big, the calculator displays it in scientific notation, as shown in Figure 7.8.

Figure 7.8

The standard calculator

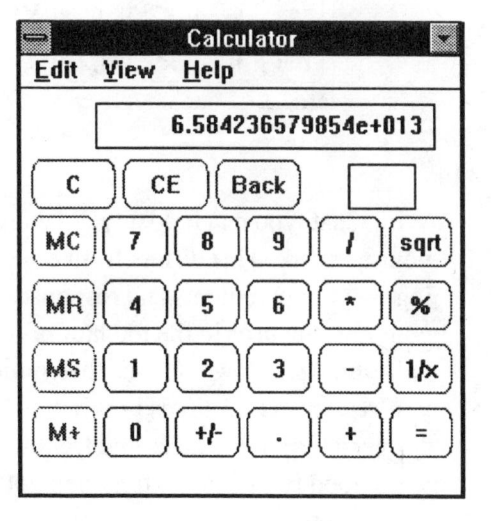

Scientific View

To use the scientific functions of the Calculator, select Scientific from the View menu. Now you can enter numbers in binary, octal, decimal, or hexadecimal base (bases 2, 8, 10, or 16). Calculator gives you trigonometric, statistical, and logarithmic functions, factorials, and many others. Figure 7.9 shows the layout of the scientific calculator keys.

The calculator will beep at you if you try to enter binary, octal, or hexadecimal numbers longer than it can store. If you do so in decimal mode it will convert the number to scientific notation. Consult the online Help system for information on particular functions.

Figure 7.9

The scientific calculator

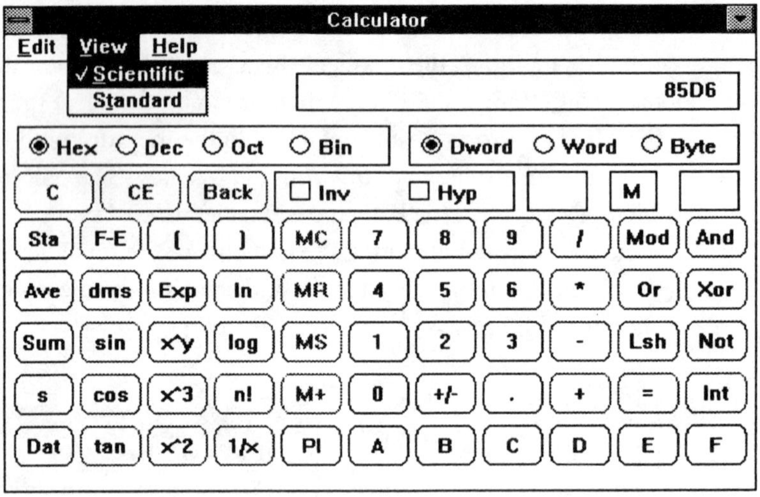

Chat

With Chat, you can hold a typed conversation with someone else on your network. This differs from e-mail, in that you are actually conversing — your comments and responses can overlap each other. Your comments appear in the top half of the Chat window, while the lower half of the window contains the comments from the person with whom you're conversing. This program is best suited to two types of usage: conversational messages and troubleshooting. Since Chat is so simple, it's a good first-thing to try when you're testing out your network connections.

Chat can be useful if you want to send a quick note to someone and you know they're at their workstation. If you want them to be able to save the note easily, though, or if you need to send a message of some length,

Getting More Productive with Windows for Workgroups Utilities

you'd be better off using e-mail, rather than hold a real-time dialog. Chat is of no use if no one is at the computer you're trying to call. It can be useful in some cases, though, and it's fun, so here's how to use it.

Placing a Call

To place a call with Chat, either select Dial from the Conversation menu or select the Dial button on the Chat Tool bar. The Computer Name field stores the names of all the computers you have called through Chat, and the Computers window shows all the workgroups and computers to which you can currently connect, as shown in Figure 7.10.

Figure 7.10

Selecting a computer for chatting

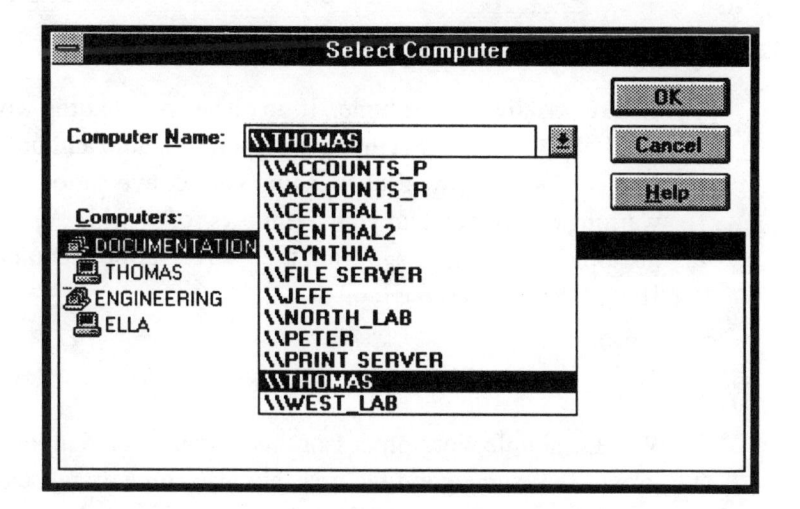

If someone on another computer calls you, the Chat icon will appear on your desktop and, if you have Sound turned on (on the Chat Options menu), your computer will beep or, with the right sound drivers, it will actually ring. Double-click on the Chat icon and you will be up in a Chat window. If you already have a Chat window open you can answer a call by either selecting Answer from the Conversation menu or by selecting the Answer button on the Chat toolbar. Figure 7.11 shows a sample conversation using Chat.

Figure 7.11

Coversing in Chat

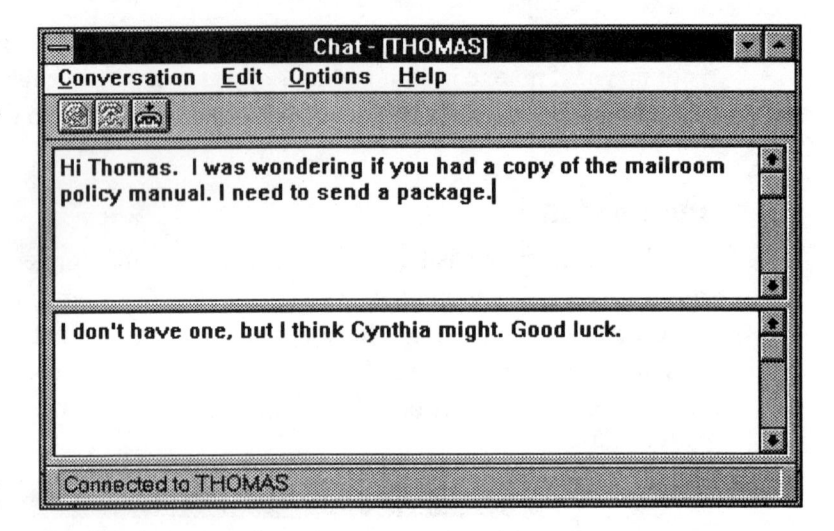

Chat works like a telephone. If no one answers at the workstation you are dialing, be sure to hang up after a reasonable amount of time. You also need to hang up after finishing your conversation, or you will get warnings when you end your Windows for Workgroups session. To hang up, either select Hang Up from the Conversation menu or select the Hang Up button on the toolbar.

Write

Write, a simple word processor that comes with Windows for Workgroups, has some good features, but also some drawbacks. If you plan to do a lot of word processing with multiple files and sophisticated formatting, consider getting a more complete word processor, such as Word for Windows or Ami Pro. For smaller jobs, though, Write may be quite adequate.

You can have only one document open at a time in Write, so if you have one open and then try to open another (from the File menu), Write saves and closes the first one. Within an open document, you can print, change fonts, change character sizes, add headers and footers, insert pictures and other objects, change paragraph spacing, and much more. You type your text using the conventions that hold throughout Windows for Workgroups for deleting text, moving around in the document, marking, cutting, and copying. (See Chapter 4 for the basics on moving around in Windows for Workgroups, and Appendix B for some keyboard shortcuts.)

Write has some useful features. You can undo the last deletion, format, or other change by selecting Undo from the Edit menu, or by typing CTRL+Z. Search for a particular text string by selecting Find from the Find menu. After you find one occurrence of the string, you can find the next one by just pressing the F3 key. You can replace all instances of a text string with another string by using the search-and-replace feature — select Replace from the Find menu. For easier formatting, Write has a ruler and toolbar; you can view them by selecting the Ruler On menu item from the Document menu. On the tool bar, you can select the type of line spacing to use and what style of text justification you want, and you can set tab stops. Figure 7.12 shows a Write window with the tool bar and ruler in use.

Figure 7.12

Formatting text with Write

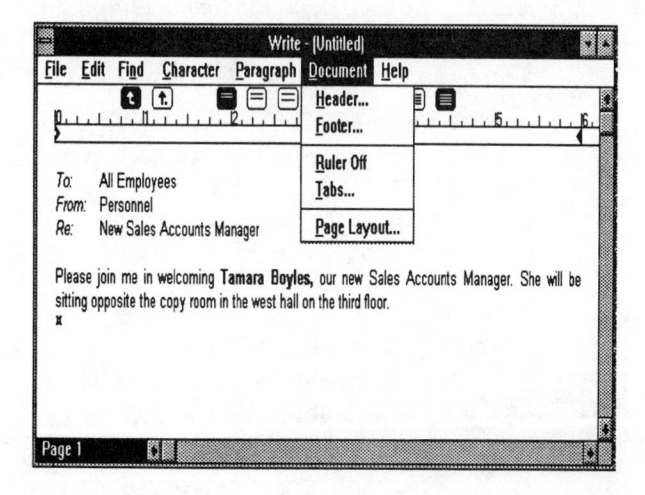

Note that you can create bold and italicized text. Select these and other effects from the Character menu. To import special symbols, use the Character Map utility.

The Write menus reveal all the available commands. Explore and use the online Help system as needed. Though limited, Write can be very useful.

Character Map

This utility, as shown in Figure 7.13, lets you insert into your documents special symbols that do not appear on your keyboard. It gives you access to mathematical notations, printers' symbols, and letters from other alphabets. In the Character Map window, the Fonts box lists all the fonts available to you; scroll through them until you find the one that contains the symbol you need. Click on that symbol to select it. Now the highlighting box is around that symbol. The Characters to Copy box contains all the characters you are going to copy into your working document. To get a highlighted character into the Characters to Copy box, click on the Select button on the right side of the screen. When you have collected all the characters you need, click on the Copy button on the right side of the window and Character Map will copy your characters to the Clipboard. Now return to your working document and select Paste from the Edit menu (or hold down CTRL and press V). The characters now appear to the left of the cursor in your document.

Character Map has two especially useful features: when you point to a character in the map and hold the right mouse button down, Character Map displays an enlarged picture of the character so you can see the detail, as shown in Figure 7.13. At the same time, in the lower-right corner of the Window, Character Map is showing you the keystroke sequence you can type to get the same character. For the character in the figure, for instance, you would hold down the ALT key and type the numbers 0195, then release the ALT key.

Figure 7.13

The Character Map screen

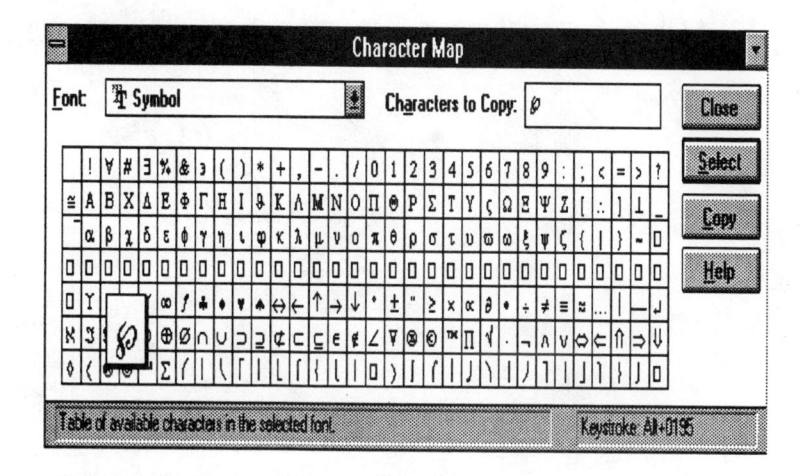

> **NOTE:** You must be using the same font in your document as you are in the Character Map. Otherwise, your selected characters will map to different characters in your current font. For instance, the character that maps to ALT+0195 in the Symbol font is "+," but in the Times New Roman font that same sequence will give you "_." So before copying the selected characters in from the Clipboard, change fonts in your working document, then copy the characters in. Now you can change back to your regular font and continue typing.

Paintbrush

Paintbrush is a simple drawing package. It can work with files in Bitmap format, having the extension .BMP, as well as .PCX, .DIB, and .MSP files. You can also use Paintbrush to edit drawings that already exist in these formats. To do so, choose Open from the File menu. You will see a file list of drawings that Paintbrush can edit. Choose your file in the usual way, moving around in directories until you find the one you want. Paintbrush will bring it up in its workspace, as shown in Figure 7.14.

Figure 7.14

The Paintbrush window

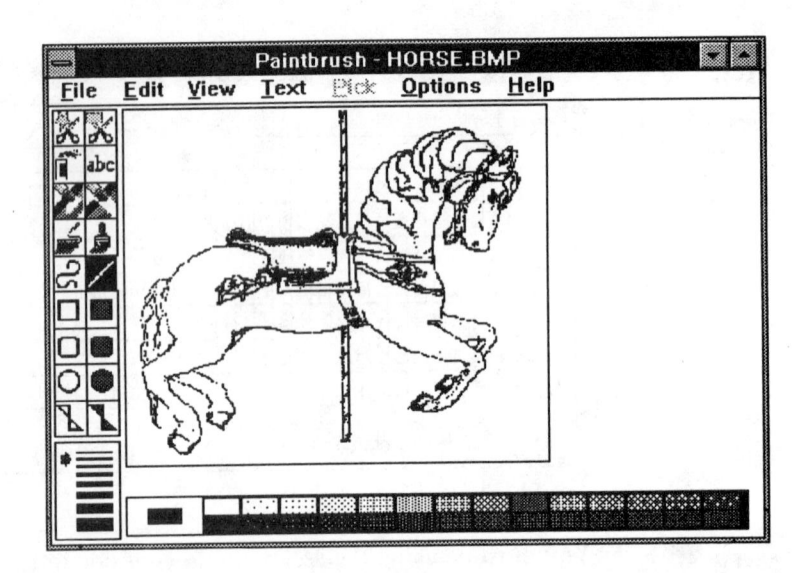

To get a sense of the capabilities that are available, try commands from the menus and the toolbar. You can draw shapes, like circles and rectangles, as well as free-formed shapes, lines, and rounded boxes. To do so, click on the associated boxes on the left side of the drawing area. You can create filled regions by clicking on the filled shapes. Like Write, Paintbrush only lets you work on one file at a time, so it closes the current one when you open a new one. Also like Write, it lets you make mistakes. If you do, select Undo from the Edit menu or press CTRL+Z.

Paintbrush also lets you work with text; see the Text menu. You can change sizes and fonts and use boldface and underlining. The text color, your current drawing color, is shown at the left side of the palette.

To see the entire drawing, press CTRL+P. This will zoom the drawing to fill the screen. You can get back to the work area by pressing a key on the keyboard or by pressing a mouse button. To zoom in on a particular area of the drawing, hold down CTRL and press N. Paintbrush will draw a zooming frame — move it to the area you want to study, and click. You now have a view of the selected area that allows you to edit the individual pixels. To zoom back out, hold down CTRL and press O. These viewing commands are also available from the View menu.

Paintbrush includes far more features than we can cover here. With it, you can tilt, flip, and sweep selected areas of your drawing; create custom colors, draw curves, ellipses, and polygons; and print your drawings with headers and footers on the page. It may be the only drawing tool you'll need.

Notepad

Notepad is a simple text editor without any of the formatting options that you get in Write. This makes it ideal for editing files that must not have any format characters in them, such as your AUTOEXEC.BAT or CONFIG.SYS. It is also useful for managing small files such as lists, but remember, files must be less than 50 K. This seems like a high limit until you run up against it, possibly losing data. Another danger of Notepad is in the line wrapping. Without wrapping, you must press RETURN to get the text to move to the next line; otherwise you will see one long line of text trailing from the screen to the right. If you select Word Wrap from the edit menu, Notepad will let you type your text without pressing RETURN, and will wrap the text to fit within its window. But when you print it out it will still be one long line of text, trailing off the paper.

If you only use it to edit short files with short lines, Notepad will be fine. But if you have more elaborate needs, you might want to keep looking. Shareware utilities are available that provide the same functions with better features — we'll look at how to get them later in this chapter.

Recorder

This utility can be very useful. It records a sequence of mouse and keyboard movements, and lets you replay that sequence on command. If you are editing a file and need to do the same operations to several parts of the file, for instance, it would be convenient to assign those operations to a single control key so you could just move to the desired part of the file and press that control key. This is exactly what Recorder lets you do. These combinations of control keys and command sequences are called *macros*.

To record a simple macro, move to the application for which you want to create a macro and start up the Recorder application from the Accessories program group. Select Record from the Macro menu. You will see a dialog box like the one in Figure 7.15.

Figure 7.15

Setting up Recorder to record a macro

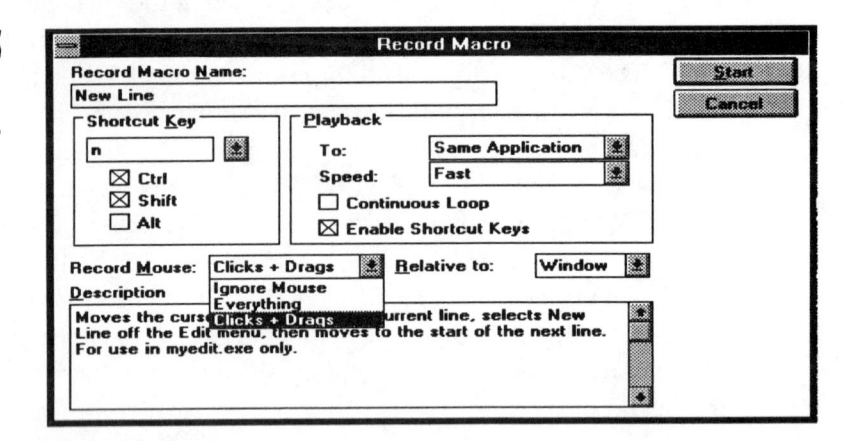

In this dialog box, you can name the macro in the Record Macro Name box, or define a shortcut key in the Shortcut Key box. You must do one or the other, since you will run the macro using either the name or the shortcut key. Note that the shortcut key can be any of a number of combinations, but it must include some combination of CTRL, ALT, and SHIFT; and it must also include at least one of the other keys, such

Getting More Productive with Windows for Workgroups Utilities

as letters, numbers, or symbols, that are available on the keyboard. Our example macro will be invoked by holding down CTRL and SHIFT and pressing the N key.

> **NOTE** It's actually best to avoid using the ALT key in your macros, since so many of the Windows shortcuts already use it. Your macro could become confused with a standard Windows shortcut5 key.

Enter a description in the lower box so you know what the macro does and the application in which it works. When you're ready, select the Start button. You are now back in your application, so perform the action you want to record. When you are done, switch back to Recorder by clicking on the Recorder icon, which is flashing. The box that now appears is illustrated in Figure 7.16.

Figure 7.16

The Recorder status window

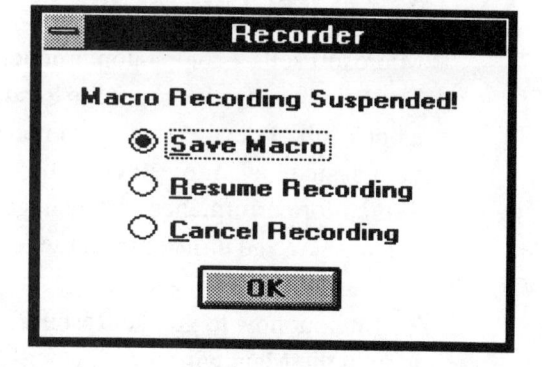

To save the set of actions as a macro, select Save Macro and OK. If you aren't done with your sequence, select Resume Recording. If you made a mistake or changed your mind, you can still Cancel.

Now, when you view the Recorder window, you see an entry listed by the shortcut key name. Every time you use that shortcut key, Windows for Workgroups will perform the actions you recorded. If you press the key sequence in an application other than the one for which it was recorded, Windows for Workgroups will move you to that application if possible, then play it back. Save the macro so that it will still be available when you restart Windows for Workgroups.

You can use macros to speed up your work in a number of ways. We have looked only at macros within a single application, but you can also create macros that work between applications and on Windows for Workgroups itself. Explore the other options on your own.

In our example, we have selected Fast for the playback speed, which means that Windows for Workgroups will replay the macro as fast as your computer will permit. But if you select the other speed, Recorded Speed, the macro will replay at the same speed at which you recorded it, an ideal feature for demonstrations.

Utilities from the Resource Kit

Microsoft sells a companion product to Windows for Workgroups called The Windows for Workgroups Resource Kit. When you order it, you get a book full of detailed technical notes about networking, configuring your system, and more. You also get a diskette filled with useful utilities to monitor performance and manage your desktop. This section will discuss selected utilities from the Resource Kit.

To find out how to get the Resource Kit, double-click on the ReadMe icon in the Main window. This will bring up the Write utility with the file README.WRI, which contains instructions for ordering the Resource Kit and other useful information.

Graphics Viewer

You can use Paintbrush to view graphics files, but for the times when you don't need to edit drawings, the Resource Kit provides you with a smaller, faster utility called Graphics Viewer. It displays graphics files in bitmap, MetaFile, and icon formats (files ending in .BMP, .WMF, and .ICO). It also includes a bonus feature: if you are viewing a bitmap file and press the load button, Graphics Viewer loads the current graphic as your new wallpaper as in Figure 7.17.

Figure 7.17

Viewing a graphic with Graphics Viewer

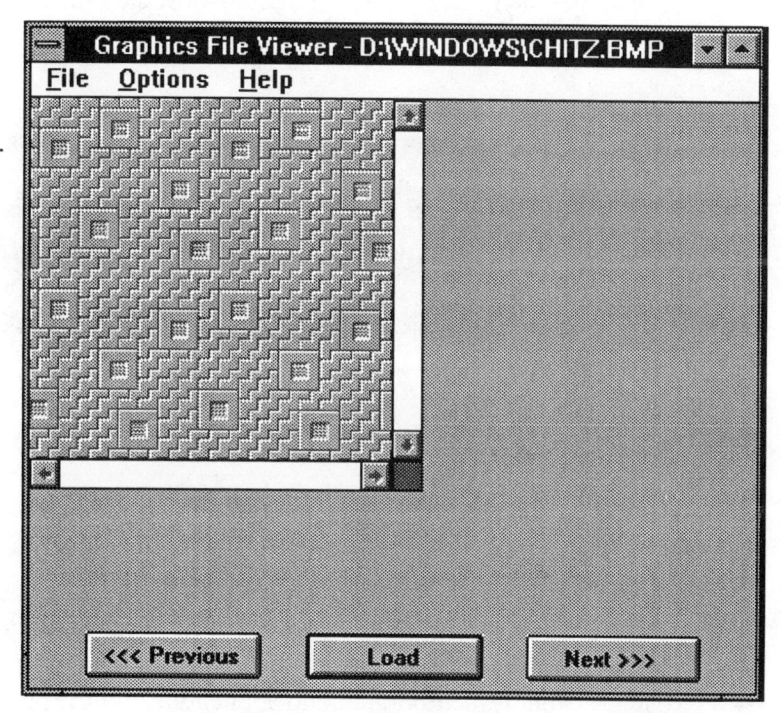

Top Desk

Top Desk provides a graphical representation of your desktop, and lets you switch between multiple applications that are running concurrently by using your mouse. Top Desk is useful if you prefer using the keyboard instead of a mouse to move around in Windows.

Top Desk displays your programs as blocks in a grid. One of the blocks is the desktop. (See Figure 7.18.) As you start each of your applications, Top Desk creates a box for it on the desktop area. If you drag that program's box off the desktop, it disappears from your Windows desktop as well. When you drag it back, you are reactivating it. Think of the Top Desk desktop box as your current screen area, and the regions around it as areas off screen. When you drag your programs off screen, they are still running but they are not cluttering your workspace. It is easy to get them back with Top Desk — just drag the box back onto the desktop area.

Figure 7.18

Top Desk

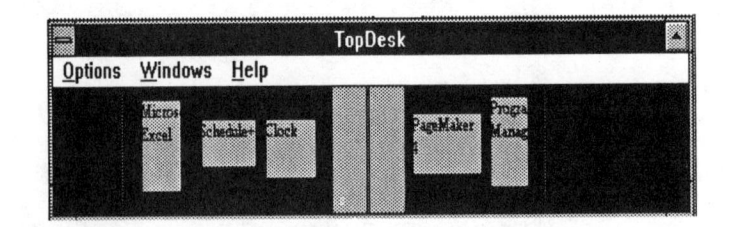

Document Management with Windows for Workgroups

With Windows for Workgroups, Microsoft released a facility called Network DDE (dynamic data exchange). This is not directly usable by end users but is incorporated into applications for the purpose of sharing information across applications and people.

In this section we'll explore the options of sharing both documents and pieces of information across a network. First we will introduce a few new concepts for sharing information, they are: objects, linking and embedding. Then we will present an example of using the ClipBook Viewer and showing how Network DDE can work in a workgroup setting.

Object Linking and Embedding

If you have heard much about Windows, you've probably already come across the term *object linking and embedding*, or OLE (pronounced o-lay). OLE is a method of sharing information between different applications on the same computer, the same application on different computers, or the same application on the same computer but used in a different part of a document.

In OLE, *object* refers to a piece of information, such as a chart, a drawing, an image, or a sound or video file. In some cases, text is also considered an object.

Linking and embedding refer to how the object gets into a document or file. If an object is *linked*, information is placed with it about its origins. A linked object will contain an invisible piece of information about the application that generated the object. If in the originating application you make in the object, the changes will be reflected immediately in the destination document.

Embedding, on the other hand, makes a copy of the object, as it exists, in the destination document or file. If, after you have embedded the object, you make changes in the original, those changes won't automatically be reflected in the copy embedded in the second file.

OLE in Action

OLE is easiest to understand by means of an example. Say George creates a graph in his Windows spreadsheet. Sam is writing a status report and wants to include George's graph. OLE lets Sam use George's graph without having to recreate any information. And, depending on what method is used (linking or embedding), Sam can print the up-to-date status report – if George's graph changes, so will the graph in Sam's status report – immediately, without any additional effort.

OLE can be a real time saver. You simply highlight and select the object, copy it or link it, then paste it into the new document. You don't have to re-key information and send it out to a file and import it again, so you also aren't as likely to make mistakes in the course of transferring material.

Using OLE and ClipBook Viewer

In Chapter 4 we introduced the ClipBook. In this section, we'll develop a scenario that illustrates how to share information from several computers, using the ClipBook Viewer.

Four members of the Currid & Company office team, Smith, Lab, Currid, and Davison are working together on a report. The report is divided into 13 chapters, and today we are finishing the last one. Davison has been working up some travel expense charts in Microsoft's Excel spreadsheet program. Smith has been editing text that was written by Currid and Lab is pulling it all together.

As each member of the team completes their part of the work, he or she posts it to the ClipBook. Notice, in Figure 7.19, that Davison has posted two versions of the travel chart and the original Chapter 13.

Figure 7.19

Davison's ClipBook with Travel Charts

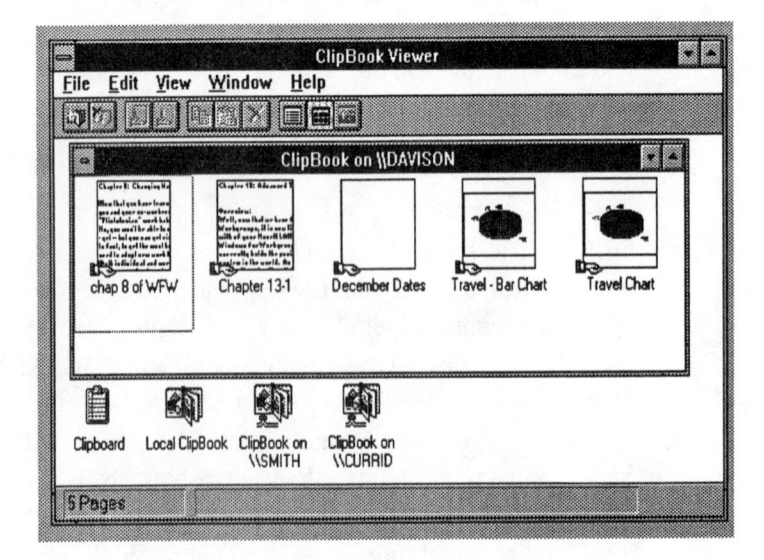

Note, in Figure 7.20, that Lab has posted a version of Chapter 13, which he called *"#2 Edit of Chapter 13-1."*

Figure 7.20

Lab's version of ClipBook with Chapter 13

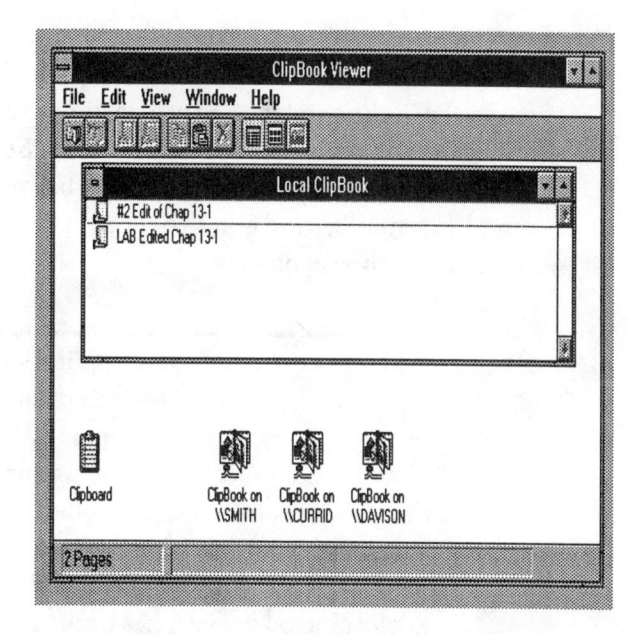

For Lab to combine Davison's graphs and the edited report, he must copy the pages from these ClipBooks to his local application software, in this case, Microsoft's Word for Windows. He would first copy the ClipBook page called #2 Edit of Chapter 13-1 to the Clipboard, then paste it into a new Word document.

Lab would then pick up the graphic from Davison's ClipBook and paste it into the Word document, using the same copy procedure. With just a few clicks of the mouse, Lab has been able to combine information created by different people using different applications on separate computers. He was able to embed an object (the graph) into a document using only his ClipBook in conjunction with his word processor.

Let's make this a little more complicated. What if Davison's graph information changes a lot? If Lab were to *embed* Davison's graph into

Chapter 13, the graph would reflect only the numbers entered up to the point in time when he embedded the information.

If the graph is likely to change, it might be better to *link* the graph to the chapter instead of embedding it, so the changes will be automatically reflected in the chapter. Lab can get up-to-the-minute access to Davison's changes if he chooses the Paste Special... option from Word's Edit command. This creates a live link between his report and Davison's spreadsheet. When the graph changes in the spreadsheet, it will also change in Lab's report chapter.

> **NOTE** Linking between different applications on different computers is a technical miracle! From a user point-of-view the process is easy, but the technology behind the scenes is still new, and complicated. If you use links, there are a few rules that you must follow to make the links work reliably. Make sure the object is properly copied to the Clipboard and marked for sharing, and that the option for starting the application on connect has been checked. This sets up the proper background so the link will stay active.

Shareware and Freeware Utilities

What Is Shareware?

Software probably accounts for a large portion of your computing budget. Most off-the-shelf programs cost hundreds of dollars. You spent a significant amount of money buying Windows for Workgroups, but it doesn't provide every function you need. It's tricky to round out your selection of utilities and still stay within budget. Fortunately, off-the-shelf software is not the only choice. With some exploring, you can benefit from the rich and varied world of shareware and freeware.

Shareware is inexpensive software that is distributed by its developers, who generally do not advertise or package it. Since their costs are low, your price stays low: you can register most shareware for under $100. An important feature of shareware is that you can try it out before you pay. The copy you have before you register it is only an evaluation copy. If a program does not do all you had hoped you can just stop using it, but you can also still give evaluation copies to other people who might have a use for it. If you decide you want to keep and use the program, you'll follow instructions that are included by the developer in the evaluation copy for registration.

When you register your shareware program, you might get diskettes, a manual, and the next three updates to the program, or you might get nothing more than the permission and gratitude of the developer. Either way, we encourage you to register, because by doing so you make it possible for the developer to keep fixing bugs in and adding features to your copy of the program. You also help support a system that gives everyone lower prices and a higher selection of software solutions from which to choose.

Freeware Is Freely Available

Freeware is exactly what its name implies. Freeware programs are those that the developers give away. Don't assume "you get what you pay for" here — many freeware programs are of excellent quality. So why are they free? To some freeware writers, the free distribution channel is a political statement. They believe the explosion of personal computers to be the advent of a similar explosion of information, and that no one should have to pay for information. Whether or not you agree with the philosophy of freeware, you can still benefit from the results.

Finding Shareware and Freeware

You can find shareware programs in a number of places. The most common and popular sources are bulletin boards, such as CompuServe or Prodigy (both worth exploring in their own right). Many good books on the market describe these information systems, so we will not do so. Other sources of shareware are books: often a book on a computer utility or system will come with a diskette full of shareware utilities for you to try. A third source is friends and coworkers. Ask around; probably many people you know have clever utilities to improve their working styles. If these utilities are shareware, they can give you copies, but read license agreements carefully before handing out copies yourself! And, a word of warning, be careful to check all shareware for harmful programs called computer viruses. (See Chapter 10, for information about protecting your network from computer viruses.)

When you start working in the Windows for Workgroups environment, a world of utilities opens up to you. Some are very useful, others have a few good features, and some are more cumbersome than helpful. In this chapter we described some of each, and gave you information about finding out more about them and others.

CHAPTER 8

SECURITY AND THE WORKGROUP

CHAPTER 8

FEATURING:

- Who Is Responsible for Security
- How Security Works
- Basic Password Concepts
- Sharing Directories and Security

Ideally, you might want to share just about everything with members of your local group. But in many cases, complete access to files and printers isn't appropriate. With Windows for Workgroups, you can have a completely open system, or you can set up restrictions. You can share use of the payroll files with Peter and your spreadsheets with Sam, and specify that Richard can just read your documents. Or, you can set up certain directories on your hard disk so that everyone can have access to all the files within that directory. The options are yours.

In this chapter, we'll talk about the differences between peer-to-peer network operating systems like Windows for Workgroups, and file-server-based systems like Novell's NetWare and Microsoft's LAN Manager. We'll cover the use of passwords and how to assign them. We'll also talk about sharing your files — who to give access to and how much to give. Finally, realizing that at some time you may forget your password, we'll also discuss regaining access to the workgroup.

Who Is Responsible for Security?

In mainframe or minicomputer systems, the responsibility for security rests with a specially trained administrator. The security administrator is charged with granting users' privileges, from accessing the system to use of printers and data files. Frequently, organizations also layer on extra security in the form of security software. Then the security administrator assigns the user a special name to use with the computer (called the logon i.d.) and issues users access rights to the various resources. Some large computer security systems are very sophisticated and require constant monitoring and updating to keep the right people in or out of sensitive material and resources.

File-server and client-server networks, composed primarily of PCs rather than minicomputers or mainframes, also require a specially trained person to take responsibility frequently for security. In this case, the responsibility may not be as great as that of a mainframe security administrator, but it is important and time consuming.

With Windows for Workgroups, or other peer-to-peer operating systems, things are very different. Security rests with the individual user, not necessarily an administrator. The operating environment is set up so that users themselves are in charge of sharing and unsharing their resources. While this provides a great deal of freedom, it also makes everyone responsible for making sure that an appropriate level of security is applied to his or her individual (shared) resources and files. And, a word of caution, since Windows for Workgroups essentially runs on top of the MS-DOS operating system, full security of every file is nearly impossible to achieve. This is because the MS-DOS operating system does not have security built in to it.

How Windows for Workgroups Security Works

There are four layers of security within Windows for Workgroups. They are:

- ▲ Logon Security
- ▲ Directory Sharing Security
- ▲ Printer Security
- ▲ Application Security (e.g. Mail & Schedule+)

With the exception of Application security, each is controlled directly by the end user, not a systems administrator.

How Logon Security Works

When a user logs into Windows for Workgroups, the system checks the logon name and password against a security file located on the local PC. If both the name and password match the entry in the security file, the user is granted access to the workgroup and to all of the devices that have been specified for his or her use. This includes printers, disk drives, and other network resources.

Each user in the workgroup can have different access security. For example, Sam and Joe may share Harry's printer, but Beth and Bill want to share Mary's printer instead. Ted may want Joe to work with his spreadsheet files, but he may not want Sally to see them. By creatively assigning passwords to access files, the combinations of security options are almost limitless.

Basic Password Concepts

Passwords are the heart of logon security in Windows for Workgroups. You should establish a personal password that is known only to you. By

SECURITY AND THE WORKGROUP

changing your password from time to time and keeping it private, you can ensure that no one is able to gain unauthorized access to your resources.

Why Use Passwords

Your password, a special word that only you know, gives you a private key into the system. Passwords can be any combination of as many as 14 letters and numbers. If you are creative and careful with your password, it can be virtually impossible to guess.

Making Passwords Effective

Your password must be one that cannot easily be guessed, and that no one else knows. Creating a secure password is easy, but there are some tips to follow and traps to avoid. Table 8.1 lists some of the good and bad points to consider when you create or maintain your password.

Table 8.1 Rules for Secure Passwords

Do	Don't
Use more than five characters	Use less than five characters
Use words or phrases that you'll remember	Use words or phrases that are too complex to remember
Change your password every few months	Write down your password

Passwords to Avoid

Some passwords should never be used — unfortunately, they are also the type most commonly used — names of your family members, pets, or friends. Although they are easy to remember, these passwords are too easy to figure out, and reduce the added measure of security that a proper password can offer.

Sharing Directories and Security

Another layer of security is available in the form of sharing directories. You, the user, are in complete control of sharing directories on your own computer. As described in Chapter 4, you can use the File Manager to share or unshare files in a directory. When you decide to share a directory on your PC, you have the option of giving workgroup members Full access, Read Only access, or Depends on Password access. (This password should be different from your personal logon password.) Keep in mind that whatever access you grant to a directory is passed along to subdirectories below it. For example, if you give full access privileges to the directory C:\WORDFILE on your hard disk, you have automatically given full access to any files that exist in:

    C:\WORDFILE\JAN
    C:\WORDFILE\FEB
    C:\WORDFILE\MAR
    C:\WORDFILE\APR

and so on. Even though you didn't explicitly define those subdirectories when you shared C:\WORDFILE, they inherit the access privileges of the directory above it.

Deciding Who Should Have How Much Access

When deciding how to share your resources, you must consider what you want to share and with whom you want to share it. Anyone who is

Security and the Workgroup

connected to your workstation via the network can use your resources if you share them. In some cases, you will want to offer FULL access to everyone. For example, you'll want everyone to have access to the laser printer that was purchased for the group. But you may want to limit access to Joe's color printer or the one in Harry's office. Also, you may want to limit access to some other resources, such as the directory containing the corporate accounting files. Limiting access can be accomplished either by selecting to limit it for all users or by requiring those users with access rights to know the designated password.

You'll want to be careful in granting access privileges to your directories. While most users will not intentionally destroy your data, there are plenty of ways to have an inadvertent "oops!" Also, some users may not understand the importance of certain documents. All too often the greatest threat to your data is an accident. A user who has Full access may delete your files, thinking that he or she is cleaning up his or her own hard disk instead of yours. Thinking "I don't recognize ANY of these files; oh well, I guess I can delete them," has destroyed a lot of data. Fortunately, the damage can only be done if other users are granted Full access to your directories.

In granting access to a directory, sometimes it is wise to grant Read Only access. There are two main reasons for this.

First, once the program is installed and configured for the workgroup, you will want to be sure that the configuration is not changed. Users in a workgroup tend to forget that the application is being shared by all users. The problem arises when a user modifies a configuration, and in doing so affects all the users who use it. To prevent users from modifying the applications configurations that affect everyone, restrict access to Read Only.

Assigning Read Only access will also prevent inexperienced users from saving files into application directories instead of placing them in personal directories. If users save files to the application directory, it becomes very difficult to separate any program files from data files when it comes time to delete or upgrade the application.

Printer Security

In most cases, you will want to grant access privileges to peripheral devices, such as printers and plotters, to all users, so everyone can use them. Few workgroups insist on using tight security or a password assignment for a printer, because it is so cost-effective to allow many people to use one printer.

But there are cases when printers are used for printing sensitive documents. For example, an executive may not want to allow others to share his secretary's printer so that they cannot see the documents being printed. A workgroup in the human resources department might need to print confidential information about employees, so they may need to print to a place where their document would not accidentally be picked up. You may also want to restrict the use of equipment that's particularly expensive to use, like a color printer or a linotype typesetter. In these cases, you can set up the printer to be shared only by users that know the proper password.

Application Security

Beyond sharing and securing physical devices, such as printers, or files in directories, there is a need to secure certain types of applications. You may have instances where a certain application, perhaps an accounting package, is reserved for only select members of the workgroup. In this case, even password security to the directories of the accounting system isn't enough. You'll want to provide extra security within the use of the application. This is called application security and is not built in as a part of Windows for Workgroups.

Application security rests with the application. Whether it is an accounting system, a parts-order system, or a manufacturing application, it must provide for security internally. This requires that the application have security of its own.

An example of how application level security works can be seen in the Mail and Schedule+ applications of Windows for Workgroups. As you may have already noticed, your Mail user name and password don't necessarily have to match your Windows for Workgroups logon name and password. In fact, most security specialists would recommend that you do not use the same password, to add an extra amount of protection to your mail and schedule files.

What to Do When You Forget Your Password

No matter how careful you are, the inevitable has a way of happening -- you've forgotten your password! Are you permanently locked out of the network? No -- regaining access to the network is not very difficult.

The first step is to delete your password table. This is accomplished by viewing the SYSTEM.INI file in the Windows directory. You can view the contents of this file by using any editor that lets you view an ASCII file. You can use the Notepad supplied in Windows, the SYSEDIT utility or the DOS editor EDIT.EXE. Look for the Password Lists section of the file. In this section, you will see one or more user names along with the path and location of the users' password table, such as:

[Password Lists]
*Shares=C:\WIN\Shares.PWL
CURRID=C:\WIN\CURRID.PWL

Write down the name and location of the .PWL file that contains your logon name. (In our case, the file name would be CURRID.PWL that is located in the C:\WIN directory.) Then exit from the program you used to view the file. If you use an editor to view the file, make sure you don't change or save SYSTEM.INI file.

Resetting the password table is a simple matter of deleting the .PWL file. The file will then be rebuilt when you log back into the network.

Resetting Your Mail Password

If you forget your User Name and password for Mail, you cannot reestablish it yourself (unless you are the mail administrator). Modifying the mail password has to be done on the station that contains the workgroup postoffice, and therefore the WGPO directory. The mail administrator can log in at that location and easily change your password under the Postoffice Manager option of the Mail menu.

Regaining access and resetting passwords is not a difficult task, but it can be time consuming. The best way to avoid having to follow these steps is to select a password that you are sure to remember.

In this chapter, we examined the importance of providing security for the workgroup. We began by looking into the basics for setting and maintaining passwords, which are the most important part of maintaining a secure environment. Then we moved on to consider just how much access is appropriate, and where security is needed. Finally, we closed by examining where security is located in Windows for Workgroups, and how to get back into our secure environment, having found the right password.

CHAPTER 9

ADMINISTRATIVE CHORES FOR THE NETWORK

CHAPTER 9

Featuring:

- Selecting a Backup System
- Available Tools and Products
- Providing Training and Support
- Protecting Against Viruses

More than just cabling and computer systems, the procedures and policies of a workgroup enable a group of people to use their network system effectively. As we have seen in previous chapters, networks can provide us with real gains in productivity. Yet, if the proper procedures and policies aren't in place, networks actually can be counterproductive. For example, exposure to data loss is increased as we share more and more data and concentrate into shared directories information that is critical to the efforts of the workgroup. With common sense and regular housekeeping, the challenges presented by workgroup computing can be managed so that users get maximum benefit from the system. This chapter covers some key administration tasks necessary in the Windows for Workgroups environment. These include:

▲ Backing up files,
▲ Monitoring disk space utilization,
▲ Defragmenting hard disks for increased performance,
▲ Training and supporting users,
▲ Maintaining configuration information,

▲   Protecting against computer viruses, and

▲   Managing the Mail system's disk space.

Protecting Data by Backing Up Files

Everyone who has stored information on computers on a regular basis has experienced loss of data. Hard disks, because they are mechanical devices, are one of the more likely points of failure in a computer system. Besides mechanical failure of the disk, data might be lost or damaged through computer viruses, unexpected problems in software programs, natural disasters, or, most often, human error. Many things can go wrong, but if you have backup copies of the files on hand, downtime due to loss of data will not be as great. In fact, your loss is limited to the changes made to the files during the time that has elapsed since your last backup.

A Backup Strategy

A good backup strategy minimizes the exposure of workgroup members and the organization as a whole to loss of important data. There are two types of backups. The first, a *full backup,* is a copy of all the files on the hard disk. An *incremental backup* copies only those files that have been changed or added since the last backup.

It is important to make periodic full backups, capturing the operating system, configuration files, and all applications on your workstation. To restore your system after a disk failure, you need more than just your data; you need your whole PC work environment. If your hard disk is completely wiped out and you have a full backup, you can easily restore the files to a new disk and be up and running in a morning.

Many novices fall into the trap of making one backup every day, using the same single set of tapes or floppy disks day after day. If some files on the hard disk have been corrupted that you are not aware of and you copy the corrupted files from the hard disk to your backup tape, you will have wiped out the last good copy of that data. Various tape rotation strategies exist to minimize this possibility and to ensure that a valid backup of all data exists.

A commonly used backup schedule is to do a full backup of each system every week or two. The full backups are kept for one to three months. A daily incremental backup is also performed, capturing all the new data on tapes or disks that are rotated day by day. Using this strategy, you are protected from data problems that might not be discovered right away, and you have a greater chance of recovering data that is valid.

It is important to check the validity of your backups periodically. By performing a "restore" of the backups onto that extra system, you can verify that your entire procedure works. Do this on an extra system, or one that does not contain critical data.

When you make backups, you are generating new information that must be tracked. It is important that all backups be marked and dated carefully. Going through stacks of tapes to find the one you need can be a trying experience.

Storing backups at an offsite location is an important part of any backup strategy. Computer systems have become a critical part of our businesses, and if we hope to recover from a natural disaster or fire, we must have stored our data and programs elsewhere. Insurance can replace the building and systems; but no insurance policy, other than a carefully applied backup strategy, can preserve the information and programs that keep our businesses organized and running efficiently.

Many businesses keep a copy from the previous week in an offsite safe deposit box. If you don't do that, keeping copies at another safe alternate location does provide some degree of protection.

Designating Responsibility

Even the best backup strategy is useless if it is not carried out. The workgroup's systems and data are assets and protection of those assets should be taken seriously. The key to this is that all members of the workgroup must understand whose responsibility it is to maintain the backup.

If each member is individually responsible for data on his or her system, this policy should be made clear and each member must be trained to use the backup system. The manager of the workgroup should then verify that backups are being made on a regular basis.

As workgroups become larger, it may be more efficient to make a single individual responsible for backing up systems in the workgroup. This individual might be an administrative aide or a member of the corporate Information Systems staff.

Selecting a Backup System

Most of today's personal computers have large hard disks —100-200 MB. It is not uncommon for systems to include up to 500 MB of disk storage. While any means of copying data will work for backing up your system's data, in practice you want an organized system that is designed for backing up large amounts of data. Faced with hundreds of MB of data, backing up onto floppy disks could take all day. If the backup chore is too onerous, people will find excuses not to do it. Unfortunately, it is when things are busiest in the office (and when the most data is generated), that people don't want to take the time to properly back up their systems.

You should select a backup system based on the dependability of the backup media, the system's ease of use, speed, storage capacity, and finally the cost. The physical size of the storage media can also be an important issue. As discussed above, you will want to keep a set of backups and cycle through them. The smaller the physical size of the storage media, the less space needed to store your backups. Consider the space needed by one high-capacity cartridge versus that needed by 20 or more diskettes.

The most common backup systems use magnetic tape. Vendors of backup systems usually offer complete systems of tape drives, controller cards, and programs to perform backups.

Most tape drives use 1/4" tape cartridges that hold 60-120 MB of data. Newer backup systems use 4mm digital audio tape (DAT). These hold between 1.1 to 2 GB (gigabytes) of data on a single tape. In addition, the new DAT cartridges are very convenient for storage as they are smaller in size than the 1/4" cartridges.

For larger systems or large workgroups, you may want to consider the new 8mm helical-scan digital tape drives. These drives write data in diagonal strips using sets of rotating heads, allowing the tape surface to be used more efficiently than it is when data is written in several parallel tracks the length of the tape. Helical-scan systems can store as much as 2.2 GB of data on a single tape.

In choosing which type of tape drive to use, think about how your backups will be organized. If all of your systems have less than 120 MB of storage, the 1/4" tape systems should do fine. Each workgroup member will need five tape cartridges, each labeled with the day of the week, on which to do incremental backups, and at least four tape cartridges for doing the full backup once a week.

Choosing Where to Place the Backup System

You should carefully consider the question of which workstation will have the tape backup system attached to it. If members of the workgroup are to back up their own systems, the workstation must be easily available to them. If you have delegated a single individual to make the backup, you should have the tape system attached to his or her system.

It is probably cost-prohibitive to attach a tape system to each person's system. However, it may be worthwhile to consider putting a controller card in each person's system and placing the backup software on a shared directory. Then the tape unit itself could be checked out and used to back up the disks at the workstation. Having the tape system attached to the system you are backing up will speed up the backup process, because you will have eliminated the network link (you don't have to pass all that data over the network).

An alternative way to perform backups is to copy the important data to a file server. This is an option if you are connected to another network such as LAN Manager or NetWare.

Performing the Backup

If one member of the workgroup is responsible for backing up all data, then each member needs to share the root directory of each disk drive. (If this is done, we recommend that a password be used to limit access to each PC.) The person doing the backups will connect to the shared drive and perform the backup over the network. Be aware that whatever backup software you choose to use, it will need to have full access to the directory. It is a good idea to have a naming convention, such as the one shown in Figure 9.1, for sharing your disk drives for backups. You can make good use of the comment field as well, for example, to note the contents of the backup.

Note that the dialog box that shows the available directories on the network will also identify each group member's drive, as shown in Figure 9.2.

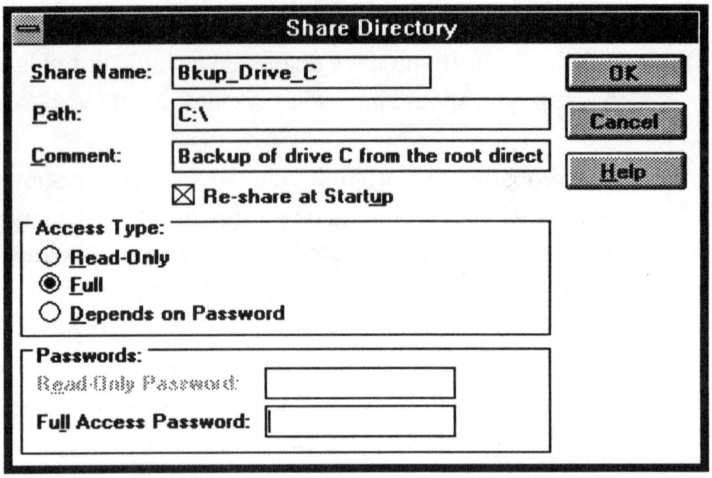

Figure 9.1

Sharing the disk drive for backup

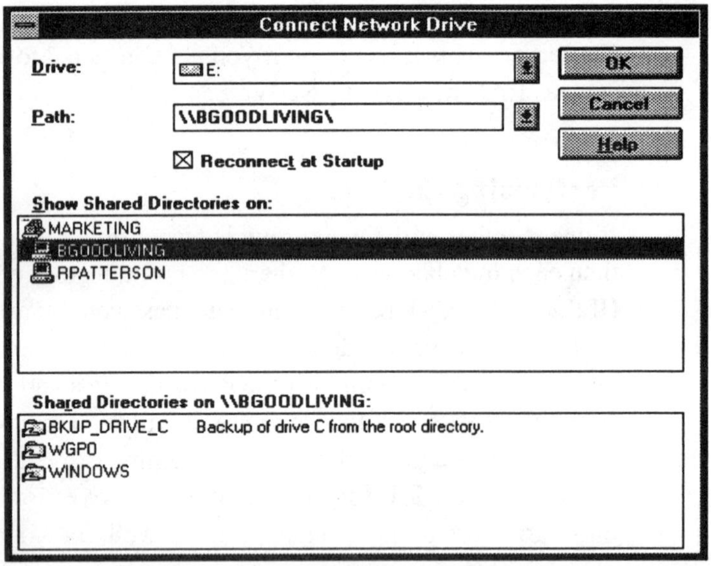

Share Directory

- Share Name: Bkup_Drive_C
- Path: C:\
- Comment: Backup of drive C from the root direct
- ☒ Re-share at Startup

Access Type:
- ○ Read-Only
- ● Full
- ○ Depends on Password

Passwords:
- Read-Only Password:
- Full Access Password:

[OK] [Cancel] [Help]

Figure 9.2

Connecting to the shared drive

Connect Network Drive

- Drive: E:
- Path: \\BGOODLIVING\
- ☒ Reconnect at Startup

Show Shared Directories on:
- MARKETING
- BGOODLIVING
- RPATTERSON

Shared Directories on \\BGOODLIVING:
- BKUP_DRIVE_C   Backup of drive C from the root directory.
- WGPO
- WINDOWS

[OK] [Cancel] [Help]

The full path name, \\BGOODLIVING\BKUP_DRIVE_C, provides a good label for the tape, with all the information needed to associate the tape with the proper system and drive. Using conventions such as these can eliminate the possibility of mislabeling backups. Consistency in naming will allow indexing of workgroup members' backups so that

Administrative Chores for the Network

they can be located without any fuss. See Figure 9.3 for an example of the full path name.

Figure 9.3

The full path name

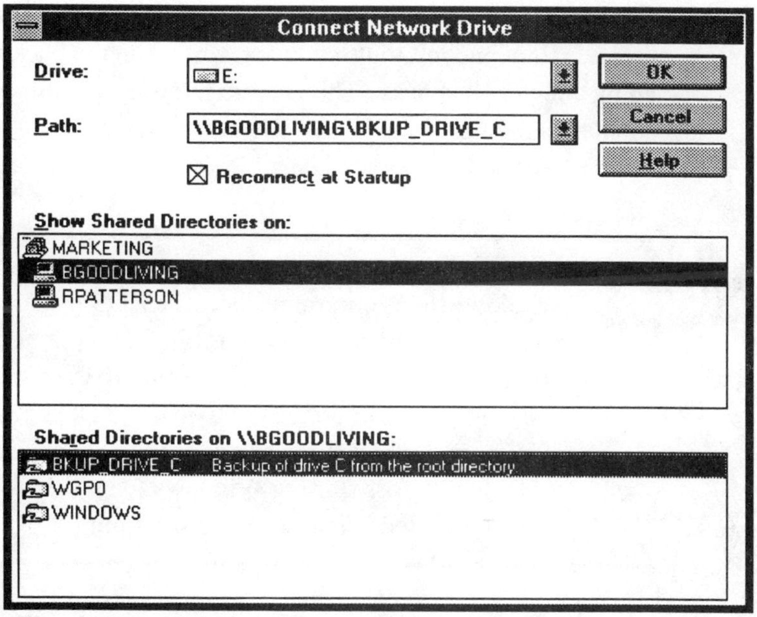

[Connect Network Drive dialog box showing Drive: E:, Path: \\BGOODLIVING\BKUP_DRIVE_C, Reconnect at Startup checked. Show Shared Directories on: MARKETING, BGOODLIVING, RPATTERSON. Shared Directories on \\BGOODLIVING: BKUP_DRIVE_C (Backup of drive C from the root directory), WGPO, WINDOWS.]

Available Tools and Products

Backing up is done using the tape system vendor's software. You should select a system that was designed for the Windows 3.1 environment. We further recommend that you verify that the software can back up shared directories over the network before buying it. Another key feature to look for is the ability to selectively restore files from a backup. Most backup software will allow you to choose between making a quick-and-dirty disk image or a file-by-file backup of your system. Many of the Windows backup utilities present an interface similar to File Manager, where you can select the files and directories to backup or restore. This makes it easier to back up your Windows for Workgroups network.

Another important feature to look for is automated scheduling of backups. Several backup programs for Windows, notably Maynard's MaynStream for Windows and Gazelle's Back-it for Windows, provide automated scheduling and background operation. When backups are automated, one of the big problems associated with them — people forgetting — is eliminated. Windows applications can run in the background, allowing you to use your system while the backup program is going about its business. This feature removes a common complaint about backing up — the loss of use of the system while the backup is being performed.

> **NOTE** Many DOS backup programs will not run correctly under Windows for Workgroups, because DOS backup programs rely on being in complete control of the system, and Windows for Workgroups is always running even when we are working in a DOS box. If you do use a DOS backup system, you will need to run your backups on each workstation either before starting Windows for Workgroups or after you have exited Windows for Workgroups.

Some backup systems that work in Windows are:

- ▲ Central Point Software's Central Point Backup Version 7.2,
- ▲ Emerald System's Xpress Librarian™ Software,
- ▲ Maynard Electronics' EZTape 3.1 for Windows and their MaynStream for Windows, and
- ▲ Gazelle System's Back-It for Windows.

These vendors and others, who have previously marketed backup programs for Windows, will most likely be creating products specifically for Windows for Workgroups. You should watch for reviews of products that are compatible with Windows in the major trade publications (*Infoworld, PC World, PC Magazine, PC Week, Windows,* and *Windows User Magazine*).

Keeping the Hard Disks in Order

As people use up available disk space, purchase requests for more and larger hard disks will come in. These requests, however, must be cost-justified, like purchase requests for other tools and supplies. Are the disks currently available being utilized as efficiently as they can be? Do you need all the files that are on your disk? Whether it is done by a designated administrator or by consensus, the workgroup's disk space must be managed.

Often, we keep various files around because we are unsure of whether we should delete them. This uncertainty fills disks with irrelevant information that is not being used. There are several administrative ways to deal with this. Periodically the administrator or manager of the workgroup can send out an e-mail message asking that users delete any unnecessary files. If files need to be archived, they can be stored best on tape, by making a backup of those files and keeping the tape in a safe place. This tape should be clearly marked as to its contents and the reason the information is being archived. Moreover, this tape should not be one of those used in the daily or weekly backup cycle.

If there is a designated administrator, that person can monitor the disk usage of each member in the workgroup. This can be done when backups are performed. The disk-utilization figures for the shared directory \\BGOODLIVING\BKUP_DRIVE_C are shown on the status line in the File Manager window shown in Figure 9.4. On the left side of the status line, the amount of free space on the disk is shown. Total capacity for the hard disk is also given. You can compute the percentage of utilization using this information; in this case the disk is 63 percent utilized.

Hard disks in a workgroup can be viewed as a common resource. By looking at the percentage of the hard disk storage used by each of the systems, the administrator can get a good idea of total usage and how much is still available. If one person is running out of space, the administrator can ask a group member with extra space to create a shared

Figure 9.4

Disk usage on shared drives

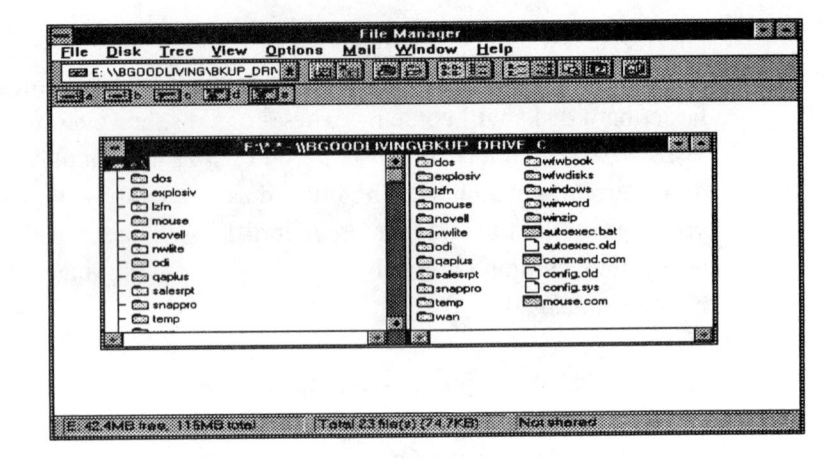

directory, and then the person who needs more space can connect to that directory and use it as an additional drive. The ability to share disk space among the workgroup creates a flexible storage area that can be allocated according to the needs of workgroup members without physically modifying systems.

A common rule of thumb for disk utilization is to use no more than 80 percent of the disk. When you start bumping up against this threshold, it's a good idea to think about purchasing additional disk space. There are two reasons for this:

- ▲ Performance suffers when the disk is nearly full, because the operating system must place blocks of data in areas of the disk that are not physically close together.
- ▲ A buffer is necessary to prevent work stoppage and loss of data if the disk becomes completely full. The buffer is necessary because Windows uses the disk for *swap* and *temporary* files. The impact of swap and temporary files on performance is discussed in Chapter 12.

Many Windows applications create temporary files in which to store information while performing their tasks. If these files cannot be created because you don't have sufficient disk space, you will be unable to use the application. You also need space in which to save the files you are working on. There are few feelings worse than having worked for an hour or so, and then getting a message indicating that your work cannot be saved because there is insufficient disk space.

Defragmenting for Increased Performance

On a newly formatted hard disk, each file gets created by stringing together "blocks" of disk space. If they are together on the disk, we say they are using *contiguous* space. Contiguous blocks can be read or written in one pass of the disk's read/write heads, resulting in better performance, because the system does not spend time waiting for the disk's read/write heads to be positioned multiple times.

As you create and delete files on your hard disk, the operating system keeps track of the unused blocks of data, even if they are not contiguous, and chains them together. These blocks may be in widely different areas of the disk. When the system goes to the list of free blocks, it may find that it has to scatter different parts of a file over a wide area of the disk.

Vendors of operating system utilities have written programs, called *disk defragmentation utilities*, that move all of the files to contiguous blocks on the disk. A defragmentation utility looks at the way the files are stored on the disk and creates a map. Then it figures out a scheme for copying blocks from one place to another so that all the blocks for a particular file will be contiguous.

If you create, delete, or edit files frequently, you may experience a small gain in performance through defragmenting your files. For optimal performance, defragmentation can be performed once a day.

Most defragmentation programs are DOS utilities. They should not be run in DOS under Windows or Windows for Workgroups because when you run a DOS application under Windows, there is at least one other program running — Windows — which may potentially be using the file system. If you try to run these utilities under any type of Windows environment, they may corrupt the file system, resulting in loss of data. Therefore, you should run defragmentation utilities before loading, or after exiting, Windows for Workgroups.

Symantec Corporation's Norton Utilities and the PC-Kwik Corporation's Win Master toolbox both contain disk defragmentation utilities. Many other vendors provide defragmentation utilities either by themselves or bundled with other utilities.

Providing Training and Support

Windows for Workgroups and the personal productivity software used in conjunction with it are tools. As with all tools, people must be trained in their use if they are to get the most from them. A key administrative chore is to ensure that all members of the workgroup know how to use the system to best advantage. Windows for Workgroups can be a real aid in providing support and getting information on how to use new tools.

We have discussed sharing information through shared directories. You could set up a shared directory and put files there that explain how to accomplish various tasks. Then workgroup members could browse the files to find information on new tools or on overcoming a problem they may have encountered, and print whatever information they need.

If one person has encountered a problem, it is likely that other people in your group are experiencing it. To get the word out quickly, you might create a Personal Group in Mail. From the Mail menus, choose Personal

Groups... from the Mail menu. Then create a new Personal Group and add the names of all the members of your workgroup who should receive the bulletin. Figure 9.5 shows a list for TECH_BULLETIN.

Figure 9.5

An e-mail personal group for support

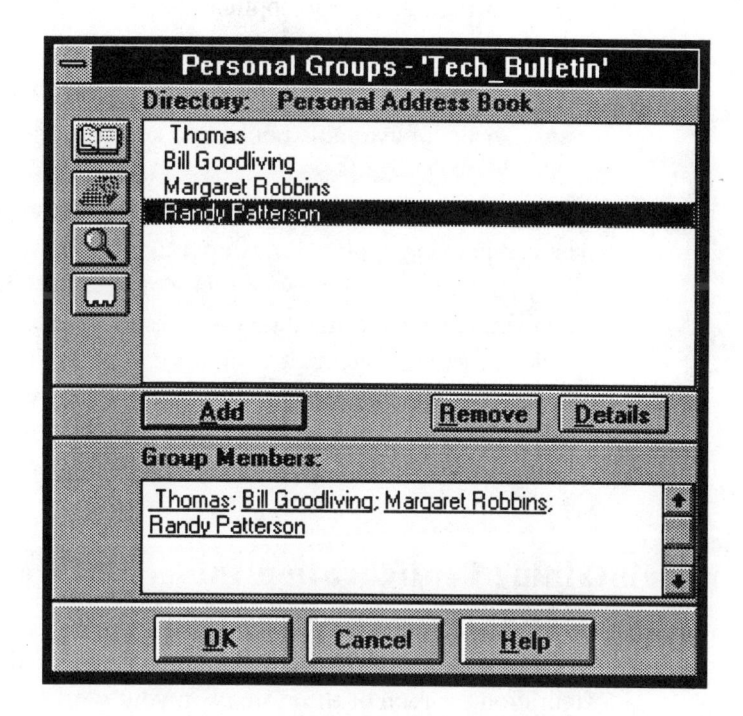

The documentation that comes with your applications (and books such as this one) provide detailed information on how to use your systems and the applications that run on them. You might want to keep a library that includes at least one copy of each manual and a selection of reference books about each standard application your workgroup uses. It is also a good idea to put together a short introductory training session about your computing environment for new employees. If you have a small workgroup this need not be formal, but you should identify the key information necessary for someone to get up and running productively on your system. Topics you might cover include:

- ▲ How to log on to the system,
- ▲ Bringing up basic applications, such as the word processing and spreadsheet programs,
- ▲ How to run tutorial software on the applications, and
- ▲ A list of available books and key sections of manuals.

Most network headaches happen when new software is installed, or when an existing application is upgraded to a newer version. Because of this, you should install new software only when it makes sense, i.e., only when you have determined that there is real benefit to the new features provided by the software. Check for compatibility between versions, or convert everyone in your workgroup to the new version at one time. Productivity losses can occur when you cannot share files with a co-worker because he or she is on a different version of the software.

Maintaining Configuration Information on Your Network

In Chapter 3, we discussed making an inventory of the hardware configuration for each of the systems in your workgroup. You should keep this inventory up-to-date, tracking any new devices that are added to workstations on the network. The inventory will be useful when you're troubleshooting problems or calling for technical support.

You should also keep an inventory of software used in your workgroup. This will help in doing software upgrades and in estimating how much an upgrade might cost. It will be useful in troubleshooting problems to know which programs might be interacting over the network.

Maintaining the software inventory will help you to keep in line with licensing requirements. The ability to share programs over the network increases temptation to use software for which users are not licensed. If the LAN administrator or manager of the workgroup knows what is out there, it will be easier to enforce compliance.

Protecting against Computer Viruses

Computer viruses are programs that, much like their biological counterparts, multiply by infecting other host systems with copies of themselves. Computer viruses may infect a host but be relatively benign, existing only to replicate themselves, or they may be intentionally malicious programs that alter or destroy data with disastrous effects.

Altering or destroying data, or causing the malfunction of another program, can potentially have far-ranging and very serious consequences, sometimes bringing an entire organization to a standstill. For example, the order processing department of a business might be affected, rendering that business incapable of handling the transactions through which it survives and prospers.

Viruses enter the host computer through one of its input devices – typically when a floppy disk containing an infected program is used, or when a program is copied from one system to another over a network – in other words, when files are shared. Because file sharing is a key component of workgroup computing, it is important that steps be taken to guard against infection.

Several preventive measures may be taken:

- ▲ Make sure that all programs installed on workgroup systems are clean. Install only from write-protected program disk masters.
- ▲ Never boot a hard disk system from a floppy unless there is no other way to get the system up.
- ▲ Use care when installing shareware programs. Programs pulled down from bulletin boards can introduce a computer virus into your network environment.

▲ Encourage use of antivirus software. Hard disks should be scanned for infection regularly. Before using floppy disks, scan them with a virus-detection program.

Available Antiviral Programs

Antiviral programs can be used to scan floppy disks for infection before you copy files from them. They also can be used to scan hard disks to detect any infected files. If an infected file is encountered, many of the same products can "repair" the file.

Among the vendors offering antivirus programs are:

▲ Symantec Corporation's Norton Desktop™ for Windows, which has an antivirus program that operates from the Windows environment and can provide continuous background checking for virus infection,

▲ FlashPoint Development's WinNAV™ set of utilities provides Virus SCAN,

▲ Microcom, Inc.'s Virex - for the PC, and

▲ Central Point Software's Central Point Anti-Virus for Windows.™

If your system is infected by a virus that these programs do not know how to repair, you will have to perform a low-level format of your hard disk and reinstall all of your programs from original master disks. You should then restore only your *data* files from your most recent backup. Do not restore any program files from backup disks or tapes, as they may be infected.

> **NOTE** Earlier in this chapter, we discussed effective backup strategies that will be helpful in containing and repairing any potential damage from viruses.

Managing the Mail System's Disk Space

Because the Mail system doesn't actually delete the message until the messages are compressed, and because when you used the delete option, the system merely marked the message to be deleted, deleted Mail messages continue to take up space in shared folders.

The workgroup member who is managing the e-mail system is responsible for monitoring the status of shared folders and recovering unused disk space by compressing shared folders following these steps:

1. You should not compress shared folders while other workgroup members are using them. First, ask all members to close any shared folders they are using. You can do this by sending a Mail message, or calling them on the phone. It is a good idea to perform this operation in the evening, or some other time when the Mail system is not being used.
2. Choose Postoffice Manager from the Mail menu on the Mail administrator's system. This is the system that was used to set up the Postoffice. (See Figure 9.6.)

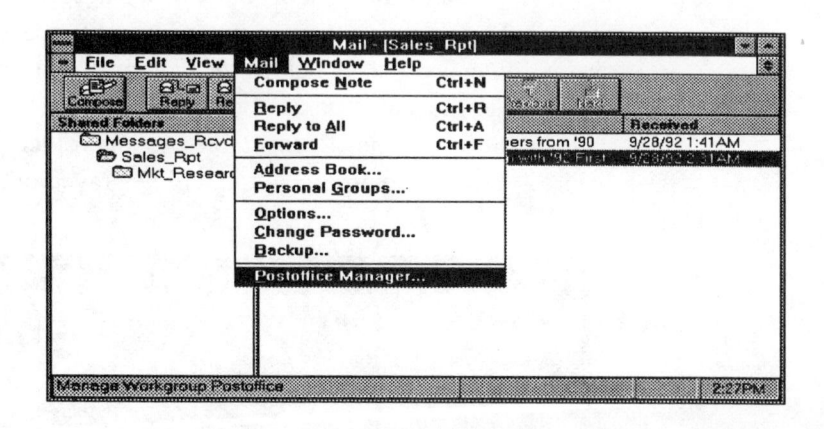

Figure 9.6

Opening the Postoffice Manager dialog box

3. When the Postoffice Manager dialog box appears, choose Shared Folders by clicking on the Shared Folders... button on the right side of the box, as shown in Figure 9.7. This will bring up the dialog box for managing shared folders.

Figure 9.7

Selecting shared folders

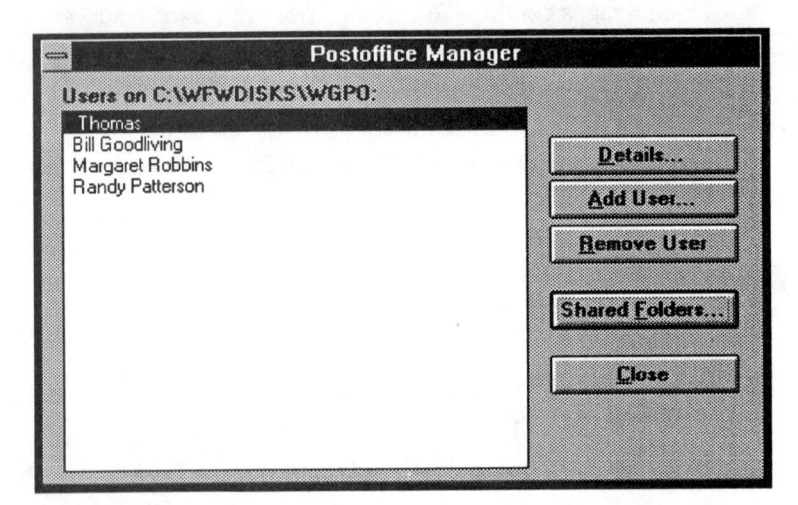

[Postoffice Manager dialog box showing Users on C:\WFWDISKS\WGPO: Thomas, Bill Goodliving, Margaret Robbins, Randy Patterson, with buttons Details..., Add User..., Remove User, Shared Folders..., Close]

4. The Shared Folders dialog box, shown in Figure 9.8, gives information on the number of folders, messages, and recoverable bytes in the folders. If there is any recoverable space in the shared folders, you can click on the Compress button on the right side of the dialog box and recover the space. If there is no recoverable space, the "Recoverable bytes in folders:" entry will read "0" and the Compress button will be grayed out.

Figure 9.8

Selecting Compress

[Shared Folders dialog box — Current Status of Shared Folders: Number of folders: 3; Total messages in folders: 5; Bytes used by messages: 8,423; Recoverable bytes in folders: 1,532. Buttons: Compress, Close]

If the shared folders contain a large number of messages, compressing may take a long time, so be patient.

In this chapter we looked at some of the key administration chores to be done in the Windows for Workgroups environment. We discussed a strategy for handling backups and reviewed some of the tools to perform backups on the network. We looked at how performance of the disk system can be improved by using disk defragmentation utilities. We discussed the need for an introductory training plan for new workgroup members, and how Windows for Workgroups can actually help us with training and support.

The threat of computer viruses on the network was discussed, along with strategies for prevention of infection and recovery of system operation. Finally, we discussed the task of managing the disk space of Shared Folders in the Mail system.

CHAPTER 10

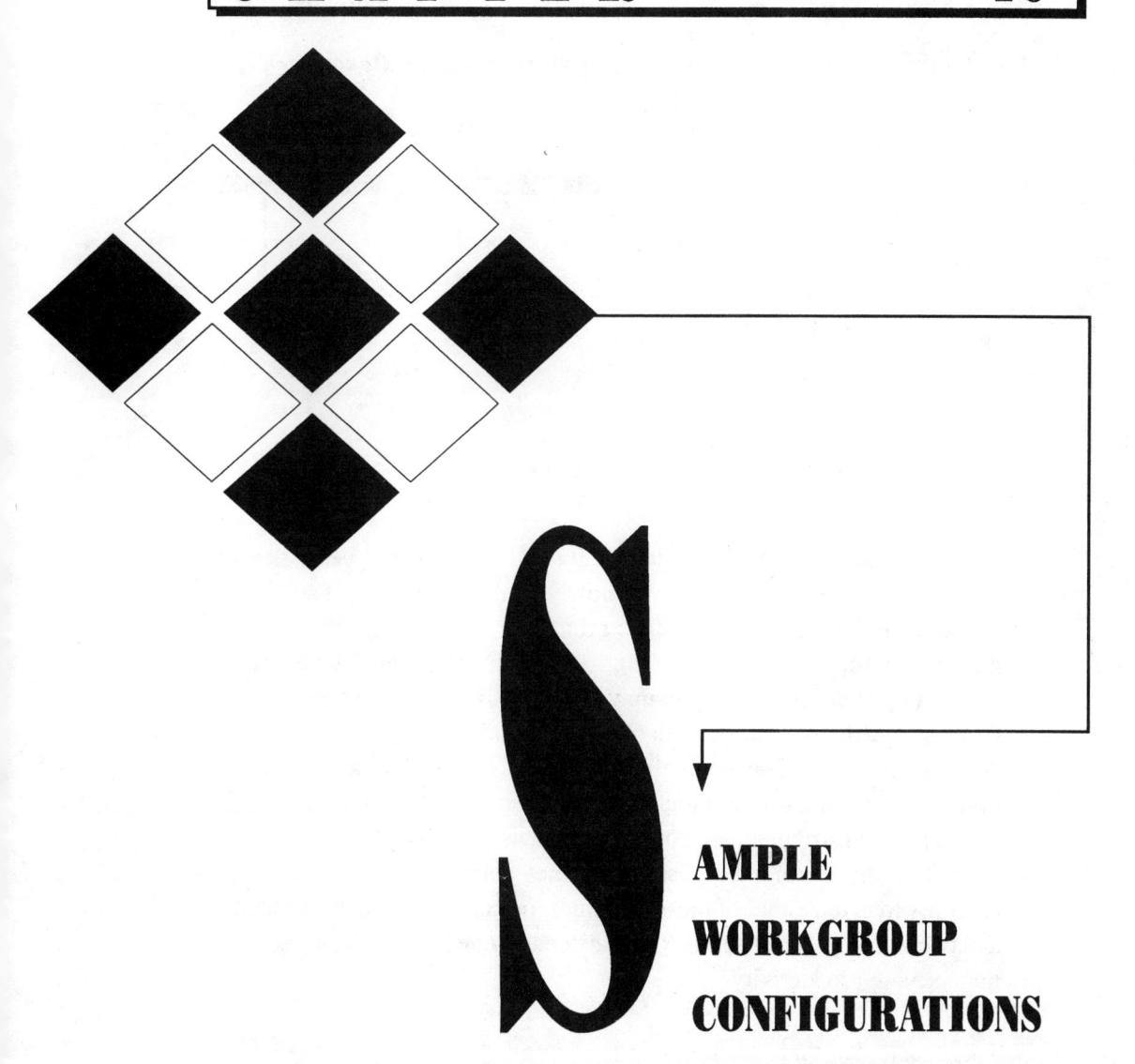

SAMPLE WORKGROUP CONFIGURATIONS

CHAPTER 10

Featuring:

→ **Organizing Your Workgroups**

→ **Allocating Network Resources**

→ **Sample Workgroup Configurations**

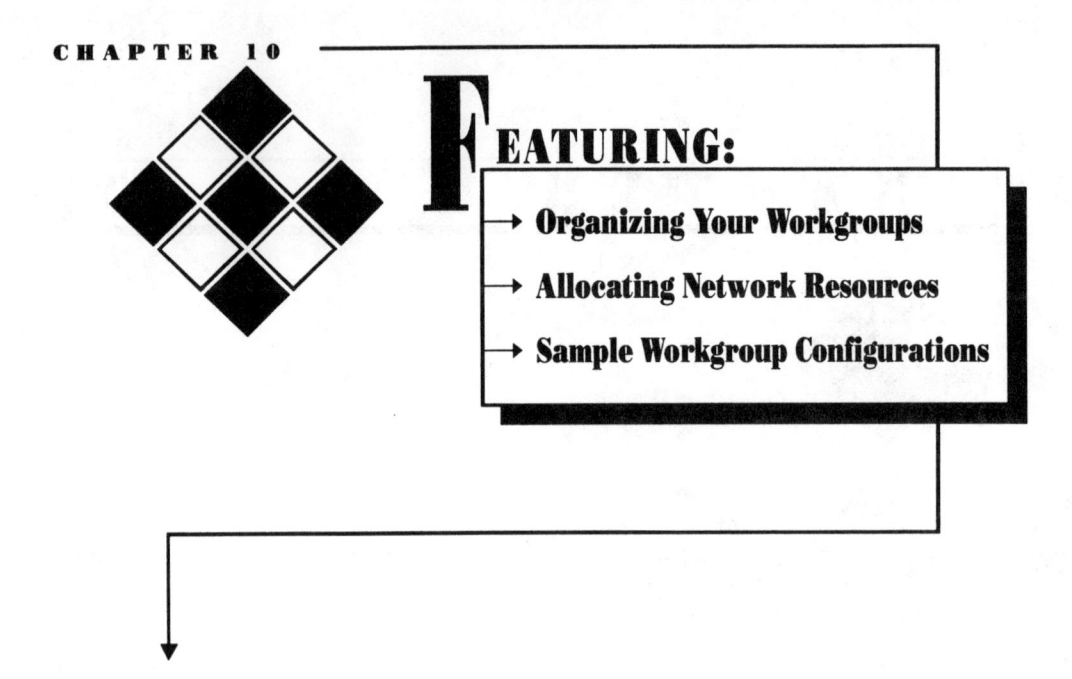

Two factors will determine the extent to which your new network will help you become more productive: how you allocate the physical resources and how you organize the groups. If you arrange the equipment neatly for fast, efficient throughput, but haven't organized the right groups of people sharing it, you may find that some people spend extra time trying to communicate with others, or making uninformed decisions because they were not adequately informed of events. On the other hand, if you arrange your groups carefully by project, but the system resources are unevenly distributed, people may have to spend extra time and effort to print documents or get access to files they need. Plan your network carefully to avoid either of these extremes, because doing so will ensure a network that is useful and helpful, instead of one that could actually impede your productivity.

This chapter has three sections:

1. Guidelines for organizing your workgroups.
2. Guidelines for allocating network resources.
3. Sample workgroup configurations.

We will look first at two aspects of setting up workgroups: the grouping of people and the allocation of resources. Allocation of resources will depend on several factors, including what types of computers you have, how many workstations you plan to link together, how you use each system, and what resources (such as files and printers) need to be shared. And of course, how you group people within workgroups will depend on the tasks you need to accomplish. Finally, we'll go over some examples of workgroup arrangements, and discuss the reasons and trade-offs involved in creating the structures.

Guidelines for Organizing Your Groups

The amount of information available to us is enormous and constantly growing. We are surrounded by sources of information — voice mail, electronic mail, memos, news services, and more. No one can keep up with it all. We must find ways to focus on the sources that are necessary and block out those that are not. This is the task that confronts you when you begin to plan the organization of your workgroups.

Workgroup organization is the key to efficient work. Workers who often share information with each other will be more efficient and productive if they can communicate with each other readily. You have probably noticed that whenever a company goes through a reorganization, many people move to different offices. They move around to be closer to the people and information they need to get their work done.

The same thing happens with electronic workgroups. Just as you would want all the people responsible for publicity, for example, to have offices in the same building, you would want them to all to be in the same workgroup on your network. You want to make sure that they can easily get the information they need, when they need it.

This is why organizing your workgroups carefully is one of the most important things you can do when setting up your network. Think about how people work together in your organization and what tasks they perform, and organize them accordingly. Consider some examples.

In most companies, we group people organizationally; that is, people in the same department have offices near each other, and departments that work closely together are placed nearer each other than those that have less frequent interactions. In a computer manufacturing firm, for instance, the engineering department might be in a section of the building near the manufacturing area but somewhat far from the sales department. The sales department, on the other hand, is close to the marketing and finance departments.

Within departments, it's often a good idea to group people together who have similar tasks or who work together on the same projects. In an engineering department, for example, you might place the people responsible for writing the system documentation in one area, near the people who designed the system, while those people working on developing the new product would be in another area. They should be near those who are performing support work on the existing product, however, so the support personnel can advise the developers of the problems of the existing products and prevent them from making the same mistakes again.

But, as we've mentioned before, many of the projects in a company cross departmental boundaries. To bring a new product to market you might need input from every department in the company. Someone in manufacturing might have to make sure they have materials and equipment ready when the product goes into production. Someone from engineering would have to be on hand to make sure manufacturing gets the right diagrams and instructions for making the product, and someone from marketing must be there to ensure that the new product literature is accurate, and that it's in the hands of the customers when the product is ready to ship.

You could handle this by sending memos to everyone in the company about every detail of every project, but that could just lead to an information overload. The result would probably be that no one would have time to really read any of the memos and many details of the project would get overlooked. You need to limit the amounts of information people have to deal with, but be sure that people still get the information they need to do their jobs. You'd probably organize a team formed of representatives from each of the departments involved in the project.

The same points apply to electronic workgroups. You want to organize them to maximize information flow but prevent information overload. You could organize by department, with one workgroup per department, and in small companies this might be the ideal configuration. As your company gets larger, though, you may have many projects within the same department, and you might want to partition things further. You will probably also have interdepartmental projects that need to share information on a regular basis.

As another example, perhaps you have several computer systems and a printer at your home and are tired of carrying diskettes back and forth to move information between them or to print a file. You want to link these systems together instead, so that you don't have to have the same files duplicated on every system. By setting up a Windows for Workgroups network for your systems, you gain the ability to share directories and print from any of your systems.

Now that you have analyzed the information needs of your organization, you are ready to build the workgroups for your Windows for Workgroups network. It is a simple matter to add someone to a workgroup: choose the Networks icon in the Control Panel group. A dialog box pops up which looks like the one in Figure 10.1.

You can enter the workgroup name in the space labeled "Workgroup," or you can click on the arrow and choose a workgroup. Notice that you can

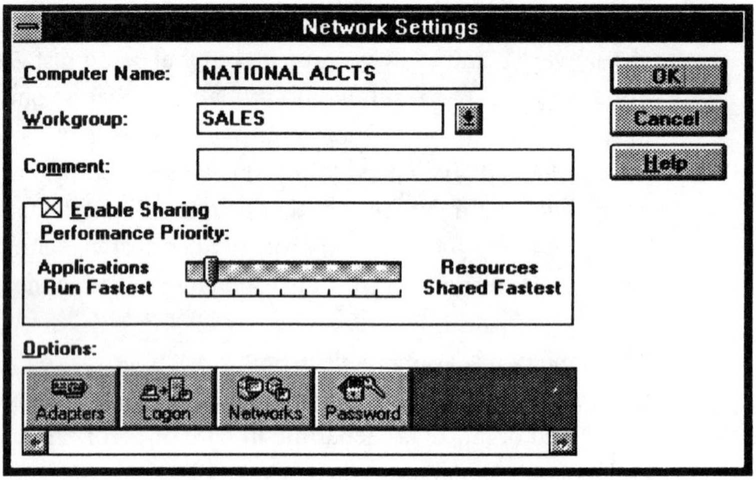

Figure 10.1

Network Settings dialog box

also enter a comment, which will appear to the right of the computer name in network listings like the one in Figure 10.2. This is a good place to enter any information that will help others identify this system, because the computer name, like the workgroup name, can be only 15 characters long, and it's hard to be very descriptive in that amount of space.

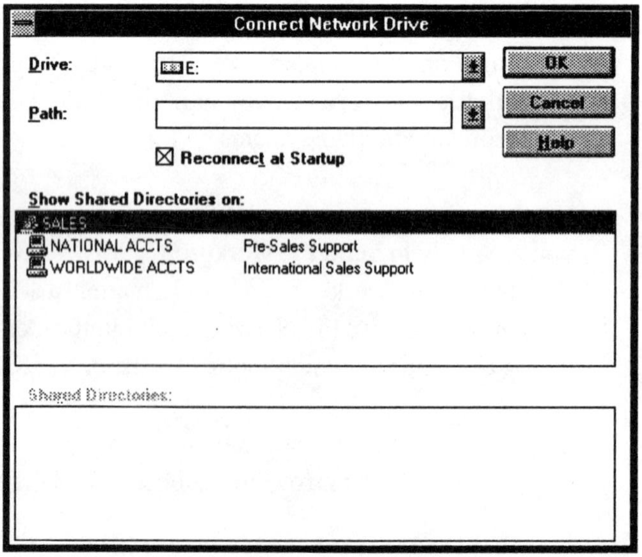

Figure 10.2

The newly added system appears in the Group List

Sample Workgroup Configurations

When naming your workgroups, remember that the system allows workgroup names to contain up to 15 characters, and can contain letters, numbers, and the following characters:

! # $ % & ( ) - . @ _ ' ~

Workgroup names cannot, however, contain spaces, and Windows for Workgroups will change any lowercase letters to uppercase. Select workgroup names that are easy to remember; the best way to do this is to select names that relate to the purpose of the group. The name FIELD_SALES, for instance, would suit a group that is responsible for meeting with customers regarding sales calls.

You might be tempted to use a person's name for the group name, such as the name of the group's manager, but resist that idea. The person might get promoted, or leave the company, and then everyone in that workgroup would have to change their group name in the Network Settings box. Or you might consider naming the stations in your workgroup after the nine planets, but what will you do when you get a tenth computer? This is a slightly silly example, but it illustrates a point: be sure to allow room for growth when you create your workgroups.

Once you have entered a new workgroup name in the Network Settings box, you will need to restart your computer before the name will take effect. After you restart it, you will be able to connect to that system from any other system in the network. Just bring up the Connect Network Drive box in the File Manager, and the new system will appear as a member of the group.

Placing people in workgroups does not, by itself, restrict or bestow access to any resources. Anyone on the network can use any directories or printers on the network, as long as the person responsible for those devices has designated them as 'shared.' By organizing into workgroups, however, you gain the same advantages that you get when you organize the files on your disk into directories. If you put all your files into one directory, it would take you a long time to find a file once you had more than about 30 files on the disk. If you remembered only what the file contained, and weren't quite sure what the name was, it could take even longer. But if you had organized them according to what they contained, your search would go a lot faster. The same idea goes for workgroups. You can look at a Browse list of all the computers in your network, and if everyone is in the same workgroup, you'll have to look at every line to see if it's the computer name you want. This is not a problem if you have around 10 computers, but when you get up toward 20 it will be slow. If you have them organized into groups, though, first you can search for the group you need, and then for the computer within that group, which will greatly simplify the task.

One Windows for Workgroups organization that does restrict access is the *mail group*. A mail group is a group of computers that all have accounts on the same Workgroup Postoffice (WGPO). People in different workgroups can connect to the same WGPO, but only those people who have accounts on the same WGPO can receive electronic mail and meeting notices from one another. Mail's mailing list features make it easy to create groups of users to whom you often send messages (see Chapter 5 for more information on Mail). You can create mailing lists to send mail to people in a number of different workgroups, as long as they all have accounts on the same postoffice.

If you are in doubt about how to organize your groups, it's probably best to keep things simple. Create just one or two groups in the beginning. Although it will be some trouble, you can go back later and divide your groups differently if necessary, after you have learned more about Windows for Workgroups and what it can do for you.

Guidelines for Allocating Network Resources

In a company that has unlimited money and space, you might not need to set up a network at all. You would just buy everyone a computer, a laser

Sample Workgroup Configurations

printer, and a very large disk drive, and would not be concerned if these items were not always fully in use. But very few of us operate in such an environment. Laser printers are expensive, as is disk space, so it makes sense to share these resources across the group to get the most for your money. This section gives you some general guidelines to sharing those items efficiently. Note that this process involves a set of trade-offs; some of these issues will apply more to your particular working environment than others. Try to determine which factors relate the most to your particular situation, and consider them more heavily when balancing conflicting needs.

> **NOTE** If you buy any new PCs for your network, we urge you to get 386 processors in the computers you buy if at all possible. They cost more, but they can do much more than 286 processors, and are a smarter long-term investment.

The resource allocation guidelines and notes appear below, in no particular order. For more information about fine-tuning the performance of individual computers, see Chapter 11.

Shared access is not possible on 286-based computers.

Keep in mind that you cannot share resources on 286-based PCs. You can access shared resources *from* these computers, but other people cannot access information on the 286-based PC. Do not plan on these PCs making any resources available to other PCs.

Place printers near those who use them most.

Whenever possible, try to minimize users' running-around time. If just a few group members use the printer often, they'll really appreciate having it nearby.

Printing charts and graphs can use a lot of system resources.

If you need to do a lot of this kind of printing, consider getting one PC that you can dedicate to printing. Otherwise, the person to whose workstation the printer is connected may experience slow performance when running his or her own programs because someone else is currently printing a graphical image. A PC that handles only printing and is not used as a workstation is often called a *print server*.

Minimize the number of large files you send over the network.

Heavy traffic over the network slows down network response time for everybody. If you have one station that often needs to print large files or charts, for instance, consider attaching the printer to that PC.

File access can slow down a workstation.

Users who work on systems that contain a lot of shared files that others are frequently accessing may find that their own tasks run unacceptably slowly. To prevent this, consider setting one machine aside for file access only, with no one using it as a workstation. A computer configured in this way is called a *file server*. Alternatively, you may want to re-evaluate the way the group has implemented file sharing. Most companies using Windows for Workgroups should not find it necessary to use a dedicated file server.

Large files and programs benefit from lots of RAM.

The more RAM in your PC, the faster you can access the data. This becomes an issue when files get big — perhaps 100,000 bytes or more. Files smaller than this should fit within the minimum amount of memory that Microsoft recommends (4 MB) without too much trouble (depending on what else is running on that system). Moreover, multitasking with several applications benefits from the PC having ample amounts of memory.

Calculations go faster on a faster processor.
Generally, programs will run faster on PCs with faster processor chips. If you need to do a lot of calculations (in complex spreadsheets, for example), consider using a 486-based PC rather than a less-powerful 386-based computer. (Microsoft recommends running Windows for Workgroups with no less than 386-based PCs.)

Make sure you have enough disk space.
The more data you have to store and access, the more disk space you will need. Graphics files (those that contain pictures instead of just text), for instance, can take up surprising amounts of disk space, sometimes as much as 1 MB (a million bytes) or more apiece, so plan accordingly. A small disk drive contains under 100 MB of storage space, and large ones can hold hundreds or thousands of megabytes.

Organize workgroups according to who works together.
This could mean grouping people by department or by project. The idea is to make sharing information as easy as possible. Earlier in this chapter we discussed workgroup organization.

Sample Networks

In this section we will examine some sample workgroups and look at the trade-offs made in arranging them.

A Simple Three-Person Workgroup

Let's start by looking at a very simple network. Patricia, Bill, and Harold work in a small five-person graphics design firm that owns three computers and one printer. Patricia does the graphics design and documentation for the company, and Harold does the accounting and financial tracking. Bill is the office manager and does the word processing and order entry tasks as necessary. The other employees are a sales executive and the president. These two use the computers occasionally, but Harold, Bill, and Patricia do the bulk of the computer work in the office.

When the company purchased the systems, they knew they would be storing a lot of graphics files, so they outfitted one of the systems with a larger hard drive than the others. They knew also that the financial work Harold does would require a lot of calculations on some large complicated spreadsheets, and that this sort of work would go more quickly if it ran on a system with a powerful PC with plenty of RAM. Bill, on the other hand, could do his word processing and order entry comfortably on a system without any special enhancements. Finally, they bought a printer for all the office's broad printing requirements — they print all the financial data, letters, orders, graphics drawings, and other miscellaneous reports on the same printer.

They connected the PCs and printer as shown in Figure 10.3, and they decided that, since Patricia would often be sending the drawings to the printer, they would attach the printer to her PC rather than having her send them over the network to another system, which could reduce network response time for the other two workstations. This also gives Patricia the advantage of having the printer near her workstation, which made sense because she will be using printing more than anyone else. Bill does the word processing and order entry tasks on his system, and occasionally sends a file to Patricia's machine for printing. The more powerful PC is in Harold's work area, where he can run spreadsheet calculations without impacting anyone else. When he finishes his calculations, he can send the reports to the printer with a simple command.

Since Harold does not have room on his PC to keep all his spreadsheet data files on the hard disk, he stores the ones he uses less often in a shared directory on Patricia's workstation. When he wants to link to it, he brings up the File Manager on his system and selects Connect Network Drive from the Disk menu. This brings up a list of possible network directories, as shown in Figure 10.4.

SAMPLE WORKGROUP CONFIGURATIONS

Note that Harold has selected the "Reconnect at Startup" option, so that whenever he restarts his computer it will automatically connect to the "1991 Data" directory on Patricia's PC, if her PC is available.

For more information on setting up shared drives and printers and connecting to them, see Chapter 4.

Figure 10.3

A sample network configuration

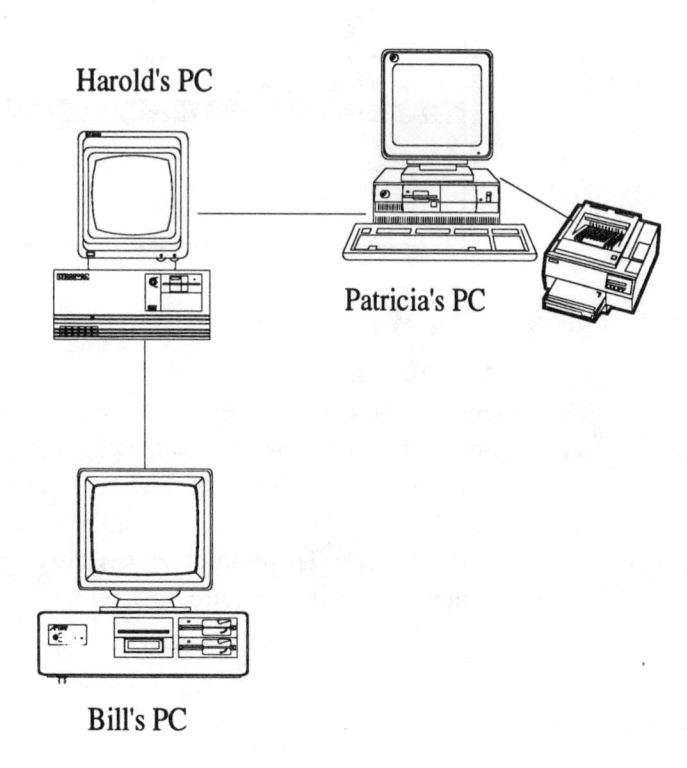

Figure 10.4

Connecting to a shared directory

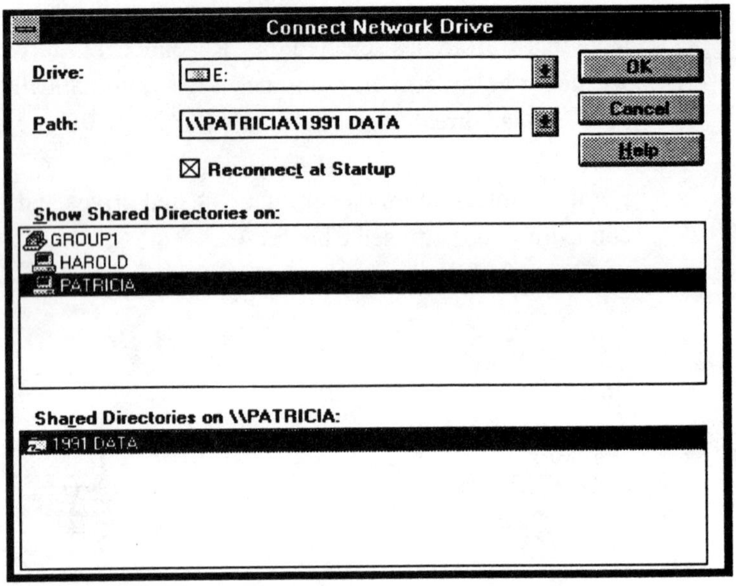

A Seven-System Workgroup

Let's look next at a small company that does professional typesetting. Their clients are the major university in the area, which uses their services for publishing doctoral dissertations, and a law firm that needs legal documents typed and printed. The same three people from the company are assigned to work on each of the client's documents every time there is a project. Therefore, they have two workgroups, each with its own printer, as shown in Figure 10.5.

SAMPLE WORKGROUP CONFIGURATIONS

Figure 10.5
You can share resources between workgroups

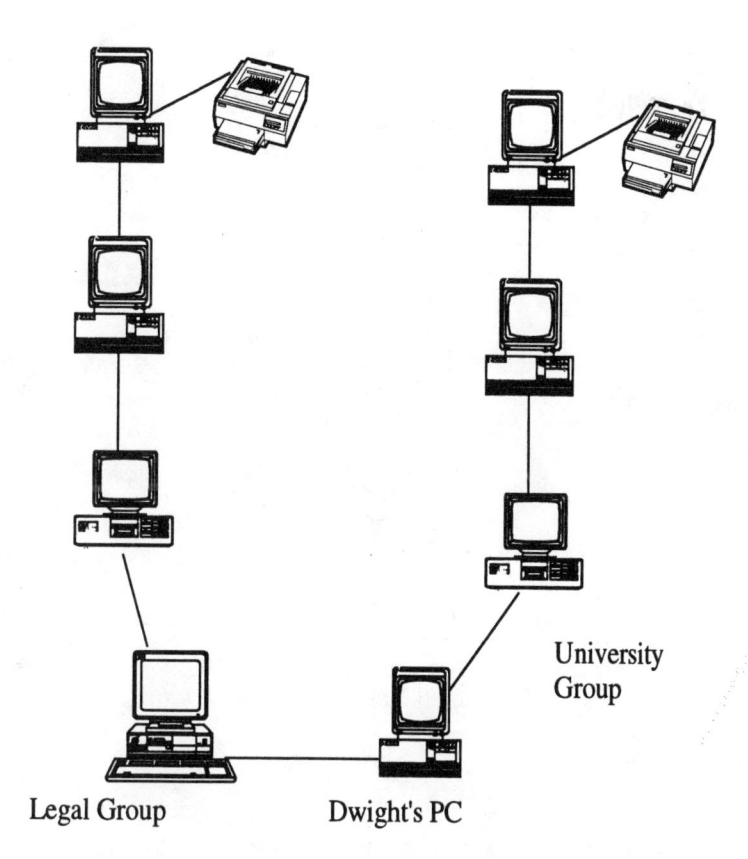

Legal Group   Dwight's PC   University Group

Dwight, the office manager, has created two workgroups, one for the legal documents and one for the university documents, and has attached a printer to one of the stations in each group. He is not a member of either workgroup, but can connect to any shared directories or printers on any of the systems in the network. Similarly, anyone in the Legal group can connect to shared directories in the University group. The browse list from the "Connect to Network Drive" window in the File Manager's Disk menu illustrates this capability in Figure 10.6.

Figure 10.6

Users can connect to any shared resource on the network, no matter what workgroup they belong to.

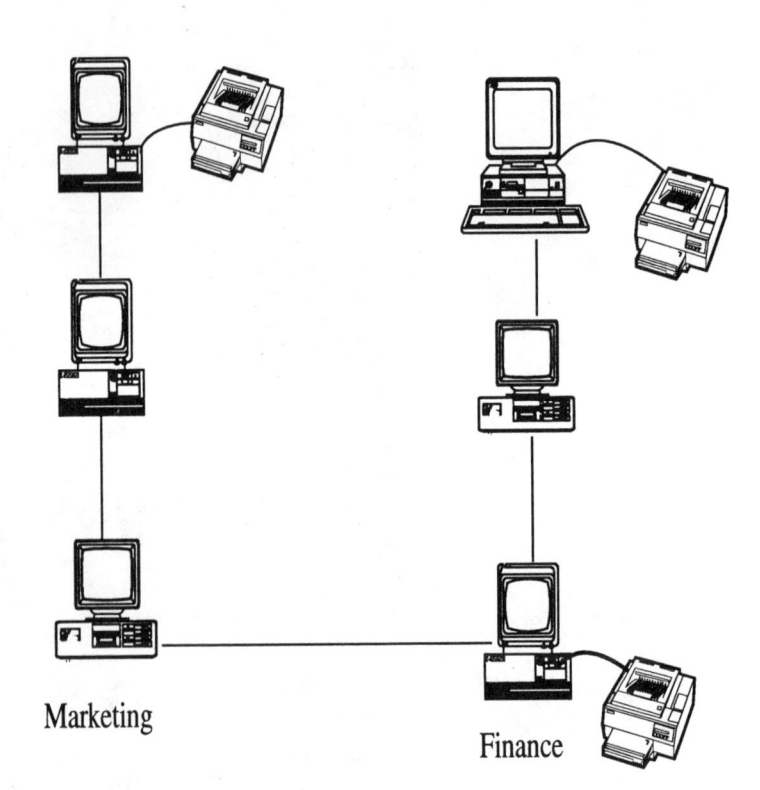

Marketing

Finance

Attaching to a Novell NetWare Network

Finally, let's look at a more complex network. This one links together a marketing department of 15 people. Seven of them work on product marketing, and eight on public relations. So they have created two workgroups, one called Products and the other called PublicRel (Windows for Workgroups will put these names into all uppercase when you enter them into the system). Two printers belong to the PublicRel group and one to Products. Furthermore, they have a link to the company's Novell NetWare server, and so they can access any of the drives on that corporate network. See Figure 10.7 for an illustration of this configuration.

Figure 10.7

A Windows for Workgroups Network connected to a Novell Network

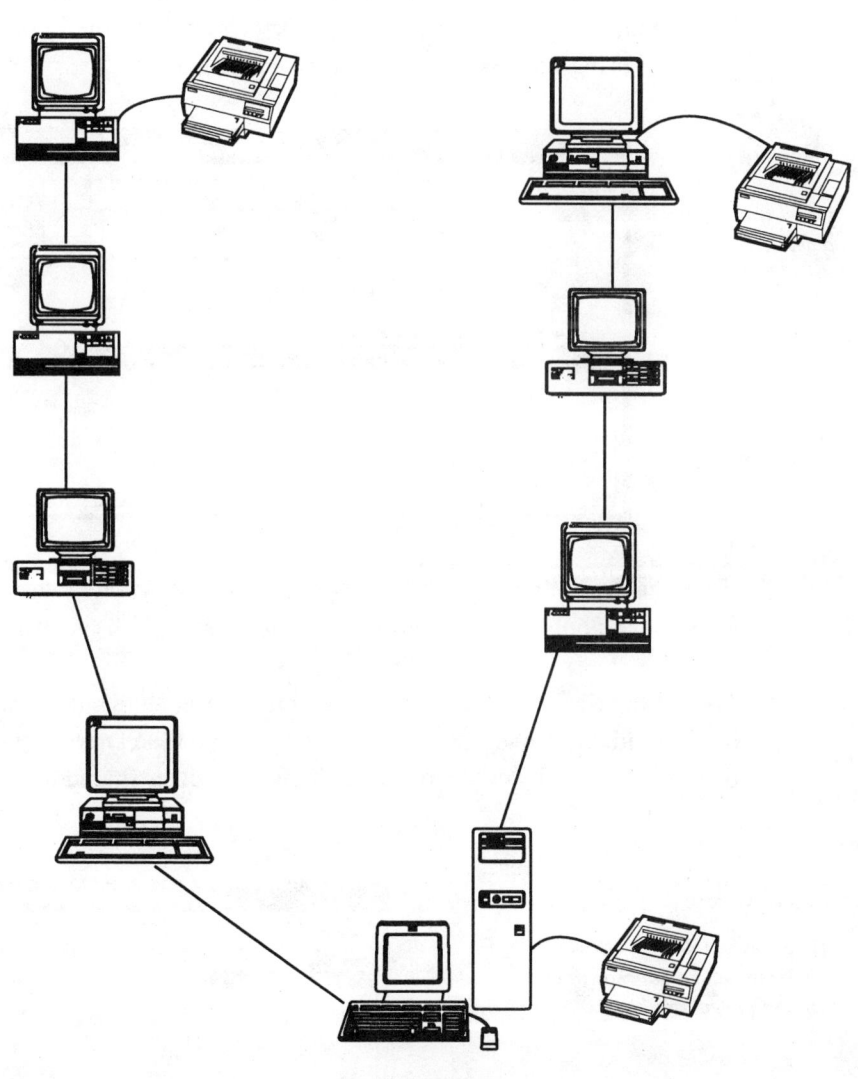

Novell Server

Now a user in Marketing can access files on the Novell server. Suppose Abigail in Products wants to access the latest product information from Engineering. She knows that they keep it on the NetWare server, so she just needs to open her File Manager and choose the Connect Network Drive button or the Connect Network Drive item from the Disk menu. This will bring up a window like the one in Figure 10.8.

Figure 10.8

Connecting to a network drive

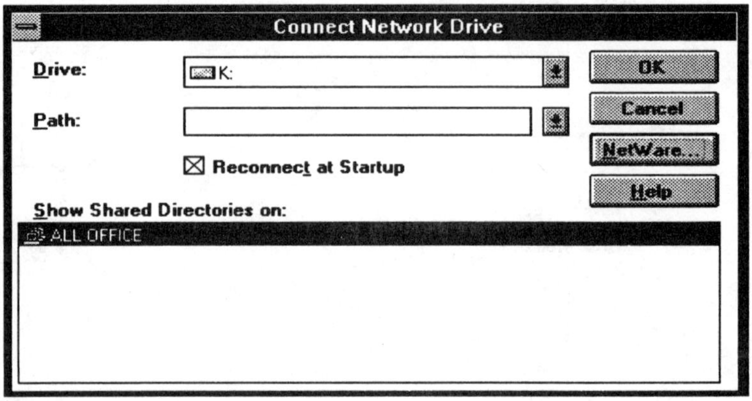

If you have access to a Novell network, your File Manager window will give you the option of searching the Novell drives.

To find the file she needs, Abigail selects the NetWare button, and the list of available Novell network drives appears in the Drive Connections box, along with the drives on her computer, and her shared drives. (See Figure 10.9.)

Figure 10.9

Drives available on a Novell NetWare network appear in the Drive Connections box.

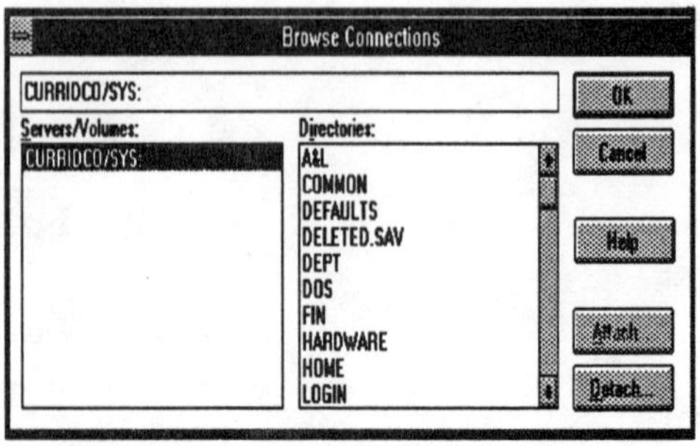

Sample Workgroup Configurations

Now she can access the NetWare drives just as she would any of her other drives, moving around between directories and drives as usual. (See Chapter 12 for information on connecting to your Novell network.)

In this chapter, we outlined the issues you need to consider when you are setting up your Windows for Workgroups network, including organizing your groups according to your tasks, making sure everyone has the best possible access to the resources they need, and planning for future changes in the group. We also examined three sample group configurations that illustrated some basic principles of workgroup organization. You now have some good general guidelines for creating an efficient network and knowing what pitfalls to avoid.

CHAPTER 11

ADVANCED TOPICS: CUSTOM SETUP AND TUNING

CHAPTER 11

FEATURING:

→ **Changing the Look of Your Workspace**
→ **Organizing Program Groups**
→ **Running DOS in Windows**
→ **Virtual Memory and Swap Files**

This chapter focuses on the ways you can personalize your environment to reflect your work habits and tastes. It has two sections: Customization and Tuning. In the first section, we will look at the many ways in which you can personalize your working environment with Windows for Workgroups. Many of the tricks we discuss in this section are for fun; they may not directly improve your productivity, but they will amuse you! The second section talks about what you can do to enhance the performance of your system — making it run as fast as possible.

Customizing Your Workspace

Windows for Workgroups provides you with a number of features that you can use to personalize your workspace. You can change the background of your desktop, change the colors of your windows, make your screen go blank (or display interesting patterns) when the system is not in use, and even change the language conventions used by your system.

You can also change the way your programs run, and, if you often run the same ones, you can set them up to run automatically when you start Windows for Workgroups. This section outlines these features and more.

Changing the Look of Your Workspace

You can change your workspace appearance in a number of ways. One of the most visible (and entertaining) ways is by changing your desktop background and colors, which we'll talk about first. You can also change the response rates of your keyboard and mouse, change the system date and time, and make the system play you a song when you start running it. Most of these features can be accessed by opening the Control Panel icon in the Main program group.

Changing the Desktop Background and Colors

We'll look first at what you can do to make your workspace look different in two ways: changing the colors that Windows uses to display things, and changing the background display of the desktop. The desktop is Windows for Workgroups' name for the area on which it displays all the windows, including the Program Manager window. When you first install your system, the Desktop is a solid gray. This is the "default" desktop, the one it uses if you have not chosen any other desktop features. This section is about changing those defaults.

One way you can see your desktop is to minimize all your programs so that they run as icons. You do this by clicking in the Minimize box in the upper-right corner of each window, or by selecting Minimize from the window's Control menu. (For more information about these and other basics of using Windows, see Chapter 4.) Figure 11.1 shows a sample desktop, with the Program Manager window open and two applications running as icons. The gray background is the Desktop surface.

Figure 11.1

A sample desktop with the Program Manager window open

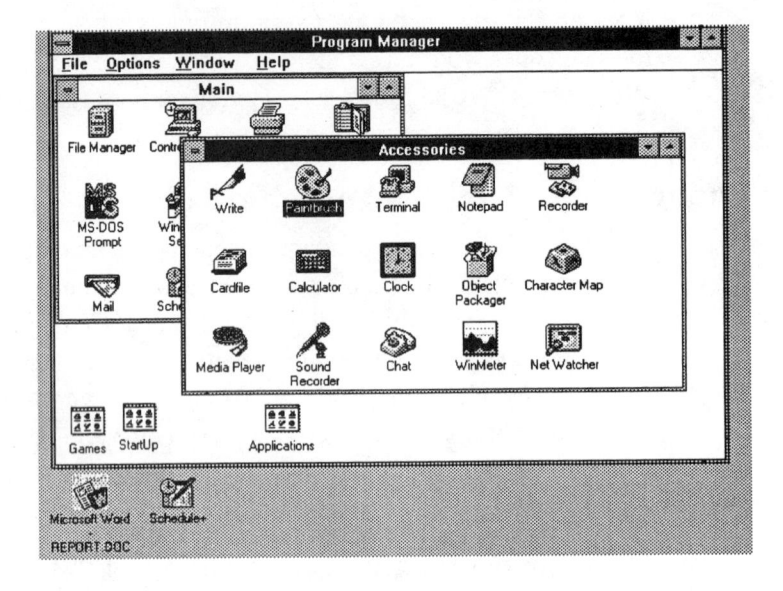

Changing Colors

To change the colors Windows uses, open the Control Panel icon in the Main program window by double-clicking on it. This opens a program group with about a dozen icons in it, as shown in Figure 11.2.

Figure 11.2

The Control Panel

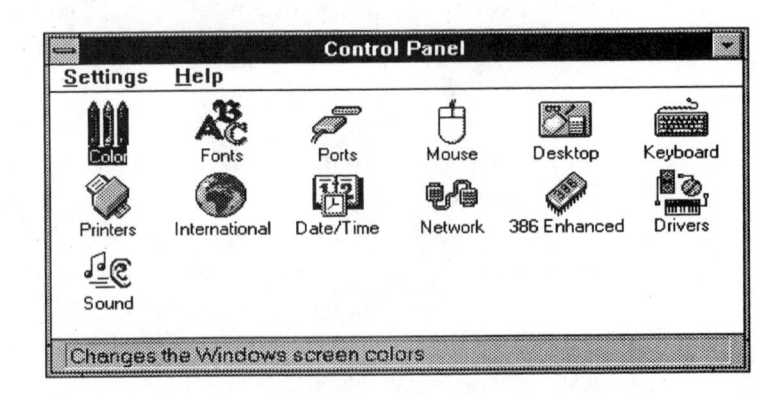

Note the Color icon is selected. Open the Color dialog box by double-clicking on the icon; you will see a box like the one in Figure 11.3.

ADVANCED TOPICS: CUSTOM SETUP AND TUNING

Figure 11.3

The Color dialog box

Open the Color Schemes list (near the top of the Color box) by clicking on it. Windows for Workgroups will present you with a list of possible color combinations for your desktop, your menu bars, buttons, text, and so on — 21 different window elements in all. Using the arrow keys, move up and down in the list and watch the color combinations change. The middle section of the Color box displays a sample of each combination, so you can see what each one will look like before you install it.

Don't see any color combinations that you like? You can create your own. Select the Color Palette button and the Color box opens up to the right. At the top of this new section is a list box titled Screen Element. Move through this list to select a window element, such as Menu Bar, then click on one of the 48 color boxes. When you do so, you select a color for the selected window element. Windows displays your choices in the sample area to the left, as before, so you can try out different combinations before you commit to them. The expanded Color box is shown in Figure 11.4.

Figure 11.4

Selecting colors for window elements

Perhaps you've experimented with all the possible combinations of colors and screen elements, and still can't find a color scheme that suits you. No problem. Windows for Workgroups provides you with all the tools you need to create up to 16 of your own colors. Just click on the Define Custom Colors box in the lower right of the expanded Color box, and a new box pops up, titled Custom Color Selector, as shown in Figure 11.5.

Figure 11.5

Custom color selector box

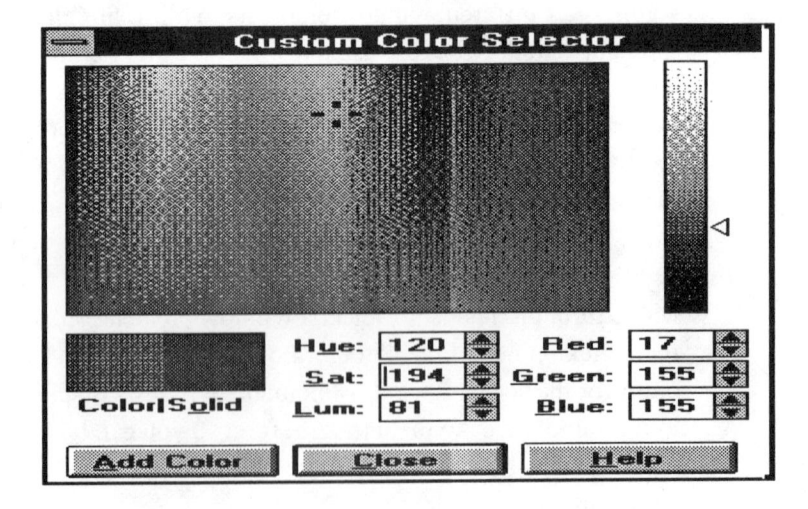

Advanced Topics: Custom Setup and Tuning

Figure 11.5 provides you with three different ways to define a color: pointing to it, defining RGB (red-green-blue) values, or defining HSL (hue-saturation-luminosity) values. The Color|Solid box displays your custom color on the left, and the nearest matching solid color on the right. When you have achieved the desired color, select one of the Custom Colors boxes, then click on the Add Color box.

Pointing to a Color

Drag the star-shaped cursor around in the color field to select a color. You can adjust luminosity by dragging the arrow up and down the length of the luminosity bar.

RGB Color Creation

To custom mix a color, type into these boxes the values for Red, Green, and Blue, or use the arrows beside the boxes. Simply use the mouse to point to the up or down arrows and press the left mouse button.

HSL Color Creation

Type into these boxes the values for Hue, Saturation, and Contrast, or use the arrows beside the boxes, to create custom colors.

Solid and Nonsolid Colors

Nonsolid colors are patterns of colored dots. The dots are so close together that they appear to blend into a single color on some monitors. Solid colors are those supported directly, without blending, by your display adapter. To create a solid color (which is faster to display), double-click on the right side of the Color|Solid box before selecting the Add Color button.

Changing Patterns

Once you have chosen satisfying colors, you will want to experiment with patterns that change the texture of your background. A selection of patterns is available in the list box. Patterns use two colors from the color scheme that you set up above: the background is the Desktop color, and the foreground is the Window Text color.

To select patterns, select the Desktop dialog box in the Control Panel group. A sample Desktop box appears in Figure 11.6.

Figure 11.6

The Desktop dialog box

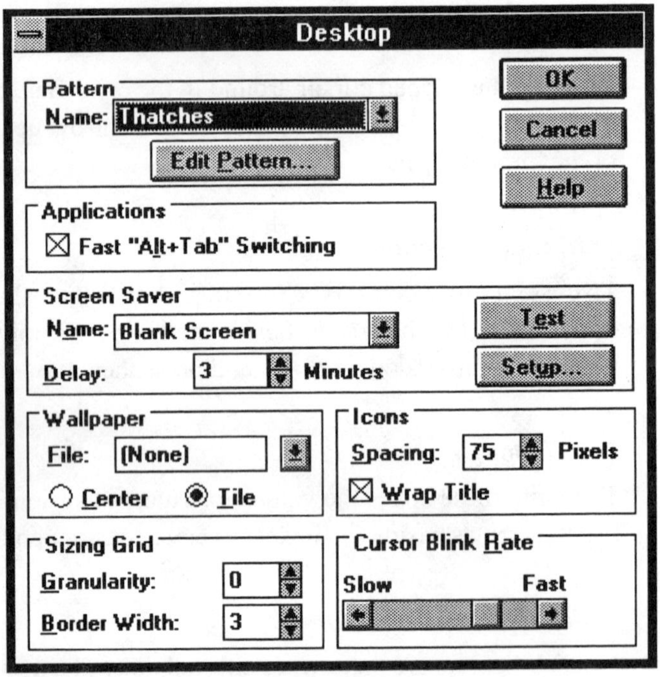

Choosing a Pattern

In the Pattern box (at the top left of the desktop box), click on Name to see a list of the available patterns. Select one, then press OK to see the results on your desktop.

Creating a Custom Pattern

Under the list of patterns is a button called Edit Pattern. When you select Edit Pattern, it brings up a box in which you can edit the current pattern by clicking boxes in the master pattern. The results of your editing appear on the left, as shown in Figure 11.7. When you have a pattern you like, you can either save it on top of the old one (if you do, the original pattern will be gone), or save it to a new name. To save it over the old one, select Change. To save it to a new name, type the new name in the Name field, then select Add. Finally, select Close or OK and you will be back in the Desktop box, with the new name (if you added one) now available in the Patterns list. You can now select that name as before, and when you select OK, Windows for Workgroups will display your new pattern on your desktop.

Figure 11.7

Editing a pattern

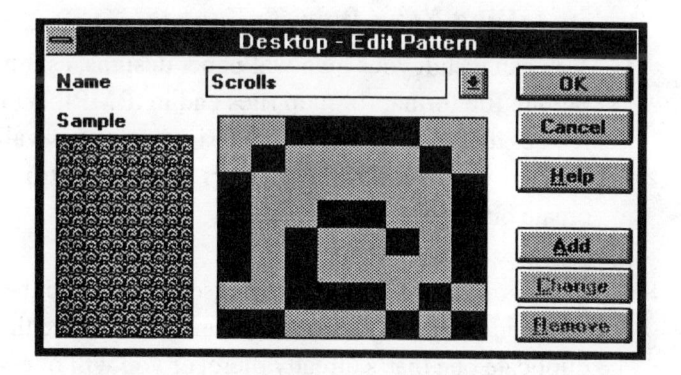

Displaying and Changing Wallpaper

There are limitations to patterns — they are small, and displayed in only two colors. What if you want to display a larger graphic design on your desktop, or a multicolored one? Windows is ready for you, with designs called *wallpaper*. Windows for Workgroups includes several wallpaper designs from which to choose, and it's also easy to install your own.

Selecting Wallpaper

The wallpaper list in the Desktop dialog box (see Figure 11.6) contains a list of all the wallpaper designs available to you. You must select a wallpaper design and click the OK button, as you did in Pattern, before Windows for Workgroups will install your chosen wallpaper.

Tiling and Centering

Below the Wallpaper list you'll see a pair of buttons labeled Tile and Center. These buttons are meaningful if your wallpaper design is smaller than the screen (as is the case for all the wallpapers supplied with Windows for Workgroups). If you select Center, Windows for Workgroups will place your wallpaper design on the screen once, at the center of the screen, and your pattern will show around it. If you select Tile, Windows for Workgroups will repeat the design across the screen as many times as necessary to cover the entire desktop.

Installing Your Own Wallpaper

You can install your own wallpaper designs, as long as they are in a bitmap file format (bitmap files end in .BMP). Windows Paintbrush creates these files, so you can design your own wallpaper with Paintbrush if you like. Several vendors also make utilities that you can use to create bitmap files.

Once you have a bitmap file to use, copy it into the directory where you installed Windows for Workgroups. (Make sure the file name does not duplicate one that's already there, or you will overwrite the original.) Now your new design will appear when you bring up the list of wallpapers, and you can select it.

Some Practical Matters

Changing the appearance of your workspace can have some practical benefits. If you are color blind, for instance, the color customization features let you select combinations that are easy to distinguish.

On a plasma display (such as on many notebook computers), bright color schemes will take more energy than dark colors and will run down your battery faster, so you will want to select colors accordingly. Windows for Workgroups comes with a color scheme designed especially for these types of display adapters.

ADVANCED TOPICS: CUSTOM SETUP AND TUNING

If your screen updates (redraws) slowly, try switching to solid colors, which will update faster. The Windows for Workgroups default color scheme is made up of all solid colors, which run faster than nonsolids.

Finally, solid colors will take up less of your computer's memory than patterns or bitmaps. If you are low on memory or run out of memory, try switching your wallpaper selection to (None), your pattern selection to (None), and your color scheme to a set of solid colors.

Other Desktop Features

There are a number of other desktop configuration features that you can experiment with. These can help you customize your PC to suit your individual taste and needs.

Fast Switching between Applications

This box enables and disables the option to switch quickly between programs by holding down the ALT key and repeatedly pressing the TAB key. A window comes up in the center of your screen that displays information about the programs you're running, one at a time. This feature is described in more detail in Appendix B.

Screen Savers

Windows comes with several *screen savers* — moving patterns that appear on your screen when your system has been idle for some specified period of time. Screen savers serve two purposes: they prevent your screen from getting an image burned into it, and they provide you with some privacy when you leave your system unused. When you press a key or move the mouse, the screen saver vanishes and your screen returns to your original application.

Selecting a Screen Saver

In the Desktop dialog box (see Figure 11.6), open the list of screen savers in the name field and select one. Press the test button to see it, then press any key or move the mouse to end the test. Set the delay (the number of minutes that will elapse before the screen saver is activated) in the number box below the list.

Customizing a Screen Saver

Many Windows for Workgroups screen savers can be customized. The Marquee, for instance, is a banner of text that scrolls continuously across your screen. You can make it print any message you wish. Some of the other screen savers allow you to select colors or animation speeds. Several have password options as well. To customize a screen saver, select it, then select the Setup button. Experiment with the settings until you find the screen saver you like best.

Other Screen Savers

Several vendors make screen saver packages. Among the most popular are After Dark (whose flying toasters are so famous that After Dark now markets a line of clothing as well) and Intermission. Both of these allow you to install a password, so the actual screen can't be viewed by anyone but you.

Icon Spacing

To allow room for the title of an icon (in a group window or on the desktop), Windows for Workgroups leaves three lines below the icon. If you have the Wrap Title option checked, Windows will wrap the titles into a horizontally smaller space, allowing up to three lines. Otherwise the titles will appear in one line and the titles of icons could run into those next to each other. To keep that from happening, adjust the icon spacing in the number box.

Cursor Blink Rate

Drag the button from side to side to select a rate at which you'd like your cursor to blink. Both the button and the cursor on the right will blink at the new rate as you adjust it. Find a balance: setting this rate too slow could make it hard for you to find the cursor, but setting it too fast could make it irritating.

More Features You Can Customize

The Control Panel offers a number of other ways to customize your Windows environment. Here are some of the more frequently used ones; we encourage you to explore to find other features to improve your workspace.

Keyboard and Mouse

To set the delay for holding down a repeating key, open the Keyboard icon. This option allows you to specify the amount of time you can hold down a key before Windows for Workgroups starts repeating the key. You can also set the repetition rate.

In the Mouse box, you can set the delay between double-clicks, so if you like to double-click more slowly, the system will still recognize what you are doing. Here, you can also reverse the left and right mouse buttons, which might be useful if you are left-handed.

Date and Time

To set the date and system clock, select the Date/Time icon from the Control Panel window. Type in new values, or adjust the values by using the arrows at the end of the entry boxes. The new values will take effect when you click the OK button.

Support of Other Languages

Windows for Workgroups selects currency formats, date and time formats, list separators, and a number of other parameters according to the conventions of different countries as you choose. Figure 11.8 shows the International dialog box.

Figure 11.8

The International dialog box

[Figure 11.8: The International dialog box, showing fields for Country (United States), Language (English [American]), Keyboard Layout (US), Measurement (English), List Separator (,), Date Format (10/21/93, Thursday, October 21, 1993), Currency Format ($1.22, ($1.22)), Time Format (12:13:45 PM), Number Format (1,234.22), with OK, Cancel, Help, and Change buttons.]

If you want to change countries or customize some aspect of international format, this is the box. These settings will affect Windows for Workgroups and any Windows applications, but may not affect other programs, such as programs that run under the MS-DOS operating system.

> **NOTE** Selecting a different country in this dialog box will not change the actual language in which Windows for Workgroups operates, but Windows itself is available in other languages. Contact your dealer for more information.

Customizing Your Work Environment

Just as Windows for Workgroups provides dozens of ways you can customize the appearance of your workspace, it also allows many ways to change your work environment. We will cover some of the more useful features, but we certainly won't cover everything. For additional information, refer to the available on-line Help.

Organizing Program Groups

When you install Windows for Workgroups, it creates up to five program groups (possibly fewer, if you asked it not to install everything). These groups — Main, Accessories, Applications, Startup, and Games — contain icons for each of the programs you can run. In the Main group, for instance, you will see icons for File Manager, Control Panel, Mail, and several other programs. You can easily change their organization by moving programs between groups. Open both the group from which you want to move a program and the group to which you want to move it. Now drag the program icon into the new group window. Or, if you want a copy of the program to stay in the old group, hold down the CTRL key while you drag the icon.

The Startup Group

Any program in this special group will get started automatically when you start Windows. When you initially install Windows, the Startup group will be empty. If you have one or two programs that you use consistently, save yourself some time by copying them into this group — they'll be there, conveniently ready to use every time you enter Windows. This feature is even more useful coupled with the Run Minimized feature, discussed below.

Run Minimized

If you select the Run Minimized feature for a program, that program will start itself, be minimized to an icon at the bottom of your Desktop, and be waiting there for you to work in — you won't have to change windows to get to that program's icon. Whenever you want to use it, just double-click on its icon on the desktop. When you're done, click on the application's Minimize button and it will drop back to an icon, out of the way but conveniently ready to use the next time you need it. This can be very useful for programs you use often (but not constantly) during a work session.

To set this feature, select the application's icon in its group window. Now select the File menu from the Program Manager menu bar, and choose the Properties menu item. Figure 11.9 illustrates this process.

Figure 11.9

Changing the properties of the Clock accessory

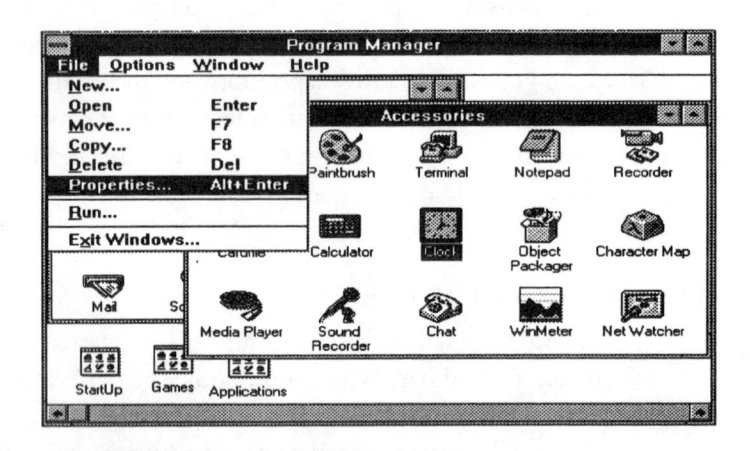

Now you see a dialog box that displays the properties of your application. Click on the Run Minimized box. After this, whenever you start the application, it will run as an icon until you double-click on it. Figure 11.10 shows the Properties dialog box.

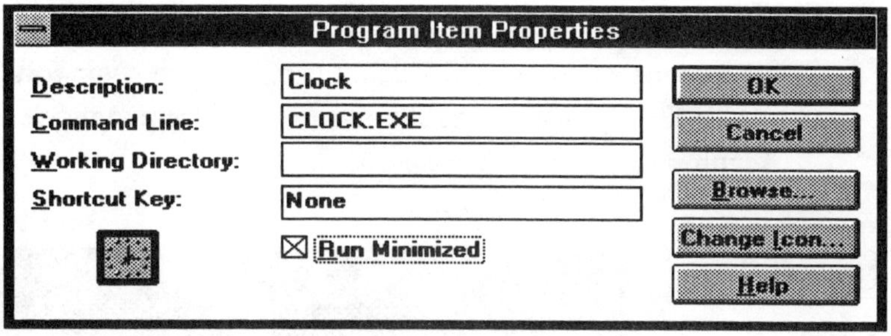

Figure 11.10

Program Item Properties for the Clock accessory

Program Item Properties	
Description:	Clock
Command Line:	CLOCK.EXE
Working Directory:	
Shortcut Key:	None
	☒ Run Minimized

Buttons: OK, Cancel, Browse..., Change Icon..., Help

Running Your DOS Applications in Windows

Many of the applications discussed in this book are designed for Windows and run within the graphical environment that is common to Windows for Workgroups and Windows itself. These applications have buttons, scroll bars, and Control menus, and you can share information between them. But if you have some applications you want to run that were not written for Windows, you can still get the benefit of some of these features, because Windows and Windows for Workgroups provide for running DOS applications (those not written for a Windows environment) in their own windows.

Some examples of DOS applications include Quicken 5.0, WordPerfect 5.1, Lotus 1-2-3 for DOS, and the MS-DOS prompt. When Windows for Workgroups installs these programs, it sets them up to run on the full screen, so that you can see the entire Quicken, WordPerfect, or DOS screen, but you can't see your desktop or any of your other icons. So it *looks* like a DOS screen, but actually Windows for Workgroups is still running. When you are running a DOS program in the full-screen mode you can get back to your Windows for Workgroups desktop with the ALT+TAB key combination, but there is an easier way.

To demonstrate, open the MS-DOS prompt from your Main program group. Your screen looks like old-fashioned DOS, with that one program running on the entire screen. Now press ALT+ENTER (hold down the

ALT key while pressing ENTER). Voila! Your desktop is back, with all your icons, and the DOS Prompt is running in a window. Press ALT+ENTER again, and it will run in full screen mode again. (See Figure 11.11.)

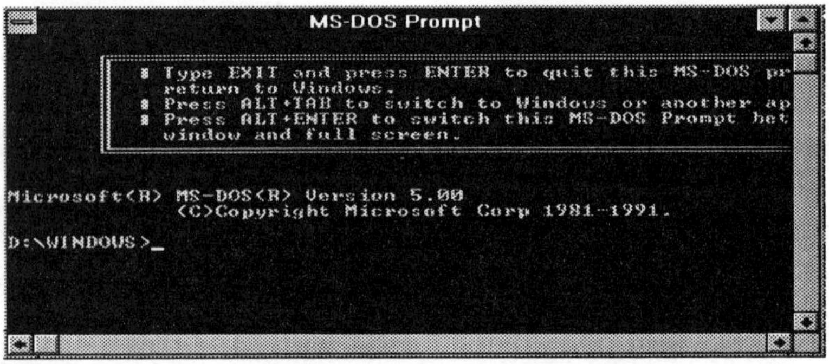

Figure 11.11

Running the DOS prompt in a window.

Now, how can we arrange things so that the DOS prompt always starts up in a window this way? When Windows for Workgroups installs a DOS program, it creates a PIF (Program Information File) for that program. The PIF file contains information Windows uses to run that program — we are now going to change that information.

Open the PIF Editor in the Main program group. Select File/Open from the PIF Editor menu. A list of PIF files appears. The PIF file names are usually the same as the program names, so if you want to edit the PIF for B.EXE, select the B.PIF file from the list. In our case, we are changing the DOSPRMPT.PIF file, so select that one. (See Figure 11.12.)

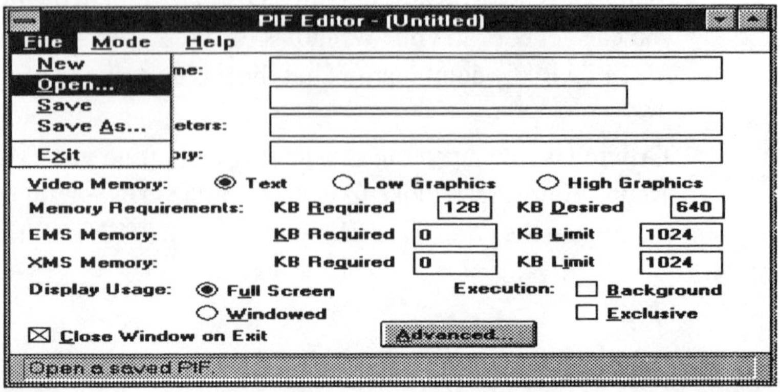

Figure 11.12

Opening a PIF for editing

Advanced Topics: Custom Setup and Tuning

Now the information about your PIF is loaded into the fields in the PIF Editor. Near the lower part of the box, next to the label Display Usage, you will see a pair of buttons — one button says Full Screen, the other says Windowed. Select the second one (Windowed), as shown in Figure 11.13.

Figure 11.13

Changing the Display Usage Field

To save the change you've made, select File/Save from the menu, and the next time you start up a DOS prompt it will start in a window.

> **NOTE**
> Unfortunately, not all DOS programs can run in windowed mode. If yours cannot, Windows for Workgroups will give you a message saying so. Running an application in windowed mode also takes up more memory than running it full screen. If you have plenty of memory in your computer, this may not be a problem for you. Otherwise, you will receive a "low on memory" message from Windows indicating that you cannot run the software.

Changing Fonts in DOS Applications

One problem with running DOS applications in Windows is that you see only a small part of the screen at a time. Fortunately, this is easy to fix. Windows provides ten different sizes of text fonts for DOS programs.

To change the text size of a DOS program window, select the Control menu button in the upper-left corner of the window, then select the Fonts... menu item. Figure 11.14 shows you how.

Figure 11.14

Selecting the DOS Text Fonts menu item

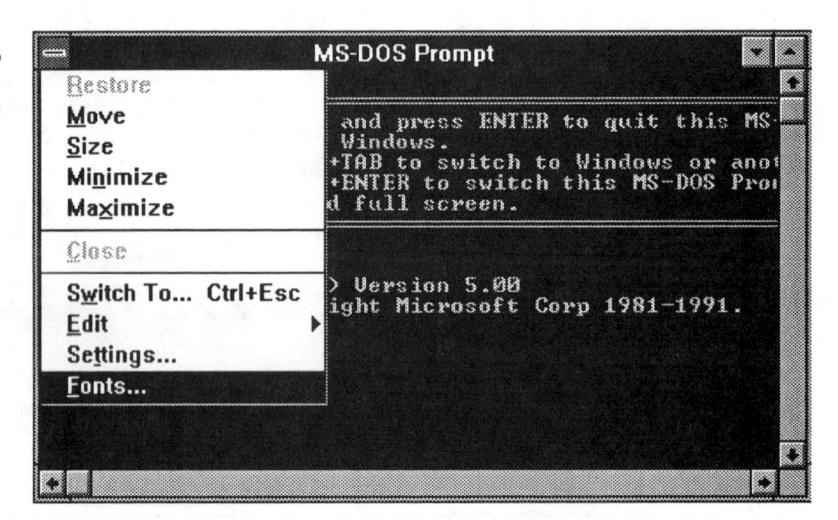

Now you will see a dialog box in which you can select a new text size. As you select each text size, the sample window at the bottom of the box shows what that size will look like in your window. (See Figure 11.15.)

When you have selected a size, click on the OK button, and your window reappears with the new text size. Adjust the window size if necessary until you can see everything in it.

Figure 11.15

The Font Selection window

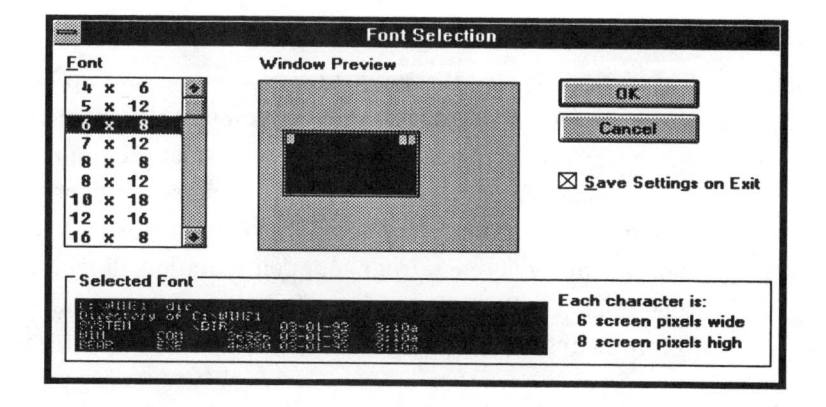

Tuning for Better Performance

In this section we will discuss things you can do to maximize performance in your systems. We'll cover memory needs, disk usage, and the efficient running of processes. First we'll discuss areas to examine if your computer appears to be running slowly.

Random Access Memory

You can do several things with your computer's memory to improve your performance, but probably the most significant is making sure you have enough. Microsoft states that you need at least 4 MB (megabytes) of RAM, or *random access memory,* in your computer to run Windows for Workgroups successfully. We have found that Windows runs on computers with only 4 MB, but fairly slowly. In our experience, 8 MB appears to be a more realistic need. If you have less than 8 MB of RAM, check the manual that came with your computer to see whether you can put more memory into it. If you decide to do so, shop around. Prices for RAM have dropped significantly in recent years, and they vary widely from store to store. RAM prices at a computer dealer, for instance, might be as much as 50 percent higher than at an electronics parts store.

Memory-Resident Programs

These are programs that are loaded before you start up Windows for Workgroups, and are always in your computer's low memory (below the first 640K). This leaves less memory for other programs to run. Check the documentation that came with the memory-resident program to see whether you can load it in such a way that it takes up less low memory. You can also remove it from your configuration altogether if you no longer need it. See Microsoft's *Windows for Workgroups User's Guide* for more tips on keeping memory-resident programs to a minimum.

SmartDrive

Your computer can get information from memory much more quickly than it can from your hard disk. SmartDrive is a program that comes with Windows for Workgroups and that stores data from your hard disk in memory so you can access that data faster. It is called a *disk cache* (pronounced "cash") program, and if it is running efficiently it can greatly increase your disk access speed. SmartDrive was installed on your computer automatically when you installed Windows for Workgroups. If things seem slow, be sure it is still running by checking for a line in your AUTOEXEC.BAT that looks something like this: C:\WINDOWS\SMARTDRV.EXE.

Program Tuning Issues

Some applications can run in full-screen, exclusive, and background modes. The mode in which you choose to run your programs will affect performance. In this section we outline some of the issues involved in running programs in various modes. Keep in mind that we are presenting only guidelines — you will have to weigh the benefits against the costs for your particular configuration.

Running Applications in Full-Screen Mode

As we discussed before, running DOS applications in windows takes more memory than running them full-screen. However, when you run

DOS applications in full-screen mode you cannot share information between them and other programs. If this is acceptable to you, running DOS programs full-screen could improve performance significantly.

Exclusive and Background Use

You may be able to improve the speed of a DOS application by setting Exclusive Execution for that application, and by turning off Background Execution for other DOS applications. Using the PIF Editor (discussed earlier in this chapter), you can set a DOS application to run in Exclusive Execution mode, which means that if the application is running full screen, all other applications are suspended while it runs. If the application is running in a window and Exclusive Execution is set, other DOS applications are suspended while it runs. If Exclusive Execution is not set, other applications run as usual when this one is running.

If Background Execution is set, the application will continue to run while other applications are active. The application will still get suspended, however, if the active application has Exclusive Execution set.

Figure 11.13 (earlier in this Chapter) illustrates the PIF Editor window. The Execution settings are in the lower-right portion of the window.

Monitoring Performance with WinMeter

The WinMeter program generates a chart indicating what types of programs are using your system's resources, and periodically it updates that chart. You can adjust the frequency the chart is updated from as little as ..... five seconds to as much as every ten-minutes by changing its settings. If you installed Windows for Workgroups using the default setup, the WinMeter icon was placed in the Accessories group of the Program Manager. If WinMeter shows that a lot of your resources are being used by shared programs and relatively little by your own, you may want to change the Enable Sharing or the Performance Priority settings in the Network Settings box, as described below. Figure 11.16 shows the WinMeter window.

Figure 11.16

The WinMeter Window

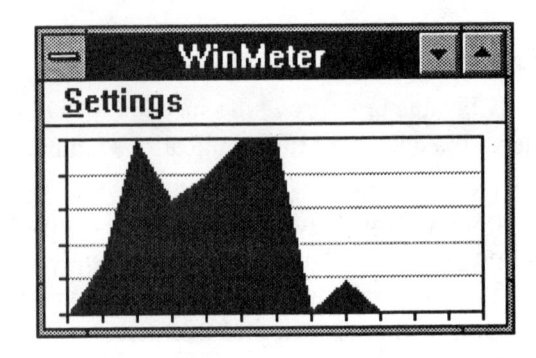

Disabling Sharing

In the Network Settings dialog box of the Control Panel, you will find a check box labeled Enable Sharing. If this box is not checked, other people on your network will not be able to link to directories or printers on your computer, even if you have designated them as Shared. Blocking access in this way could improve the speed of your programs, because no one else's programs will be running on your computer. If other people in your workgroup need access to your resources, however, this may not be an option for you. (See Figure 11.17.)

Figure 11.17

The Network Settings dialog box

Performance Priority

You can control how fast your own programs run in relation to those that are running from other computers, by using the Network Settings dialog box. For maximum speed in your own programs, move the sliding box pointer to the left. If you are setting parameters for a server (a computer that will only be sharing resources and not running any programs locally), move the pointer to the right. (See Figure 11.17.)

Looking at Virtual Memory and Swap Files

In the PC environment, programs can run in only a small area of memory, often called *low memory*. Windows for Workgroups can run far more programs at once than will fit into low memory. It does this by using something called virtual memory. Virtual memory allows a program to access more memory than is physically in the box. It does this by storing an image of the complete memory on disk, and paging parts of physical memory to and from the disk as needed. A program, when it is not running, is not taking up space in low memory, but instead is waiting for its turn to run again. It is possible to run enough programs to fill up all memory. If that happens, Windows will write the idle programs to disk, then read them off the disk when it is their turn to run again. The place on the disk to which it writes these programs is called the *swap file*. The swap file acts as virtual memory for applications. Disk access is much slower than memory access, so you want to minimize swap file usage and maximize its efficiency as much as possible.

Minimizing the Need for the Swap File

The fewer programs you are running, the less memory you will need. However, being able to run several programs at once is one of the best things about Windows, so it would be silly and inconvenient to close everything down except the program you are currently using. For efficiency, avoid running unnecessary programs and close down unused programs when you are finished with them.

Permanent and Temporary Swap Files

We recommend that you create a permanent swap file, especially if you have only 4 MB of RAM in your computer. Otherwise, Windows will spend a lot of time trying to find places to put data temporarily, and will do it in inefficiently small chunks. Creating a permanent swap file can speed things up dramatically.

Determining Swap File Size

Microsoft recommends that your swap file be at least twice as big as the amount of RAM in your computer. So if you have 4 MB, you would need an 8 MB swap file, but if you have 16 MB you would need a 32 MB swap file, larger than some hard disks! When Microsoft calculates your swap file size in Setup, they look at how much RAM you have and double that number, then they look at how much disk space you have and cut that number in half, then they use the larger of the two numbers. In our experience, however, 8 MB is plenty for the swap file on most computers. Knowing this, you might be able to free up some precious disk space. 8 MB (megabytes) is 8192 K (kilobytes). This is the number you will enter into the Virtual Memory dialog box in the 386 section of the Control Panel, as shown in Figure 11.18.

Figure 11.18

Changing the size of the swap file

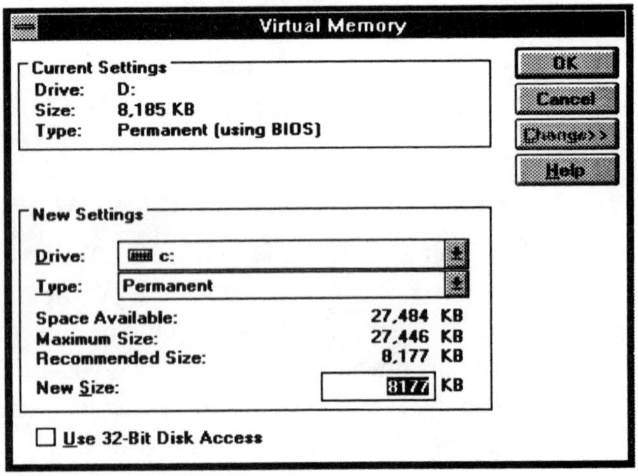

Swap File Notes

If you use disk compression utilities such as Stacker or SuperStor, you must reserve a drive that is not compressed for your swap file. Windows for Workgroups will not run if the swap file resides on a compressed drive.

Disk Usage Issues

Your computer spends a lot of time looking for files. The following guidelines will help you find ways to keep that time to a minimum.

> **NOTE** Keep seldom-used files off the disk.

As a disk fills up, it takes longer for the computer to find files on it because it has more places to look. If you have any files on your hard disk that you do not often use, consider moving them to another system with more space, or even to storage on diskettes or magnetic tape.

> **NOTE** Fragmentation slows disk response.

Sometimes a file will be stored on the hard disk in pieces — one piece will be on one part of the disk and the rest of it somewhere else. This slows down disk access time, because the computer has to find the next piece of the file before it can return the data to you. Keeping files all in one piece on the disk (sometimes called *contiguous files*), on the other hand, allows you faster access time. Several vendors sell disk defragmenting utilities; see Chapter 9 for more information. Be sure to exit the Windows for Workgroups environment before running any such utilities, because these utilities don't run optimally in a multitasking environment.

Removing Windows for Workgroups Components via Windows Setup

Chances are good that you will not use all components of Windows for Workgroups at all times. When you are not actually using some components, there is no need to leave them on your disk. If you need them later you can always reinstall them from the original installation diskettes. You can both remove and reinstall components by opening the Windows Setup icon in the Main program group. You will see a dialog box that displays information about your system and has two menus, Options and Help. Select Options, then the Add/Remove Windows Components menu item, and you will see a box like the one in Figure 11.19.

Figure 11.19

Selecting Components of Windows to add or remove

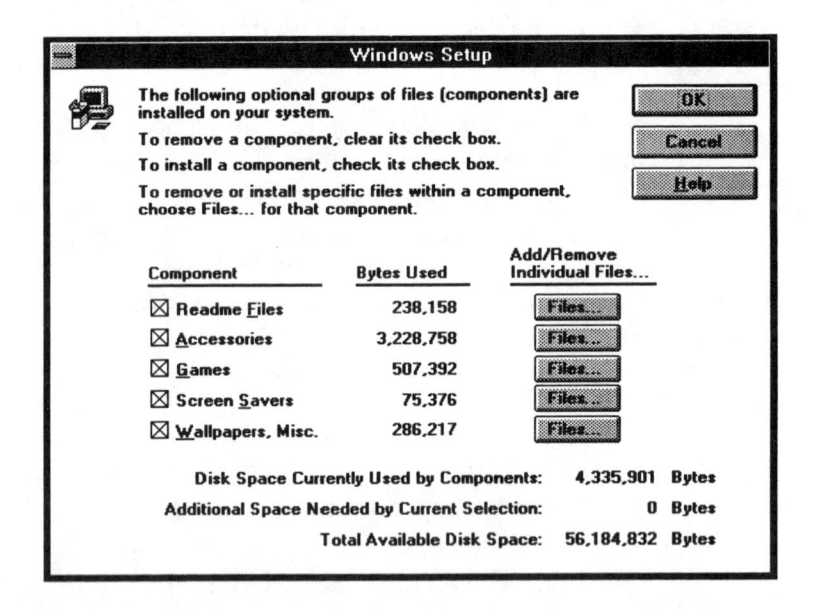

This screen divides the components into several categories, including Games, Wallpapers, and Readme files. All of these are good candidates if you need to free up some disk space. If, however, you have a favorite wallpaper that you use all the time, you can remove all but that one by selecting the Files box to the right. Now you can see exactly how much space each file or set of files consumes, and delete elements accordingly.

Advanced Topics: Custom Setup and Tuning

This chapter outlines just a few of the many ways that Windows for Workgroups allows you to customize your work environment and organize it to perform efficiently. Spend some time getting familiar with these features, then start exploring. With the concepts and guidelines learned in this chapter, you can find many other ways to adjust your work area to suit your needs and tastes.

CHAPTER 12

ADVANCED TOPICS: WINDOWS FOR WORKGROUPS ON A NOVELL LAN

CHAPTER 12

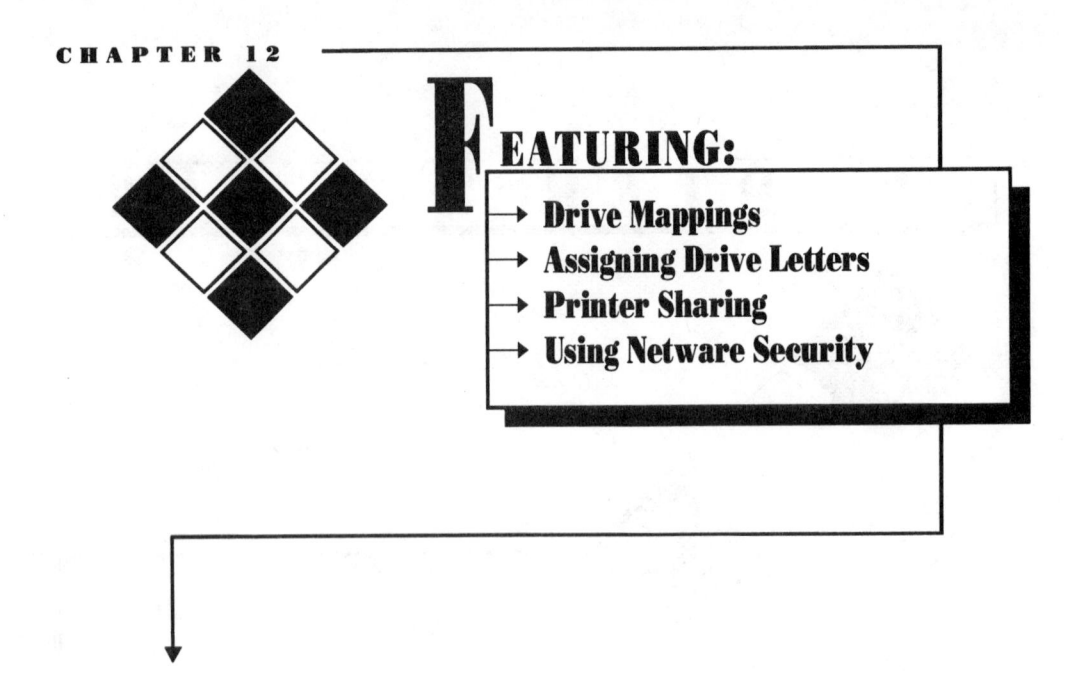

FEATURING:

- **Drive Mappings**
- **Assigning Drive Letters**
- **Printer Sharing**
- **Using Netware Security**

The Microsoft Windows operating environment and the Novell NetWare network operating system both enjoy the highest distinction in their respective software categories: they are both market leaders with very large install bases worldwide. Windows 3.1 currently is installed on millions of desktop workstations, and NetWare is the most popular LAN operating system in the world. As can be expected, many Windows-based systems are also part of a NetWare LAN. Unfortunately, Windows and NetWare have not always worked harmoniously — until now. Windows for Workgroups was designed with integration into a larger network specifically in mind. Windows users on NetWare LANs can benefit tremendously from upgrading to Windows for Workgroups, which integrates the *workstation* operating system with the *network* operating system.

Windows for Workgroups integrates the two operating systems by replacing the Novell supplied IPX driver with MSIPX. The MSIPX driver is a Microsoft NDIS driver. The MSIPX is a fully Novell compatible driver, but it is designed to work seamlessly with Windows.

A second advantage is that NDIS drivers allow a network card to operate with different protocols (such as TCP\IP and IPX). Therefore, the MSIPX driver, which the installation process generates, provides more features than IPX and works better with Windows.

In this book we have referred to Windows for Workgroups as a peer-to-peer network operating system. Windows for Workgroups can, however, co-exist very nicely with the client-server based system of Novell NetWare. NetWare offers many strong features, such as increased security and support for additional resources, that can be great assets to Windows for Workgroups; while Windows for Workgroups brings to the relationship its own strong features, such as the robust graphical user environment, built-in mail and scheduling applications, and user management from the desktop.

In this chapter, we will look at some of the considerations for setting up Windows for Workgroups within a Novell NetWare environment. Because each operating system is slightly different, we will look at potential conflicts between the systems, as well as ways the two systems can complement each other. We will conclude by examining the memory requirements for running both protocols, and methods you can use to reduce the load on your system.

Potential Conflicts

There are several areas where Novell NetWare and Windows for Workgroups can conflict with each other. Awareness of these areas will make it easier for you to avoid or eliminate these problems as you set up your network.

Drive Mappings

Although the two operating systems have many differences, there is one important similarity: both products require drive letters to indicate where directory resources are located. Each drive letter is assigned as one of two types:

- ▲ A **network drive** letter is assigned to a shared directory. The shared directory is either a shared resource in Windows for Workgroups, or a directory to which the Novell user has been given access rights.
- ▲ A **search drive** letter is used only by NetWare. This is a drive letter that is assigned to a Novell directory, but this drive is also placed in a list of drives that are searched when the system is looking for the requested executable file (similar to the path on a DOS workstation). Novell allows a maximum of 16 search drives (drive letters Q: through Z:).

Assigning Drive Letters

A NetWare file server can contain thousands of directories and subdirectories, and it is easier to remember to save your memos to drive I: instead of having to remember to save to the directory I:\DEPT\PUBLISH\WORD\MEMOS. Therefore, you will need to have a separate drive letter for each NetWare directory resource you want to access quickly.

Novell provides *drive pointers* (drive letters) to point to a specific directory on the network. In Windows for Workgroups, users click on drive pointers to access shared directories that are located on different workstations.

> **NOTE** Although a network drive letter is designated to a certain directory, you can change the pointer location by using the DOS Change Directory command (CD) or by using the Windows File Manager. For example, if drive H: is assigned to \HOME\SMITH, and you CD to the WORDS subdirectory, then drive H: is now assigned to \HOME\SMITH\WORDS.

The problem is that there are only 26 drive letters. If each system is using a large number of pointers, they will both run out of available letters and the systems will fight for available letters.

If you started with a Novell LAN that uses batch files to load drivers and login users, the first problem you might encounter is that the line to change your current drive to F: no longer works. This is because the default setting in your CONFIG.SYS was changed to LAST DRIVE = P by the Windows for Workgroups installation procedure. When you load the shell for accessing the NetWare server, the LAST DRIVE line sets the login drive to Q: (the next available drive).

Once you log into your NetWare LAN, you will notice other changes. The drive maps that you have set in your Novell login scripts will remain the same, but if you try to map a search drive before Q:, you will be informed that all drives are in use. You will also find as you add NetWare drive letters that you will be required to delete the local pointer that is already using that letter. Reassigning the drive letter is easy for a network drive as Novell will ask if you want to use the local drive letter for the network drive pointer.

Both of these errors are occurring because LAST DRIVE = P is causing all, or most, of your available drives to be listed as local drives. Classifying drives A: through P: as local drives reduces the number of search drives that are available to NetWare to 10 (Q: to Z:). If you are currently using more than 10 search drives, you will not be able to map them all as there are not enough search drive pointers available.

If you are using 10 search drives the NetWare command line utility NDIR won't work because NDIR maps a dynamic search map to perform its function. As there are no more free drives to be created as a search map, the utility cannot function.

To solve the problem you can:

- ▲ Modify your AUTOEXEC.BAT file,
- ▲ Modify your CONFIG.SYS file,
- ▲ Minimize the NetWare drive mappings, or
- ▲ Log in to the NetWare LAN before logging in to Windows for Workgroups.

Modify Your AUTOEXEC.BAT File

The easiest drive problem to solve is the loss of drive F:\LOGIN. Most networks use the AUTOEXEC.BAT file to place the user into the NetWare login directory. By Novell default, the drive pointer for this directory is F:, as shown below.

```
@ECHO OFF
CLS
PROMPT $P$G
PATH C:\;C:\DOS;C:\WINDOWS
C:\WINDOWS\NETSTART
C:\WINDOWS\MSIPX
C:\WINDOWS\NETX
F:
LOGIN
```

Unfortunately, Windows for Workgroups automatically sets the LAST DRIVE option to drive P:. Therefore the login directory has been "moved" to drive Q:. By simply editing the batch file to change to Q: instead of F:, you will be able to log into the network without having to remove all of the drive letters that have been designated for Windows for Workgroups.

Modify Your CONFIG.SYS File

As far as NetWare is concerned, the important line in the CONFIG.SYS file is the one designating the LAST DRIVE. The last drive line is used

Advanced Topics: Windows for Workgroups on a Novell LAN

by Novell to tell its operating system how many local drives you have on your system. By default, Windows for Workgroups tells Novell that it is using drives A: to P:. In order to regain needed search drives, you will need only to modify the CONFIG.SYS file to read

LAST DRIVE = J

This will leave drives A: to J: for use by either Novell or Windows for Workgroups network maps, and also offer the full 16 search drives for Novell to use. Unfortunately, this will change your first available network drive to K: . Then you have to change your AUTOEXEC.BAT file so that the login directory is K:\LOGIN.

Minimize Your Drive Mappings

Although it is a very effective means of reducing the number of drives that are needed by your Novell LAN, reducing the number of drive maps is not a simple solution. Typically, the designation of NetWare drives is controlled by the network administrator.

> **NOTE** If you use dynamic mapping with Windows or your network menu system, you can reduce the required number of search maps to four — one to the PUBLIC directory, one to your DOS directory, one to a utility directory (if you have one separate from PUBLIC), and the last one to your menu program or Windows.

If you do require more than 10 search maps, all that is required is to change the statement in CONFIG.SYS to read LAST DRIVE = K. This will give Novell 16 available search maps, which is the maximum number that Novell can handle.

Login the NetWare LAN before logging in to Windows for Workgroups

There are two main reasons for logging into the NetWare LAN before starting Windows for Workgroups. The first concerns the environment that is set up by the Novell LAN. Generally (especially if the LAN came first), the network will setup a working environment. This environment can be anything from setting up simple drive mappings to notifying you that there are e-mail messages waiting for you to read. The Novell environment is set up by the system's Login Script.

Printer Sharing

A printing problem may be encountered when working with a Novell LAN. Novell uses a redirection of the hardware port. This means that if you designate LPT1: to be a network printer, you will not be able to print to the printer that is physically attached to the computer's parallel port, or to a Windows for Workgroups printer that you have designated as being on LPT1:. As a result, even though you set up Windows for Workgroups to print to the Compaq PageMarq on LPT1:, you will actually print to the network print queue HP_LASER_III that is designated as the printer on LPT1: by the Novell CAPTURE command. Anyone who has ever wandered the halls looking for lost print jobs can appreciate the problem.

The solution to this problem is to reconfigure your Novell CAPTURE statement to use LPT3:. We suggest LPT3: because very few systems actually have three parallel ports, and therefore any local printers that you set up will be able to accept print jobs. This leaves LPT1: for your actual local printer and LPT2: for designating any shared printers within Windows for Workgroups. If you need to access several printers on the Novell LAN, or more printers within the workgroup, you will need to work with your Novell system administrator to find the correct configuration for you.

Complementary Features

Once you have worked past all of the potential conflicts between Windows for Workgroups and Novell NetWare, you will see that there are many ways to set up the two to complement each other, offering you some of the best features from each product.

Using NetWare Security

One feature that has made Novell NetWare so widely accepted is the increased security provided by a server-based network operating system. All of the data stored on the server is protected at all times by the system's stringent security. Depending on the setup, access to data can be strictly controlled by a network administrator who assigns access privileges to users. Otherwise, if a user has the Access Control Right (A) for a directory, then he or she can grant access to any other user on the Novell network by using the GRANT command.

In a peer-to-peer network like Windows for Workgroups, access to a data is protected only from users who are accessing the drive from across the network, not from a user who is working on the same physical machine. There is no protected central repository for sensitive data. Moreover, each user on Windows for Workgroups decides the security fate of his directories and resources, as opposed to having one administrator control it all.

Placing the Postoffice on a Novell Server

If you are using a dedicated server for your Novell LAN, your server can handle multiple requests from all of your users. The dedicated server is also the ideal place to install the Windows for Workgroups Postoffice. This will reduce the workload on one of your workstations (because it will not have to act as a Postoffice and a workstation) and provide a secure location for your mail messages.

Setting up the Postoffice on your server is not difficult — it can be accomplished by following a few simple steps:

1. Login to the NetWare network as a Supervisor.
2. Create a directory for the Postoffice.
3. Grant rights to the Postoffice directory.
4. Assign a drive letter to the Postoffice directory.
5. Start Windows for Workgroups and the Mail application.
6. Setup the Postoffice using the NetWare drive letter.

The first step is to designate a directory on your server for the WGPO directory (for example, use P:\WFWPO) and grant everyone in the workgroup the following rights to that directory:

R — Read
W — Write
S — File Scan
C — Create
E — Erase
M — Modify

Next, start Windows for Workgroups and open Mail. When you open the Mail program for the first time, it will ask if you want to create a Postoffice. If you answer yes, Mail will then prompt you for the path to locate the WGPO directory. At the prompt enter the path P:\WFWPO\WGPO (for our example), and this will create the Postoffice on your file server. Whichever Windows for Workgroups user name you are currently using will be assigned as the Postoffice Manager.

> **NOTE** If you have already been using Mail and want to move the Postoffice, be sure to rename or delete the MSMAIL.INI file from your WINDOWS directory. If this .INI file is found by the system, it will not let you create a new Postoffice.

Software Installation

Your NetWare file server was designed to provide a large amount of shareable disk space. In this capacity, setting up the NetWare server can provide several advantages, including that it will allow for quick backup and restore of the local drives in the workgroup. Each user can be given the task of backing up his or her own hard disk to the file server. This is accomplished by simply logging into the server and mapping a drive to a backup directory. Generally, this task will be handled by a batch file that has been configured by the system administrator, but any user can also accomplish this task.

> **NOTE** Before backing up data to a Novell server, you will want to check with the system administrator to be sure that there is sufficient storage space.

Or you can use a backup program like Norton Backup. This will compress the files and save space on the server.

Next the user will copy all of the data and the directory structure from the local drive to the server. The central file server can then be backed up using a tape unit, making yet another copy of the data, and therefore, more protection against data loss. Because access time for the server is faster than that of any tape unit, you will be able to complete backup and restoration of the local drives considerably faster time than if you were relying strictly on a tape unit.

> **NOTE** If you want to save space on the file server, the local hard drives can be backed up using a program like Norton Backup. These programs will compress the data and save disk space.

You can also use the central server as a means for installing software. For example, if you need to install Word for Windows on 10 workstations, you could perform the installation on each system (one for each license). Or, more simply, you could copy all of the Word for Windows disks to the file server then log on each station, and perform the software installation from the server. To do this, you would replace the path to your floppy drive (for the location of the installation disks) with the path to the directory on the server. Once again, the access time from the server will be much faster and make the installation much easier.

If disk space is at a premium on the workstation, you can use the Novell server to run Windows for Workgroups. By using the installation switch /A, you will copy all of the Workgroup files into a directory on the server. Next, the administrator will need to grant Read (R) and File Scan (S) rights to any user that needs to access Workgroups from the server. Then, by running SETUP /N on the workstation, you will install only the necessary files for launching Workgroups. In this way, you can dramatically reduce the amount of disk space used for each user (either on the workstation or from a user's directory on the network). By using the server in this manner, users that do not have a hard disk or enough disk space at their workstation can still run Windows for Workgroups.

There are two additional advantages to using the server to install programs. The first is that many Microsoft products allow you to control the way the software is installed by modifying an .INF file. This gives you a way to standardize the installation and ensure that all of the users are set up in the same way. The second is that you automatically have a backup for your installation disks. If one of your diskettes gets damaged, you will still be able to install workstation software from the server.

As a closing note, we must point out that not all software can be installed in this manner. Some products require a unique serial number on each installation. Further, using this form of installation for many workstations when you have purchased only one copy of the software is illegal. We recommend that you read the licensing rights to your software products before installing them on a server or workstation.

Printer Sharing

Although we mentioned that printer sharing might be an area of conflict between NetWare and Windows for Workgroups, it can also be worked to your advantage. Novell offers a complete set of printing utilities that can be utilized by the workgroup. Dedicated print servers can eliminate several of the burdens that are associated with Windows for Workgroups' shared printers.

Each output request to a shared printer in Windows for Workgroups must be serviced by Print Manager on the PC that has the printer locally attached. This requires that particular workstation to use memory, storage space, and processor time both to receive the print request and to route the job to the printer. Of course these activities will temporarily affect the performance of the PC, and they may lead to a very frustrated user.

On the other hand, using NetWare to manage print requests allows the central file server to handle the job spooling and routing. The printer is most likely to be directly attached to the file server or to a dedicated print server, so no user workstation will be adversely affected. Shifting all of the printing tasks to NetWare will improve the performance of any station that would otherwise have had a printer attached. It will also reduce the amount of memory and disk space needed to accept spooled print jobs.

One other advantage is that Novell can use old and slow machines, like those 512 K XT machines you've stored in the closet, as print servers. You'll continue to get value out of the hardware that you have purchased in the past.

Memory Considerations

Although computer memory is not as expensive as it once was, the efficient use of memory is still of great concern to network administrators and end users alike. There are some issues to consider when using both Novell NetWare and Windows for Workgroups on a LAN.

Workstation Memory

When new features are added to any user's workstation, the user will be concerned with how much memory it is going to use. Unfortunately, Windows for Workgroups linked to a NetWare LAN does cost some memory. Memory, from the DOS base 640 K, is required to run the drivers for connecting to Novell NetWare. The NetWare protocol shell, IPX, requires about 17 K of base memory. The NetWare network shell, NETx, needs 44 K of memory. This might appear to be a great deal of memory, particularly for users who run large applications (such as Lotus) or a lot of TSR programs (such as memory resident antiviral programs like Vshield). One way to reduce memory usage in the base 640 K range is to use one of the two upper memory shells (XMSNETx and EMSNETx) provided by Novell. These shells can be used in place of NETx.

XMSNETx, a high memory shell that is solely designed for use with extended memory, requires the use of HIMEM.SYS. EMSNETx, an expanded memory shell, requires a LIM memory manager such as EMM386. Either XMSNETx or EMSNETx can be used to load the NetWare shell into upper memory. The result will be a reduction of about 64K in the amount of base memory used.

> **NOTE:** If you are already utilizing the upper memory block by loading other TSRs high, there may not be enough memory space for the NetWare shell. For example, if you use HIMEM.SYS to load DOS high, there may not be enough space for XMSNETx to load. If there is not enough memory, you will not be able to load the shell and, therefore, will not be able to access the file server.

Server Memory

The good news is that linking Windows for Workgroups to a Novell server does not have any measurable ill effect on server performance. If Windows is being run across the network (i.e., loaded on the file server instead of the workstations), or if the swap file has been placed on the server, memory allocation is required from the server, which tends to bog down network communication. Because of this, we recommend that you install Windows for Workgroups on the local hard disks, and leave the NetWare server for storing data and performing printing services.

This chapter was designed for advanced users, to point out how Windows for Workgroups can work in harmony with Novell NetWare on the same LAN. We looked at potential areas of conflict and some possible remedies for those situations. Then we looked at the advantages of using both network operating systems at the same time. Overall, with a few modifications to your Windows for Workgroups and Novell configurations, you will be able to effectively link the two operating systems together.

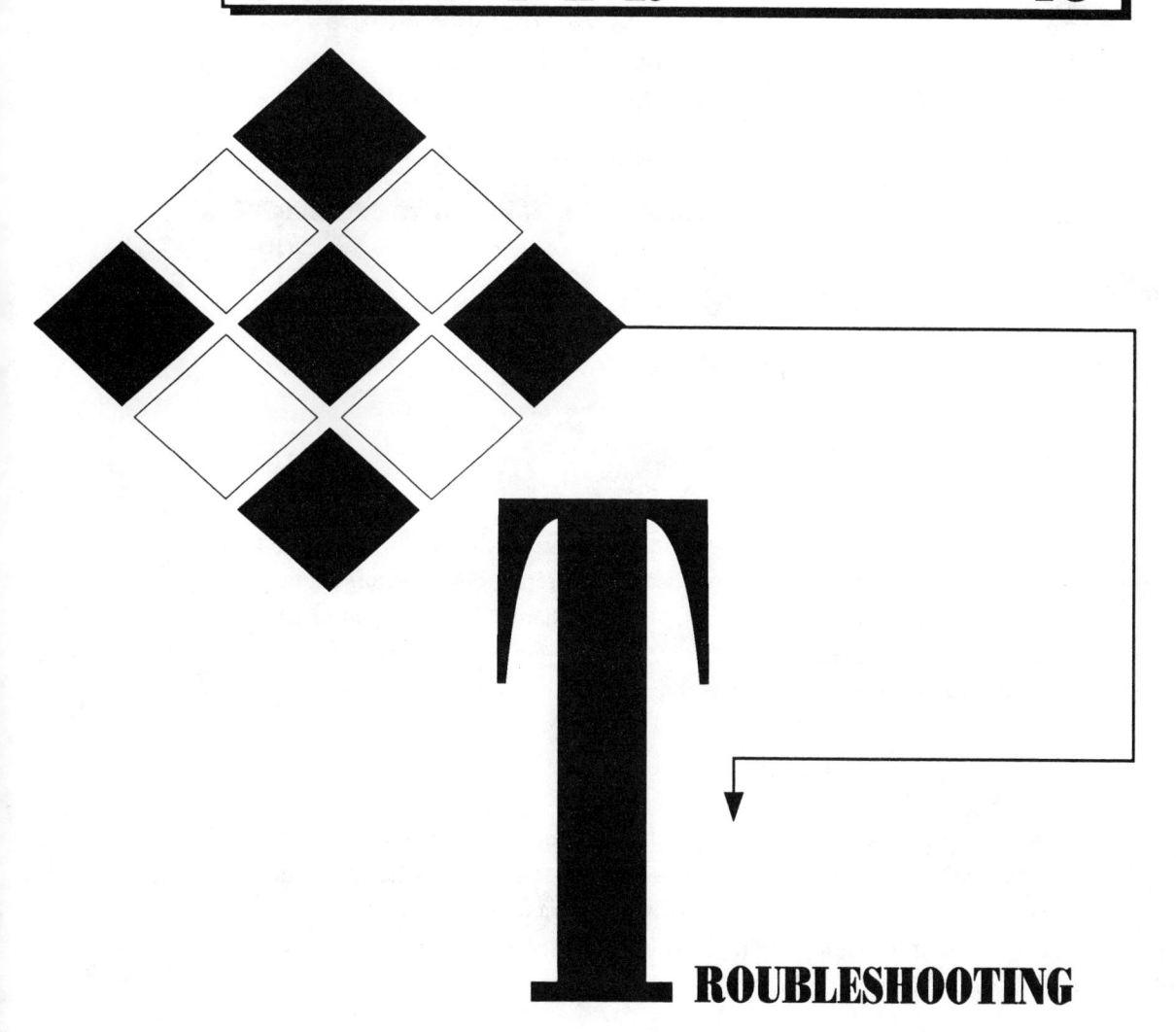

CHAPTER 13

TROUBLESHOOTING

CHAPTER 13

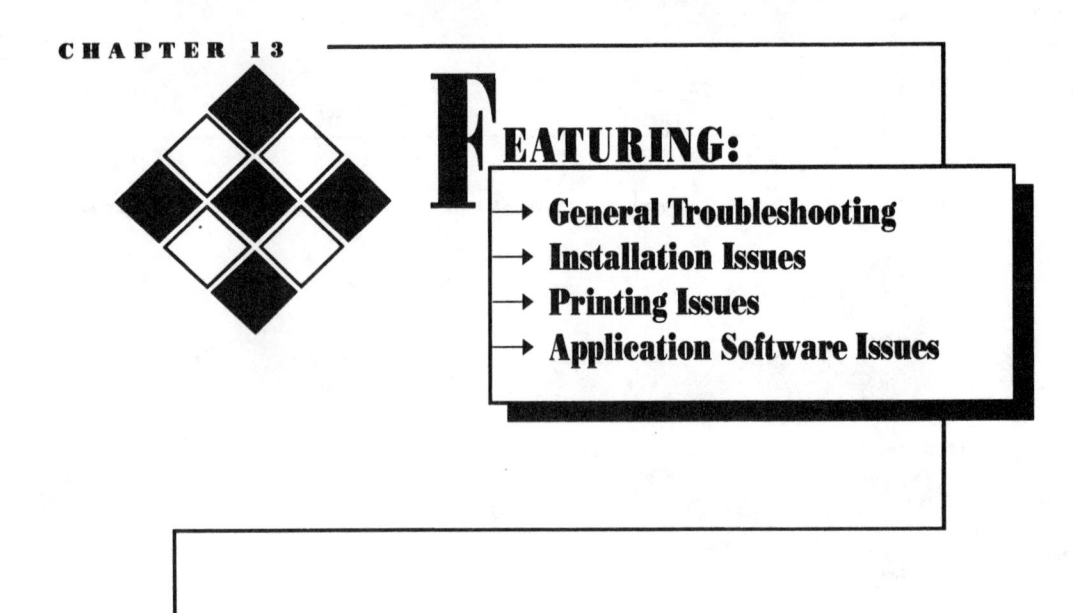

Featuring:

- → General Troubleshooting
- → Installation Issues
- → Printing Issues
- → Application Software Issues

LAN technology is generally stable. Some LANs run trouble-free for years, while others need only an occasional repair call. But any technology that is comprised of so many pieces — hardware, cable, and software — has potential for problems. And, of course, when problems occur it is always at the least convenient time.

This chapter is devoted to common problems — and solving them quickly. We'll begin with practical tips for what to do first if something goes wrong. Then we'll divide up the probable points of failure — the places where things can go wrong — and describe both what you can check yourself and what to leave for a qualified repair technician. We'll close with information on how to contact Microsoft support services directly.

General Troubleshooting Guidelines

As in life, the first thing to remember when something goes wrong with your network is: *don't panic.* Sure, it's frustrating when the printer

suddenly stops printing, or the disk drive doesn't read the diskette anymore. But maintaining a cool head and using a step-by-step approach to problems will more than pay for itself, and often the user or administrator can solve the problem if armed with the right information.
Here are a few basic rules for approaching technical problems:

1. Look for the obvious first.

Many problems can be solved by a quick check of the fittings on cables and plugs. Repair technicians who've responded to "emergency" calls often walk away after just turning on the power switch or plugging in a loose cable.

2. Read (and reread) the manual.

If there's still a problem after you've checked the obvious, locate the manual for the hardware or software that seems to be failing. Here's where things can get confusing. Sometimes what appears to be a hardware problem turns out to be software, or the other way around.

Generally, however, you can find clues. If, for example, you can't get a document page to print from Word for Windows, but all your spreadsheets print fine from Excel, chances are something's gone astray with the word processing software, rather than the printer or the cables. Knowing this, you'd look for troubleshooting tips in the Word for Windows manual.

Often, just skimming through manuals will provide lots of clues. Look carefully at the installation instructions and ask yourself if everything was followed to the letter. Then look at those parts of the manual devoted to troubleshooting. Many software and hardware vendors anticipate potential conflicts and document them in their manuals.

Even if you don't find your specific problem outlined in the manual, you will have eliminated some possibilities and narrowed your search for the cause of the problem.

3. Change only one thing at a time.

It's all too easy to reinstall software, change out a driver, slap in a new network card, and change the cable in one fell swoop. If, after this, things start working, then fine, you're set. If they don't, you may have inadvertently introduced new complications into the scenario, confusing your search and adding to your problems.

We know of one workgroup installation that took days (instead of hours) because the installers weren't careful about their process. It turned out that two problems existed: faulty cables and a bad Ethernet hub. Unfortunately, the installers persisted in spinning their wheels by reinstalling the software and changing network cards and PCs about six times.

If you do change several variables at once and things start working, you still have a problem: you'll never know what went wrong in the first place. The symptoms could recur, and you'd have to go through that whole time-consuming process to fix it. Experienced network troubleshooters gather up all the clues and take one step at a time to find the right solution.

4. Know your own technical limitations.

Don't try to exceed your own technical limitations. While hardware, software, and network vendors make every effort to simplify the installation and configuration processes, sometimes this technology is best left in the hands of experts. This is especially true if you've chosen to install Windows for Workgroups over a pre-existing network. You may be loading software or drivers that conflict with Windows for Workgroups. The individual workstations might include other adapter cards, extra boards with extra serial ports, internal modems, scanner boards, game boards, or other devices that conflict with your network board. Or, if you try to use a unsupported network card, you may cause a problem.

Give yourself a time budget, say thirty minutes or an hour. If you can't solve the problem by then, don't waste your valuable time. Call someone who can take care of it quickly.

5. Call the manufacturer's Help line for support.

If you've checked the obvious, not changed more than one thing at a time, read the manual, and still think you can do it within your budgeted time, the next step is to call a Help line for support. Be ready to describe the symptoms. Try to paint a complete picture of the problem — it's not very helpful to say "my printer doesn't work." Instead, tell the support person about the whole problem. It's more helpful to say, "my printer doesn't work in Excel, but it does in PowerPoint." Or, "my printer won't print anything from any software package, and I've already checked the cables, power cord, printer assignment, and print manager print queue."

Often, the manufacturer's Help personnel can diagnose and solve your problem in a short time. If you are working in an organization with in-house technical support, it is also an option to get help there.

6. Call a local repair shop.

Some problems just seem to defy detection. No matter how knowledgeable you and your help line staff might be, there are times when you'll just have to call in technical experts. At this point, you should contact a local repair facility. Make sure you describe the problem in complete detail so they can dispatch the right kind of expert. A networking guru probably isn't the best person to fix a broken printer. Likewise, a software specialist probably doesn't know if the RJ-45 connector on your network cable is improperly made.

Be forewarned, too, that lots of witch doctors and charlatans disguise themselves as LAN consultants. There aren't any certification programs for repair technicians that specialize in Windows for Workgroups, so you are on your own to find someone that is qualified. The best way to find competent practitioners is through personal referral from a satisfied customer.

Aside from that, interview your candidate by phone or in person about his or her previous networking experience. It will help if the firm has previous experience with other peer-to-peer networks, such as Lantastic or Novell NetWare Lite. Make sure that your vendor has also had some exposure to the Windows environment.

Troubleshooting Basic Problems

We will focus here on those more common glitches that can be inspected by a non-technical person — installation, printing, setting up applications, and running DOS applications. If you have specific network issues, such as working with Novell NetWare, see chapter 12.

NOTE If you want more technical details on troubleshooting, consult Microsoft's Windows for Workgroups Resource Kit, which is available as a separately purchased product.

Windows for Workgroups Won't Install

Installation problems can point to hardware conflicts, unsupported hardware, or networking problems. Table 13.1 outlines some common problems and suggested actions. If these don't work, refer to your users guide or Microsoft's Windows for Workgroups Resource Kit, which is available separately. Otherwise, contact a qualified local network installation company.

Table 13.1 Installation Issues

Problem	Cause / Solution
PC doesn't power on (or PC powers on, but nothing comes up on the screen) after network card is installed.	The network interface card (NIC) has a conflict with some other adapter card in the PC. Remove the NIC and reconfigure any jumpers or dip switches. Consider running the Microsoft Diagnostics program (MSD.EXE) to determine which IRQs and base I/O ports memory are available. MSD.EXE is on disk 4 of Windows for Workgroups. You can run it from the disk before WFW is installed.
The network interface card doesn't fit inside the PC.	Check to make sure you are using the correct type of card for your PC. Your PC will support ISA, EISA, or Microchannel. Make sure your NIC is the appropriate type. (See Appendix A for hardware installation details.)
The COM2 port doesn't work anymore.	You have set your NIC for IRQ 3. Reset the NIC for a different IRQ. If the card supports it, try IRQ 10 or IRQ 11.
The installation software (SETUP) stops running before it's complete.	Try running SETUP again to see if it can complete the installation. SETUP will recognize that it had a problem and attempt to pick up where it left off. Or —

Table 13.1 Installation Issues (continued)

	The SETUP program may be having trouble detecting your network hardware correctly. Try running SETUP in custom installation mode. From DOS, type SETUP /I, which will bypass the automatic hardware detection part and let you specify your system information. Or — Check to make sure you had no other program, application, or TSR running on your computer prior to running SETUP. Or — Check to make sure you are running a supported version of MS-DOS on your computer. We strongly recommend that you upgrade to at least MS-DOS 5.0, although MS-DOS 3.3 will work.
The computer doesn't find other computers on the network.	Check network cables to make sure your PC is connected to the network. Or — Use a diagnostic utility (usually supplied with your network interface card) to make sure your computer can send and receive packets across the network. Or —

Table 13.1 Installation Issues (continued)

Check your installation, and make sure you correctly specified the network interface card and the protocols. From the Control Panel, choose the Network icon. Then, from the Network Settings dialog box, choose the button labeled Adapters. From the next dialog box, choose the Setup button. Then on the next dialog box choose the Protocol button. The list displayed should confirm you are running the NetBEUI protocol (and others if you have other networks).
Or —

Check to make sure other computers are presently powered on.

Printer Won't Work

Printer problems can be among the most frustrating of LAN maladies. It seems that printers only fail to work when you need them most. Again, we suggest that you take slow and careful steps to debug printing problems. Use common sense techniques first. Then, look for more technical issues. Table 13.2 provides some guidelines for looking at printer problems.

Application Software Doesn't Install Correctly

In theory, Windows for Workgroups shouldn't have an effect on the way other software installs. If a program is compatible with the regular version of Windows (release 3.1), it should run under Windows for Workgroups.

Table 13.2 Printing Problems

Problem	Cause / Solution
You can't get a local printer to work.	Check cables, connections, and configurations first. Do you have the correct set of cables? Is the printer turned on? Is it getting power? Does it have toner, ribbon, and paper? During installation, did you correctly select the driver for your printer? Double-check everything. Then, turn the printer off and on again before you retry printing. Or — Check to see if the printer will print from MS-DOS. From the C:\ prompt, type PRINT C:\AUTOEXEC.BAT. If the file prints, check whether you have correctly set up the printer in Windows, and whether you have more than 2 MB free disk space on your local drive. If the file doesn't print, recheck your cable connections.
A shared printer doesn't work.	Check whether the printer works from the local PC (both from MS-DOS and Windows). See the above instructions if it does not print from either Windows or MS-DOS on the local printer. Or — From the Print Manager icon, make sure the printer has been shared correctly.

Table 13.2 Printing Problems (continued)

The printer works but isn't printing documents correctly.	Make sure you've correctly identified the printer. Use the Print Manager to verify the type of printer you specified during installation. Or —
	If you have connected your printer with a serial connection, try slowing it down. Consult with your printer manual for the procedure to use a slower rate. Or —
	If the printer prints only part of a page, or prints only some pages of a document, you may not have enough memory in the printer. (This is an especially annoying problem with laser printers that are trying to print from a graphics program.)

In practice, however, things can go wrong in a shared environment that don't occur in a stand-alone environment. Table 13.3 covers some problems that can creep up when networking application software.

Contacting Microsoft

Microsoft, the maker of Windows for Workgroups, offers several ways for you to contact them.

You can use a voice mail (and fax back) support service that allows access 24 hours a day by touch-tone telephone. Telephone (206) 635-7245 for a recorded message about Windows that will let you request

Table 13.3 Application Software Issues

Problem	Cause / Solution
Windows applications don't share across the network.	Some Windows-based applications will work fine if you run them across the network, but you cannot guarantee it. Many, like Excel, PowerPoint, or communications software, require special initialization files (.INI files) that are located in your individual Windows directory.
DOS applications won't run.	Windows for Workgroups will run in such a way as to let most DOS applications run without a problem. If you are also loading other network protocols, drivers, or TSR programs, you may not have sufficient memory left to run your DOS applications. Or — Check your memory use by running the MSD.EXE program from your Windows directory. If your free memory is below that required for your application software, remove some of the nonessential drivers or programs. (You may want to consult a qualified networking specialist before changing anything in configuration files.)
My application software won't install.	Check the amount of free disk space. Some software installation routines don't do a very good job of checking or forewarning you of impending problems. If it is a disk space problem, delete unnecessary files (including those in the directory of the failed software) and try to install the application again.

TROUBLESHOOTING

more information, which will arrive by fax or mail. You can also access Microsoft via electronic mail through services such as CompuServe.

(For CompuServe, the forum can be accessed by typing GO MICROSOFT at any prompt.)

You can speak directly to a technical support person by calling Microsoft's Product Support between 6:00AM and 6:00PM (Pacific time) on weekdays. The number is (206)637-7098. Be sure to have on hand your product serial number (located on the inside back cover of your Getting Started manual) and all of your Windows for Workgroups documentation. You should also be prepared to describe your hardware configuration (make, model, amount of memory, disk space, etc.) and what version of DOS you are running. If an error message came on screen when your problem occurred, write down all the information that was displayed in the message so you can describe it.

CHAPTER 14

CHANGING HABITS, WORKING SMART

CHAPTER 14

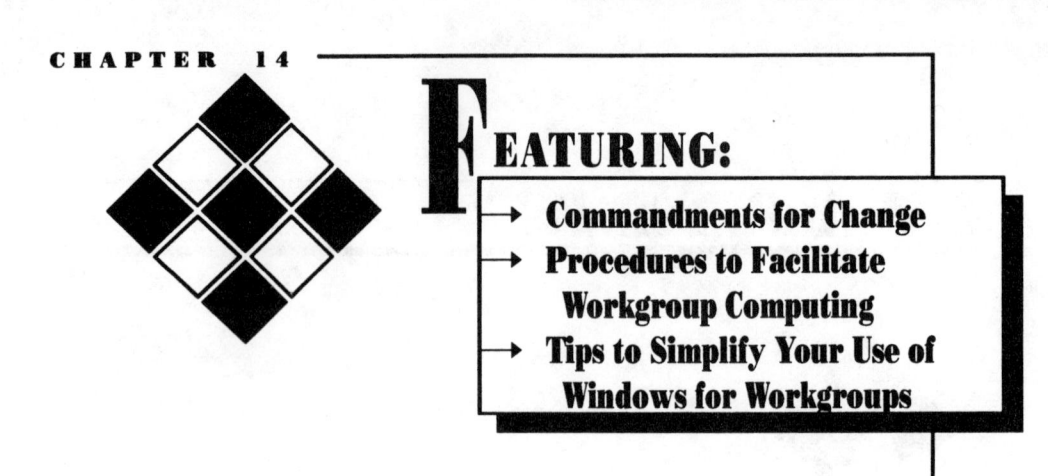

FEATURING:
- **Commandments for Change**
- **Procedures to Facilitate Workgroup Computing**
- **Tips to Simplify Your Use of Windows for Workgroups**

Now that you have learned how Windows for Workgroups will help you and your coworkers get organized, give up your Flintstonian work habits and move into the age of George Jetson. No, you can't just talk to your computer and have it respond — yet — but you can get rid of paper and pencil for many common activities. In fact, to get the most out of Windows for Workgroups, you really need to adopt new work habits and develop a few new procedures.

Both individual and workgroup habits should change to maximize this application's benefits. Individuals should ban paper calendars from their desks, do away with calculators, and tear up notepads. Windows for Workgroups has an electronic replacement for those tools. Workgroups should begin electronically exchanging memos, phone messages, and documents. This can save time and reduce conflicts and misunderstandings.

With just a few slight modifications to your work routine, you can become much more productive. And a funny thing will happen over time: the more you use your desktop computer, the more proficient you will become. Soon you will wonder how you ever got along without your computer network and Windows for Workgroups.

In this chapter, we'll make suggestions on how you can modify your habits to make the most of Windows for Workgroups. We'll discuss the need for your workgroup to agree on a few common file-naming conventions and procedures that will help you take advantage of Windows for Workgroups' great features. And finally, we'll include some tips that save time and facilitate the use of various applications.

Commandments for Change

Throughout the years, we have all developed personal work habits, which can increase or decrease our productivity. For many people, the morning office ritual goes something like the one described in Chapter 1: arrive at the office, turn on the PC, get a cup of coffee, listen to voice mail, look over the day's schedule, and chat with fellow employees. Most of these activities help you get ready for the day ahead.

As the workday progresses, the ritual becomes a little less predictable. The phone rings. A coworker stops by your office. The boss wants to see you. Reports get delivered to you. You have meetings to attend. And so on. Many of these diversions waste your time and take away from the "real" work at hand.

With a few new habits and methods to deal with these diversions, you can become more productive. For instance, when you take a phone call for a coworker, don't write down the message and walk it down the hall to her desk. Instead, bring up e-mail and send a quick message. You never have to leave your desk. Likewise, when you need to schedule a meeting with your project team, don't go around asking who is available when. Let Schedule+ determine the best meeting date and time.

This brings us to Currid & Company's Commandments for Change — a set of rules that we developed over the years that will wean you away from inefficient habits and bring you forward into the age of workgroup computing.

The First Commandment of Change:
Thou Shalt Not Compute Alone

In a workgroup environment with multiple PCs, a network is needed. It can be a complex client-server network with many peripheral devices, or a peer-to-peer network with simple file and resource sharing. Either way, networking is better than exchanging information on diskettes and wheeling printers around on carts. Standalone computing is virtually worthless to an organization; data is redundant (or worse yet, inaccessible), expensive resources are duplicated, and time is wasted. If your organization doesn't have one already, you should demand a LAN.

The Second Commandment of Change:
Place Thy PC on Thy Desk

A PC belongs on a desk, not on a back bar, credenza, or table across the room or down the hall. The only way that people can integrate the PC into everyday work habits is if the PC is within reach.

Of course, the corollary to this commandment is that the PC must be *turned on* and *used*, not just kept for a desktop ornament. If dust gathers on the keys of your keyboard, you aren't using that PC enough!

> **NOTE** If your desk is too small or too cluttered for a PC, get rid of some now nonessential items: your calendar, your calculator, your Rolodex, etc. Windows for Workgroups can replace all of these items.

The Third Commandment of Change:
Thou Shalt Not Keep a Paper Calendar

Paper calendars are passe. Among the most time-robbing rituals of corporate civilization is the process of setting up group meetings or activities. With Schedule+, you can keep your own calendar and check others' schedules as well. Schedule+ can save time and money. If everyone adapts to electronic calendars, the company doesn't need to buy new paper calendars and DayTimers every year! Moreover, you'll gain some desk space. (The only negative side here is that many people will lose their favorite place to doodle!)

If you enjoy looking at the pictures or cartoons on your paper calendar and can't bear to give them up, look for the electronic equivalent. Amaze! has some very creative calendar programs featuring popular cartoons such as "The Far Side" and "Cathy." Softhoughts, Inc.'s Heartwarmers has a calendar with a new motivational message every day. These and other products can make it fun and inspirational to look at your electronic calendar each day.

The Fourth Commandment of Change:
Thou Shalt Stuff Thy Calculator in a Drawer

Your desktop calculator should be relegated to a drawer, the trash can, or a garage sale. If you need to add numbers quickly, use the calculator in Windows for Workgroups. If you need to remember the numbers, use a spreadsheet and save the file. Here again, your company saves money: no more buying batteries or rolls of paper for the calculator. And getting rid of the calculator reclaims some of your desk space.

The Fifth Commandment of Change:
Thou Shalt Give Up Thy Notepaper

Don't use notepaper. Enter your notes into a notepad on the computer. If you need to share the notes, send them through e-mail. Think how neat your work area can be without little scraps of paper tacked all over the walls and without sticky notes stuck to your monitor. You won't lose notes under stacks of paper, and you'll never have problems reading your own or someone else's handwriting.

Get rid of those little pink phone message slips! Enter phone messages directly into e-mail. They'll be delivered promptly and they won't get misplaced. As long as Mail is running in the background, Windows for Workgroups will "beep" the recipient when a phone message comes in.

The Sixth Commandment of Change: Thou Shalt Stop Using Handwritten "To Do" Lists

Little scraps of paper with your "to do" list on them belong in the trash can with the calculator. Use the task list in Schedule+, or an electronic notepad. Schedule+ can even remind you when a task must be done. And if you make your list accessible to other people, they may even perform your tasks for you if are out sick for a day or two.

If the workgroup needs a joint "to do" list, try using the shared clipboard feature. As you'll learn in the Ninth Commandment, shared clipboards are the electronic answer to white boards and other shared lists.

The Seventh Commandment of Change: Remove Thy Rolodex

Chances are that the people in your workgroup all have their own Rolodex files or address books, many of them including the same names. Get rid of all those little paper cards and start using a group version of an electronic address book. If you have a company phone directory, save the time and expense of printing and distributing it to all employees.

Your electronic address book can be used by all for client names, sales contacts, employee listings, vendor contacts, and more. Give everyone Read and Write access so you can all enter names for new acquaintances.

Some of the better products on the market let you mark entries as private or public, so you can even keep personal names in the group book.

Windows for Workgroups does not currently include an address book feature, so you will have to shop for a third party product. As a minimum, we suggest you look for a product that can hold the following information: contact name, prefix (or salutation), company, title, department, address, city, state, zip code, business phone, home phone, fax number, and note. Another field that we find quite handy is electronic mail ID.

Keeping your addresses in electronic format means you can access them from almost anywhere. And take a copy of the file with you on the road in your notebook computer. You don't need to be at your desk, rifling through a thousand stray business cards, to find that one contact that is important at the moment.

An added benefit of electronic address books is that the entries can often be flagged and merged with a document to create a "custom" letter for a large group of recipients. This sure beats typing in many different addresses and salutations to the same letter!

The Eighth Commandment of Change: Thou Shalt Remember to Multitask

One of the greatest features of Windows for Workgroups is that it allows you to quickly flip among your favorite applications. Jump from word processing into your daily schedule, move from mail to your spreadsheet, and so on. There's no need to completely back out of one application before switching to another.

Get into the habit of loading all of your most frequently used applications when you first start up Windows for Workgroups. For instance, you may want to load Mail, Schedule+, a word processing program, a spreadsheet program, and the address book all at once. Keep the applications minimized until you need to use them. Windows for Workgroups will keep an icon on the screen to remind you that the applications are ready for use at a moment's notice.

Switching from One Application to Another

There are a number of ways that you can quickly switch from one application to another. We suggest you try them all and decide which method works best for you.

ALT+TAB

Press and hold down the ALT key and then press the TAB key repeatedly. As you continue to press TAB, the title of each application currently running in Windows for Workgroups appears at the center of your screen. When you see the application you want, release ALT+TAB. The new application appears in the foreground.

Task List

Press CTRL+ESC to bring up the Task list menu. From the menu, highlight the application you want to switch to and double-click with the left mouse button, or click on the Switch To button. You can then maximize your application and begin working.

Icons

Minimize the application that is currently active. From the Windows desktop, double-click on an icon for another application. The new application becomes the active one.

> **NOTE** Before you minimize any application, it would be wise to save all open data files that you may have been working with in that application.

The Ninth Commandment of Change:
Thou Shalt Use No More White Boards

Workgroups often get together to brainstorm, and write all of the great ideas on a white board (or chalk board). At the end of the meeting, someone copies the notes from the white board onto paper, then types them up and distributes copies of the notes to everyone. How inefficient! Wouldn't it be easier to enter the original ideas onto an electronic white board (clipboard), so that everyone has immediate access?

In another common scenario, a project manager keeps a white board in the office with a task list or status report for all of the team members. The team members can access the information only by calling the project manager and asking for details, or, worse yet, walking down the hall to look directly at the board.

Windows for Workgroups has shared clipboards that everyone can write on and read from. Even workgroup members in remote locations can share the information on the electronic white board. What's more, the information can be moved into an e-mail message or formal document if the need arises. And the information is written only once.

The Tenth Commandment of Change:
Thou Shalt Not Recreate the Wheel

Get into the habit of entering information into the computer system only once. If you need the same information in another format, look for a shortcut method of reusing the data. For example, if you are addressing a letter to an acquaintance, look up the address in your electronic Rolodex, highlight the pertinent information, use the Windows Copy and Paste features, and drop that address right into your letter. If you have more than one letter to generate, use the document merge feature in your word processing package. You certainly don't want to have to retype dozens of addresses that already exist in your electronic Rolodex. And share your information with others electronically. Don't type someone's list into your computer — find a way to transfer the file.

There are so many ways that Windows for Workgroups and the Windows-based application software packages can help to eliminate retyping. Cut (or copy) and paste. Object linking and embedding (OLE). Dynamic Data Exchange (DDE). The Clipboard feature. File conversions. File imports and exports.

Once data has been entered into a computer, retyping it into another application should be your last resort. Look for some simple way to paste it, link it, embed it, import it, or transfer it. These techniques can save you countless hours as you become more proficient with Windows.

Procedures to Facilitate Workgroup Computing

Now that you have seen our commandments for change, don't stop here. It's time to establish a few new procedures to make workgroup computing easier. Everyone in the group has to agree to abide by these rules to simplify routine activities. As you gain more experience with Windows for Workgroups, you'll discover other procedures that will keep your office running smoothly. We suggest that you broadcast your ideas through e-mail or the shared clipboard, so that your coworkers can review and agree to them.

The Postoffice PC

In setting up Windows for Workgroups, you designated a particular PC as the hub for the workgroup Postoffice. It is important to keep this PC running at all times so that mail and other messages can be delivered. If you turn all the other office PCs off at night, keep the Postoffice PC on.

PCs with Printers Attached

If you designate a locally attached printer as sharable by workgroup members, keep the printer and the PC it is attached to turned on, as described in Chapter 4. In fact, the PC must be running Windows for

Workgroups and the Print Manager (in either the foreground or background), in order to handle print requests. Otherwise, documents directed to the printer may be hung up or lost.

Load Mail and Schedule+ at Startup

You have already learned how useful the electronic mail and scheduling programs can be. To get the most use from these applications, you should have them loaded and in the background even when you are not using them. That way, you can be notified with a pleasant little beep when messages arrive or with an on-screen message when an appointment is approaching. We suggest you put Mail and Schedule+ in your Windows Program Manager Startup group so that they are loaded as soon as you start up Windows for Workgroups.

File-Naming Conventions

Creating file-naming conventions will take some forethought and a concerted effort from all of the group members. Windows for Workgroups uses the standard DOS file-naming convention — one-to-eight characters for the file name, a period, and then an optional one to three character file extension. For most applications that you will use in Windows for Workgroups, the file name is not particularly important, but the extension is very important because it determines the application associated with the file.

For instance, if George sends Fred a note with an attached document, Fred should be able to simply double-click on the icon of the attached document and have Windows for Workgroups launch the application that supports that file (i.e., Word for Windows, Lotus 1-2-3, Harvard Graphics, etc.). Windows for Workgroups uses the file type (actually the file extension) of the attached document to determine what application to launch. Some of the most common associations are listed in Table 14.1.

Table 14.1 Files Extensions and Associations

File Extension	Common Association
.DOC	Word for Windows
.XLS	Excel
.PPT	PowerPoint

Some applications (like WordPerfect) do not use standard or default file extensions. Therefore, the workgroup should come up with its own standard extensions, and then use File Manager to create an association between these extensions and the appropriate application.

Creating a File Association

To create an association, follow these simple steps:

1. Double-click on the file cabinet icon in the Main window to get into File Manager.
2. Open up the File command and choose the Associate... option.
3. Type in the extension for your file, as shown in Figure 14.1.
4. Tab down to the box that says Associate With: and either select one of the listed programs or type in the full path and file name for the executable file of the program of your choice. For example, C:\WPWIN\WPWIN.EXE for WordPerfect.
5. Click on OK to create the association. Then exit File Manager.

Figure 14.1

Associate window of File Manager

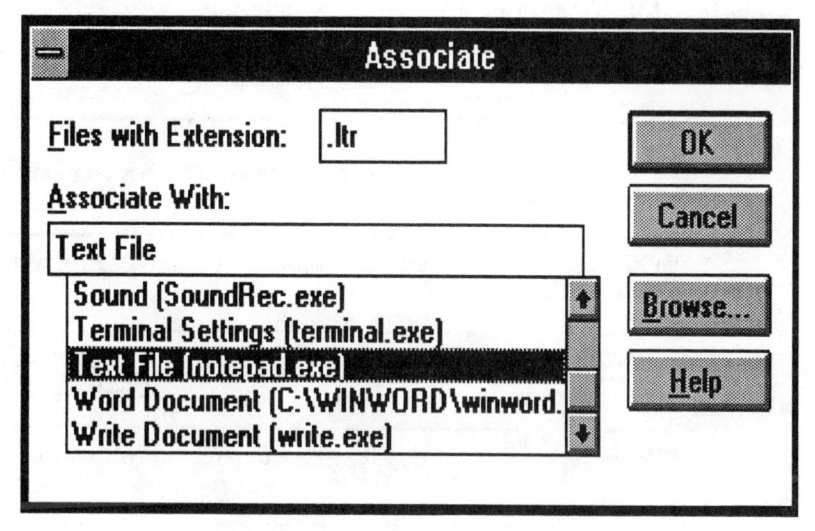

[Associate dialog box: Files with Extension: .ltr; Associate With: Text File; list showing Sound (SoundRec.exe), Terminal Settings (terminal.exe), Text File (notepad.exe), Word Document (C:\WINWORD\winword.), Write Document (write.exe); buttons: OK, Cancel, Browse..., Help]

6. Test your association by sending mail to yourself with an attached document. The document should have the extension you specified in Step 3 and be saved in the file format of the application you specified in Step 4. When you receive the e-mail note, open it and double-click on the icon for the attached note. If Windows for Workgroups launches the appropriate application (in this case, WordPerfect), then you have created the proper association. If Windows for Workgroups cannot launch your application, carefully check your file extension and application name specified in Steps 3 and 4 above. Chances are you mistyped an extension or path.

Table 14.2 contains a list of our suggestions for standard file extensions. The specific nature of the extension will help you recognize the contents of the file. Of course, this list assumes that your group uses only one word processing package (such as Word, WordPerfect, or Ami Pro).

Table 14.2 File Extensions, Contents, Association

File Extension	File Contents	Association
.DOC	any text-based data	Word for Windows
.WPW or .WP5	any text-based data	WordPerfect for Windows
.PW	any text-based data	Professional Write
.AMI	any text-based data	Ami Pro

If your workgroup uses more than one word processing package, for example, both Word and WordPerfect, you may have to be more generic in your file extension to simplify the association process. Otherwise, co-workers may want to use the .LET extension for both Word and WordPerfect files. This would make it impossible to create a unique file association. Table 14.3 contains a few of our suggestions for generic file extensions.

Table 14.3 File Extensions and Associations for Word Processing Documents

File Extension	File Contents	Association
.TXT	any type of text	Notepad, word processing
.LTR or .LET	letter	word processing
.OUT	document outline	word processing
.PRO	proposal	word processing
.ASC	any ASCII file	word processing
.FAX	facsimile material	word processing
.REF	reference material	word processing
.BRO	brochure	word processing
.LST	a list of some sort	word processing
.PRG	program file	word processing

Tips to Simplify Your Use of Windows for Workgroups

Here are a few tips and tricks that make using Windows for Workgroups much easier. Pass them along to your friends and colleagues!

Minimize, Don't Close

As you work with various applications throughout the day, get into the habit of minimizing them when you are done. This way, each application stays loaded and is ready for use at a moment's notice. You can switch to a minimized application using the techniques described previously in this chapter.

Minimizing applications does have one drawback. Each application requires computer memory (RAM) to stay in the background. If your PC has 4 MB of memory or less, you may quickly run out of memory to run your applications. Or, you may notice a slowdown in the processing of applications. To temporarily resolve this problem, close down some of the applications. To permanently resolve the problem, add more RAM to your computer. We recommend at least 8 MB of RAM for optimal performance.

Keep Your Icons Handy

You will have three or four applications that you use frequently. We recommend that you place the icons for these applications at the top of your application window. When you install Windows for Workgroups, the placement of icons is determined by the setup routine. You can rearrange your icons to make them convenient for your own use.

Keep Mail and Schedule+ Loaded and Minimized

As we mentioned earlier, loading Mail and Schedule+ as you log in to Windows for Workgroups is a good habit to develop. When you aren't actively using these applications, keep them minimized and running in the background. This will allow you to receive clues from the system that mail has arrived or an appointment is approaching.

If you receive a lot of mail throughout the day, don't feel compelled to check your in box every time a new message comes in. Wait until several messages build up, and then check the mail. Otherwise, you'll interrupt your workflow and reduce your productivity.

Putting It All Together

It takes more than new hardware and software to make workgroup computing effective — it also takes a change of work habits and procedures. In this last chapter we presented guidelines for changing those personal habits that have been ingrained over the years, and we looked at electronic alternatives to manual processes such as computing and scheduling. We talked about the need to formalize a few procedures to keep Windows for Workgroups running smoothly. Finally, we shared some tips that will get you up to speed and proficient in Windows for Workgroups in practically no time!

Now it's your turn. Networking with Windows for Workgroups offers a real opportunity to improve your personal and workgroup productivity. We've opened the first set of doors — but there's more. As you work with the features and utilities of Windows for Workgroups you'll find more ways to tailor it and shape it to your own needs. We encourage you to master the basics, then experiment with some of the advanced techniques.

Like Craig Gilbert, the subject of our Chapter 1 opening, you too can harness the power of computing. The adventure continues.

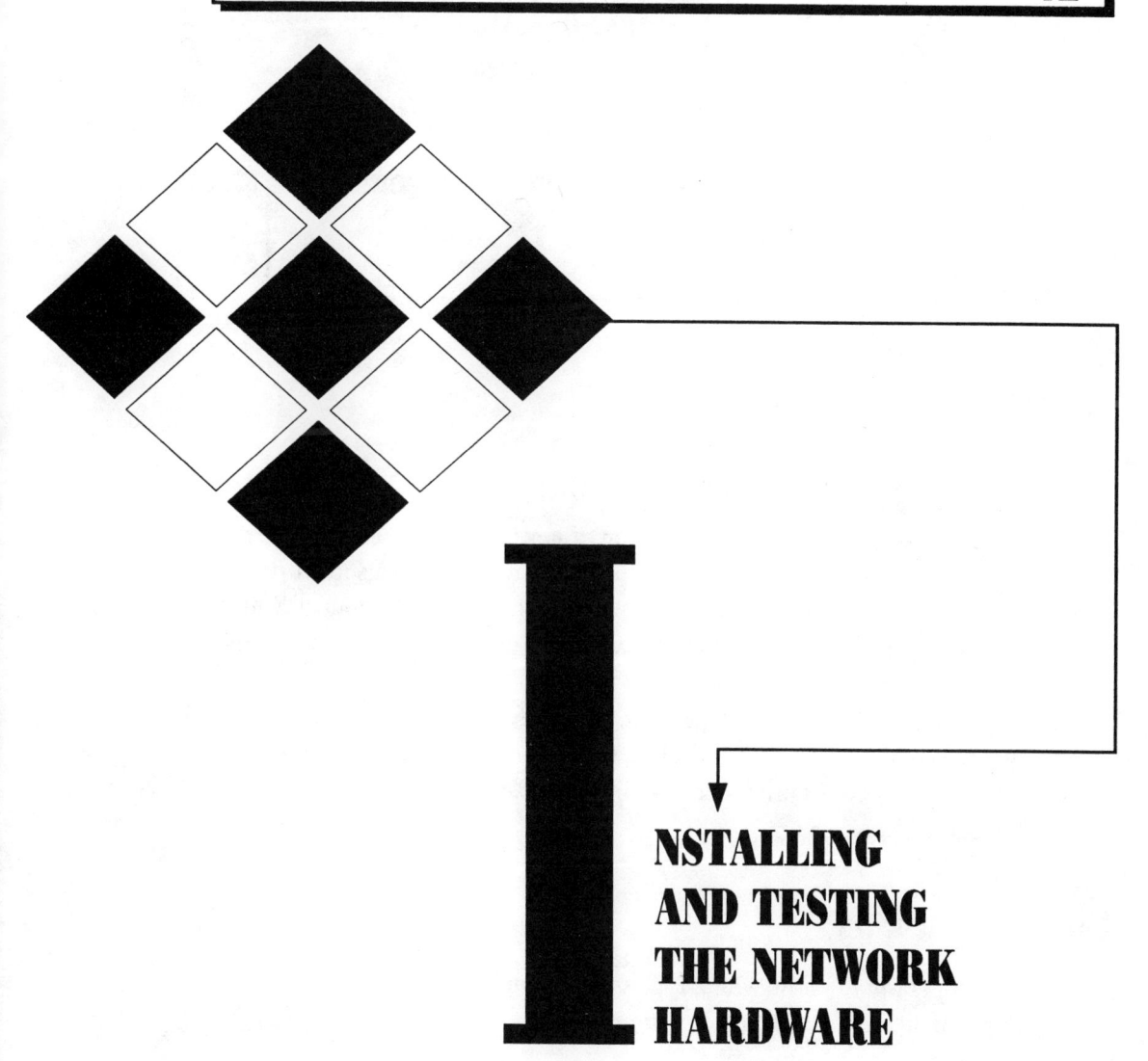

APPENDIX A

Installing and Testing the Network Hardware

APPENDIX A

FEATURING:
- Planning the Workgroup
- Installing Windows for Workgroups
- Defining Passwords

Installing network interface cards (NICs) is not difficult. Most PCs are designed to allow easy installation of new cards that will upgrade or enhance the capabilities of the machine. If you can wield a screwdriver, then you are capable of adding a network card to a PC. Of course, you must be careful and follow the correct procedures.

In this section, we will take you through hardware installation procedures. We will begin with installing the cabling, and will proceed step-by-step, from configuring and installing the card all the way to testing the network.

Choosing a Bus

It is important to know which type of bus your computer has, because this will determine whether a particular network interface card (NIC) will work in your computer.

In PCs, there are three types of bus architectures, MCA, EISA, and ISA. Micro Channel Architecture (MCA) is used in most IBM PS/2s and

NCR PCs; Enhanced Industry Standard Architecture (EISA) is used on some models of high-end computers from manufacturers such as Compaq, Acer, and AST; and Industry Standard Architecture (ISA) is used in most other brands. Examples of ISA computers include the desktop models of Compaq, Acer, Dell, and Hewlett Packard. You can add functionality to your computer by plugging adapter or interface cards into expansion slots on the bus. Figure A.1 shows an example.

Figure A.1
A 16 bit ISA expansion card

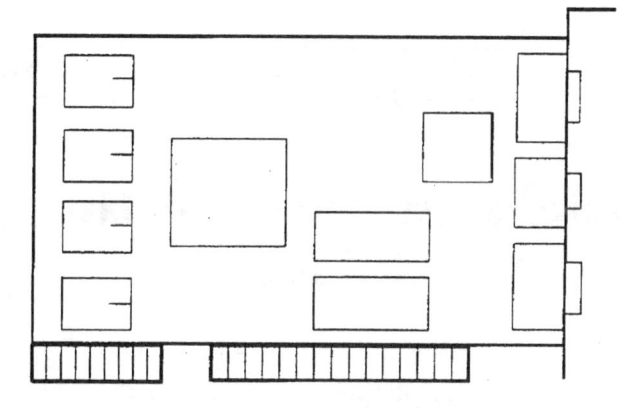

> **NOTE** All EISA expansion slots can be used for either EISA cards or ISA cards. If you are using an ISA NIC in an EISA machine, you will set up the network card as if you were installing it into a plain PC (ISA) system. Micro Channel slots, by contrast, will only work with MCA NICs.

Selecting Your Network Interface Card

Once you have determined which type of computer you have, verify that the NIC is one of the more than one hundred cards that have been tested and certified as compatible with the Windows for Workgroups operating system. See Microsoft's Windows for Workgroups reference manual for a compatibility list. If your NIC is not listed, it may or may not work with the software.

Table A.1 Expansion bus architectures

Bus Type	Cards Used	Bit Size
MCA	MCA	32-bit
EISA	EISA	32-bit
	ISA	8- or 16-bit
ISA	ISA	8- or 16-bit

Hardware Installation Task List

There are six easy steps to installing the network hardware.

1. Gather the necessary equipment.
2. Install the cabling system (run the cables and install hubs/concentrators).
3. Install the network interface cards.
4. Connect the cables to the PC.
5. Test the network hardware.
6. Install the network software.

The following section contains a detailed description of each step.

Gather the Necessary Equipment

Before you are able to start the installation procedure, it is important that you have all of the necessary equipment on hand. The requirements will depend on which step you are performing. In the case of cabling, you will need the necessary cable and cable ends for your network. Some of the tools that will help you complete the cabling job include: a weighted

Installing and Testing the Network Hardware

string for guiding the cable through the ceiling and walls; a saw for cutting holes in the wall for the face plates; a screwdriver for mounting the faceplates; and face plates.

Finally, if you are building your own cables, you will need special tools. All of your cables will need some type of cable end (depending on your type of network cabling). In order to prepare the cable, you will need tools that are designed to remove the outer coat of shielding, (also called stripping the cable). Once the cable has been striped and the end attached, you may need a crimping tool to ensure that the end will not come loose.

The next items to collect are the manuals for all of the systems you are going to be working with. For example, you may need the workstation's manual to help in setting the configuration of the NIC. The manuals for the NICs will also be important. Finally, you will want to have the manuals of the software. The software manuals will clear up any final questions as to what is supported and how it can be installed.

If you are installing network interface cards, you will have to have a PC tool kit. This kit will have a collection of screwdrivers to match most PCs. Most manufacturers use a Phillips head screw driver, but there are a few that require a flat blade. Others, Compaq being the most notable, use a special driver called a Torq head. While this in not a common type of screwdriver, most PC tool kits will include at least one Torq driver.

> **NOTE** One tool that will not be in a typical tool kit, but is very useful is a set of medical hemostats. Hemostats are much like tweezers except that they allow you to lock them in place. Hemostats are great for helping you to change jumpers (described later in this appendix) and small connectors. Hemostats are available at almost all medical supply stores.

The final materials to gather are the software disks. You will need the disks for installing the NIC, such as configuration disks and testing utilities. You will also want to have the operating system disks so that you can quickly complete the installation for each workstation.

Once you have collected all of the needed equipment, you are now ready to roll up your sleeves and jump right into the installation of your hardware.

Installing the Network Cabling

Cabling a network can be very straightforward, but if not planned well, it may be time consuming and difficult. Therefore, planning the layout of your network is extremely important. Improperly laid cable is the number one cause of network downtime, and can result in frequent and expensive visits from a network repair technician. For a more detailed look at planning your cabling scheme, refer to Chapter 2.

As suggested in Chapter 2, decide which topology to use: star-shaped (one cable for each computer), or bus (all computers on one cable) topology. Star-shaped topology has the advantage that only one computer is affected if a cable is cut or damaged. The disadvantage is that a star-shaped topology requires much more cable. The bus topology is easy to install and add stations to, but a cut or damage to almost any location on the cable will result in problems or downtime for all of the stations on the network.

For a small workgroup that has a limited number of workstations in the same office, we recommend that you use the bus topology. For a larger workgroup, or one that includes users spread out over multiple offices, we recommend one of the star-shaped topologies.

There are some important matters to consider when laying out your cable. First, ensure that your cables are long enough. Adding patches to lengthen a cable segment only weakens it and can result in a significant loss of performance. Further, the cable must be carefully routed in the walls and ceiling. Placing cables over light fixtures or near electrical conduit can cause interference with the network transmission. This can result in data loss and network downtime.

If you are not sure about how to properly cable your network, contact a professional cabling company. Many phone and computer resellers provide network cable installations at a reasonable cost.

Installing the Network Interface Card

To install your NIC, you will first need to gather up the following materials:

- ▲ The NIC board,
- ▲ Manuals for your computer and the NIC,
- ▲ Configuration or setup disks supplied by the NIC manufacturer
- ▲ A screwdriver, and
- ▲ Cables and connectors to connect to the network.

Configuring the Network Card

For the network interface card to function properly in your system, it must be configured to work with the other components in the computer. To achieve this, most cards require that you assign a value to the following settings:

- ▲ Interrupt,
- ▲ Base I/O (Input/Output) port, and
- ▲ Memory address.

Each of these settings controls how the computer's Central Processing Unit (CPU) communicates with the NIC. Every component of your computer has to have its own unique setting for interrupt request line (IRQ) and Base I/O address. If two cards have the same setting, a conflict will occur and the computer will not operate properly.

The network interface card can be configured in one of two ways: hardware configuration, or software configuration.

Hardware configuration utilizes switches or jumpers, as shown if Figures A.2 and A.3, to assign a value to each setting. Switches assign a value of *on* or *off*, and jumpers are plastic blocks that, when placed over a set of pins, short (or jump) the pins.

> **NOTE** Be careful when handling a card with switches. If something accidentally hits the switches, the card's configuration can be changed.

Figure A.2
Two types of switch blocks

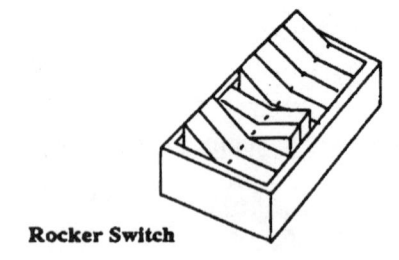

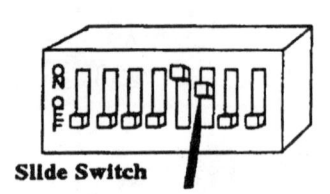

Rocker Switch   **Slide Switch**

Software configuration is accomplished by using either a setup utility for the system (in the case of EISA or Micro Channel machines) or a DOS-based program that is provided by the card manufacturer. For example, the Intel Ether Express 16 (ISA) cards do not have any jumpers or switches. The IRQ, Base I/O address, and the Base Memory address are all set by using a software utility.

Figure A.3
Pin set showing a jumper on one of the pin sets

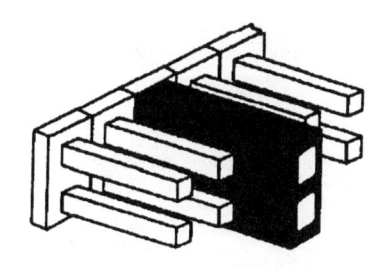

Selecting the Proper Configuration

The first step in deciding on a configuration for your network card is to record the settings for the other components in your system. You can use a purchased utility software package such as CheckIt to help tell you what settings are already in use. If you do not have access to such a program, you can physically check the equipment already installed in your computer. For example, if your computer has two serial ports (COM1 and COM2), then you cannot use IRQ 4 or IRQ 3, because your communications (serial) ports are already using them (as shown in Tables A.2 and A.3).

You can photocopy Table A.2 and use it as a form to record the settings for your system. Many components, such as communications ports (COM), printer ports (LPT), and floppy controllers, do not require the use of a Base Memory Address (Base memory in Table A.2), but some NICs do require this setting. Further, you should keep the photocopied form handy when installing Windows for Workgroups so that you can record the network card's settings.

Table A.2 Standard hardware configurations

Hardware	IRQ	Base I/O	Base memory address
COM1	4	3F8	
COM2	3	2F8	
LPT1	7	3BC	
LPT2	5	378	
Floppy Controller	6	3F0	
Hard Disk Controller	14	1F0	
Mouse			
Modem			
Network Card			
Sound Card			

NOTE The best way to configure your NIC is to leave the settings as they were when shipped from the manufacturer. These settings are called defaults, and are selected to work in as many different types of computers as possible.

Setting the IRQ

Most components in a computer require an IRQ. The interrupt is used to notify the CPU that it has a request. If two or more components share the same IRQ, then the computer will not know which component to work with. The result is that all of the conflicting cards will cease to function properly, and can possibly cause the entire computer to "crash."

For most PCs, the NIC can be set for either IRQ 2, IRQ 3, IRQ 5, or IRQ 10. These settings are generally available, however, consult with Table A.2 to determine if they are used in your system.

If the suggested settings are in use in your computer, or if you want to use a different setting, consult Table A.3. This table lists the interrupts and the devices that use them. An available IRQ will be one of the ones marked as Available, or one listing a component that is not in use in your system.

> **NOTE** If your NIC supports setting the IRQ to 10, we suggest that you use this setting. IRQ 10 is rarely used, and will work well with almost any computer.

Although Table A.3 applies to most computer systems, it is possible that your system will require a modification to the table. If you have a problem with one of the settings, be sure to check your system's manuals. For example, some VGA cards require IRQ for their exclusive use. If this is the case, simply note that on Table A.3 and select a new setting for your NIC.

> **NOTE** Some manufacturers of clone I/O boards do not release the IRQ even after the port is shut off. For example, a card that is capable of having two serial ports may use both IRQ 4 (for COM1) and IRQ 3 (for COM2) even if there is only a COM1 in the system.

Table A.3 Standard devices and their IRQ

IRQ	PC/AT Component
2	EGA\VGA
3	COM2, COM4
4	COM1, COM3
5	LPT2 (if present) otherwise available
6	Floppy Disk Controller
7	LPT1 (first Parallel port)
8	Real-time Clock
9	Redirects to IRQ2
10	Available
11	Available
12	Available
13	Math Coprocessor
14	Hard Disk Controller
15	Available

Installing and Testing the Network Hardware

If the network interface card fails to function after selecting an available IRQ, then switch the setting and try again.

Setting Up the Base I/O Port

The Base I/O Port is the hexadecimal address that is used by the CPU to communicate with each device. The NIC will require a unique address if the computer is going to be able to communicate with it and the other components in your PC. Table A.4 lists the commonly used port addresses. Setting your network card for any of the listed addresses may result in a failure for the NIC or the listed device.

If your computer does not (or will not) have a game port, then it's a good idea to use port address 200-20F. Otherwise, feel free to use another address that will not conflict with other installed components. Once the Base I/O has been set, you are ready to select the Base Memory Address.

Setting the Base Memory Address

Depending on the NIC card you use, you may not have to set a base memory address. Some NICs require memory space to load operating information in the computer's memory. This memory is typically information that is copied from a ROM chip on the NIC to the computer's RAM for faster access. A typically free memory address is D8000. Other NIC cards have memory installed on the card and don't require you to select a base memory address.

> **NOTE:** If you are using an expanded memory manager (such as QEMM, BlueMax, or EMM386), you may need to exclude the network interface card's Base Memory Address. Including this address range can result in network communication failures. Check your memory management documentation to see if and how you can accomplish this exclusion.

Table A.4 Used I/O port addresses

Port Address	Device
200 - 20F	Game Port
230 - 23F	Bus Mouse
270 - 27F	LPT3
2F0 - 2FF	COM2
320 - 32F	Hard Disk Controller
370 - 37F	LPT2
3B0 - 3BF	LPT1
3C0 - 3CF	EGA/VGA
3D0 - 3DF	CGA/MCGA (EGA/VGA in color video modes)
3F0 - 3FF	Floppy Disk Controller, COM1

Placing the NIC into the PC

The first step to installing the NIC into your PC is to turn off and unplug the computer. Turning off the computer will protect the components from damage when you place a new card into the system, and disconnecting the power cable will protect you from getting an electrical shock.

Next, remove the outside cover from the computer as in Figure A.4. Most computer cases require you to remove one to three screws from the back of the case. Once the screws are removed, the case cover slides forward or upward.

Figure A.4
Cover being removed from a desktop case

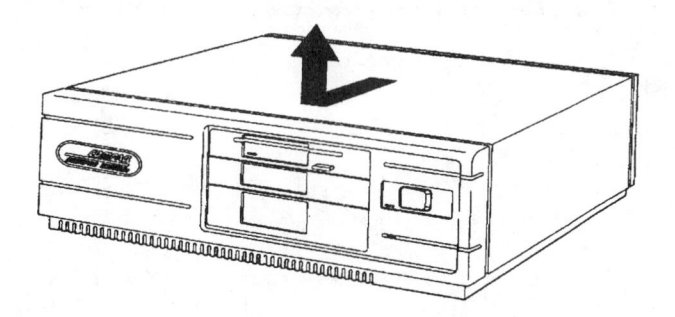

With the case cover removed, you should be able to see the bus expansion slots as shown in Figure A.5.

Figure A.5
Looking down on the PC's expansion sockets

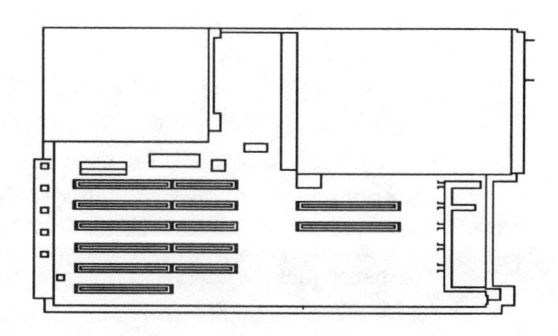

Next, you must select the appropriate expansion slot for your NIC. In ISA and EISA systems, the expansion slots will have one socket (8-bit) or two sockets (16-bit) to plug the card in. MCA computers will only have one type of expansion slot. Some slots may have three sockets, these are special 32-bit sockets and are not to be used for the NIC.

For ISA computers, it is preferred that you place an 8 bit card into an 8 bit socket (although it can be placed in a 16 bit socket). A 16 bit card, on the other hand, cannot be placed in an 8 bit socket; it has to be set in a 16 bit socket.

After you have selected the proper slot, you will need to remove the protective slot cover from the back of the case as shown in Figure A.6.

Figure A.6
Removing the slot cover plate

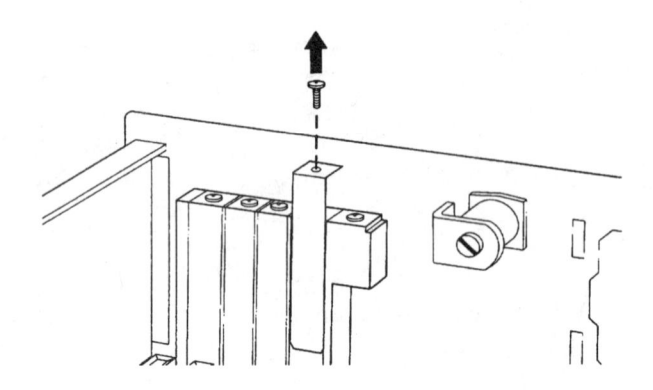

Next, the network interface card is seated into the slot. Be sure the card is firmly plugged into the slot and that you are able to put the holding screw back into place. If the card is not seated correctly, it can damage your computer and the new network interface card. (See Figure A.7.)

To ensure that the card remains in the slot, replace the screw that you removed from the protective cover, and use it to hold the NIC in place.

Figure A.7
Inserting the NIC into the socket

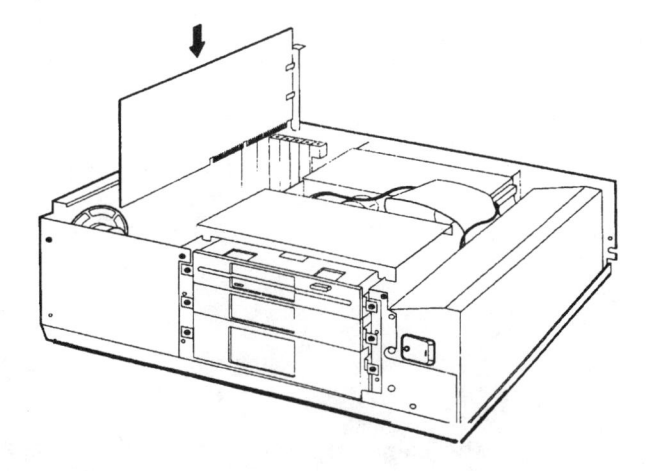

To complete the installation, replace the case cover and plug the computer back in. Turn on the computer to ensure that the system will boot up and work properly.

> **NOTE**
> If the NIC that you have just installed requires configuration, perform that task now. Consult the section of this appendix on configuring the network card to find the appropriate settings for your card.

Connecting to the Network

Now that you have successfully installed the NIC, it's time to attach the computer to the network, which task is simply a matter of attaching the network cable to the new NIC. The type of cable attachment that you will use depends on the type of network that you are installing.

Thin Ethernet is a linear topology. This means that the cable connecting all of the computers on the network runs to each station as shown in Figure A.8.

Figure A.8
Attaching a workstation to a Thin Ethernet network cable

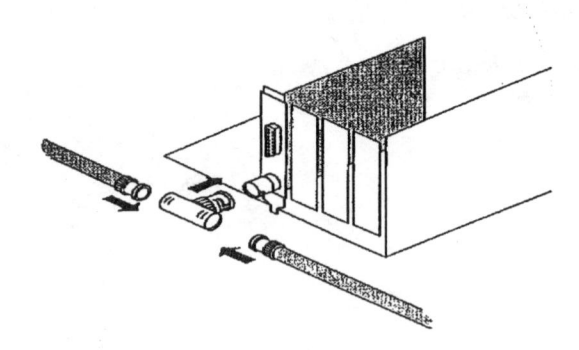

The cable comes in to one side of a T connector and leaves out of the other side. The cable continues this way from station to station. Capping the cable at each end is a terminator. The terminator completes the circuit and allows the stations to communicate up and down the line.

> **NOTE** If you break the cable at any point (between the terminators), the network will not be able to function, be sure that all of the users are logged out of the network before you add a new cable length or cut the cable to add a new PC.

Twisted Pair Ethernet uses a connector that looks like a big version of the one on the end of your phone line. The connector plugs in the same way. This connector is plugged into the NIC at one end and to a concentrator at the other end, as shown in Figure A.9.

The concentrator has plugs for several computers, and sends the network transmissions to any other station that is plugged into the concentrator.

Token Ring also uses twisted pair cable, but the connector for the NIC is different. As shown in Figure A.10, the cable plugs straight into the adapter card at one end and connects to a Multistation Access Unit (MSAU) at the other end.

Figure A.9

Three workstations connected to one concentrator

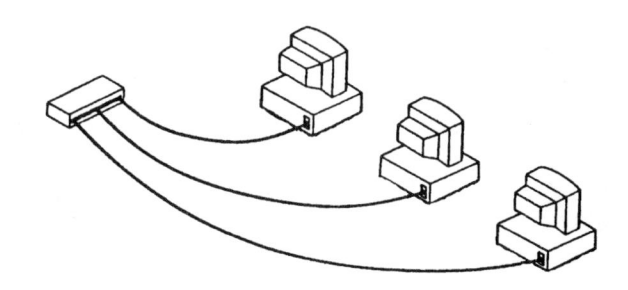

An MSAU works just like a concentrator for Twisted Pair Ethernet, but each MSAU is connected to the next one in the chain, making a ring (hence the name).

ArcNet network cable connections work in the same manner as Twisted Pair Ethernet. The main difference is that ArcNet utilizes coaxial cable, and connects to the workstation using a BNC connector (see Figure A.11).

All of the workstations are attached to each other by a hub. In the case of ArcNet, there are two types of hubs, active and passive.

Figure A.10

Connecting Token Ring cable to a workstation

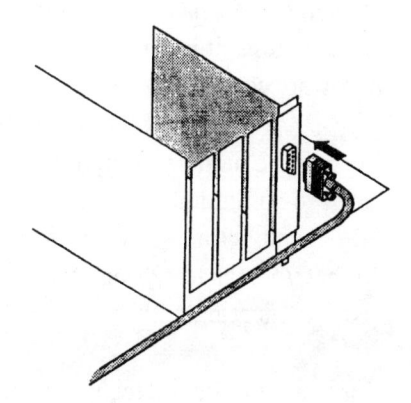

Figure A.11
Connecting a workstation
to ArcNet cable

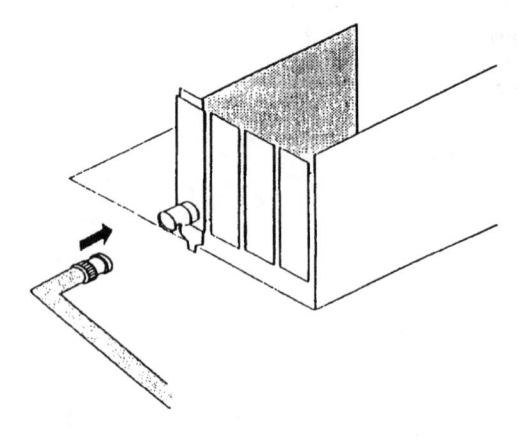

> **NOTE:** ArcNet passive hubs have a history of being unreliable and difficult to diagnose. Therefore, we recommend that you only use active hubs on your ArcNet networks.
>
> For more information on cabling and network topologies, see Chapter 2.

Testing the Network

Once the NICs have been installed and cables are connected to the workstations, it is time to test the network to make sure that all of the hardware components are functioning properly.

Testing the hardware requires a utility software program that allows the cards to communicate without using a network operating system. Several NIC manufacturers, such as Proteon and Intel, provide just such a utility so that you can test your network cards and cables by sending packets to (communicating with) the other stations on the network.

For example, Intel's testing utility, called Softset, involves setting up one station as a receiver and a second station as a sender. The sending station simply sends modulated pulses down the network cable. The receiving unit picks up the pulses and checks to see if they are within specifications. If the network is not functioning properly, you can check to see if the problem is with a NIC in one of the machines or with the cable that connects the two computers.

Testing the network hardware before you install the operating system is helpful because it signals problems related to hardware or the network installation, rather than software malfunctions. For example, if the cards are unable to communicate, either the problem will be found in the NIC and its configuration, or it will be the result of faulty cables.

If you wait and test the network using the operating system, then your list of potential problems grows to include the network operating system, Windows for Workgroups, the user's configuration, and the network hardware. Since 90% of correcting a problem is knowing where it is, limiting the list to hardware problems will make diagnosis and repair easier and less time consuming.

Install the Network Software

Now that all of the hardware has been installed and tested, it is now time to install the operating system. Installation of the operating system should be much easier now that you know all of the hardware is functioning properly. Further, you also have a list of all of the types of NICs for each machine and their settings. For a detailed explanation of the software installation, please read Chapter 3.

In this appendix, we examined the steps to install the hardware needed to turn stand-alone computers into a functioning network. We also provided a step-by-step list of how to install the hardware and ensure that it is functioning properly.

With network hardware installed and functioning properly, you can install the Windows for Workgroups software. See Chapter 3 for details.

APPENDIX B

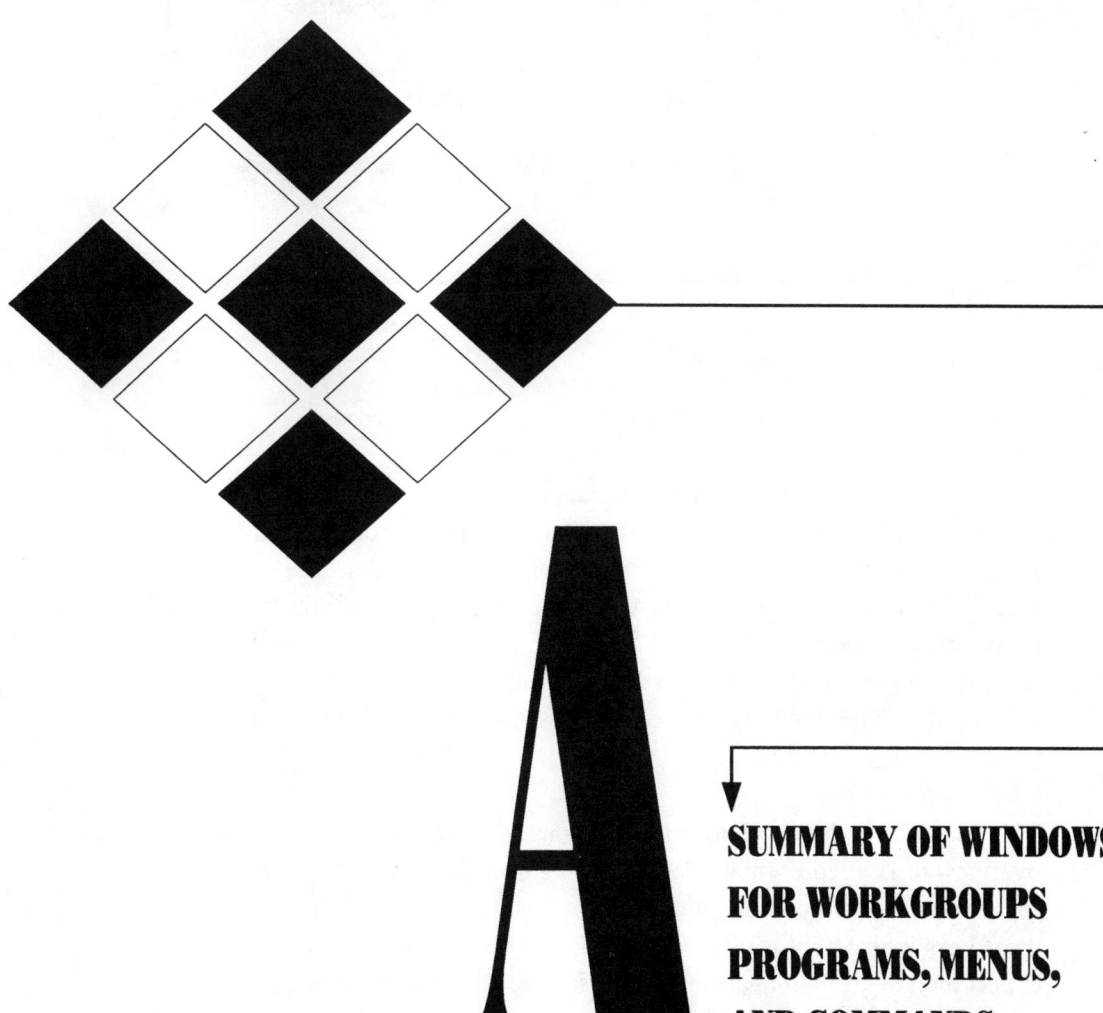

A SUMMARY OF WINDOWS FOR WORKGROUPS PROGRAMS, MENUS, AND COMMANDS

APPENDIX B

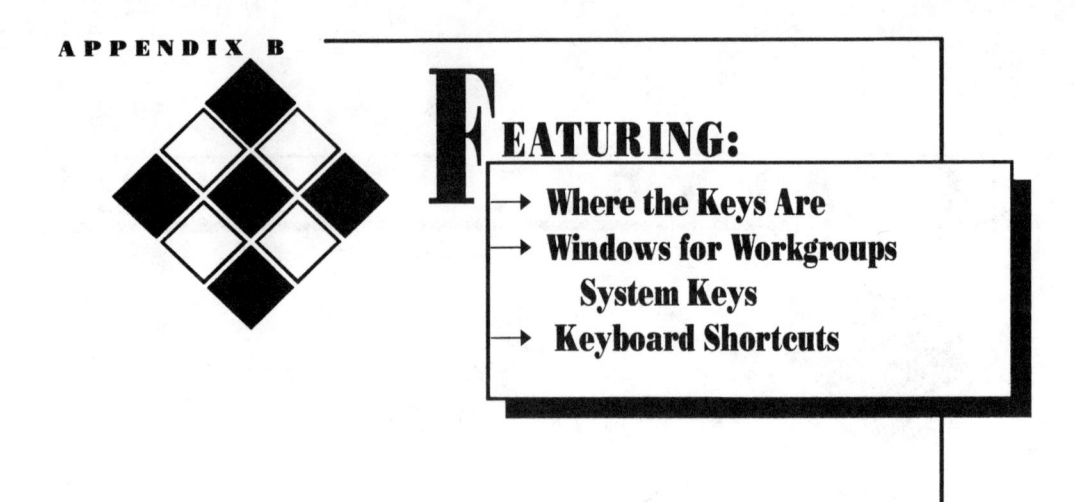

FEATURING:

- Where the Keys Are
- Windows for Workgroups System Keys
- Keyboard Shortcuts

This appendix contains a list of programs that come with Windows for Workgroups, and the keyboard shortcuts you can use to control them. It's handy to know these shortcuts when you don't have a mouse, or you don't have the room to use one — when you're using a laptop on an airplane, for instance. As you learn them, you may find that you prefer using the keyboard shortcuts for some commands even when you have a mouse. Most experienced users tend to go with a mix of keyboard- and mouse-driven commands.

This appendix is divided into seven sections. The first will give you an overview of key representations, describing how the control keys are represented in this book. Because many software manufacturers use these keys in different ways, this section also describes what you can expect the keys to do in various circumstances. Remember, though, these are just guidelines; what the keys actually do in a given application depends on the software manufacturer.

In sections 2 through 6, we'll discuss the system keystrokes. We'll divide up keys within menus, dialog boxes, editing keys, cursor movement keys and keyboard shortcuts for Windows programs. These are keystrokes that are common across Windows applications, including Windows for Workgroups. Finally, we'll talk about keystrokes to control the programs that come with Windows for Workgroups. Most of these will be covered in sections 2 through 6, but if a Windows for Workgroups program has unique keyboard shortcuts, this is where you will find them. This section includes a short description of each application that comes with Windows for Workgroups, to give you an idea of what features are available.

Not every program command or action will have a keyboard equivalent. Some actions, like drawing, are impossible to do from a keyboard. But the keyboard sequences described here will enable you to do almost everything else in the system without a mouse.

Where the Keys Are

In this section we represent the keys in capital letters. The letter and number keys are probably obvious, but most of the other ones can look different and appear in different places on different keyboards.

ARROW Keys: PAGE UP, PAGE DOWN, HOME, and END: The **ARROW** keys move the cursor up, down, left, or right. On some keyboards they appear on the number pad, while on others they appear in a block of keys separate from the rest. Typically, they move the cursor one "step" in the direction in which they point; the size of the step depends on what you're doing.

You will usually find the **PAGE UP** and **PAGE DOWN** keys on either the number pad or on a block of keys to the left of the number pad. They move the current object up one screen or one "page," whatever makes sense for your application.

The **HOME** and **END** keys also appear on the numeric keypad, or within a block of keys to the left of the numbers. A common convention is for HOME to move the cursor to the top or left-most edge of what you're currently working on (the top of a screen or the start of a line, for instance), while pressing END often moves the cursor to the bottom or the right edge of whatever you're working on.

Your keyboard might have one or two SHIFT keys, either toward the lower left of the letters or at both lower corners. They all do the same thing: when you hold them down and press a letter key, the capitalized version of that letter appears on your screen. Some applications also use the SHIFT keys to increase the number of operations you can perform from the keyboard; thus, holding down the SHIFT key and pressing HOME does something different than just pressing the HOME key.

The **CTRL** (Control) key is usually found to the left of the letters. You hold it down while striking another key. Such sequences are often reserved for special system functions.

The **ALT** key is found to the left of the letters on the keyboard or possibly on either side of them. This is another key that you usually hold down while depressing another key. It's also a special function key.

The **Backspace** key is found on the upper right of the keyboard. It is used to erase a character to the left of the pointer.

The **ESC** (Escape) key may be on the upper left of the keyboard or the upper right. It can be used to cancel whatever you're currently doing and restore a previous value.

The **ENTER** key is found in the same place on a computer keyboard as on a typewriter: to the right of the letter keys. It completes the current action or tells the computer to process some input that you have typed.

As on a typewriter, the **TAB** key is to the left of the letters. When you are working in a window that has several boxes, or fields, the TAB key will move you to the next field, and holding down the tab key and pressing SHIFT will move you back to the previous one.

A row of keys across the top of your keyboard or a double row down the left side are your **FUNCTION** keys (F1 through F12). You probably have 10 or 12 of them, depending on your keyboard. What they do depends on your current application.

You will probably find the **DEL** key on your numeric keypad or the block just to the left of it. Use it to delete characters to the right of the pointer (or cursor). Conversely, the backspace key deletes characters to the left of the pointer. (See BACKSPACE key, mentioned earlier in this chapter.)

Typically used to switch between inserting and overstriking, the **INSERT** key is probably near the DEL key, either on the number pad or in a block to the left of it.

Windows for Workgroups System Keys

In some cases you must press two or more keys to complete an action. For some actions you press keys one after another, and for others you must hold down one key while you press another. When we show keys with a comma (,) between them, it means you should press the first one, then the next; when we show them with a plus sign (+) between them, it means you need to hold down the first one while pressing the second. For instance, a command might require you to press the ESC key, then the F2 key, which would look like this: ESC, F2. Another command might require you to hold down the ALT key and at the same time press the TAB key, which will look like this: ALT+TAB.

The following key sequences are available whenever you're running Windows for Workgroups, except as indicated.

ALT+TAB: You may find ALT+TAB to be one of the most useful key sequences. To understand what it does, picture a list of the programs you have currently running, either full screen, in windows, or minimized as icons. This key combination switches you to the next program in the list. It's very useful when running a DOS-based application (like a DOS prompt) on the full screen instead of a window, because when a program is running full screen, you have nowhere to click your mouse to switch to another window.

But this key combination has another, even niftier feature. Hold down the ALT key and tap the TAB key without letting up on the ALT key. A window pops up in the middle of the screen showing the next program in your list of running programs (see Figure B.1). Now, still holding the ALT key, tap the TAB key again. The window now shows the name of the next program in your list. Continuing in this way, Windows will show you the names of all your running programs, and will circle back to the one you started with. If you release the ALT key while the pop-up window is showing, Windows will switch you to the program whose name is in the window at that time. This can be a big time saver.

Figure B.1
ALT+TAB pops up a window showing the next program in the list

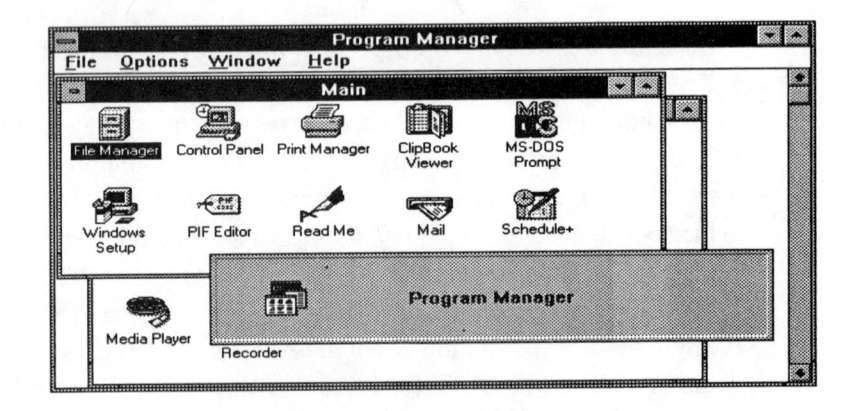

If you hold down the SHIFT key while executing this key combination, it will go through the list of running applications in reverse order.

If you execute this key combination while you are running a DOS-based program in full-screen mode, you'll see a full-screen window listing the names of the programs instead of a pop-up window in the middle of your screen.

ALT+ESC: This key sequence switches you to the next application. If it is running in a window or full screen, Windows makes it the current window; if it is running as an icon, Windows activates that icon (and highlights the name under the icon). If you press ENTER while an icon's name is highlighted, Windows will enlarge it to a window.

If you are running a full-screen DOS-based application when you press ALT+ESC, Windows will minimize your DOS-based program to an icon before switching to the next program.

CTRL+ESC: This key combination brings up the task list in a window in the center of your screen (see Figure B.2). If you are running a full-screen, DOS-based application when you press CTRL+ESC, Windows will minimize your DOS-based program and switch you to a Windows-based program before it displays the Task list.

Figure B.2

The Windows for Workgroups Task list

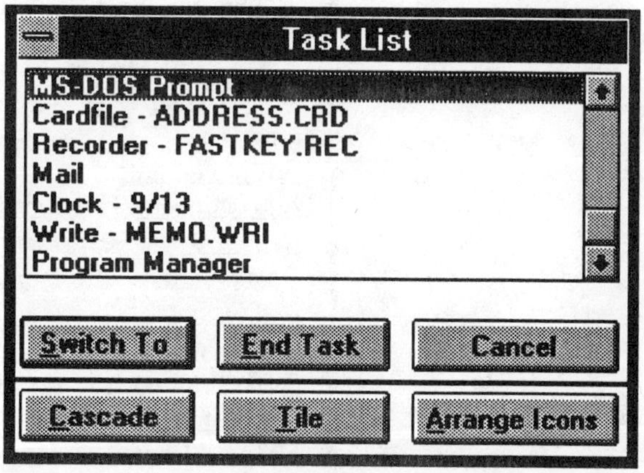

PRNTSCR: When you press this key, Windows for Workgroups will take a snapshot of your screen and copy it to the Clipboard (see Chapter 4 for more information about using the Clipboard).

ALT+PRNTSCR: Similar to PRNT+SCRN, but this key combination copies an image of the active window to the Clipboard, rather than the entire screen.

F1: Software manufacturers generally reserve the F1 function key for on-line help. A sample help screen is shown in Figure B.3. That way, no matter what program you're running, you can always press F1 get more information. This can make a new program much easier to learn. All programs that come with Windows for Workgroups follow this convention, but other programs might not, so beware.

Figure B.3

A sample Help screen: help for Cardfile ALT,spacebar or ALT+spacebar

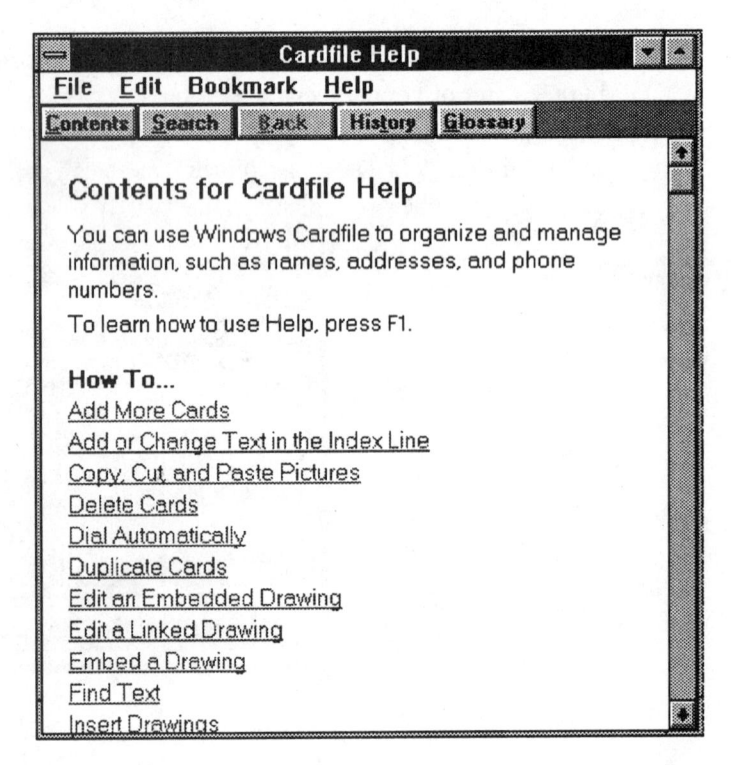

ALT+spacebar: When a Windows-based application is running in the current window, this key sequence opens the Control menu for that window. All windows have a Control menu (as shown in Figure B.4). See Chapter 4 for more information on what Control menus do.

Figure B.4

A sample Control menu: The Clock program's Control menu

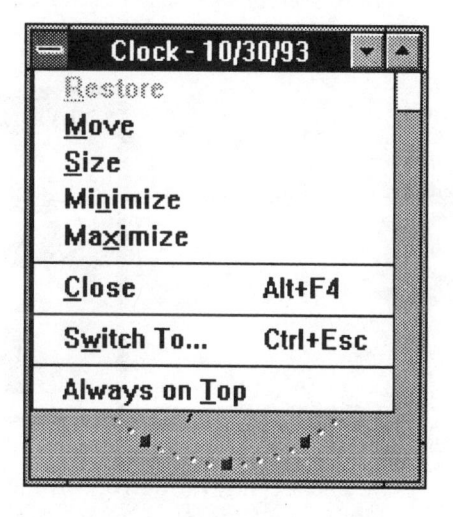

ALT+spacebar: When a DOS-based application is running in the current window, this key sequence opens the Control menu for that window. See Figure B.5.

Figure B.5

Control menu for a DOS program running in a window

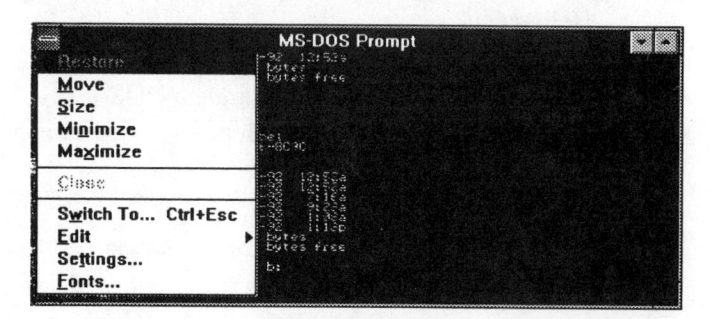

ALT,dash or ALT+dash: When the current window is a document window rather than an application window, this sequence opens the Control menu for the window.

ALT+F4: This sequence closes the current window. If the current window is an application window, it will also exit the application. The application may prompt you to perform some actions before exiting, such as saving files, as shown in Figure B.6. Depending on the application, some DOS-based or Windows applications may not allow you to exit this way.

Figure B.6

Dialog box to confirm Exit command

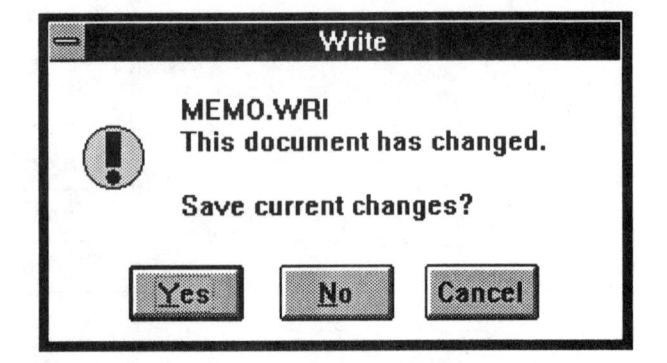

CTRL+F4: If the current window is a document window, this sequence will close it. If the current window is a group window (for example, from the Main group in your Program Manager), it will close that group. See Chapter 4 for more about group windows and document windows, or run the Windows for Workgroups tutorial from the Program Manager Help menu.

ALT+ENTER: If you are running a DOS-based application in a window, this sequence will switch it to run full screen; if it's already running full screen, this switches it to run in a window.

ARROW Keys: Among the things you can do from a window's Control menu are resizing and moving the window. If you select one of those operations, the arrow keys then let you do the moving or resizing. Press ENTER to complete the operation, and the ARROW keys revert to whatever function the current window has for them.

Keys You Can Use within Menus

In Chapter 4 you saw a description of the parts of a window. One important part is the menu bar. This section describes the keys you can use to perform actions in menu bars. Refer to Figure B.7 for a sample menu bar.

Figure B.7

Sample menu bar with a drop-down menu opened

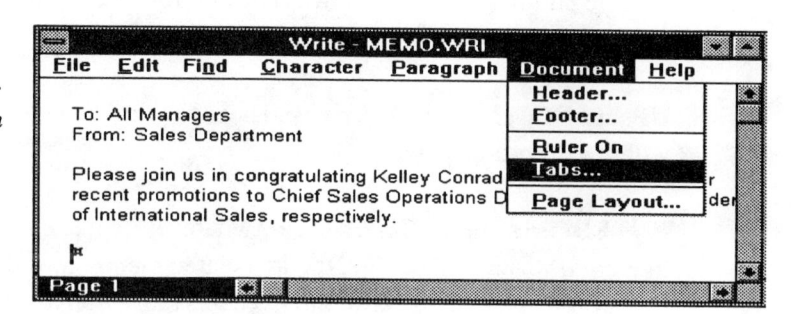

ALT or F10: This is the key you use to activate the menu bar. As shown in Figure B.8, it highlights the first menu on the bar, making the menu keystroke sequences available to you. If a menu is already highlighted, pressing ALT or F10 unhighlights it and returns you to your previous task (as does pressing ESC).

Figure B.8

Menu bar with Edit menu highlighted

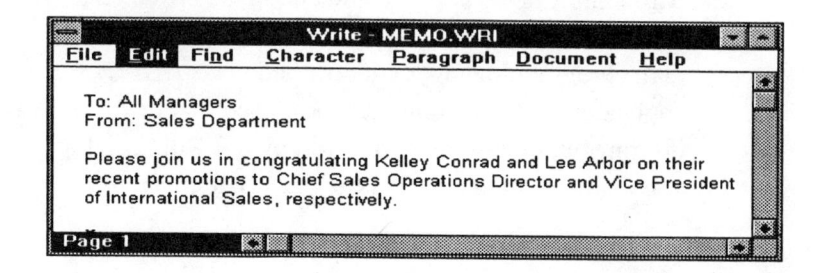

Underlined Letters: As you can see in Figure B.7, each of the menu names across the menu bar has one of its letters underlined, as do all the items in the drop-down menus. These letters serve as shortcut keys: when the menu bar is active (one of the menu names is highlighted), typing the underlined letter will take you directly to that menu and drop it down. If you are already in a drop-down menu, typing the letter will execute the menu item. ALT+ the letter will also pull down the menu.

LEFT and RIGHT ARROW Keys: These keys move you between the possible menus on the menu bar, including the Control menus and the Restore button (see the Windows Tutorial for more information about these menus).

UP and DOWN ARROW Keys: These keys move you up and down within a drop-down menu.

ENTER: Pressing ENTER chooses whatever item is currently highlighted. If it is a menu name, the associated menu drops down. If it is an item within a menu, the program executes the action associated with that item.

ESC: If a pull-down menu is visible, pressing ESC will close it, but leave the menu name highlighted. If a menu name is highlighted with no menu open, pressing ESC will return you to your application task.

An example of executing menu commands from the keyboard: to exit Windows and return to the DOS prompt without using the mouse, switch to the Program Manager window and press ALT, f, x. If you have any applications running that must be closed before you exit, Windows will inform you; otherwise it will present you with a dialog box asking you if you really mean to exit. Pressing ENTER confirms the action, and Windows exits.

Keys You Can Use within Dialog Boxes

When Windows or your application need some information from you, you will see a dialog box. (See Figure B.9.) These key sequences are available when you are within a dialog box. See Chapter 4 for information on the parts of a dialog box.

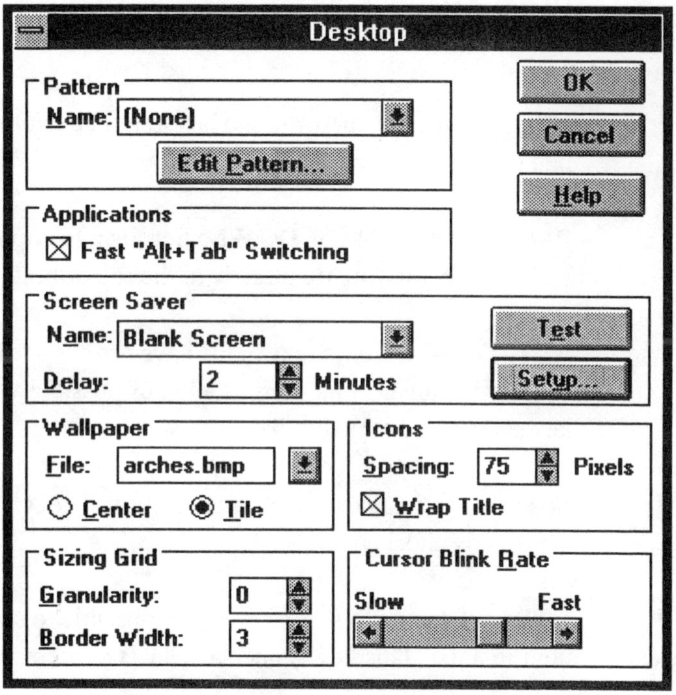

Figure B.9

A dialog box with text, lists, radio buttons, check boxes, and command buttons

TAB: The parts of a dialog box (text boxes, list boxes, check boxes, radio buttons, and command buttons) are called *fields*. The TAB key moves you between the fields of a dialog box. The field that is currently active will be outlined darker than the others, or will have a dotted line around it. The TAB key will skip any boxes that are not available for the current operation.

SHIFT+TAB: Like TAB, moves you between fields, but in reverse order.

ALT+letter: This key sequence takes you to the field that has that letter underlined.

ARROW Keys: The ARROW keys move you between options within a field.

HOME: Moves the cursor to the first item in a list or the first character in a text box.

END: Moves the cursor to the last item in a list or after the last character in a text box.

PAGE UP and PAGE DOWN: Scrolls a list up or down one screen. Has no effect if you are already at the top or bottom of the list.

ALT+DOWN: Some text fields have arrows at the right edge of the box, which means that there is a list of possible values available. This key sequence opens that list.

Spacebar: Clears or selects a check box. The X in the box indicates that the item is checked.

CTRL+/(slash): In some cases it is possible to select more than one item in a list. This key sequence selects all items in the current list.

CTRL-\ (backslash): When you have selected more than one item in a list, this key sequence will deselect all items except the one on which the cursor currently rests.

SHIFT+ARROW Key: If you are selecting multiple list items or characters, this sequence selects another one in the direction of the arrow. If you have already selected the items, it will cancel the selections one at a time.

SHIFT+HOME: When selecting multiple items, this sequence selects everything from the current cursor position to the first character in the list. When items are already selected, this cancels them.

SHIFT+END: This sequence is like SHIFT+HOME, but it goes to the end of the box instead of the beginning.

ENTER: Selects the command button that is currently active. Common command buttons are **OK** (executes the action of the box), **Cancel** (leaves the box without doing anything), and **Help**.

ESC or ALT+F4: Closes the dialog box without performing the action.

Editing Keys and Where You Can Use Them

When your cursor is within some text, such as a document in a Write window (see Figure B.10) or a file name in a dialog box, these keys will let you perform simple editing on that text, including selecting text to be copied, moved, or deleted. Depending on what type of text you are editing, not all of these key sequences will be available.

Figure B.10
Text window with a block of text selected

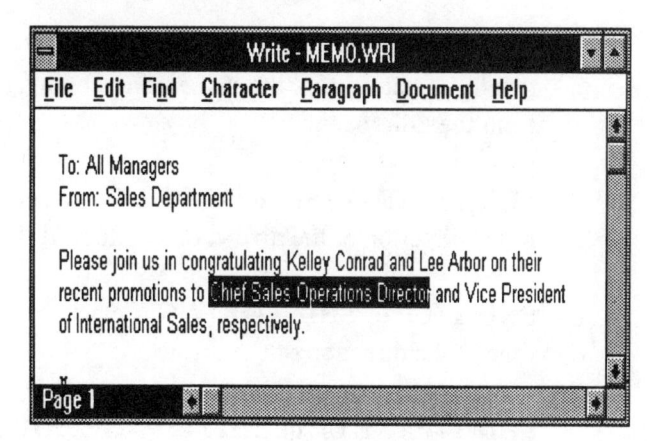

Backspace: Erases the character to the left of the cursor. Backspace has no effect if the cursor is at the beginning of the line. Depending on the application, however, backspace will move the cursor to the end of the last line. If you have selected some text, such as a word or sentence, the backspace key will delete it.

DEL: Erases the character to the right of the cursor. DEL has no effect if the cursor is at the end of the line. If you have selected some text, such as a word or sentence, the DEL key will delete it.

CTRL+INS or CTRL+C: When you have selected some text, these sequences will copy the block onto the Clipboard. The text remains selected.

SHIFT+DEL or CTRL+X: When you have selected some text, these sequences will cut the block onto the Clipboard, deleting it from your document.

SHIFT+INS or CTRL+V: These sequences will paste text from the Clipboard into your document at the point where the cursor currently rests. If you have not placed anything on the Clipboard, these sequences will have no effect.

ALT+Backspace or CTRL+Z: The "undo" command; restores your text to its state before the last editing command. Undo is also available from the Edit menu.

SHIFT+LEFT or SHIFT+RIGHT: Selects text one character at a time in the direction of the arrow, or deselects it if it is already selected.

SHIFT+UP or SHIFT+DOWN: Selects or deselects text one line at a time in the direction of the arrow.

SHIFT+PAGE UP or SHIFT+PAGE DOWN: Selects or deselects everything from the current cursor position to one screen above or below it.

SHIFT+HOME: Selects or deselects text to the beginning of the current line.

SHIFT+END: Selects or deselects text to the end of the current line.

CTRL+SHIFT+LEFT: Selects or deselects to the start of the previous word.

CTRL+SHIFT+RIGHT: Selects or deselects to the start of the next word.

CTRL+SHIFT+HOME: Selects or deselects everything from the current position to the start of the document.

CTRL+SHIFT+END: Selects or deselects everything from the current position to the end of the document.

Keys to Move the Cursor Around

These keys will help you move around more quickly when you are working in text blocks.

UP: Moves the cursor up one line.

DOWN: Moves the cursor down one line.

RIGHT: Moves the cursor to the right one character. Sometimes it will wrap you back to the end of the previous line if you're at the start of a line, but this depends on the application.

LEFT: Moves the cursor to the left one character, and possibly to the start of the next line if you're at the end.

CTRL+RIGHT: Moves you to the start of the previous word.

CTRL+LEFT: Moves you to the start of the next word.

HOME: Moves you to the beginning of the current line.

END: Moves you to the end of the current line.

PAGE UP: Moves you up one screen.

PAGE DOWN: Moves you down one screen.

CTRL+HOME: Moves you to the top of the current document.

CTRL+END: Moves you to the end of the current document.

Keyboard Shortcuts for Windows for Workgroups Programs

This section examines each of the programs that comes with Windows for Workgroups and lists the keyboard shortcuts that each program supports. Note that each program has many more functions that do not have keyboard shortcuts; the functions listed here are just the most frequently used. Refer to the menu bars and toolbars for each program to see what other functions they offer.

Program Manager

The Program Manager is the first program that you see when you start Windows for Workgroups, and it is the program that runs all the others. It contains *groups* of programs, represented by icons. Figure B.11, for instance, shows the Program Manager window with the Main group open and icons for the Startup, Games, Applications, and Accessories groups. Every program in a group has an icon, and sometimes two programs will have the same icon. You can tell them apart by the name under the icon.

ARROW Keys: These keys move you between program icons in the current group. They have no effect if you do not have a group open.

CTRL+F6 or CTRL+TAB: These sequences move you between groups, whether they are open windows or group icons.

Figure B.11

The Program Manager window with the Main group open

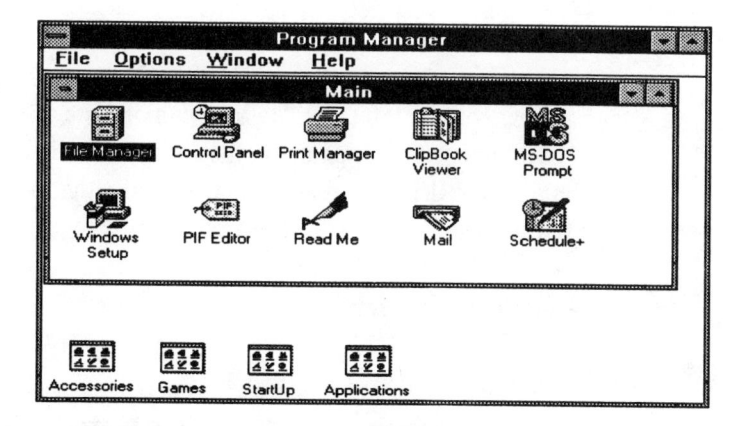

ENTER: Starts the currently highlighted application if you're in a group window, or opens the group window if you're currently on a group icon.

SHIFT+F4: Moves all your open group windows so they do not overlap. This is known as *tiling* your windows.

SHIFT+F5: Moves your open group windows so they overlap with just the title bar of each one showing. This is called *cascading* your windows.

CTRL+F4: Closes the window of the current group. Has no effect if there is no currently open group window.

ALT+F4: Closes down the Program Manager; this will exit Windows. Windows will ask you to confirm the operation before it drops you back to a DOS prompt.

File Manager

The File Manager does exactly that: manages the system files. From it you can move, copy, and delete files, search for particular files, and look at what files you have on all available drives. It has three main sections: the directory tree box (which lists all the directories on the current drive and appears on the left), the file box (which lists all the files in the current directory and appears on the right), and the drive box (which lists all the possible drives and appears just below the toolbar), with different key sequences in each. (See Figure B.12)

TAB or F6: moves you between the Directory Tree, File List, and Drive boxes.

Figure B.12
The File Manager window

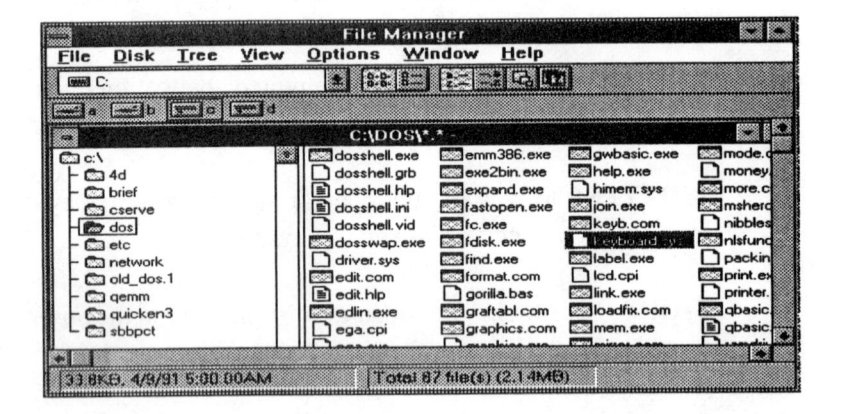

Directory Tree Box

LEFT or BACKSPACE: Moves to the directory above the current one.

RIGHT: Moves to the first directory below the current one, if any.

ENTER: Switches between displaying and hiding subdirectories.

SHIFT+ENTER: If you are currently on a directory, this key sequence opens a new window in which you can view the contents of that directory.

UP or DOWN: Moves to the directory above or below the current one.

CTRL+UP: If there is another directory at the same level as this one but before it, this key sequence moves there.

CTRL+DOWN: If there is another directory at the same level as this one but after it, this key sequence moves there.

PAGE UP: Moves to a directory that is one screen up from the current one.

PAGE DOWN: Moves to the directory that is one screen down from the current one.

HOME or \(backslash): Moves to the root, or top, directory.

END: Moves to the last directory in the tree.

A letter key: Moves to the next directory that has that letter as its first letter.

File List Box

PAGE UP: Moves to the file or directory one screen above the current file.

PAGE DOWN: Moves to the file or directory one screen below the current file.

HOME: Moves to the first file or directory in the current directory.

END: Moves to the last file or directory in the current directory.

A letter key: Moves to the next file or directory whose name starts with that letter.

SHIFT+ARROW Key: Lets you select more than one file or directory at a time, or cancel the selection if they are already selected.

CTRL+/(slash): Selects everything in the current list.

CTRL+\(backslash): Deselects everything in the current list except the current item.

SHIFT+F8: Lets you select several items that are not next to each other in the list. After pressing SHIFT+F8, a blinking cursor will signal you that you can move around in the list with the arrow keys and select (or deselect) items with the spacebar.

ARROW Keys: These keys move the currently highlighted item by one in the indicated direction. If the next item in that direction is outside the current window, the File Manager will scroll the contents automatically.

Spacebar: Selects or cancels selection of items that are not next to each other. See SHIFT+F8 for full information on this key.

ENTER: If the cursor is currently on a directory and you press ENTER, File Manager will open that directory and display its contents in the current window. If the cursor is on a program file, File Manager will start that program for you.

SHIFT+ENTER: If the cursor is on a directory, this key sequence will open that directory and display its contents in a new window.

Drive Box

CTRL+Drive letter: Moves to the drive icon corresponding to that letter, if any.

LEFT or RIGHT: Moves between the icons for the available drives on your system.

Spacebar: Changes the currently selected drive to become the current drive.

Control Panel

Each icon in the Control Panel window (see Figure B.13) opens a dialog box in which you can enter the new settings for that feature. For key information, therefore, refer to the section above on dialog boxes. This section contains a brief description of each feature; see Help on each one for more detailed information.

Figure B.13
The Control Panel window

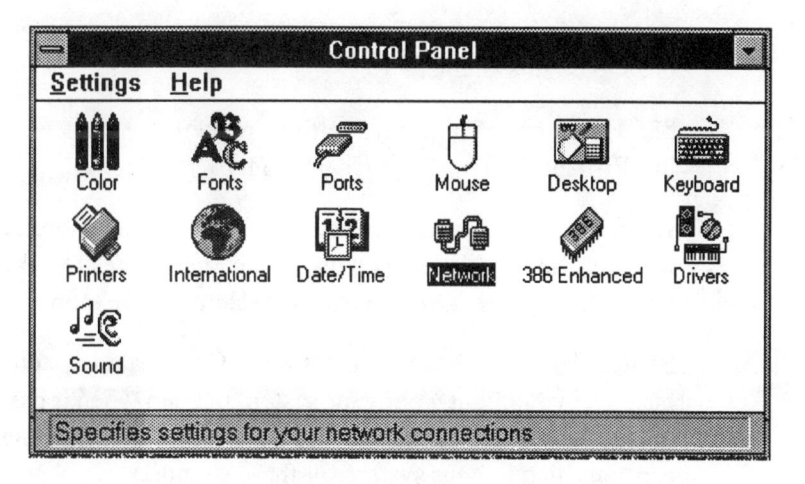

Color: Lets you change the colors of your windows, menu bars, etc. Offers several color schemes, or lets you create your own.

Fonts: Lets you add fonts to your Windows applications, or remove them.

Ports: Configures settings for your communications ports, including their base addresses and interrupts.

Mouse: Adjusts how fast your mouse responds.

Desktop: Lets you define a screen saver, change your wallpaper (see Chapter 11: Custom Setup) and set other characteristics of your screen appearance.

Keyboard: Sets speed features for your keyboard, like how long to wait before starting to repeat a key that you're holding down.

Printers: Tells Windows how to find your printer.

International: Sets parameters that differ between countries, like keyboard layout, how currency values are represented, and how dates are represented.

Date/Time: Sets the current date and/or time for your system.

Network: Configures settings that have to do with how your system talks to other systems.

386 Enhanced: Configures settings related to Enhanced mode, including Virtual Memory. (See Chapter 11.)

Drivers: Installs or removes device drivers, such as sound boards or music devices. This lets you use special hardware. The dealer or the instructions for that hardware device should have more information.

Sound: Windows lets you attach sounds to certain system events; for instance, you might want your system to beep when it has completed an operation. This is where you can set that up. (You must have a sound card installed in your system for these sounds.)

Print Manager: The Print Manager lets you edit and display a list of files currently waiting to be printed on your local printer.

DEL: If your cursor is currently on a print job line and you press this key, Windows will delete the file from the list (after asking you to confirm).

F5: Tells Windows to redisplay the list of files waiting to be printed. This will give you an updated list if anything has changed since the last time the list was displayed.

ALT+F4: Closes the Print Manager window.

ClipBook Viewer

This is the program that lets you look at the contents of your Clipboard and view the Clipboards of other people's systems in your workgroup. See also the keystrokes for editing text, above, for more about getting information onto the Clipboard.

DEL: Clears the current contents of the Clipboard, to make room for something else.

Windows for Workgroups Setup

This is the same program you ran when you first installed Windows for Workgroups. With it you can add new programs to your application group, change your system settings, and remove some of the Windows for Workgroups files from your hard disk to save space. See Chapter 11 for more information. Setup is just a set of dialog boxes, so it follows the dialog box key conventions.

PIF File Editor

A dialog box that lets you change the system information about a non-Windows application, such as whether it runs in a window or on the full screen, how much memory it runs in, where the program can be found on your disk, etc. Follows dialog box key conventions.

Mail

The Mail utility is one of the most important features of Windows for Workgroups. It lets you send text, files, graphics, or any data to others in your workgroup and on your secondary network. See Chapter 5 for a complete discussion of Windows Mail.

CTRL+M: If you have a message or a folder selected, this sequence brings up a dialog box so that you can move the selected item to your InBox, another folder, or the Wastebasket. Has no effect if nothing is selected.

CTRL+D: If you have selected a message or a folder, this sequence deletes it (you will be asked to confirm). If nothing is selected, this key sequence has no effect.

ALT+ENTER: Brings up a dialog box in which you can change the sharing status of a particular folder.

CTRL+P: Prints the selected message(s) if your printer is set up.

CTRL+T: Displays the toolbar if it is not already visible, or hides it if it is visible.

CTRL+N: Brings up the form for creating a new Mail message.

CTRL+R: Allows you to reply to a message. Only active if you are on a message that you have received from someone else. Brings up the Compose a Note form with the From, To, and Subject fields already filled in (but you can change them).

CTRL+A: Allows you to reply to both the sender of the original note and all recipients. Opens a Compose a Note form with the To and Subject fields filled in, and with all the Copy recipients included in the To field.

CTRL+F: Allows you to forward the current message to another workgroup member. Brings up a form for a new note with the subject and text from the current message; just type the recipient's name (or recipients' names) into the To box.

Schedule+

Another very useful program and an important part of Windows for Workgroups, Schedule+ is described in detail in Chapter 6. Key shortcuts for Schedule+ are as follows:

CTRL+P: Prints either your appointments or your task list, depending on what you're viewing when you select it.

CTRL+E: Displays the details about the current appointment in a window so that you can edit the information.

CTRL+Y: Copies the selected appointment to the Clipboard.

CTRL+O: Moves the selected appointment to a new time slot. All comments and other information about the appointment move with it.

CTRL+D: Deletes the selected appointment from your schedule.

CTRL+F: Finds specified text in your appointments or notes.

CTRL+G: Goes to a specified date.

CTRL+N: Creates a new appointment.

CTRL+A: Finds the next time slot which all attendees of a meeting have free. This is the Auto-Pick command, which is available only from the Planner, not from the Appointment Book.

CTRL+R: Creates a new Recurring appointment. These are appointments like regularly scheduled meetings that you don't want to have to enter every week.

CTRL+SHIFT+T: Blocks out a time slot as tentatively filled. This slot will appear free to others who view your schedule.

CTRL+SHIFT+P: Creates an appointment that will not be visible to other users, including your assistant if you have one.

CTRL+SHIFT+R: Sets Schedule+ to send you a reminder when the indicated event occurs or some configurable amount of time beforehand (see Chapter 6).

CTRL+T: Creates a new task for your Task list, prompting you for the details.

CTRL+SHIFT+V: Tasks can be grouped into projects, and can be viewed either by project or all at once. Pressing this key sequence will alternate you between the two types of views.

Write

Write is a simple word processor that comes with Windows for Workgroups. A simple memo written in Write is shown in Figure B.14. It recognizes the following key sequences:

F3: Repeats the last text search operation. Has no effect if you have not done a Find command since you started the program.

F4: Go to Page... command. Prompts you for page number, then brings up that page if it exists.

F5: If you have selected a special character style (like boldface, italic, or underline), pressing this function key will return you to standard style.

Figure B.14
Write gives you a selection of character styles

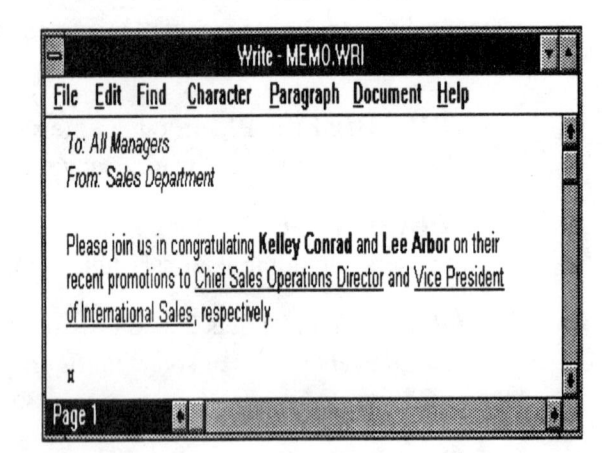

CTRL+B: If you are using non-bold characters, this will cause the next characters you type to be displayed in boldface. If you are already using boldface, this will return you to non-bold.

CTRL+U: Switches you between underlined and non-underlined characters.

CTRL+I: Switches you between italicized and non-italicized characters.

Paintbrush

This simple drawing package (see Figure B.15) comes with Windows for Workgroups. To make best use of it, you will need a mouse, but here are the keyboard shortcuts it offers you:

CTRL+S: Saves the current drawing, prompting you for a file name if necessary.

CTRL+N: Zooms in. You get a frame to move around on the drawing to select the area to zoom into. After Ctrl+N, you use the arrow keys to position to Zoom box. Tab zooms the contents of the Zoom box.

Figure B.15

Create charts and drawings with Paintbrush

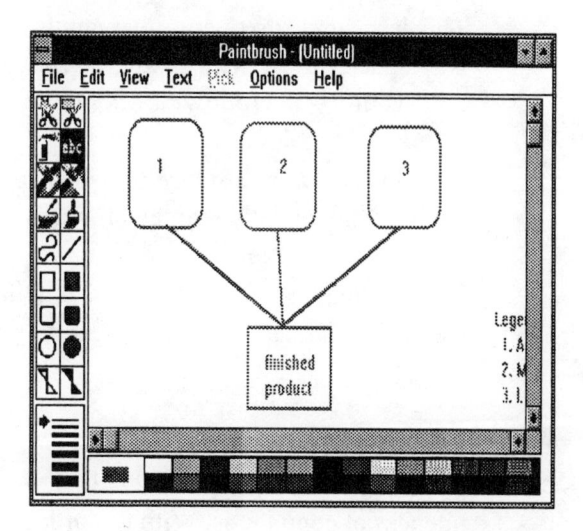

CTRL+O: Zooms out. The entire drawing appears in the window.

CTRL+P: Expands the current drawing to fill the entire screen. Press any key or a mouse button to return to the window view.

CTRL+B: Switches you between boldface and non-bold text.

CTRL+I: Switches you between italicized and non-italicized text.

CTRL+U: Switches you between underlined and non-underlined text.

Terminal

This program allows you to dial up an external system and transfer data between the two systems. Other than the standard key sequences, it has only one key shortcut:

CTRL+SHIFT+INS: Sends the selected text in the Terminal window to the other system. Has no effect if nothing is selected.

Notepad

This is a simple text editor that comes with Windows for Workgroups. It is intended for use with small text files such as notes, time logs, and to-do lists. It has the following shortcut keys:

F3: Finds the next instance of the current search string. Has no effect if you have not already searched for something.

F5: Automatically enters the date and time into the current note; it is useful for maintaining a consistent note format.

Recorder

A very useful program, especially if you find yourself repeating sequences of commands. With Recorder you can tell Windows for Workgroups to store the sequence and play it back when you enter a specified key sequence, thereby creating your own keyboard shortcut. However, it does not have any keyboard shortcuts of its own.

Cardfile

This program provides a way to create index cards on your screen, allowing entry, for example, of names, addresses, and phone numbers. It even has a feature that lets you automatically dial a telephone number if you have a Hayes-compatible modem attached to your system. See Chapter 7 of this book, or Cardfile Help, for more information. Cardfile has the following shortcut keys:

F3: Finds next instance of the current search text. Has no effect if you have not already searched for text.

F4: Goes to the card that has the specified text in its title.

F5: This feature lets you automatically dial the phone number on the current index card. If no search string has been delivered, F3 brings up the Find dialog box.

F6: Creates a new card with an index line. You can later display all cards sorted by this index text. F6 also allows you to edit the index line of the current card.

F7: Adds a new card to your file. Cardfile will prompt you for the title line, then display the new card.

Character Map

This program allows you to copy special characters and symbols into a document. See Help for more information.

Media Player

This program lets you play multimedia files from various devices, including CD players, videodisk players, and MIDI (Musical Instrument Digital Interface) devices. See Help on Control Panel and Media Player for information about installing these devices and their drivers.

Sound Recorder

If you have a sound board installed in your system, you can use Sound Recorder to record and play back sound files. It has no keyboard shortcuts. See Sound Recorder Help for more information.

Clock

Windows provides a clock program that displays a clock on the screen and keeps it up to date. If you start the clock and minimize it, the icon will also display the correct time. It has no keyboard shortcuts.

Chat

Chat is a simple program that lets two workgroup members exchange live text messages. It is useful for quick notes and to verify your network connections. (See Figure B.16)

Figure B.16
Sample Chat conversation

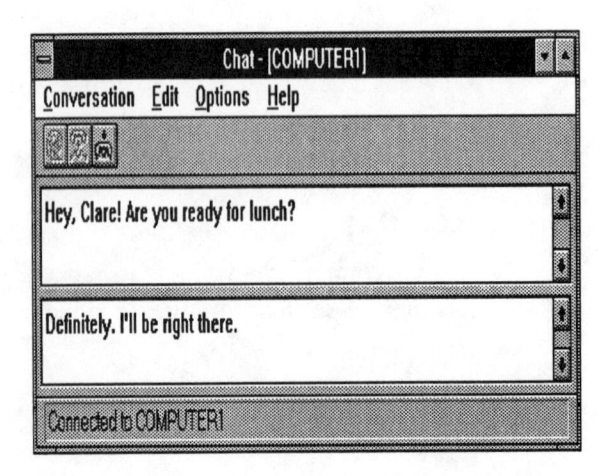

WinMeter

A program that shows a graph of how much of your system is being used by your applications and how much by remote applications. See Chapter 11 for more information. No shortcut keys.

NetWatcher

Gives you a listing of all the connections to your system from other systems. It's a good idea to check here before you unshare a resource or shut down your system; otherwise you might interrupt someone's work. It offers two key shortcuts:

ALT+ENTER: Displays a screen of detailed properties about the currently selected connection.

F5: Refreshes the list of connections. This will update the screen with any information that is new since the last time you redisplayed.

Minesweeper

One of the three games that comes with Workgroups for Windows, Minesweeper, as shown in Figure B.17, is a strategy game that offers an excellent way to practice your window and mouse skills. It has some keyboard commands, but you need a mouse to play.

F2: Starts a new game.

Solitaire

This is an electronic version of the old standby. You can specify the rules you play by — Las Vegas, Standard, or No scoring, how many cards to draw at once, and even what design appears on the back of the cards (try the island scene). No keyboard shortcuts — you'll need a mouse with this one.

Figure B.17

Minesweeper in play

Figure B.18

Solitaire offers a variety of options

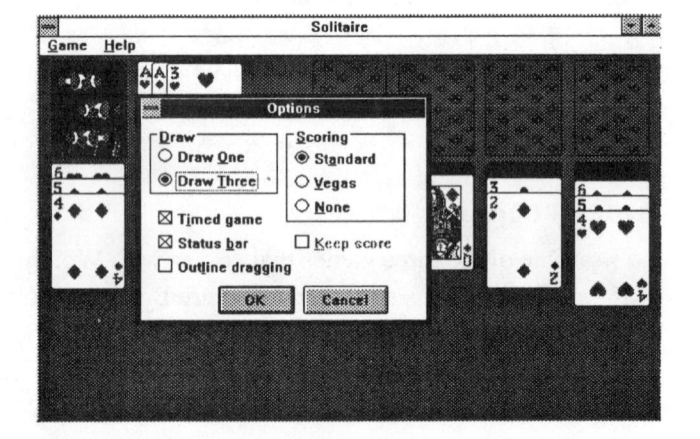

Hearts

This game is designed to be played by up to four members of a workgroup. If you have fewer than four players, the dealer's computer will play for the missing players. Like Chat, it is a good way to test your network connections and verify that everything is working correctly. You will each need a mouse to play, but it does support some keyboard shortcuts. As shown in Figure B.19, Hearts can be played with one to four players.

F2: If you are the dealer, you must wait until everyone else is in the game before you begin. To begin the game with the current players (perhaps just yourself), press F2. The game will begin automatically if four people join before the dealer presses F2.

F8: If you have a sound board in your computer, this key will turn on or off the special sound effects for the game.

F9: Displays the current score card for all players.

Figure B.19
You can play hearts with one to four players

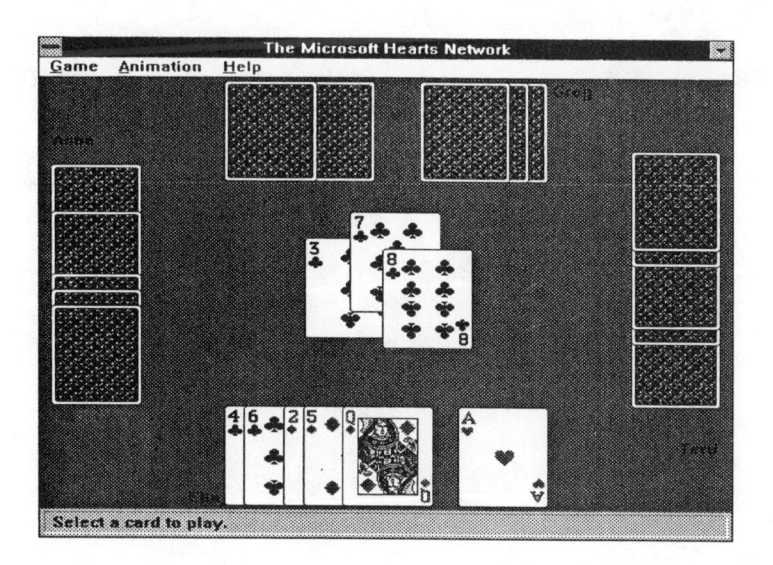

APPENDIX C

The Workgroup Connection

APPENDIX C

FEATURING:

- Installing Workgroup Connection
- Starting Workgroup Connection
- Using Mail with Workgroup Connection

To get into the wonderful world of Windows for Workgroups, you'll have to make a steep investment in hardware resources. The very best results come from fast 386 or 486 processors heavily endowed with RAM. The Windows environment will not operate very well on PCs with 286 processors or those that aren't equipped with a graphics monitor. But you may already have some of these PCs, and you may be unwilling or unable to convert to newer, more powerful machines just yet. You can use these older machines in a limited way on your Windows for Workgroups LAN.

Windows for Workgroups comes with a utility for DOS-based computers called the Workgroup Connection. With this utility, you can perform some limited networking functions on non-Windows computers. Table C-1 shows the a list of what you can and cannot do with Workgroup Connection.

Table C.1 Workgroup Connection Capabilities

Function	Available
Connect to Network	Yes
Share your local disk drives	No
Use files from another's hard disk	Yes, with security
Use Schedule+	No
Send and receive e-mail	Yes
Use Clipboard or ClipBook Viewer	No
Share your local printer	No
Use another's printer	Yes
Use Windows application software	No
Use Chat utility	No
View Netwatcher	No

Installing Workgroup Connection

Like its Windows counterpart, the Workgroup Connection has a very sophisticated, easy to install SETUP utility. The entire SETUP procedure is contained on one disk and is provided with your software.

To install the Workgroup Connection, place its SETUP disk in one of your floppy disk drives (either drive A: or drive B:). Close the disk drive door and enter A:SETUP or B:SETUP depending on which drive you placed the SETUP disk. After a few seconds, you should see a Welcome screen that looks like Figure C.1.

Figure C.1
The Workgroup Connection Welcome screen

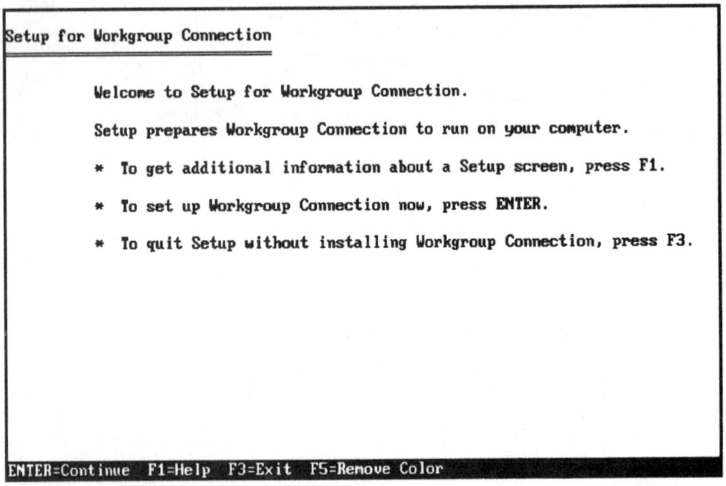

```
Setup for Workgroup Connection

    Welcome to Setup for Workgroup Connection.
    Setup prepares Workgroup Connection to run on your computer.
    * To get additional information about a Setup screen, press F1.
    * To set up Workgroup Connection now, press ENTER.
    * To quit Setup without installing Workgroup Connection, press F3.




ENTER=Continue  F1=Help  F3=Exit  F5=Remove Color
```

To confirm that you are in the right place, press the ENTER key. If you want to read the Help text, you can press the F1 key, or if you want to exit and abort the installation, you can press the F3 key (both are located at the top of your keyboard).

If you've chosen to go forward, your next screen will ask you to verify where you want the Workgroup Connection files to be placed. As a default, the SETUP program will place them in the C:\DOS directory, as shown in Figure C.2.

Figure C.2
Specifying the directory for the Workgroup Connection

```
Setup for Workgroup Connection

    Setup will place your Workgroup Connection files in the
    following directory.
    If this is where you want these files, press ENTER.
    If you want Setup to place the files in a different
    directory, type the full path of that directory, and
    then press ENTER.

    C:\DOS



ENTER=Continue  F1=Help  F3=Exit
```

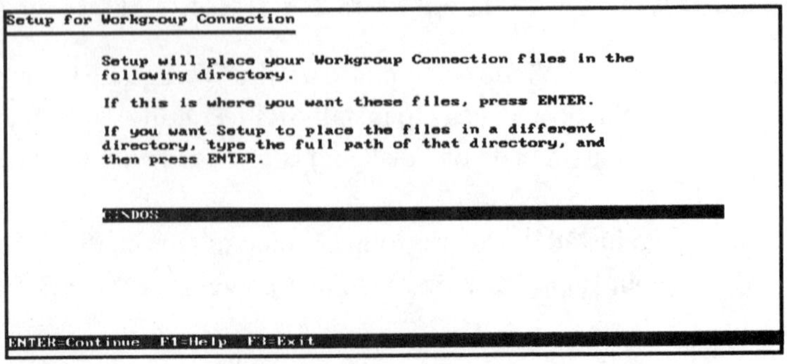

The Workgroup Connection

SETUP will take a few minutes to analyze your system for its networking connections. A screen will ask you to wait while SETUP determines your system files. The next screen will display a list of NICs, and ask you to choose from the list the NIC installed in your computer. To quickly find the one you need in the list, use the arrow keys and the page up and down keys to move through the list, or type the first few letters of the NIC name into the text box, as shown in Figure C.3.

Figure C.3
The list of supported network interface cards

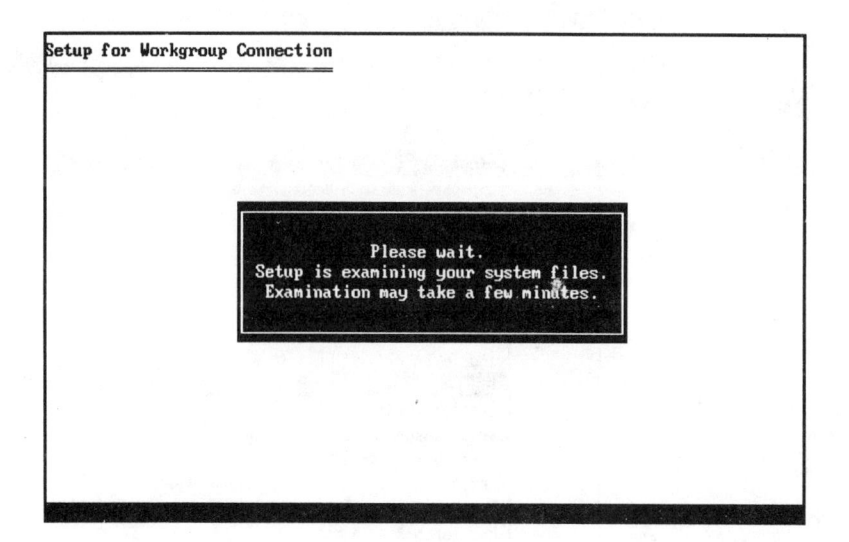

> **NOTE** If your NIC is not on the list, check with your manufacturer to see if there is a special NIC driver for Windows for Workgroups. You might try choosing other supported cards on the list, selecting one that your card emulates. We recommend that you exercise great caution in using cards that are not directly supported by the software — they may cause the PC to fail to operate correctly when connected to the network.

After you have selected a card, you'll be asked to provide a computer name for your computer. Choose a name that is not used by any other computer in the workgroup. As with the Windows version of the software, you can choose a name that is up to 15 characters in length.

The next screen will prompt you for the Workgroup Name. Use the name that has been established for use by your workgroup.

When these questions are answered, SETUP will confirm your selections and make some assumptions about your desired installation. The screen looks like Figure C.4.

Figure C.4

Setup for Workgroup Connection

```
Setup for Workgroup Connection

    Select the type of network card that is installed in your
    computer, and then press ENTER.

    IBM Token Ring
    IBM Token Ring (MCA)
    IBM Token Ring II
    IBM Token Ring II/Short
    IBM Token Ring 4/16Mbs
    IBM Token Ring 4/16Mbs (MCA)
    Intel EtherExpress 16 or 16TP
    Intel TokenExpress EISA 16/4
    Intel TokenExpress 16/4
    Intel TokenExpress MCA 16/4
    National Semiconductor Ethernode *16AT
    National Semiconductor AT/LANTIC EtherNODE 16-AT3
    NCR Token-Ring 4 Mbs ISA
    NCR Token-Ring 16/4 Mbs ISA
    NCR Token-Ring 16/4 Mbs MCA
    NE1000 Compatible

ENTER=Continue  F1=Help  F3=Exit
```

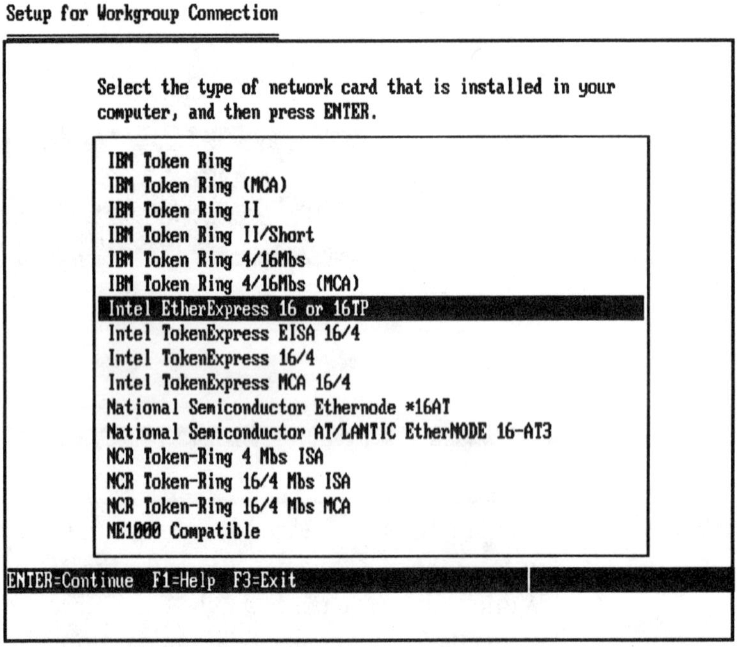

If you agree with all the information on the screen, press the ENTER key to continue. Otherwise, you can correct any entry by using the up or down arrow keys to move to that entry, highlighting the information you wish to change, and then pressing the ENTER key for other options.

The Workgroup Connection

When you agree with all the information, press the ENTER key. Depending on what brand NIC card you are using, SETUP may ask about the parameters for my NIC (such as IRQ, or base memory). Be prepared to enter that information if asked. Next, SETUP will begin to copy files into your directory, changing any necessary configuration information on your computer. SETUP will also modify both your AUTOEXEC.BAT and CONFIG.SYS files. Your computer uses these two files each time it is started. SETUP has copied network driver information and information about where the Workgroup Connection is located into them, so that the connection can be made.

When SETUP is complete, a screen that looks like Figure C.5 will appear. Remove the SETUP disk and store it in a safe place in case you need it again. Finally, restart your computer.

Figure C.5

Setup for Workgroup Connection confirmation

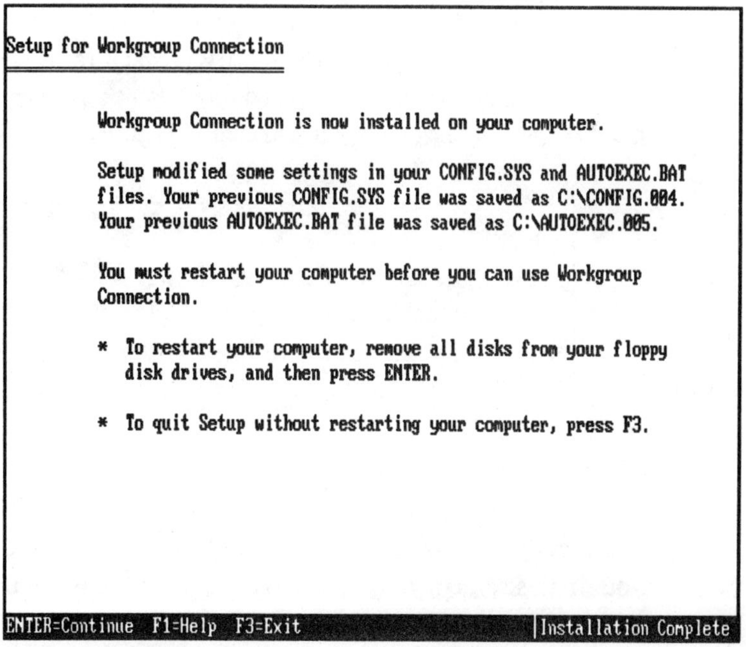

```
Setup for Workgroup Connection

         Workgroup Connection is now installed on your computer.

         Setup modified some settings in your CONFIG.SYS and AUTOEXEC.BAT
         files. Your previous CONFIG.SYS file was saved as C:\CONFIG.004.
         Your previous AUTOEXEC.BAT file was saved as C:\AUTOEXEC.005.

         You must restart your computer before you can use Workgroup
         Connection.

         *  To restart your computer, remove all disks from your floppy
            disk drives, and then press ENTER.

         *  To quit Setup without restarting your computer, press F3.




ENTER=Continue  F1=Help  F3=Exit                       Installation Complete
```

> **NOTE:** Do not try to use the network until you have restarted your computer. SETUP installs special drivers that are only loaded by the computer after it is restarted. If you do try to use the computer before it reads these files, the PC will not be able to access anything on the network.

Starting Workgroup Connection

After your computer restarts, you can access the network by issuing the NET command from DOS. The NET.EXE program will be located in the directory that you specified during the system setup. If you want to access the network each time you start your computer, you can add that command to your AUTOEXEC.BAT file.

After issuing the NET command, you will have to log into the network. Your computer will ask you to identify yourself (or if you have logged on to the system before, it will recognize you as the user of the computer). The Logon screen is illustrated in Figure C.6.

Figure C.6
Logon screen from DOS on a Workgroup Connection computer

```
C:\WC>net
Type your user name, or press ENTER if it is GOULDING:
Type your password:********
Please confirm your password so that a password list may be created:********
```

Next, you will see a popup screen (like Figure C.7), that lets you connect to directories on other computers and that shows the printers available to you. In this screen, you can use the tab key to move to the next field and the up or down arrow keys to select an item. You can get help at any time by pressing the F1 key.

THE WORKGROUP CONNECTION

Figure C.7
Disk Connections screen

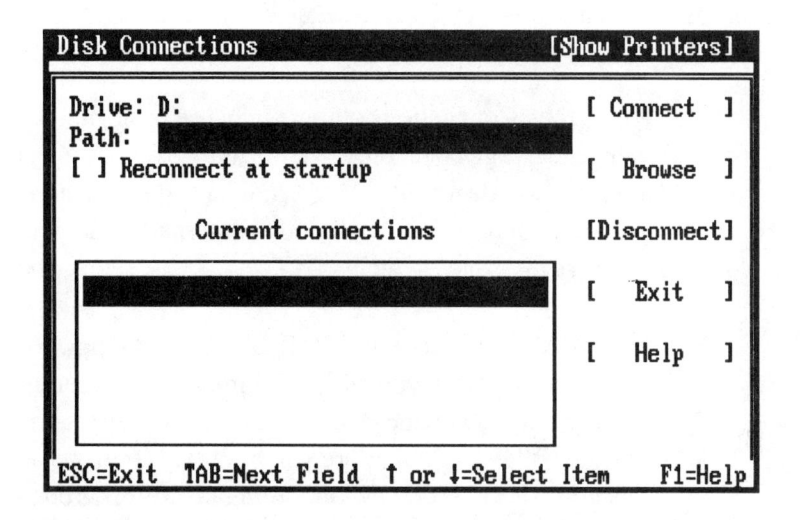

```
Disk Connections                          [Show Printers]
┌─────────────────────────────────────────────────────────┐
│ Drive: D:                                  [ Connect  ] │
│ Path:                                                   │
│ [ ] Reconnect at startup                   [ Browse   ] │
│                                                         │
│           Current connections              [Disconnect] │
│         ┌─────────────────────────┐                     │
│         │                         │        [   Exit   ] │
│         │                         │                     │
│         │                         │        [   Help   ] │
│         │                         │                     │
│         └─────────────────────────┘                     │
│ ESC=Exit  TAB=Next Field  ↑ or ↓=Select Item   F1=Help  │
└─────────────────────────────────────────────────────────┘
```

If instead you choose the Show Printers field (on the previous screen) you will see another popup window (similar to Figure C.8). Here, you can connect to another workgroup member's port, browse a list of printers, disconnect from the printer, or show the print queue. If you select a printer on the network, you can make that selection valid for future sessions by checking the Reconnect at Startup box. (Please note that, as a Workgroup Connection PC, you cannot share your own printer.)

Figure C.8
Printer Connections

```
Printer Connections                       [ Show Disks  ]
┌─────────────────────────────────────────────────────────┐
│ Port: LPT                                  [ Connect  ] │
│ Path:                                                   │
│ [ ] Reconnect at startup                   [ Browse   ] │
│                                                         │
│           Current connections              [Disconnect] │
│         ┌─────────────────────────┐                     │
│         │                         │        [   Exit   ] │
│         │                         │                     │
│         │                         │        [   Help   ] │
│         │                         │                     │
│         └─────────────────────────┘        [Show Queue] │
│ ESC=Exit  TAB=Next Field  ↑ or ↓=Select Item   F1=Help  │
└─────────────────────────────────────────────────────────┘
```

Using Mail with Workgroup Connection

A Workgroup Connection computer can use basic mail services and exchange messages with others in the workgroup using a DOS-based Mail utility. While this utility does not have the attractive look and intuitive feel of its Windows-based counterpart, it does allow you to send and receive messages to others.

To use the Mail system, type MAIL at a DOS prompt. If it is your first time using the system, you will be prompted with a series of screens to setup the Mail system and establish a link to the appropriate workgroup Postoffice (WGPO). Make sure you have the name of your workgroup and location of the WGPO when setting up a Workgroup Connection to Mail.

This appendix gave you a quick tutorial on setting up the Workgroup Connection for your DOS-based computers. We examined the feature and function list to determine how a Workgroup Connection computer participates on the network, and we proceeded with an installation. Then we looked at logging on to the system for the first time, and setting up for accessing disks and printers on the network. Finally, we looked at setting up access to the electronic Mail system, Mail.

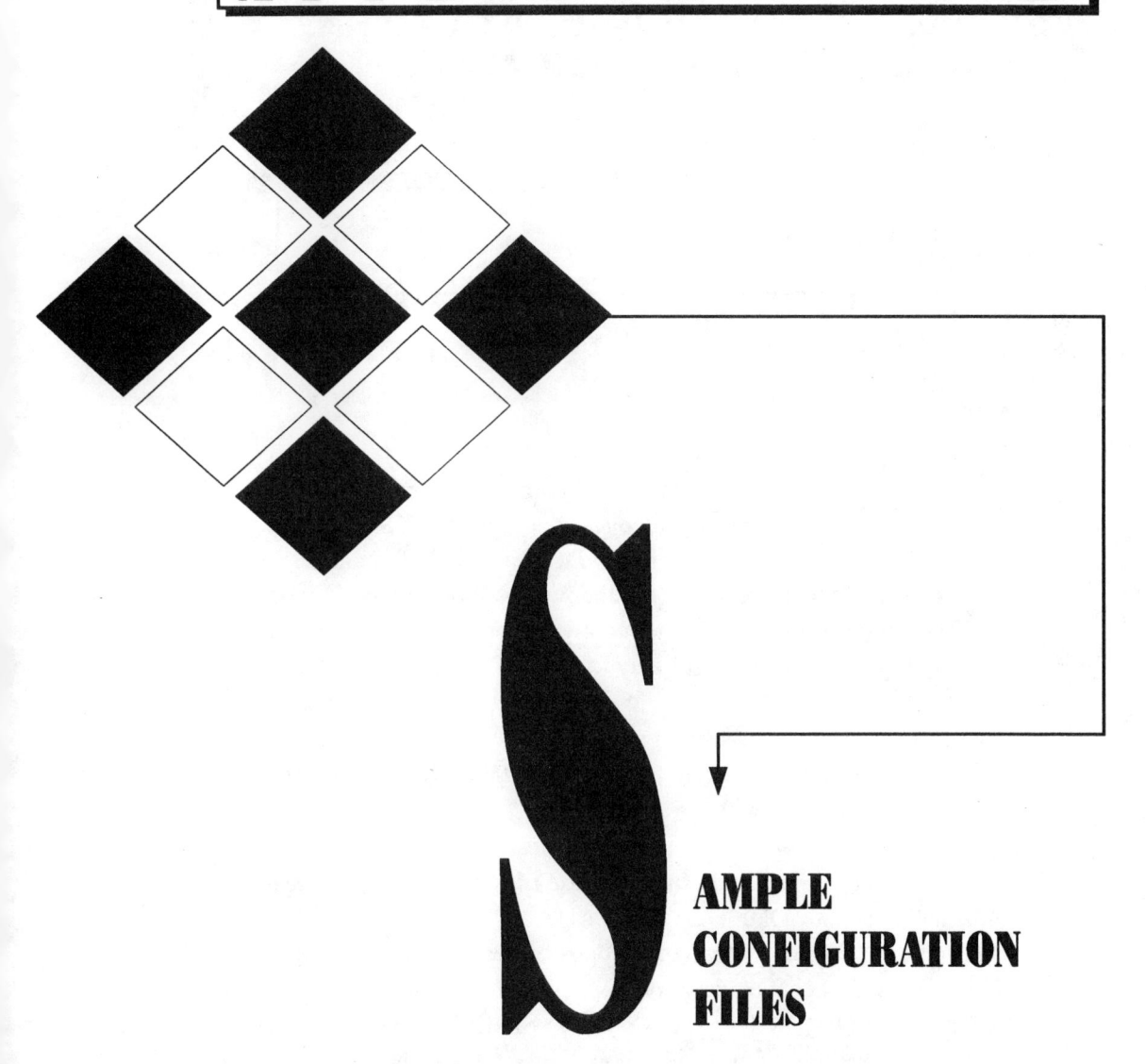

APPENDIX D

Sample Configuration Files

APPENDIX D

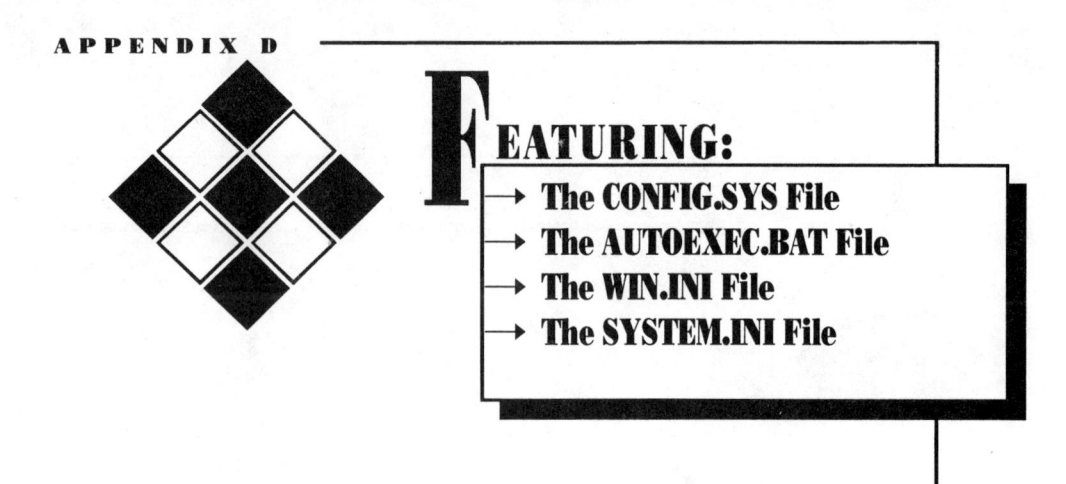

FEATURING:

→ The CONFIG.SYS File
→ The AUTOEXEC.BAT File
→ The WIN.INI File
→ The SYSTEM.INI File

In this appendix we'll look at the configuration files from several different systems. The files we'll cover are CONFIG.SYS and AUTOEXEC.BAT, which are used by DOS, and WIN.INI and SYSTEM.INI, which are used by Windows for Workgroups. Windows for Workgroups uses several other configuration files as well, but these two are the ones you are most likely to need.

The files we show in this section are all from working systems. If you have problems, it might help to take a look at these files and determine how they differ from yours.

We will not have room to discuss all these files in detail. For more information about CONFIG.SYS and AUTOEXEC.BAT, consult your DOS manuals. Windows for Workgroups comes with several files in Write format that contain descriptions of some of the Windows configuration files: look at NETWORKS.WRI, SYSINI.WRI, and WININI.WRI with the Write utility. For details about the Windows .INI files, consult the Windows for Workgroups Resource Kit. It is full of detailed technical notes about networking, configuring your system, and more. You also get a diskette full of useful utilities to monitor performance and manage your desktop. To find out how to get the Resource Kit, double-click on the ReadMe icon in the Main window. This will bring up the Write application with the file README.WRI, which contains instructions on ordering the Resource Kit and other useful information.

A note about viewing these files: All the files we'll discuss in this section are plain text files, which means you can edit them with a standard text editor (Notepad, for instance). But Microsoft also provided SysEdit to make editing easier. SysEdit brings up the editor windows for four files WIN.INI, SYSTEM.INI, AUTOEXEC.BAT, and CONFIG.SYS. As you make changes in one, you can see the effect your changes have elsewhere. Run SysEdit from the File Manager by double-clicking on the program SYSEDIT.EXE. It is in the System directory, under the directory where you installed Windows (probably C:\WINDOWS, so the full path is C:\WINDOWS\SYSTEM\SYSEDIT.EXE). Click the maximize button in the upper-right corner of the window, then select Tile from the Window menu to get the four windows on the screen together without overlapping. Figure D.1 shows the SysEdit screen configured this way.

While you are editing the Windows configuration files, don't do anything else that might change them. Do not, for instance, move over to your Control Panel and change your screen colors while editing your WIN.INI file. The color information goes into the WIN.INI file, and if you're changing it in both places, one of the versions will get lost. It's safest to make your changes, save them, and leave the editor before you do anything else.

The CONFIG.SYS File

We'll look first at the CONFIG.SYS file. This is a file that DOS reads when you turn on your computer to determine what device drivers to run and how to configure some low-level parameters about your system.

Figure D.1

Editing your configuration with SysEdit

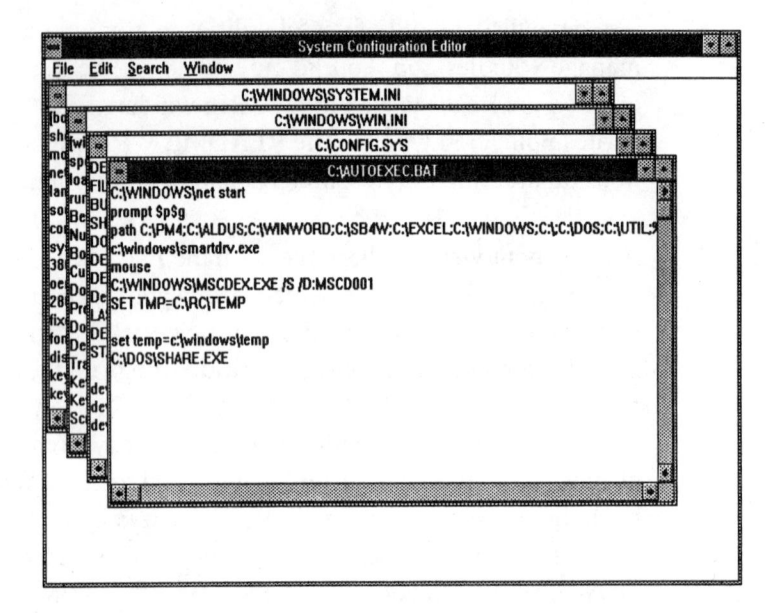

Device drivers are programs that provide specific instructions for devices like Network cards, CD-ROMS, disk drives, and some other peripherals. Some are built in to DOS (most hard disks, keyboards,etc.), others are loaded from config or devicehigh= if you have DOS 5. Device driver lines in CONFIG.SYS always start with the 'device=' such as: DEVICE=C:\WINDOWS\HIMEM.SYS

In the following example, we are running HIMEM.SYS, SETVER.EXE, and some network drivers. All Windows for Workgroups systems must load PROTMAN.DOS (the Protocol Manager), and WORKGRP.SYS. The other drivers required depend on the network configuration and the set of peripheral devices attached to the system.

The CONFIG.SYS file below, for instance, belongs to a system that has an Intel EtherExpress 16 network interface card, so it uses the EXP16.DOS driver. It also links to an external Novell network, so it needs the MSIPX.SYS driver.

Installing and Testing the Network Hardware

```
DEVICE=C:\DOS\SETVER.EXE
DEVICE=C:\WINDOWS\HIMEM.SYS
DOS=HIGH
files=30
buffers=30
SHELL=C:\DOS\COMMAND.COM /p
STACKS=9,256
device=C:\WINDOWS\protman.dos /i:C:\WINDOWS
device=C:\WINDOWS\msipx.sys
device=C:\WINDOWS\workgrp.sys
device=C:\WINDOWS\exp16.dos
LASTDRIVE=P
```

Note that this CONFIG file explicitly states that the boot shell is the DOS command interpreter, COMMAND.COM. The CONFIG file below, on the other hand, is for a computer that is using a Novell Anthem NE2000 network adapter, for which the driver is NE2000.SYS. It does not attach to a secondary network.

```
DEVICE=D:\WINDOWS\HIMEM.SYS
device  = c:\dos\setver.exe
DOS=HIGH
FILES=30
LASTDRIVE=P
STACKS=9,256
device=D:\WINDOWS\protman.dos /i:D:\WINDOWS
device=D:\WINDOWS\ne2000.dos
device=D:\WINDOWS\workgrp.sys
```

Finally, this CONFIG.SYS file loads a mouse driver. Generally you won't need to do this to run Windows for Workgroups, but you may need it for other programs, such as DOS applications from outside of Windows for Workgroups.

```
files= 30
DEVICE=C:\DOS\SETVER.EXE
DEVICE=C:\WINDOWS\HIMEM.SYS
DOS=HIGH
STACKS=9,256
device=C:\dos\mouse.sys
device=C:\WINDOWS\protman.dos /i:C:\WINDOWS
device=C:\WINDOWS\workgrp.sys
device=C:\WINDOWS\exp16.dos
device=C:\WINDOWS\msipx.sys
LASTDRIVE=P
```

The AUTOEXEC.BAT File

This file is a batch file that DOS runs every time you restart your computer. It is a good place to set up your DOS environment and load TSR (terminate and stay resident) programs that you want always running. You can also start WFW as the last line in AUTOEXEC.BAT. Some people also put their network login commands in their AUTOEXEC.BAT file, so they log on to their network whenever they restart their computer, as shown below:

```
C:\WINDOWS\net start
C:\WINDOWS\msipx
C:\WINDOWS\netx
SET dPalette=C:\DPALETTE\dpalette.cfg
C:\WINDOWS\SMARTDRV.EXE
PROMPT $p$g
PATH
C:\WINDOWS;C:\DOS;C:\WINWORKS\EXEC;C:\DPALETTE;
MOUSE
SET TEMP=C:\DOS
Q:
LOGIN
```

Installing and Testing the Network Hardware

The "net start" command in this file appears in the AUTOEXEC.BAT of every Windows for Workgroups system. The "msipx" and "netx" lines are to attach the user to the Novell network as well as the Workgroups network. Note that this file also loads a mouse driver, defines the style of the DOS prompt, and sets the Path and other DOS environment variables.

The next AUTOEXEC.BAT file contains sets some environment variables for the Brief text editor.

```
D:\WINDOWS\SMARTDRV.EXE
D:\WINDOWS\net start
echo off
prompt $p$g
path D:\WINDOWS;c:\dos;c:\brief;c:\etc
set temp=c:\dos
set bpath=;c:\brief\macros;c:\brief\misc;c:\brief
set bhelp=c:\brief\help
set bfile=c:\brief\state.rst
set bpackages=default,m,asm:r;doc-txt:r,wp;h,c-c,l,y:s 0 0 1
set bflags=-i120l200M120dga -mMLR -mrestore -mtu100z -mmlr -msavehist -mscrapper -Dega
```

Note that both AUTOEXEC.BAT files start the program SMARTDRV.EXE. This is the disk caching utility that comes with Windows for Workgroups. It gets installed automatically when you set up Windows, unless Setup detects that you have another disk caching program already running. Using a disk caching program can greatly improve your system performance.

The WIN.INI File

This is the main configuration file for Windows for Workgroups. The words in square brackets are called headings. They usually appear at the top of a group of setting lines. The headings and their groups can be in any order within the file, but you should not change the order of the settings. Windows ignores blank lines, so use them as necessary to group things. Never put spaces around the equal signs in the setting lines.

The WIN.INI file below is from a system with no applications and no special configurations. As you can see, even a simple WIN.INI file is quite complex. Before you edit it, be sure to make a copy in case your changes don't work.

[windows]
spooler=yes
load=
run=
Beep=yes
NullPort=None
device=
BorderWidth=3
CursorBlinkRate=530
DoubleClickSpeed=452
Programs=com exe bat pif
Documents=
DeviceNotSelectedTimeout=15
TransmissionRetryTimeout=45
KeyboardDelay=2
KeyboardSpeed=31
ScreenSaveActive=0
ScreenSaveTimeOut=120
CoolSwitch=1

[Desktop]
Pattern=(None)
Wallpaper=(None)

GridGranularity=0
IconSpacing=75
TileWallPaper=1

[Extensions]
crd=cardfile.exe ^.crd
trm=terminal.exe ^.trm
txt=notepad.exe ^.txt
ini=notepad.exe ^.ini
pcx=pbrush.exe ^.pcx
bmp=pbrush.exe ^.bmp
wri=write.exe ^.wri
rec=recorder.exe ^.rec
hlp=winhelp.exe ^.hlp
mmf=msmail.exe /f ^.mmf

[intl]
sLanguage=enu
sCountry=United States
iCountry=1
iDate=0
iTime=0
iTLZero=0
iCurrency=0
iCurrDigits=2
iNegCurr=0
iLzero=1
iDigits=2
iMeasure=1
s1159=AM
s2359=PM
sCurrency=$
sThousand=,
sDecimal=.

sDate=/
sTime=:
sList=,
sShortDate=M/d/yy
sLongDate=dddd, MMMM dd, yyyy

[ports]
; A line with [filename].PRN followed by an equal sign causes
; [filename] to appear in the Control Panel's Printer Configuration dialog
; box. A printer connected to [filename] directs its output into this file.
LPT1:=
LPT2:=
LPT3:=
COM1:=9600,n,8,1,x
COM2:=9600,n,8,1,x
COM3:=9600,n,8,1,x
COM4:=9600,n,8,1,x
EPT:=
FILE:=
LPT1.DOS=
LPT2.DOS=

[FontSubstitutes]
Helv=MS Sans Serif
Tms Rmn=MS Serif
Times=Times New Roman
Helvetica=Arial

[TrueType]

[Sounds]
SystemDefault=ding.wav, Default Beep
SystemExclamation=ding.wav, Exclamation
SystemStart=chimes.wav, Windows Start

SystemExit=chimes.wav, Windows Exit
SystemHand=ding.wav, Critical Stop
SystemQuestion=ding.wav, Question
SystemAsterisk=ding.wav, Asterisk
RingIn=ringin.wav, Incoming Call
RingOut=ringout.wav, Outgoing Call

[mci extensions]
wav=waveaudio
mid=sequencer
rmi=sequencer

[Compatibility]
NOTSHELL=0x0001
AMIPRO=0x0010
REM=0x8022
PIXIE=0x0040
CP=0x0040
JW=0x42080
TME=0x0100
VB=0x0200
WIN2WRS=0x1210
VISION=0x0040
MCOURIER=0x0800
_BNOTES=0x24000
PM4=0x2000
DESIGNER=0x2000
PLANNER=0x2000
DRAW=0x2000
WINSIM=0x2000
CHARISMA=0x2000
PR2=0x2000
PLUS=0x1000
ED=0x00010000

EXCEL=0x1000
GUIDE=0x1000
NETSET2=0x0100
W4GL=0x4000
W4GLR=0x4000

[Microsoft Word 2.0]
HPDSKJET=+1

[fonts]
Arial (TrueType)=ARIAL.FOT
Arial Bold (TrueType)=ARIALBD.FOT
Arial Bold Italic (TrueType)=ARIALBI.FOT
Arial Italic (TrueType)=ARIALI.FOT
Courier New (TrueType)=COUR.FOT
Courier New Bold (TrueType)=COURBD.FOT
Courier New Bold Italic (TrueType)=COURBI.FOT
Courier New Italic (TrueType)=COURI.FOT
Times New Roman (TrueType)=TIMES.FOT
Times New Roman Bold (TrueType)=TIMESBD.FOT
Times New Roman Bold Italic (TrueType)=TIMESBI.FOT
Times New Roman Italic (TrueType)=TIMESI.FOT
WingDings (TrueType)=WINGDING.FOT
MS Sans Serif 8,10,12,14,18,24 (VGA res)=SSERIFE.FON
Courier 10,12,15 (VGA res)=COURE.FON
MS Serif 8,10,12,14,18,24 (VGA res)=SERIFE.FON
Symbol 8,10,12,14,18,24 (VGA res)=SYMBOLE.FON
Roman (Plotter)=ROMAN.FON
Script (Plotter)=SCRIPT.FON
Modern (Plotter)=MODERN.FON
Small Fonts (VGA res)=SMALLE.FON
Symbol (TrueType)=SYMBOL.FOT

[embedding]

SoundRec=Sound,Sound,SoundRec.exe,picture
Package=Package,Package,packager.exe,picture
PBrush=Paintbrush Picture,Paintbrush Picture,pbrush.exe,picture

[MRU_Chat]
Order=a
a=\\MARGARET

[MRU_Files]
Order=a
a=\\ELLA\FASTBACK

Notice the Extensions heading near the top of the WIN.INI file in this example. When you double-click on a file, Windows checks the file extension to see if it has a program associated with that file. In this file, for instance, files whose names end in .CRD are associated with the Cardfile program. You can create new extensions in the File Manager by selecting a file with the desired extension, then choosing Associate from the File menu. You will see a dialog box like the one in Figure D.2.

Figure D.2

Associating a file with an application

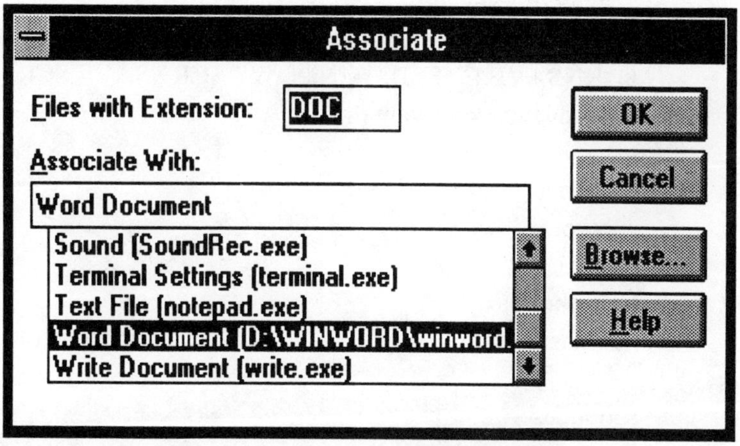

The SYSTEM.INI File

Finally, let's look at a SYSTEM.INI file. This is where Windows stores parameters about your hardware configuration and network connections. A sample SYSTEM.INI file is shown below:

[boot]
shell=progman.exe
mouse.drv=mouse.drv
network.drv=wfwnet.drv
language.dll=
sound.drv=mmsound.drv
comm.drv=comm.drv
keyboard.drv=keyboard.drv
system.drv=system.drv
386grabber=vga.3gr
oemfonts.fon=vgaoem.fon
286grabber=vgacolor.2gr
fixedfon.fon=vgafix.fon
fonts.fon=vgasys.fon
display.drv=vga.drv
drivers=mmsystem.dll
SCRNSAVE.EXE=D:\WINDOWS\SCRNSAVE.SCR
secondnet.drv=netware.drv

[keyboard]
subtype=
type=3
keyboard.dll=
oemansi.bin=

[boot.description]
keyboard.typ=All AT type keyboards (84 - 86 keys)
mouse.drv=Microsoft, or IBM PS/2

network.drv=Microsoft Windows for Workgroups (3.1)
language.dll=English (American)
system.drv=MS-DOS System
codepage=437
woafont.fon=English (437)
aspect=100,96,96
display.drv=VGA

[386Enh]
32BitDiskAccess=OFF
device=*int13
device=*wdctrl
mouse=*vmd
network=vnetbios.386,vnetsup.386,vredir.386,vserver.386,vbrowse.386,vwc.386
ebios=*ebios
woafont=dosapp.fon
display=*vddvga
EGA80WOA.FON=EGA80WOA.FON
EGA40WOA.FON=EGA40WOA.FON
CGA80WOA.FON=CGA80WOA.FON
CGA40WOA.FON=CGA40WOA.FON
keyboard=*vkd
netheapsize=20
device=vtdapi.386
device=vcd.386
device=vshare.386
device=vpicd.386
device=vpd.386
device=*vtd
device=*reboot
device=vdmad.386
device=*vsd
device=*v86mmgr
device=*pageswap

device=*dosmgr
device=*vmpoll
device=*wshell
device=*BLOCKDEV
device=*PAGEFILE
device=*vfd
device=*parity
device=*biosxlat
device=*vmcpd
device=*combuff
device=*cdpscsi
local=CON
FileSysChange=off
PermSwapDOSDrive=D
PermSwapSizeK=8185
transport=vnb.386
secondnet=vipx.386,vnetware.386
OverlappedIO=off

[standard]

netheapsize=8
[NonWindowsApp]
localtsrs=dosedit,ced

[mci]
WaveAudio=mciwave.drv
Sequencer=mciseq.drv
CDAudio=mcicda.drv

[drivers]
timer=timer.drv
midimapper=midimap.drv

[DDEShares]
CHAT$=winchat,chat,,31,,0,,0,0,0
CLPBK$=clipsrv,system,,31,,0,,0,0,0
HEARTS$=mshearts,hearts,,15,,0,,0,0,0

[network]
ComputerName=ELLA
Workgroup=ENGINEERING
UserName=MARGARET
logonvalidated=no
reconnect=yes
Comment=
EnableSharing=1
multinet=netware
reshare=yes

[Password Lists]
*Shares=D:\WINDOWS\Shares.PWL
MARGARET=D:\WINDOWS\MARGARET.PWL

[NetWare]
NWShareHandles=FALSE
RestoreDrives=TRUE

Advice About Changing Configurations

Windows for Workgroups configurations can grow complex. In this chapter we highlighted the areas what can grow and change in your configurations. We recommend, however, if you are not experienced with PC configurations, you steer clear of making modifications to any of your configuration files. Look, but don't touch. This is an area that can confuse even the experts.

GLOSSARY of Terms

GLOSSARY

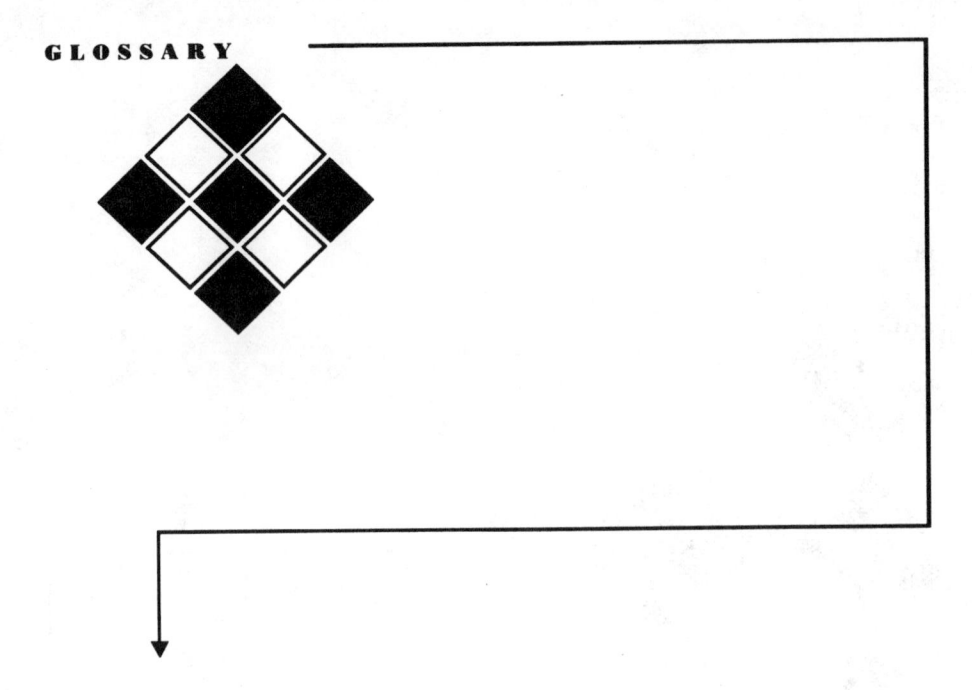

Active Hub: A networking device that connects the wires of a star-shaped network. Used most frequently with ArcNet LANs.

AppleTalk: A network protocol designed by Apple Computer, to be used for communication among Macintosh computers, printers, and other devices.

Application: A computer program used for a particular process, such as database management or word processing. "Program" is synonymous with application. *See also* Windows Application *and* Non-Windows Application.

Application Icon: A glyph that represents a running application. This icon will appear only after you start the application and then minimize (reduce) it.

Application icons also show up in the Program Manager. These icons do not represent running programs. Only icons on the desktop represent running programs.

Glossary

Application Switching: Moving from one application to another without closing the first application.

Application Shortcut Key: A key combination (keyboard shortcut) that brings an already running application to the foreground. Can be assigned through the Program Manager or in PIF (program information file). Application shortcut keys are different in the PIF and Program Manager. The shortcut key assigned in the PIF switches to the application (makes it active) once it is running. The Program Manager shortcut key will start an application. The Program Manager shortcut key only works while Program Manager is the active application.

Application Swap File: A temporary file that Windows uses to store a non-Windows application when you switch to another application. This leaves more room available in memory for running applications. Windows uses application swap files in standard mode only. *See also* swap file.

Application Window: The window that has the work area and menu bar with the application name on the top. Several document windows can be contained within an application.

Architecture: A set of rules for building programs, networks, or other structures. Networks and programs have architecture.

Archive: To back up old files and remove them from immediate access. They can be retrieved and used whenever necessary.

ArcNet: A network protocol standard that permits computer data, as well as voice or video information, to be carried across a network. It employs a token-passing star topology and is usually connected using coaxial cable.

ARROW Keys: Keyboard keys that let you navigate around the screen. Each one is marked with a directional arrow. There is an UP ARROW, DOWN ARROW, LEFT ARROW, and RIGHT ARROW key. *Also known as* direction keys.

ASCII Character Set: The American Standard Code for Information Interchange 7-bit character set. It consists of the first 128 (0-127) characters of the ANSI character set (American National Standards Institute 8-bit character set) and most other 8-bit character sets. The ASCII character set is the most universal character-coding set.

Assistant: In Schedule+, a person who is designated to work on your behalf.

Associate: To create a relationship between a file name extension and an application. The extension will belong to a certain application. From any OLE supported application, such as the File Manager or Mail system, opening a file with an extension that has been associated starts the application.

Association: A relationship between a file type and the application that created or reads the file.

Attributes: Specific information that is maintained about files. Attributes can show that the file is read only, hidden, or system, and whether it has been changed since it was last backed up. *See also* archive attribute, hidden file, read-only file, *and* system file.

AUTOEXEC.BAT File: A file with a set of commands that is automatically run by the operating system whenever the computer is started or restarted. The file generally contains basic commands that help configure the system.

Glossary

Automatic Link: A link whose Update option is set to automatic. When editing a linked object, the changes are made to the visual presentation (image) of the object in all documents that contain an automatic link to the object.

Background: An area in back of or outside the active window.

Background Application: An application that is running but is not active. The application is not available to receive input by the user but can still do work, like downloading a file. *See also* foreground application.

Base I/O Port: Base input/output port. An area of memory that must be set aside for the network interface card to work.

Base Memory Address: An area of memory used by some (but not all) network interface cards. Other adapter cards can use base memory addresses too.

Batch Program: A series of commands that are executed by the operating system. Batch programs carry a .BAT extension and are run under the MS-DOS operating system.

Baud Rate: A measurement of speed that is close to one bit per second. It is generally applied to modems: for example, a 2400 baud modem transfers information at approximately 2400 bits per second.

Binary File: A file containing information that is in machine-readable form. The file must have an application capable of reading its format in order for it to make sense.

Bitmap: An image stored as a pattern of dots (or pixels).

Boot: To start or restart your computer, loading the MS-DOS operating system from your hard disk or floppy disk. *See also* Floppy Disk, Hard Disk, System Disk. Boot comes from the term "bootstrap" — to lift yourself in the air by your boots.

Branch: A portion of the File Manager directory tree, representing a directory and any subdirectories within it.

Browse: To look through files and directories. Some dialog boxes have a Browse button, which opens another dialog box that lists files and directories for easy selection.

Buffer: A place (usually in the computer's memory) used to temporarily store information.

Carrier Sense Multiple Access/Collision Detection: A technique in which a station on a network determines that no other stations are communicating before it transmits data.

Cartridge Font: A font contained in a cartridge that plugs into your printer. Font cartridges are often used by laser printers such as the HP LaserJet. Some dot-matrix printers also use font cartridges. *See also* font cartridge

Cascade: An arrangement of open windows on the desktop so that they overlap each other, with the title bar of each window remaining visible.

Cascading Menu: A menu that opens from a command on another menu. This command will have a right arrow next to it.

Character Set: Letters, numbers, and symbols that have some relationship in common.

Glossary

Check Box: A small, square box that appears in a dialog box and that can be selected or cleared. A check box represents an option that you can turn on or off. An X appears in the box when the option is selected.

Choose: To use a keyboard or mouse to pick an item that begins an action in Windows. You choose commands on menus to perform tasks, and you choose icons to start applications.

Clear: To turn off an option by removing the X from the check box. You clear a check box by clicking the mouse, or selecting the option and pressing the spacebar.

Click: To press and release a mouse button quickly. Usually the left mouse button, unless otherwise noted.

Client/Server Network: A type of local area network that has at least one computer that is designated as the host computer for some or all of the network's applications.

Clipboard: A temporary storage location used to transfer data between documents and between applications. You can transfer data to the Clipboard by using an application's Copy or Cut command, and insert data from the Clipboard by using the application's Paste command. You use Clipboard Viewer to view the contents of the Clipboard.

ClipBook: A temporary storage area that can store multiple pages of information. A network version of the Clipboard.

ClipBook Viewer: The facility that allows you to view the contents of the ClipBook.

Close: To remove a dialog box or window, or quit an application. You can close a window by using the Close command on the Control menu. When you close an application window, you quit an application.

Color Scheme: A predefined combination of colors that Windows uses for its screen elements. You can create your own color scheme by using Control Panel or select a preexisting color scheme.

COM Port: A connection on a computer. A COM port is a serial communication channel. *See also* Serial Port.

Command: A word or phrase that you choose to carry out an action. You choose a command from a menu, or type a command at the MS-DOS prompt. You can also type a command in the Run dialog box in File Manager or Program Manager.

Command Button: A button that carries out an action. The command button is located in the dialog box and often has a label that describes the action to be carried out (i.e., Cancel, Help, or Install). Choosing a command button that is followed by an ellipsis (i.e., Browse...) causes another dialog box to appear.

Command Line: The commands you type to run an application. You can type the commands either in the Run dialog box in File Manager or Program Manager, or at the MS-DOS Prompt.

Command Prompt: The character or characters that appear at the beginning of the line, indicating that the computer is ready to receive input. *See also* MS-DOS Prompt.

Communications Settings: Settings that specify how information is transferred from your computer to a serial device (i.e., a printer or modem). *See also* Serial Port.

Compound Document: A document containing information created by using more than one application.

Concentrator: A centrally located device for connecting wires of a star shaped topology network. Concentrators serve as the traffic cop for managing network data. With a concentrator, all network segments are active at the same time. (For contention based networks, such as Ethernet.) *See also* Hub.

CONFIG.SYS File: A text file containing configuration commands used when starting your computer. Commands in the CONFIG.SYS file enable or disable system features, set limits on resources, and extend the operating-system functionality by loading device drivers.

Confirmation Message: A message that appears after you specify a certain action, prompting you to confirm the action and continue, or cancel the action. For example, File Manager displays a confirmation message before deleting a file.

Contention-Based Protocol Standard: A local area networking scheme in which all of the computers can communicate at once. Packets of information can literally collide on the network wire and be destroyed before they are delivered.

Control Menu: A menu containing commands allowing you to manipulate the window. Application icons and some dialog boxes also have a Control menu. To open the Control menu, use the Control menu box at the left of the title bar in a window, or select an application icon. *See also* Control Menu Box.

Control Menu Box: The icon that opens the Control menu for the window to the left of the title bar.

Conventional Memory: Up to the first 640K of memory in your computer, used by MS-DOS to run applications.

Copy: To put a copy of the selected text or item onto the Clipboard for transfer to another location. Most Windows applications have a Copy command on the Edit menu to perform this task. You can use the File Manager to copy entire files from one location to another.

CSMA/CD: *See* Carrier Sense Multiple Access/Collision Detection.

Current Directory: The directory you are working in. In File Manager, the current directory is selected (highlighted) in the directory tree.

Cursor: A flashing vertical bar in an application's window or in a dialog box. *See* Insertion Point.

Data File: Any file or document created within an application, for example, a word-processing document, spreadsheet, database file, or chart. *See also* Text File.

Dedicated File Server: A master computer that directs the network's operation and applications. It may not be used as a user workstation.

Default Button: In some dialog boxes, the command button that Windows automatically selects. It is identified by a bold border, indicating it will be chosen if you press ENTER. You can override a default button by choosing Cancel or another command button.

Default Printer: The printer automatically selected at the Print command if a specific printer is not selected. You can only have one default printer, chosen through the Control Panel or Print Manager. The default printer should be the printer you use most often.

Default Setting: Settings that are automatically supplied with Windows (i.e., margins are automatically selected unless you specify specific margin settings).

Glossary

Desktop: The background screen for Windows. This is where windows, icons, and dialog boxes appear.

Desktop Pattern: A design that appears across the desktop. You can create your own pattern by using Control Panel or choose a pattern provided by Windows.

Destination Directory: The directory designated to receive a selected file or files being copied or moved.

Destination Document: A document containing a link to an object in a source document.

Device: A component of the system's hardware configuration. Examples include the modem, printer, mouse, sound card, or disk drive.

Device Driver: Software that controls how a computer communicates with a device, such as a printer or mouse. A printer driver, for example, translates information from the computer into information the printer can understand.

Dialog Box: A window that appears to let you select options. It temporarily stores your responses and then carries out a command.

Dimmed: Unavailable or disabled. A dimmed button or command is displayed in light gray instead of black. A dimmed selection cannot be chosen.

Dip Switch: A small on-off switch located on a circuit board. Some network interface cards require you to set dip switches for settings like the IRQ or base memory address.

Direction Keys: Keys that indicate UP, DOWN, RIGHT, and LEFT. *See* ARROW Keys.

Directory: Place for saving and organizing your files on a disk. A directory can contain files and other directories (called subdirectories). The configuration of directories and subdirectories on a disk is called a directory tree. *See also* Directory Tree, Subdirectory.

Directory Icon: An icon that represents a directory (or folder) on your disk.

Directory Path: See Path.

Directory Tree: In File Manager, a graphical display of the directory structure of a disk. The directories on the disk are shown as a branching configuration that resembles a tree. The top-level directory is known as the root directory.

Directory Window: A File Manager window that displays the directory configuration of your disk and the files and directories on the disk.

Disk: A device (usually magnetic media) for storing information. Information stored on a disk remains permanent and intact when you turn your computer off. You can call this information up again. Information stored in memory (RAM) is lost when the computer is turned off. You cannot recall this information. A hard disk is permanently mounted inside its drive, but a floppy disk can be inserted and removed from a floppy disk drive.

Disk Cache: A fragment of memory set aside for temporarily holding information read from a disk.

Disk Drive: A device used for storing and retrieving information on disks.

Display Adapter: An adapter card that interrupts video signals and provides output to the monitor. Usually conforms to a standard, such as EGA, VGA or SVGA.

Document: Any information created in an application that you type, edit, view, or save (for example, a business report, spreadsheet, picture, or letter), and that is stored as a file on a disk.

Document File: A file whose extension has been associated with a specific application. For example, an .XLS file is frequently associated with the Excel spreadsheet. When you open a document file in File Manager, the associated application starts too, and loads with the file up and running. Opening a file in the File Manager causes the associated application to start.

Document-File Icon: In File Management, this icon represents a file that is associated with an application. Like document file, when you choose a document-file icon, the associated application starts and loads the file.

Document Window: A window within an application window. There can be multiple windows at one time. Some applications allow you to have multiple document windows.

Double-Click: To rapidly press and release a mouse button twice without moving the mouse. Double-clicking carries out an action, such as starting an application. The left mouse button is usually used unless you have a right-handed mouse.

Drag: The process of moving an item on the screen by selecting the item with the mouse and holding down the mouse button while moving the mouse. You can move a window to another location on the screen by dragging its title bar.

Drive: A mechanical device or a place in memory where data is stored. It is addressed by a letter of the alphabet such as A:, B:, C:, and so on. *See* disk drive and RAM drive.

Drive Icon: An icon that represents a disk drive. In the File Manager, icons for floppy disk drives, hard disk drives, network drives, RAM drives, and CD-ROM drives have a slightly different appearance.

Drive Letter: The letter assigned to a drive (i.e., C for hard disk drive, A or B for floppy drives).

Driver: *See* Device Driver.

Dynamic Data Exchange (DDE): A protocol for the exchange of data between applications.

Embed: To insert information (an object) created in one application to a document in another application (e.g., graph into text). The embedded object can be edited directly from within the document. To embed, both applications must support object linking and embedding. *See also* Link and Object.

Embedded Object: Information or data created in one application and inserted into another document. Embedded objects can be edited from within the destination (receiving) document. *See also* Linked Object.

EMS Memory: *See* Expanded Memory.

Emulation Mode: A mode in which a device such as a printer can emulate the actions of another. For example, an Epson printer could be set in the HP LaserJet emulation mode to make it accept the commands for an HP LaserJet.

Ethernet: A network protocol standard that permits computer data, as well as audio and video information, to be carried across a network. It was originally developed by Xerox.

Executable File: A program file. Stores the actual machine-readable code that is the application.

GLOSSARY

Expanded Memory: Memory in addition to conventional memory that some non-Windows applications use. Expanded memory is an older standard being replaced by the use of extended memory. Only EMS-compatible software can use expanded memory. Windows running in 386 Enhanced mode simulates expanded memory for applications that need it. *Also known as* EMS memory.

Extend Selection: To select more than one item. In File Manager, for example, a group of files can be selected to be moved or copied.

Extended Memory: Memory beyond 1 megabyte (MB) in 80286, 80386, 80486 computers. Windows uses extended memory to manage and run applications. Extended memory typically is not available to non-Windows applications. *See also* XMS Memory.

Extended-Memory Manager: A program designed to prevent different applications from using the same part of extended memory at the same time. HIMEM.SYS is Windows for Workgroups (and Microsoft's) Extended Memory Manager.

Extension: The period and up to three characters at the end of a file name. An extension usually identifies the kind of information a file contains. For example, files created with Windows for Workgroups' Calendar have the extension .CAL.

FDDI: Fiber Distributed Data Interface. A high-speed protocol standard for sending network data over fiber (not copper) cabling.

File: A collection of information (document or application) that has been given a name and is stored on a disk.

File Attribute: See Attributes.

File Name: The name of a file. Windows for Workgroups uses MS-DOS naming conventions.

File Name Extension: See Extension.

File Server: A computer on a network that is dedicated to managing file access requests.

Fixed Disk: See Hard Disk.

Firmware: Software that is designed for a specific task and built into a computer system's read-only memory (ROM).

Floppy Disk: A removable disk that can be inserted in the floppy disk drive. *See* Hard Disk and Disk Drive.

Flow Control: The processes used to regulate the transfer of information from one device to another. One device sends a signal to the other when information can be transferred. (Usually used with modems and communication software.) *Also known as* handshake.

Font: A set of letters, numbers, punctuation marks, and symbols that are a given size and design.

Font cartridge: A plug in cartridge for printers that contains special printing fonts. Font cartridges are often used by laser printers such as the HP LaserJet. Some dot-matrix printers also use font cartridges.

Foreground: The area of the screen that the active window occupies. *See also* Background.

Foreground Application: The application you are working with that appears in the active window. *See also* Background Application.

Format: The way text or data is set up on a page. The way information is structured in a file. To prepare a floppy disk to hold information. Formatting a disk deletes all information that was previously on it. Be careful not to format the hard disk.

Glossary

Full-Screen Application: A non-Windows application that is displayed in the entire screen. You can specify whether a non-Windows application runs in a full screen or a window by modifying the PIF or using the Control menu. *See also* PIF.

Graphics Mode: The mode that enables applications to display images in addition to text. Windows applications always run in graphics mode. Non-Windows applications can run in either graphics or text mode.

Graphics Resolution: The level of quality at which the program prints graphics. The higher the resolution, the better the quality of printed graphics. Higher-resolution graphics take longer to print and use more disk-space and memory.

Group Icon: The icon that represents a group in Program Manager when the group window is reduced. To open a group and view its contents, you double-click the group icon.

Groupware: A class of software that allows coworkers to interact via a network. Common components of groupware software are electronic mail, personal and group calendars and schedulers, task or project management aids, and document and file management.

Group Window: A window that displays the items in a group (accessories, applications, or documents) within Program Manager.

Hard Disk: A disk that is permanently mounted in its drive (fixed disk). *See also* Floppy Disk *and* Disk Drive.

Hardware: The equipment that makes up your computer system (i.e., keyboard, mouse, disk drives, and monitor).

Hidden File: A file that is not intended to be viewed in a directory listing (for example, a Windows swap file).

High Memory Area (HMA): The first 64K of extended memory.

Highlighting: Indicates that an object or text is selected. It appears in reverse video or in color on some monitors.

Hub: A centrally located device for connecting wires of a star-shaped topology network. Hubs serve as the traffic cop for managing network data. With a hub, only one send, and receiver are allowed to use the network at a time. (For token passing networks.) *See also* Concentrator.

Hypertext Form: The arrangement of information such that you can easily move from one subject to another.

I/O Address: Input/output locations used by a device such as a modem or printer.

Icons: Graphical representations of various elements in Windows (for example, disk drives, applications, embedded and linked objects, and documents).

IEEE: Institute of Electrical and Electronics Engineers.

Inactive Window: Any open window not currently being used. Also known as background window.

In box: The location where Mail places incoming messages.

Initialization Files: Files with the extension .INI that contain information that defines your Windows environment. Windows and applications use the information stored in these files.

Insertion Point: The place information (data/text) will be inserted when you type. The insertion point usually appears as a flashing vertical bar (cursor).

Interface: The connection between two devices. Interfaces carry electronic impulses from one place to another. A hardware interface, for example, would connect a host computer to a computer, a modem, or other device.

Interrupt: A signal that a device sends to the computer when the device is ready to accept or send information. Also used when a device needs the computer's attention.

Interrupt Request Lines (IRQ): Hardware lines over which devices can send interrupts (signals). Usually, each device connected to the computer uses a different IRQ.

Jumper: A small set of pins on a computer card that allow for the change of certain settings, such as specifying an IRQ port or address. Jumpers are found on some network interface cards.

Keyboard Buffer: A temporary storage area in memory that keeps track of keys you typed, even if the computer did not immediately respond to the keys when typed.

Launch: To begin working with an application.

Linear Bus Topology: A network cabling scheme in which all stations are directly connected to one linear cable.

Link: A reference in a destination document to where an object exists in a source document (n). To create a reference in a destination document to an object in a source document (v). When linking an object, you insert a visual representation of it in the destination document. Editing can take place in the destination document. When you change the source document, the destination document is also changed. *See also* Embedded.

Linked Object: A visual presentation (icon, bitmap) of an object in a destination document.

List Box: A type of box that lists available choices within an application window or dialog box (for example, a list of files in a directory).

Local Area Network (LAN): A group of computers in close proximity that are connected so that they can communicate with one another and share applications, data, and peripheral devices.

Local Printer: A printer directly connected to one of the ports on your computer.

Logon: To establish a connection with the network and identify yourself to the network operating system.

Logon ID: The unique name assigned to a user to gain access to the network.

Low Memory: The first 640 kilobytes of a PC's RAM.

LPT Port: See Parallel Port.

Macro: In Recorder, a series of recorded keystrokes or mouse actions used to simplify procedures, such as printing a document. Recorder can be used to create macros.

Maximize: To enlarge an icon to an application, or to enlarge a window to its maximum size.

Maximize Button: The small box containing an up arrow at the right of the title bar. By clicking on this button, you can enlarge a window to its maximum size. Keyboard users can use the Maximize command on the Control menu.

Memory: A temporary storage area for information/applications, such as ROM, RAM, conventional memory, expanded memory, extended memory.

GLOSSARY

Memory-Resident Program: A program loaded into memory that is available while another application is active. Also known as a terminate-and-stay-resident (TSR) program. You load memory resident programs from DOS before you start Windows for Workgroups.

Menu: A list of available commands in an application window. You open a menu by selecting a menu name. The menu names appear in the menu bar close to the top of the window.

Menu Bar: The horizontal bar containing the names of the application's menu, which appears below the title bar.

Megabyte: An amount of information roughly equivalent to one million characters. *Also called* MB.

Minimize: To reduce an application to an icon.

Minimize Button: The small box containing the down arrow at the right of the title bar. By clicking on the minimize button, you can reduce the window to an icon. Keyboard users can use the Minimize command on the Control menu.

Modem: A communications device that enables a computer to transmit information over a telephone line.

Monospaced Font: A font whose characters have fixed widths, such as Courier. Each character is one space, the "m" is the same size as the "i."

Mouse: A pointing device used to move the pointer on the screen, choose commands, press buttons, select text, and so on. It typically rests on a desk surface and fits in the palm of your hand. In a Windows environment, the mouse includes at least two selection buttons for communicating your activities to the application. In other computer environments, such as Apple's Macintosh, there is only one selection button.

Mouse Pointer: The arrow-shaped cursor on the screen that follows the movement of a mouse (or other pointing device) and indicates which area of the screen will be affected when you press the mouse button. The pointer may change shape during certain tasks.

MS-DOS Prompt: At the MS-DOS command line, the character or characters that appear at the beginning of the line, indicating the computer is ready to receive input. *Also known as* the command prompt. (>)

Multitasking: A feature of the computer and its operating system that enables more than one application to run at the same time. Windows for Workgroups allows for multitasking.

Network: A group of computers connected by cables or other means and using software to enable them to share printers, disk drives, and information.

Network Drive: A disk drive, available to users on a network, where data files may be stored .

Network Interface Card (NIC): A printed circuit board installed in a PC that allows network stations to communicate with each other. *Also* "network adapter card" or NIC.

Network Operating System (NOS): The internal set of commands and instructions that directs a network's activities. Novell's NetWare, Banyan's Vines, Microsoft's LAN Manager are examples of client/server NOS. Windows for Workgroups is a peer-to-peer NOS.

Network Printer: A printer shared by multiple users over a network.

Network Topology: A network protocol or design that permits computer data, as well as audio and video information, to be carried across a network. The network interface cards (NICs) available for network

Glossary

printers use a variety of topologies, including Ethernet, Token Ring, and Apple Talk's Local Talk.

NIC: See Network Interface Card.

Non-Windows Application: A term referring to applications designed to run with MS-DOS but not specifically with Windows and that may be capable of taking full advantage of all Windows features, such as memory management.

Object: Information such as a drawing or chart that can be linked or embedded into another document.

Object Linking and Embedding (OLE): A way to transfer and share information between applications. OLE is frequently used to update documents or spreadsheets. Linking sets up a live connection between applications or users to update an object whenever the originating application makes a change. Embedding simply makes a copy of the object at the time it is inserted into the new document.

Option: A choice, either in a dialog box or MS-DOS command line. Used to control how a command is carried out. Usually, an option starts with a slash (/). For example, you may wish to start an application in a special mode. For example, you can force Windows to start in the standard mode by typing *WIN /S*. An Option is *also called* a switch.

Option Button: A small, round button that appears in a dialog box. Within a group of related option buttons, you can select only one.

Package: A small glyph (icon) that represents an embedded or linked object. When you choose the package, the application used to create the embedded or linked object opens and displays the text or graphics.

Parallel Interface: An interface between a computer and a printer in which the computer sends multiple bits of information to the printer simultaneously.

Parallel Printer: A printer with a parallel interface connected to a parallel port.

Parameter: Information added to the command that starts an application, such as a file name or any type of information.

Parity: A process for error-checking memory chips.

Passive Hub: A small wire connector that can be used to connect certain types of network cables. Usually found on ArcNet LANs.

Paste: To copy the contents of the Clipboard into an application or document. This command is found in the Edit menu.

Path: Specifies the location of a file within the directory tree (i.e., C:\WINDOWS\SYSTEM.INI). Path also is an MS-DOS environment variable that tells Windows for Workgroups where to look for executable programs.

Peer-to-Peer Network: A type of local area network in which there is no central host or server computer. All the connected PCs are able to communicate with each other directly.

Peripheral Device: An additional tool that is connected to a PC. Examples include the printer, plotter, mouse, and modem.

PIF (Program Information File): A file that provides information about how Windows should run a non-Windows application. You can use PIF to direct Windows to run a non-Windows application in a full screen rather than in a window, or to specify a startup directory.

Point: To move the pointer on the screen to the location you select.

Point Size: A standard size for the height of a printed character. A point equals 1/72 of an inch.

Pointer: The arrow-shaped cursor that follows the movement of the mouse. This indicates the area of the screen affected when the mouse is clicked.

Pointing Device: An input device you use to move the pointer on the screen, such as a mouse. This is used to choose commands, select text, press buttons, create drawings, etc.

Pop-Up Program: A memory-resident program loaded in memory, but not visible until a certain key combination is pressed or a certain event occurs.

Port: A connection or socket on the computer. Ports are used to connect printers, modems, monitors, or a mouse to your computer. Serial ports (COM) and parallel ports (LPT) are the most commonly used ports.

PostScript: A special printing definition language, developed by Adobe, that is understood by some printers.

Printer Driver: A program that controls interaction between the printer and computer. This program supplies Windows for Workgroups with information, such as printing interface, description of fonts, and features of the installed printer.

Printer Fonts: Fonts that are stored in your printer's memory, or soft fonts that are sent to your printer before a document is printed. Window's can only approximate the font's appearance on screen because the font is located in the printer.

Print Queue: A list of files that have been sent to a printer in the order they are received, including the file currently being printed.

Print Server: A network computer that is dedicated to managing requests for a printer.

Program File: An executable file that starts an application or program. A program file contains a file extension, such as .EXE, .PIF, .COM, or .BAT.

Program Group: A grouping of applications such that their icons all appear in the same window.

Program Items: The applications and documents that make up a group in Program Manager. Program items are represented as icons in a group window.

Program-Item Icon: The icon that represents an application or document in Program Manager. By choosing a program-item icon, you can start an application or open a document. To choose the icon, double-click the mouse or use the ARROW key to move the selection cursor to it, and then press ENTER.

Proportional Font: A font whose characters have varying widths, such as Times New Roman. A Courier font is not a proportional font.

Protected Mode: A computer's operating mode that is capable of addressing extended memory directly.

Protocol: A set of rules that define how computers communicate.

Protocol Standard: A standard method for computers to communicate, such as the Ethernet protocol standard or the Token Ring protocol standard.

Queue: See Print Queue.

Quick Format: Used to format a previously formatted disk, it deletes the file allocation table and root directory of a disk, making it appear empty, but it does not delete the file information on the disk or scan the disk for bad areas.

Glossary

Random Access Memory (RAM): The internal memory used by the computer to store data and programs during task execution.

RAM Drive: A portion of memory used as a hard disk drive. RAM drives are much faster than hard disks since computers read information faster from memory than from hard disks. Information on a RAM drive is lost when the computer is turned off. This is also known as a virtual drive.

Raster Font: See Screen Font.

Read Only: An attribute given to a file or directory so that others may view the information in the file or directory but not modify it.

Reduce: To minimize a window to an icon at the bottom of the desktop by using the Minimize button or the Minimize command. An application that has been minimized continues running, and you can select the icon to make it active again.

Resolution: The number of dots that make up an image on a screen or printer. The larger the number of dots, the higher the resolution.

Restore: To return a window to its previous size.

ROM (Read Only Memory): ROM is part of a computer's memory. It differs from RAM in that ROM cannot be rewritten and is not lost when a computer is turned off.

Root Directory: The top-level or main directory of a disk. The root directory is created when you format the disk, and from this directory you can create files and other directories.

Screen Font: The font that is displayed on your screen.

Screen Saver: A moving picture or pattern that appears on your screen when you have not used a keystroke or moved the mouse for a specified period of time. This is to prevent the image from being burned into the monitor screen.

Scroll: To move through a directory or text (up, down, right, or left) in order to see parts of the file or list that cannot fit on the screen.

Scroll Arrow: An arrow on either end of a scroll bar used to scroll through the contents of the window or list box.

Scroll Box: The small box that shows the position of information currently in the window or list box relative to the contents of the entire window.

Scroll Buffer: In Terminal, the buffer holds information that does not fit on the screen.

Select: To mark an item by clicking on it or pressing a key so that subsequent action can be carried out, such as cutting the information and placing it in the clipboard to be moved.

Selection Cursor: The device used to mark where you are in a window, menu, or dialog box. It can appear as a highlight or as a dotted rectangle around text.

Serial Interface: An interface between a computer and a peripheral (like a printer or modem) that allows single bits of information to be transmitted from the computer to the device.

Serial Printer: A printer that uses a serial interface, which you connect to a serial (COM) port.

GLOSSARY

Serial Port: A connection on a computer (COM1) where you plug in the cable for a serial device. Windows for Workgroups supports COM1 through COM4.

Server: A computer that provides disk space, printers, or other services to computers over a network.

Server Application: A Windows application that creates objects that can be linked and embedded into other documents.

Shortcut Key: A key or combination of keys you press to carry out a command or action. The key combination is listed to the right of the command name on the menu if a shortcut key exists (i.e., ALT+F4 closes the active application).

Sizing Buttons: The windows buttons on the upper-right-hand corner of the Windows screen. These buttons control whether the application is minimized, maximized, or set to a specific size.

Smart Hub: A wire connector for a LAN with built-in management tools. Smart hubs can generally report statistics about the number of packets they receive or turn themselves off if they detect a problem.

Soft Font: A font installed in your computer and sent to the printer before it can be printed. They are also referred to as downloadable fonts.

Software: The set of instructions loaded into your computer to make the hardware perform tasks. Programs, operating systems, device drivers, and applications are all software.

Source Directory: The directory where files are originally located before you move them.

Source Document: The document from which a linked object originates.

Special Characters: Characters that are not found on your computer's keyboard, but are accessible through Character Map, located in the Accessories group.

Split Bar: A bar that divides the window into two parts. An example of a split bar is in File Manager, where the directory tree is on the left and the contents of the current directory are on the right.

Standard Mode: A Windows operating mode that can be used with 80286, 80386, and 80486 computers. It provides access to extended memory and enables switching between non-Windows applications. It does not allow non-Windows applications to run in the background or provide virtual memory.

Star-Shaped Topology: A network cabling configuration in which one computer is designated as a central hub and all other stations are directly connected to it.

Status Bar: Usually located at the bottom of the window in File Manager, it shows the number of bytes available on the disk and the total disk capacity.

Subdirectory: A directory within a directory.

SVGA: Super Video Graphics Array. A definition for monitor resolution of greater than 640 x 480 pixels. SVGA can be 800 x 600 or 1024 x 768 pixels and can contain up to 256 colors.

Swap File: An area of your hard disk that is set aside for exclusive use by Windows in 386 Enhanced mode. Windows temporarily transfers information from memory to the swap file, freeing memory for other information. These files can be permanent or temporary.

Switch: See Options.

Glossary

System Disk: A disk containing MS-DOS system files required to start MS-DOS, also called the boot disk. You can have more than one system disk.

System Time: The time according to your computer's internal clock.

SYSTEM.INI File: A Windows initialization file that contains settings used to customize Windows for your system's hardware.

Task List: A window that shows all the applications running and enables you to switch between them. To open Task list, select SWITCH TO from the Control menu or press CTRL+ESC.

Terminal Emulation: In Terminal, a setting causing your computer to emulate a hardware terminal. This device permits displaying data received from a remote computer.

Terminate-and-Stay-Resident (TSR) Program: *See* Memory-Resident Program.

Text Box: In a dialog box, a box used to type information needed to carry out a command. The text box may contain text or may be blank when the dialog box is opened.

Text Editor: An application used to create, view, or modify text files. Notepad is an example of a text editor.

Text File: A file containing only letters, digits, and symbols, usually consisting of characters coded from the ASCII character set.

Text Mode: The mode that enables applications to display text but not graphic images.

Text Transfer: A procedure for transferring text files from Terminal to a remote computer.

Tile: An arrangement of windows in which all windows are visible, with each window taking up a portion of the screen.

Timeout: If a device is not performing a task, such as printing, the amount of time a computer should wait before detecting it as an error.

Time Slice: The amount of processor time allocated to an application. Each application can run for a specified amount of time before the next application takes control.

Title Bar: The horizontal bar located at the top of a window, containing the title of the window or dialog box. It can also contain the Control menu box and Maximize and Minimize buttons.

Token Passing Scheme: Each computer on the network has an individual turn to accept and relay information.

Token Ring: A network protocol standard that permits computer data, as well as audio and video information, to be carried across a network. It is both the physical wiring and access scheme whereby packets of data are relayed from station to station in a logical ring configuration.

Topology: The physical layout of the cabling for a network. Popular topologies are linear bus and star-shaped.

TrueType Fonts: Fonts that are scalable and sometimes generated as bitmaps or soft fonts, depending on the capabilities of the printer. TrueType fonts can be sized to any height, and print exactly as they appear on the screen.

Upper Memory Area: The 384K area of address space adjacent to the 640 K of conventional memory. This area is usually reserved for running your system's hardware because applications cannot store information in this area. This area may be used for running your monitor.

Upper Memory Blocks (UMBs): Areas of the upper memory that contain general-purpose memory used to hold device drivers or other memory-resident programs so more conventional memory space is available for applications.

VGA: Video Graphics Array. A definition for monitor resolution of 640 x 480 pixels.

Virtual Drive: *See* RAM drive.

Virtual Memory: A memory-management system used by Windows in 386 Enhanced mode the allows Windows to run as if there were more memory than is actually present. The amount of virtual memory available equals the amount of free RAM plus the amount of disk space allocated to a swap file that Windows uses to simulate additional RAM.

Volume label: A name that identifies a disk and appears in the title bar of a directory window in File Manager.

Wallpaper: An image that is displayed on the Windows desktop background. Wallpaper can be custom made from graphics files, saved in the .BMP format.

WGPO Directory: The network directory that contains the workgroup Postoffice information. It is maintained by a designated system administrator.

Wide Area Network: A group of computers that are connected so that they can communicate and share applications, data, and peripheral devices. The computers are spread out in various geographical locations.

Wildcard: A character representing one or more other characters. In file names, the question mark (?) represents a single character and the asterisk (*) represents any character or group of characters that might match that position in other file names. "*" ignores the rest of the file name, so a*.EXE will match ABB.EXE and AC.EXE (i.e., *.EXE represents all files ending with the extension .EXE).

WIN.INI File: The initialization file for Windows that contains settings for your specific Windows environment. Certain Windows applications modify the WIN.INI file to add extra information that is used when you run those applications.

Window: A rectangular area on your screen in which you view an application or document. You can move, open, close, or change the size of most windows. You can also open several windows at one time, reduce a window to an icon, or enlarge it to fill the entire desktop. Windows can also be displayed within other windows.

Windows Application: A shorthand term for an application designed to run with Windows exclusively. They all follow similar conventions for arrangement of menus, style of dialog boxes, and use of the keyboard and mouse.

Windows Character Set: The character set, based on the ANSI character set, used to display Windows and Windows applications.

Word Wrap: A feature that automatically moves the text from the end of the line to the beginning of the next line.

Workgroup: The collection of people that you interact with on the job.

Workspace: The portion of the window displaying information contained in the application or document being used.

Glossary

XMS Memory: Extended memory that conforms to a specification developed by major PC software manufacturers. These can be accessed by using the eXtended Memory Specification from Lotus, Intel, Microsoft, and AST. Applications work with an extended-memory manager, which makes sure only one application is using a portion of memory at any one time.

INDEX

In this index, explanations of items are listed as **bold** page numbers and mentions of items are listed as roman page numbers. Figures are listed as *italics* page numbers.

A

Access Privileges. *See also* passwords; security for Schedule+, **121**
Accessories window, *141*. *See also* utilities
adapter cards. *See* network interface cards
address books, electronic, 286–287, 289
addresses. *See also* installation; SETUP
    in ArcNet LAN, 21
    for Base I/O port, **46–48**, 305–306, 308, **312**, 389
    in Ethernet LAN, 25
    for Mail, 109
administration. *See also* security
    for backup files, **183**, **189–191**
    of drive maps, 257
    of hard disks, **189–191**
    of network troubleshooting, **268–278**
    of peer-to-peer network, 15
    for Postoffice, **92–93**, **97–103**, *98*, **197–199**, *198*
    for security, 171, **174–176**
    of software, **194–195**
    of star-shaped topology, 19
    of training and support, **192–194**
    of Windows for Workgroups, 14
alarm, for urgent tasks, 118
ALT key
    for application switching, 231
    in dialog box, 333
    for DOS applications, 237–238
    and ENTER key, 330
    and ESC key, 327
    and F4 key, 330
    for macros, 159
    for Mail, 346
    for menu bar, 331
    for multitasking, 288
    and PRNTSCR key, 328
    in Program Manager, 339, 344
    for Schedule+, 116
    and spacebar, 329
    and TAB key, *326–327*
    for text functions, **336–337**
.AMI files, 294
Ami Pro, file association for, **294**
antiviral programs, **196**
application window, **58**, 387
applications. *See also* DOS; software; Windows software
    fast switching for, **231**, **288**, **326–327**, 387
    file associations for, **292–295**, *293*
    and multitasking, 287–288
    for networks, 16
    running full-screen, **242–243**
    security for, **176–177**
    starting, **65–66**
    troubleshooting, 275, **278–279**
Appointment window, *124*. *See also* Schedule+
appointments. *See also* Schedule+
    entering, **122–126**, 347
.ARC files, 135–137
architecture. *See also* protocol standards; topology
    ArcNet, **20–22**, 29, 387
    bus, **300–301**, *302*
    Ethernet, **22–26**, 29
    and LANs, **20–28**, 387
    planning for, 13–14

Token Ring, 19, **26–27**, 28, 29, 316–*317*
archive files. *See also* backup files
    and disk administration, 189, 387
    for Schedule+, **135–137**
ArcNet LAN
    cable for, **317**–*318*
    features and requirements, **20–22**, 387
arrow keys, **323**, 330, 332, 388
    in dialog box, 334
    in Program Manager, 338
    for text, **337–338**
.ASC files, 295
assistant, for Schedule+, 121–**122**, 129, 388
association, for files, **292–295**, *293*, *379*, 388
Attach window, for embedded files, **109**
Autodial, **146–147**. *See also* Cardfile
AUTOEXEC.BAT files. *See also* CONFIG.SYS files
    definition, **388**
    for NetWare, 256
    and Windows software, 43
    for Workgroup Connection, 363, **372–373**
Auto-Pick. *See also* Schedule+
    for meetings, **128**

B

backspace key, 324, 335. *See also* DEL key
backup files
    administration for, **183**, **189–191**
    and archive files, **135–137**, 189, 387
    compressing, 261
    creating, **185–187**, 288
    in NetWare LAN, 261
    strategy for, **181–183**
    systems for, **183–185**, **187–188**
    and viruses, 195–196
Base I/O port. *See also* network interface cards
    address for, **46–48**, 305–306, 308, **312**, 389

definition, **389**
base memory address, **47**
bit size. *See also* network interface cards
    in bus architecture, **302**
.BMP files
    for Paintbrush, 156
    for wallpaper, 230, 417
Borders, *58*
.BRO files, 295
Browse, 208
buffers, **190**
bus
    architecture for, **300–302**
    cable for, 18
business calendars. *See* calendars
business practice, and workgroups, 5–7

C

cable. *See also* hardware; hubs
    for ArcNet LAN, **21**, **317**–*318*
    coaxial, 23–25
    for Ethernet LAN, 19, **23–25**, **315–317**, *316*
    fiber optic, 21, **23–24**
    installing, **24–25**, 39–40, **304–305**
    for linear-bus LAN, *18*
    and network interface cards, 21
    for network setup, 13, 30
    for star-shaped LAN, *19*–20, 21
    terminators for, 316
    for Token Ring LAN, **27**
    tools for, **302–303**
    troubleshooting, **269**, **274**
    trunk, 18
    unshielded twisted pair, 19, 21, **23–27**
cache, **242**, 373. *See also* hard disk
Calculator, 285. *See also* utilities
    scientific view, **149**–*150*
    standard view, **148**–*149*
calendars. *See also* Schedule+

INDEX

electronic, 3, 6, 285
  sharing, 117, **129–130**
Cardfile
  card creation, 142–**143**
  Help window, *328*
  index for, **143**–*144*
  searching, **145**
  shortcut keys, **351**
  sound and pictures in, **145**–*146*
  for telephone dialing, **146–148**, *147*
  viewing cards, *144*
carrier sense multiple access/collision detection (CSMA/CD), in Ethernet LAN, 23, 390
cascading windows, 339, 390
Character Map. *See also* utilities
  features, **154**–*155*, 351
  for special characters, 414
character styles. *See also* Write
  selecting, *348*–**349**
charts. *See also* Paintbrush
  creating, *349*
Chat. *See also* Mail; utilities
  using, **150**–*152*, *151*, **352**
choosing. *See also* selecting
  procedure for, **60–61**, 391
client-server network, 15–**16**, 29, 391
Clipboard
  and ClipBook, **81–82**
  copying text to, 336
  PRNTSCR key for, 328
ClipBook. *See also* graphics
  and Clipboard, **81–82**
  features and tools, **85–86**, 391
  multiple open, *84*
  for sharing documents, **81–85**, *86*
ClipBook Viewer, 81, 289, 345, 391
  for document linking, **164–166**
Clock. *See also* utilities
  adjusting, **233**, **236–237**, *329*, *343*–344
  displaying, **141**–*142*

closing
  applications, 332, 391
  dialog box, 335
  Program Manager, 339, 344
  window, 330, 339
coaxial cable. *See also* cable; RG-62 cable
  for Ethernet LAN, 23–25
Color box, *225*
colors, changing for background, **223–227**, 343
COM2 port, 273, 392
Comment, for directory names, 69, 71
comments, for workgroup names, 206
compatibility
  in Ethernet LAN, 26
  for GUI, 41
  of network interface cards, 301
  planning for, 13
  of Windows for Workgroups, **48**–*49*
compression
  for backup files, 261
  for Mail system, **197–199**, *198*
  for swap files, 247
computers, 4, 7–8. *See also* file servers; hard disk; memory
  bus architecture, **300**–*301*
  choosing for LAN, **28–29**, 358
  486-class, **211**
  IBM, 26–28, 300–301
  LAN memory requirements, **29**
  location for, **30**, **284**
  names for, **38–39**
  for Postoffice, **93–94**, 290
  print servers, **210**, 263, 290
  286-class, **28**, **40–41**, **209**
  386-class, **209**, 211, 343–344
  troubleshooting, **273–275**
  UNIX-based, 37
  and viruses, **195–196**
concentrators, 316–*317*, 393. *See also* Ethernet LAN

CONFIG.SYS files, 393
   for NetWare, **256–257**
   and Windows software, **43**
   for Workgroup Connection, 363, **369–372**
configurations. *See also* installation; SETUP
   for hardware, **308**
   for network interface cards, **305–310**, *306–308*, 315
Connect Network Drive box, *206*, *214*, *218*
Connect Network Printer box, *78*. *See also* printers; sharing
connecting and disconnecting, **67**. *See also* sharing
contention-based protocol. *See also* protocol standards
   for Ethernet LAN, **23**
Control Menu box, **58–59**, 393
Control Panel window, *224*, **343–344**
copying
   and pasting, **85**, 336, 394
   text to Clipboard, 336
costs
   for ArcNet LAN, **21**
   for Ethernet LAN, **23**
   for network installation, 20
   for Token Ring LAN, **26**
CSMA/CD. *See* carrier sense multiple access/collision detection
CTRL key
   for cursor movement, **337–338**
   in dialog box, 334
   and ESC key, 327
   and F4 key, 330
   for Mail, **345–346**
   in Program Manager, **338–339**
   for Schedule+, **346–348**
   for selecting items, 61, 324
   for Task List, 288
   for text, **336–337**
cursor
   adjusting blink rate, **232–233**
   moving, **323–324, 337–338**
cut and copy, **81–82**. *See also* ClipBook

D

Datapoint LAN, 21. *See also* ArcNet
date. *See also* Clock
   changing, **233**, *343–344*
   for notes, **350**
DDE. *See* Network Dynamic Data Exchange
default devices, 394
default values, overriding, **50**
defragmentation utility, **191–192**, 247
DEL key, 325, 336. *See also* backspace key
   in Control Panel, *343–344*
department organization. *See* organization
desktop. *See also* screen
   color selection, **223–227**
   manipulating, *343*
   pattern selection, **227–231**, *228–229*
Desktop box, *228*, *333*, 395
device driver. *See* drivers
diagnosis. *See* administration; troubleshooting
dialog boxes
   closing, 335
   key function in, 332–335, *333*, 395
direction keys. *See* arrow keys
directories. *See also* drive letters; File Manager; files
   default setting for, **49–50**
   drive letters for, 71–72
   security for, **174–176**
   sharing, **66–67, 69–73**, *70*, *72*, **174**
   structure for, *67–68*, 396, 411
   and subdirectories, **67–69**, *68*
   in Windows for Workgroups, 43–44
directory tree box functions, *340–341*. *See also* File Manager
disk. *See* hard disk; floppy disk
disk compression. *See* compression
.DOC files, 292, 294

INDEX

Document window, 58, *331*–332
documents. *See also* text; Write
    linking and embedding, 163–166, *164–165*
    management of, 6, 14
    printing control for, 79, *80–81*
    sharing, 81–87, *83–86*
DOS. *See also* Workgroup Connection
    AUTOEXEC.BAT files, *363*, **372–373**
    and backup files, 188
    CONFIG.SYS files, *363*, **369–372**, *370*
    and defragmentation programs, **192**
DOS prompt in windows, *238*
    for drive letters, 254
    keyboard functions for, **326–327**, *329*, 330, 332
    in Print Manager, 76
    and security, 171
    in SETUP, 42, 50
    troubleshooting, **274**, **276**, **278**
    in Windows, 37, **237–240**, **242–243**
drive box, 342. *See also* File Manager
drive letters. *See also* directories; sharing
    assigning, **254–258**
    for directory access, 71–72
    for Windows and NetWare, **253–254**
drive mappings, in Novell LAN, **257**
drive pointers. *See* drive letters
drivers. *See also* CONFIG.SYS files
    installation and removal, **45–47**, 343–344
    for network support, 49
    for printers, 77, 409
    troubleshooting, *278*
    for Windows and NetWare, **252–253**

E

Edit window, *331*–332
editing text. *See also* text; Write
    keys for, **335–337**
    SysEd for, **369**

efficiency, in networks, 3, 13–14, 20
EISA. *See* Enhanced Industry Standard Architecture
electromagnetic interference, shielded cable for, **27**
e-mail. *See also* Mail; Postoffice
    procedure for, **90–93**
embedding objects. *See* object linking and embedding
Enhanced Industry Standard Architecture (EISA), for computer bus, **300**–*301*, *302*, 314
ENTER key, 324, 332
    and ALT key, 330
    for choosing items, 61
    in Windows, 44, 45
ESC key, 324, 332
    and ALT key, 327
    and CTRL key, *327*
    in dialog box, 335
Ethernet LAN
    cable requirements, 19, **315–317**, *316*
    features, **22–26**, 28, 398
Excel, file extension for, *292*
expansion card, *301*. *See also* network interface card
expansion of LAN, planning for, 19, 22, 24, 28, 37, 207
expansion slots, *313–315*. *See also* network interface card
extensions. *See also* files; names
    and file names, 291–295, *292–294*

F

F5 key, for print files, 344
failure of network. *See* troubleshooting
.FAX files, 295
fiber-optic cable. *See also* cable
    for ArcNet LAN, 21

for Ethernet LAN, 23–**24**
fields. *See also* dialog box
  in dialog box, *333*
  key functions in, 334
File List box, **341–342**
File Manager. *See also* files
  Associate window, *293*, *379*
  directory tree box, **340–341**
File Manager tools, *74*
  saving positions in, 63
  for sharing directories, **69–71**, *70*
  for sharing files, 56, **66**–*67*
  shortcut keys for, **339–342**, *340*
  starting, **65–66**
  using, **339–340**, 342
File Manager window, *190*
file servers. *See also* Novell NetWare LAN
  and backup files, 185
  for peer-to-peer network, 15, 394
  software installation for, **261–262**
  and workstation speed, 210
file sharing
  in peer-to-peer network, 15
  and 286-class PCs, 28, 41
files. *See also* backup files; swap files
  ASCII, 295, 388
  association for, **292–295**, *293*, *379*, 388
  compressing, **197–199**, *198*, 261
  large files, **210**
  names and extensions, **291–295**
  sharing, **66–67**, **71–74**
  sorting and viewing, **74**
  and viruses, **195–196**
floor plans, for network planning, **39–40**
floppy disk. *See also* hard disk
  LAN requirements for, **41**
  486 computers, for calculations, **211**
Font Selection window, *241*
fonts. *See also* text
  adding and removing, *343*

cartridges for, **390**
changing in DOS, **240–241**
and Character Map, 155
monospaced, **405**
proportional, **410**
screen, **411**
soft, **413**
TrueType, **416**
function keys, 328–330. *See also* specific keys

G

games, for Windows, 353–*355*, *354*
graphical user interface (GUI), 4, 41, 44. *See also* screen
graphics adapters, for LANs, **30**, 41
graphics printing. *See also* printers
  print server for, 210
Graphics Viewer, **160**–*161*. *See also* utilities
groups. *See* workgroups; Program Groups
groupware, 6, 401. *See also* software
GUI. *See* graphical user interface

H

hard disks. *See also* backup files; floppy disk; memory
  administration for, **189–191**, *190*
  defragmenting, **191–192**, 247
  disk cache for, **242**, 373
  disk space and file size, 211, **247–248**, 278
  LAN space requirements, **29**, 41
  in peer-to-peer network, 14, 15
  Postoffice requirements, *94*
  SETUP requirements, **44**
  and viruses, **195–196**
hardware. *See also* cable; installation; network interface card

INDEX

configuring, 194–195, *306–308*
installing, **302–318**
for LAN startup, 13–14, **31–32**
Hearts, **354**–*355*
Help line, for manufacturer's support, 271, **279**
Help system
    F1 key for, *328*
    using, *64*–**65**
hemostats. *See also* tools
    for jumpers, **303**
home key, in dialog box, 334
HP LaserJet, 30
HSL color creation, **227**. *See also* colors
hubs. *See also* cable; hardware
    active, 386
    for ArcNet LAN, 21, **22**, **317–318**
    for Ethernet LAN, **25**
    passive, 22
    smart, 27, 413
    in star-shaped LAN, *19*–20, 402
    for Token Ring LAN, 27

I

I/O port. *See* Base I/O port
IBM 3270 type terminal, and RG-62 cable, 21
IBM computers
    and MCA bus architecture, 300–301
    and Token Ring LAN, 26–28, 29
icons
    for appointments, **130**
    for Chat, 151
    choosing and selecting, **60–62**, 296
    for Clock, **142**
    in Control Panel window, *343*
    creation in SETUP, **49**
    in File Manager, *74*
    for Mail, *106*
    in Program Manager, 338
    programs as, **223**–*224*, 288, 386
    for Schedule+, 119–*120*
    for sharing resources, *67*
    spacing for, **232**
IEEE. *See* Institute of Electrical and Electronics Engineers
index, in Cardfile, 143–*144*
Industry Standard Architecture (ISA), for computer bus, **300**–*301*, *302*, 314
information input, and workgroup organization, 203–205
information services departments, 5, 8
information technology, 4, 7
.INI files
    in Express SETUP, 43
    for Mail, 95, 103, **260**
    SYSTEM.INI file, **380–383**, 415
    WIN.INI file, **373–379**, 418
    for Workgroup Connection, 369
INSERT key, 325
installation. *See also* planning; software
    cable, **24–25**, **304–305**
    consultants for, 271–272
    diagnostic software for, **318–319**
    file server software, **261–262**
    floor plans for, 39–40
    hardware, **302–318**
    linear-bus LAN, *18*
    Mail, **92–102**
    of network drivers, **45–47**, 343–344
    network interface cards, 305–*315*, *306–308*, *310–314*
    peer-to-peer network, 15
    Postoffice, **92–102**
    printers, **45**
    software, 14, **261–263**, 319
    star-shaped LAN, *19*–20
    troubleshooting, **269–275**
    Windows for Workgroups, 14, **42–51**, **235**,

265, 291, 307
  Workgroup Connection, 359–364, *360–363*
Institute of Electrical and Electronics
    Engineers (IEEE), Ethernet
    standard, 23
International box, *234*
  and Control Panel, *343–344*
interrupt request number (IRQ). *See also*
    network interface cards
  assigning value for, **305–310**, *306–308*
  in SETUP program, *46–48*
  for standard devices, **310**, 403
interrupts, 42
IRQ. *See* interrupt request number
ISA. *See* Industry Standard Architecture

J

jumpers. *See also* network interface card
  configuring, *306–307*, 403
  tools for, 303

K

keyboard. *See also* specific keys
  function keys, **328–330**
  key functions, **323–325**
    repeating key delay, **233**, *343–344*

L

LAN. *See* local area networks
LAN Manager network
  naming conventions for, 39
  for non-DOS computers, 37
languages, support for, **233–***234*
layout. *See* topology

linear-bus topology. *See also* topology
  for Ethernet LAN, 24
  for small workgroups, *18*
linking objects. *See* object linking and
    embedding
local area networks (LANs). *See* networks
logon
  in NetWare and Windows, **258**, 372
  and passwords, 171, 404
  for Workgroup Connection, *364*
Logon name. *See also* passwords; security
  selecting, *51*
Logon settings, *53*
low-level format, and viruses, 196
LPT port. *See also* printers
  for Novell LAN printers, **258**
  and print drivers, 77–79
.LST files, 295
.LTR files, 295

M

Mac computers, and networks, 37, 386
macros, recording, **158–160**, *159*, 350–351.
    See also utilities
magnetic tape. *See also* backup files
  for backup files, 184
Mail. *See also* Chat; passwords; Postoffice
  adding new users, **101–102**
  description, **90–92**, 345
  disk management for, **197–199**, *198*
  disk requirements for, *94*
  E-Mail window, *105*
  etiquette for, **111**
  installation, **92–102**
  key commands, **345–346**
  Mail icons, *106*
  message receiving, **109–110**
  message sending, **107–110**, *108*

INDEX

naming conventions for, **101–102**
and Personal Groups, 192–193
Send Note window, *108*
shortcut keys for, **345–346**
for 286-class computers, 41
using, **92–93**, **101–112**, 283, 285, 289, 296–297
in Workgroup Connection, **366**
and workgroup organization, 208
Main group. *See also* Program Manager
opening, 65, *339*
manuals
for hardware installation, 303
for troubleshooting, 269–270, 277
maximizing. *See* Minimize/Maximize buttons
MCA. *See* Micro Channel Architecture
Media Player, **352**. *See also* sound
meetings. *See* Schedule+
memory. *See also* hard disk
and address settings, 47
applications requirements, **239**, **241**, 278
base memory address, **47**
and color selection, 231
expanded, 399
LAN requirements, **29**, 41, **241**, 296
large file requirements, **210**
and low memory programs, 242, 245
for NetWare LAN, **264–265**
printer requirements, 277
and swap files, **245–247**
memory-resident program, **242**, 405
Menu bar, *58–59*, 405
menus, key functions for, *331–332*
Micro Channel Architecture (MCA), for computer bus, 300–*301*, *302*, 314
Microsoft, support phone number, 279
Microsoft Diagnostics, for interrupts inventory, 42
Microsoft LAN Manager
and Postoffice setup, 97

and Windows for Workgroups, 14
Minesweeper, **353**–*354*
Minimize/Maximize buttons, *58–59*
maximizing procedure, **61–62**
minimizing procedure, **62**
for multitasking, 287–288, 296
and program icons, 223–*224*
restoring procedure, **62**
Run Minimized feature, **236**
for shared ClipBooks, *84*
modem
for Autodial, 146–*148*, 405
baud rate for, 389
monitors. *See also* screen
for LANs, **30**
plasma display, **230**
mouse
adjusting response rate, **233**, *343*
driver for, 371, 373
keystroke alternatives for, **322–323**
tutorial for, **59–61**
MSAU. *See* multi-station access unit
MS-DOS. *See* DOS
multimedia. *See* sound
multi-station access unit (MSAU). *See also* hubs; Token Ring LAN
for Token Ring LAN, 27, 316–*317*
multitasking, **287–288**

N

names
for backup files, 185–*187*, *186*
for computers and users, **38–39**
for directories, **43–44**, **67–69**
for files, **291–292**
for Mail users, **101–102**
for Share Directory box, *70*
for shared directories, *73*

sorting files by, 74
for workgroups, 205–207, 206
NetWare network
   naming conventions for, 39
   for non-DOS computers, 37
NetWatcher, shortcut keys for, 353
Network Dynamic Data Exchange (DDE), 162, 398
network identification number. *See also* addresses
   in Ethernet LAN, 25
network interface cards (NIC). *See also* hardware
   for ArcNet LAN, 21
   compatibility for, 41
   configuring, 305–310, 306–308, 315
   driver installation, 45–47, 343–344
   for Ethernet LAN, 25
   installing, 305–315, 306–308, 310–314
   for NetWare and Windows, 253
   for Network Connection, 361
   for Token Ring LAN, 26, 27
   troubleshooting, 273–275
Network Settings box, 206, 244–245
networks. *See also* Windows for Workgroups; workgroups
   architectures for, 19–28, 284, 404
   compatibility of with Windows, 48–49
   consultants for, 271–272
   data transfer for, 350
   disk space requirements, 29, 41
   installation testing, 318–319
   and Mac computers, 37, 386
   and multitasking, 287–288
   name conventions for, 38–39
   NetWatcher for monitoring, 353
   peer-to-peer vs. client server, 16
   planning for, 12–14, 39–40
   resource allocation for, 208–211
   software options for, 31–32
   starter kits for, 14

systems inventory for, 40–42
topology for, 16, 17–20
and UNIX-based computers, 37
and viruses, 195–196
"New Society of Organizations, The", 7
NIC. *See* network interface cards
Norton Backup. *See also* backup files
   for file compression, 261
Norton Utilities, for interrupts inventory, 42
Notepad, 157, 285–286. *See also* utilities
   file extension for, 295
   shortcut keys for, 350
Novell NetWare LAN
   and ArcNet LAN, 22
   AUTOEXEC.BAT file modification, 256
   CONFIG.SYS file modification, 256–257
   drive letter assignment, 254–256
   drive mappings, 253–254, 257
   and Postoffice, 97, 259–260
   printer sharing, 258, 263
   and protocol standards, 29
   sample workgroup, 216–219, 217
   and Windows for Workgroups, 14, 17, 252–253

O

object linking and embedding (OLE), 163–166, 164–165, 407
   and ClipBook Viewer, 164–166
object moving, 323
offline work. *See also* Schedule+
   in Schedule+, 134–135
OLE. *See* object linking and embedding
operating systems, criteria for, 16
organization. *See also* directories
   for directory structure, 67–69, 68
   for Program Groups, 235
   for workgroups, 203–205, 207–208, 211
.OUT files, 295

INDEX

P

page up/down keys, 323
pages. *See also* documents; files
    sharing with ClipBook, 85–*86*
Paintbrush, **155–157**, *156*
    shortcut keys for, **349–350**
passwords. *See also* security
    defining, **51–53**, *52*
    establishing, **172–174**, *173*
    forgotten, **177–178**
    for Mail, **101**, 104
    in peer-to-peer network, 16
    for sharing directories, 71–*73*, *72*
    for sharing printers, *76*
Paste box, for ClipBook sharing, *85*
Path. *See also* names
    in Share Directory box, 70
patterns, changing, **227–231**
peer-to-peer network, **14–17**
performance. *See* speed
peripherals. *See also* hard disks; printers
    in Windows for Workgroups network, 14, 15
Personal Groups, **192–193**. *See also* administration
pictures. *See also* Cardfile
    for Cardfile, **145**–*146*
.PIF files, for DOS applications, 50, *238–239*, 243, 345, 408
planning. *See also* installation
    cable installation, 24, 304
    for LAN, **36–42**
    and networking architecture, **20–26**
    for networks, **12–14, 39–40**
    for productivity, **202–203**
    for workgroups, **37**
Planning window, 126–*127*. *See also* Schedule+
plasma display monitor, 230

ports. *See also* Base I/O port; COM2; LPT
    configuring, *343*
    for sharing printers, *78–79*
positioning. *See* windows; screen
Postoffice. *See also* Mail
    administration for, **92–93, 97–103**, *98*
    computers for, **93–94**, 290
    creating, **95–103**, *98*, *100*
    disk management for, **197–199**
    disk space for, **94**
    installation, **92–102**
    in NetWare LAN, 97, **259–260**
    and workgroup organization, 208
Postoffice Manager window, *100*
PostScript, for LAN printers, 30
PowerPoint, file extension for, *292*
.PPT files, 292
predictability
    of ArcNet LAN, 20
    of Ethernet LAN, 23
    of Token Ring LAN, 26
.PRG files, 295
Print Manager, 56, **75–81**
Print Manager window, *75*
Printer Connections screen, in Workgroup Connection, *365*
printers
    for Cardfile cards, **148**
    and Connect Network Printer box, *78*
    installing, **45**
    location for, 40, 209
    and LPT port, 77–79, *78*, 258
    names for, *39*
    network connections for, *343–344*
    print server for, **210, 263**, 290
    Printer Toolbar, *80–81*
    printing control for, **79–81**, 343–344
    security for, **176**
    sharing, 14, 30, 56, **75–81**, 258, 263, 365
    troubleshooting, **275–277**

privileges. *See* security; passwords
.PRO files, 295
process team structure, 5
product-centered organizations, 7
productivity
    and Mail, 297
    organization for, **202–203**
    workgroup habits for, 282–297
Professional Write, *294*
Program Groups
    description, 65, 410
    Startup Group selection, **235**
Program Item Properties box, *237*
Program Manager
    and sample desktop, 223–*224*
    and SETUP program, 49–*50*
    shortcut keys for, 338–*339*
    starting applications from, **65–66**
    for Windows, 57–59, *58*, *60*, *63*
project management. *See also* Schedule+
    groupware software for, 6
    and workgroup organization, 203–206
Properties option, and default directories, 49–*50*
protocol standards. *See also* architecture; topology
    ArcNet, 20–22
    choosing, **29**
    contention-based, **23**, 393
    Ethernet, 23–26
    for networks, 17
    token passing scheme, 20
    Token Ring, 22–28
.PW files, 294
.PWL files, for passwords, 177–178

R

RAM. *See* memory
Read-only privileges, for shared directories, 73
Recorder, **158–160**, *159*, 350–351
reduced instruction set computer (RISC). *See also* printers
    for LAN printers, **30**
.REF files, 295
reliability
    and cable installation, 24–25
    of passive hubs, 22
remote locations, network criteria for, **16**
Resource Kit utilities
    Graphics Viewer, **160**–*161*
    Top Desk, **161**–*162*
resource sharing. *See also* files; printers; sharing
    in peer-to-peer network, 14, 15
    for productivity, 202, 209–211
    scheduling for, 116, 130
    in 7-person workgroup, **214**–*215*
    in 3-person workgroup, **211**–*213*
    with 286 computers, 209
    WinMeter for monitoring, **243**–*244*
resources, allocation for, **202–203**
Restore button, procedure for, **62–***63*
RG-11 cable, for Ethernet LAN, **24**
RG-58 cable, for Ethernet LAN, **23**
RG-62 cable. *See also* cable; coaxial cable
    for ArcNet LAN, **21**
RGB color creation, **227**. *See also* colors
ring topology. *See also* topology
    and protocol standards, 17
RISC. *See* reduced instruction set computer
Rolodex files, for networks, **286–287**, 289
Run Minimized, **236**. *See also* Minimize/Maximize button

INDEX

S

safety, in cable installation, **24–25**
saving files. *See* backup files; archive files
Schedule+. *See also* Mail
    for appointments, **115–117, 122–126,** *123–125,* 133, 136
    archive function, **135–137**
    assistant for, **121–122, 129**
    Auto-Pick function, **128**
    key commands, **346–348**
    keystroke commands, **346–348**
    and Mail, **120**
    for meetings, **126–129,** *127,* 283
    for offline work, **134–135**
    Planner window, **117–***118*
    Print window, **133–***134*
    shortcut keys for, **346–348**
    Task List, **118–***119, 131–***133,** 286, 288
scheduling, in Windows for Workgroups, 14
screen. *See also* desktop; monitors; windows
    customizing, 61–64
screen savers, **231–232,** *343*
    update rate and colors, 231
    Scroll bar, description, *58–59*
security. *See also* backup files; passwords; sharing
    Access Type selection, *70–71*
    administration for, **171, 174–176**
    for applications, **176–177**
    for directories, **174–176**
    Logon Security, 172
    in NetWare LAN, **259**
    network criteria for, **16**
    for printer, **176**
    and Read Only access, **175–176**
    for resource scheduling, 130
    in Schedule+, **121**
selecting. *See also* choosing
    procedure for, **60–61,** 412

Send Note window, *108. See also* Mail
server-based network systems, 14
service-centered organizations, 7
SETUP. *See also* installation
    for network configuration, 306–307, 345
    troubleshooting, *273–274*
    in Windows for Workgroups, **42–50, 235,** 248, **273–274,** 345
    for Workgroup Connection, **359–364,** *360–363*
Share Directory box. *See also* directories; File Manager
    for sharing directories, 69–71, *70*
Share Printer box, *75–76. See also* Print Manager; printers
Shared Folders window, *198*
shareware and freeware, **166–168**
    and viruses, **195–196**
sharing. *See also* directories; files
    calendars, 117, 129
    directories, **66–67, 69–73,** *70, 72*
    disabling, *244*
    documents, **81–87,** *83–86*
    with File Manager, **66–67,** *72–73*
    printers, **75–81, 258, 263**
    in Schedule+, 120–122, *121*
    and viruses, **195–196**
    WinMeter analysis of, 243–*244*
    in Workgroup Connection, *359*
shell. *See* Program Manager; Windows software
shielded twisted pair cable (STP). *See also* unshielded twisted pair cable
    for Token Ring LAN, 27
SHIFT key
    in dialog box, *333,* 334–335
    for multiple items, 61
    in Program Manager, 339
    for text, 336

shortcut keys
    Cardfile, **351**
    cursor movement, **337–338**
    in dialog boxes, **332–335**, *333*
    File Manager, **339–342**, *340*
    for Mail, **345–346**
    in menus, *331–332*
    NetWatcher, **353**
    for non-mouse function, **322–323**
    Notepad, **350**
    Paintbrush, **349–350**
    Program Manager, **326–330, 338–339**
    for Schedule+, **346–348**
    Terminal program, **350**
    for Write, **348–349**
Show Printers screen, in Workgroup Connection, *365*
sizing. *See* windows
smart hubs, for Token Ring LAN, **27**
SmartDrive, and disk cache, **242**, 373
software. *See also* groupware; Windows software
    administration of, **194–195**
    diagnosis for, 19
    diagnostic, **318–319**
    file server, 261–262
    installing, 13–14, **261–263**, 319
    for network configuration, 306
    for network installation, 304
    options for networks, **31–32**
    troubleshooting, **269–270**, *273–275, 278*
Solitaire, **353**–*354*
sorting files. *See* files
sound. *See also* Cardfile
    for Cardfile, **145**–*146*
    configuring for, *343*–**344**, 352
    in Media Player, 352
spacebar
    and ALT key, *329*
    in dialog box, 334
speed. *See also* memory

for applications, **244–245**
of ArcNet LAN, 20
and colors choice, **231**
data processing, 4
of Datapoint LAN, 21
disabling sharing for, **244**
of Ethernet LAN, 20, 22
for graphics printing, 210
for LAN computers, 28
of Token Ring LAN, 20, 26, 27
standard 802.3, for Ethernet LAN, 23
standard 802.5, for Token Ring LAN, 26
star-shaped topology
    for ArcNet LAN, 21
    for Ethernet LAN, 23, 24, 26
    for network installation, *19–20*
    for Token Ring LAN, 26
starter kits, for networks, **14**
Startup Group, selecting for, 235
storage. *See* ClipBook
STP. *See* shielded twisted pair cable
support
    for Ethernet protocol, 23, 28
    for network standards, 22–23
    for other languages, 233–*234*
    for other networks by Windows, *49*
    for star-shaped topology, 19
    for Token Ring protocol, 26, 27, 28
    and training administration, **192–194**, *193*
    for troubleshooting, 271, 277
swap files. *See also* memory
    and disk space, 190–191
    permanent and temporary, **245–247**, 387, 414
switches. *See also* network interface card
    dip switches, 395
    for network configuration, *306–307*
symbols, inserting. *See* Character Map
SysEd text editor, 369
system keys, functions for, 325–*330, 326–329*

INDEX

T

TAB key, 324–325
    and ALT key, *326*–327
    and dialog box, *333*
    in Windows operation, 44
tasks. *See also* Schedule+
    and Task List, 118–*119*, *131*–133, 286, 288, *327*
technology. *See* hardware
Technology for Teams, 6
telephone lines. *See also* cable; unshielded twisted pair cable
    for Ethernet LAN, 24
    for peer-to-peer network, 16
telephone numbers. *See also* Cardfile
    Autodial for, 146–*147*
temporary files. *See also* swap files
    in Clipboard, **82**
    and hard disk space, **190–191**
Terminal (program), **350**
terminate and stay resident program (TSR), 405
termination, and network failure, 18
text. *See also* fonts; Write
    in charts, 350
    copying to Clipboard, 336
    cursor keys for, **337–338**
    editing in Notepad, 157
    editing keys for, **335–337**
    entering in Cardfile, 143
    manipulating, **348–349**
    in Paintbrush, 156
    pasting, 85, 336
    in Write, **152–154**, *153*
Text window, *335*, 415
Thin Ethernet. *See* Ethernet Lan
    386 computers
    Enhanced mode configuration, *343*–344
    and LANs, 209, 211

tiling, for windows, **339**, 416
time. *See also* Clock; date
    entering into notes, 350
Title bar, *58*, 416
token passing scheme. *See also* protocol standards; topology
    in ArcNet LAN, **20**
    in Token Ring LAN, **26**
Token Ring LAN
    cable requirements, 19, 316–*317*
    features and requirements, **26–27**, 28, 29
    and network topology, 17
Toolbar buttons, **67**
    for printer control, **80–81**
tools
    in ClipBook, **86**
    in File Manager, **74**
    for hardware installation, **302–304**
Top Desk, *161*–*162*. *See also* utilities
topology
    linear-bus, *18*, 304
    ring, *17*
    selecting, **13–14**, **17–20**, 28, 304
    star-shaped, *19*–20, 304
troubleshooting, **268–272**
    DOS, *274*, *276*, *278*
    installation issues, 272, **273–275**
    Microsoft telephone number, **279**
    printers, **275–277**
    software, 275, **278–279**
    star-shaped networks, 18–19
TSR. *See* terminate and stay resident program
tutorial for Windows
    after running SETUP, 50–51
    for mouse, **59–60**
    286 computers, and LANs, **28**, **40–41**, 209
twisted pair cable. *See* unshielded twisted pair cable

.TXT files, 295
type 1, 2 cable. *See* shielded twisted pair cable
type 3,4,5 cable. *See* unshielded twisted pair cable

U

UNIX-based computers, and networks, 37
unshielded twisted pair cable (UTP). *See also* cable
    for ArcNet LAN, **21**
    for Ethernet LAN, **23–26**
    for network installation, 19
    for Token Ring LAN, **27**
users
    choosing names for, 38–*39*
    for Mail, 92–93, 101–*105*, *104*
utilities. *See also* Windows for Workgroups
    Calculator, 148–*150*, *149*
    Cardfile, 142–148, *144*, *146–147*
    Character Map, 154–*155*
    Chat, **150**–*152*, *151*
    Clock, 141–*142*
    defragmentation, **191–192**, 247
    disk compression, 247, 261
    Graphics Viewer, **160**–*161*
    for network configuration, 306
    Notepad, **157**
    Paintbrush, **155–157**, *156*
    Quick Format, 410
    Recorder, **158–160**, *159*
    Resource Kit, **160–162**, *161*
    shareware and freeware, **166–168**
    for sharing resources, 66
    Softset, **318–319**
    Top Desk, **161**–*162*
    Write, **152–154**, *153*
UTP. *See* unshielded twisted pair cable

V

viewing files. *See* files
virtual memory. *See also* memory
    configuring for, *343–344*
    definition, 417
    and swap files, **245–247**
viruses, **195–196**

W

wallpaper. *See also* colors; patterns
    changing, **229–231**, 248, *343*
WAN. *See* wide area network
wide area network (WAN), and ArcNet LAN, 22
windows. *See also* screen
    positioning, **63–64**, 330
    sizing, **62–63**
Windows for Workgroups. *See also* software
    and ArcNet LAN, 20–22
    component removal, **248**
    configuring, *343–344*
    DOS applications in, **237–240**, **242–243**
    installing, **42–51**, 307
    and LAN architecture, **20–28**
    and multitasking, 287–288
    and Novell NetWare, 17
    security functions, **172–177**
    SETUP program, **42–50**, **235**, 248, **273–274**, 345
    software options, **31–32**
    system key functions, **325–330**, *326–329*
    system requirements, **40–42**
    troubleshooting, 272, 368–369
    utilities for, **56–57**
Windows software
    basics elements, **57–59**, *58*
    and DOS applications, 237–*241*, *238–240*

INDEX

    memory and disk requirements, 29
    network options, **31–32**
    Program Manager for, **56–66**, *58*, *60*, *63*
    and temporary files, 190–191
    troubleshooting, 275, *278*
    tutorial for, **50–51**
WinMeter window, **243**–*244*
wire centers, 18. *See also* hardware
wiring. *See* cable
Word for Windows, file extension for, *292*, *294*
word processing. *See* Write; text
WordPerfect, *294*
Workgroup Connection, **358–366**, *359–365*
    directory specification window, *360*
    installation, **359–364**, *360–363*
    starting, **364–365**
    Welcome screen, *360*
Workgroup Postoffice (WGPO). *See* Postoffice
workgroups, 2–6. *See also* networks
    adding members, **205**–*206*
    and Mail sharing, 96
    names for, **38–39**, 205–**207**, *206*
    network types for, **16**
    organizing, 37, **203–208**, 211
    planning for, **37**
    sample 3-person, **211–214**, *213*
    sample 7-person, **214**–*215*
    sample 15-person, **216–219**, *217*
Workspace
    customizing, **222–223**
    description, *58*–59, 418
.WPW files, 294
Write (word processor), **152–154**, *153*. *See also* fonts; text
    Edit and Document windows, *331*
    shortcut keys for, **348–349**
    Text window, *335*

X

.XLS files, 292

About the Authors

This book is the product of Currid & Company, a Houston-based information technology assessment group specializing in networking, client-server applications, mobile computing, and end-user computing. The contributors and authors to this book are:

An early pioneer with both Windows and networks in corporate environments, **Cheryl Currid** works with companies adopting new computing platforms. She has been a keynote speaker at major industry events and is an international lecturer on both technology and management. She writes regular columns for *InfoWorld* and *Network Computing* magazine and has coauthored two other Sybex books, *The Power Users Guide to RBase* and *Mastering Novell NetWare*.

Michael Ellerbe has specialized in LAN technology and computing environments for more than six years. He currently provides support on LAN design, installation, end-user education, and support.

Lenley Hensarling has over twelve years of experience in the software industry, ranging from the development of decision support systems to design of visual programming languages. He has focused on user interface issues seeking to broaden access to the power of computers.

Linda Musthaler is an industry analyst with Currid & Company. She focuses on specific technology adoption issues. Ms. Musthaler has been an information systems professional with a successful career in large corporate environments and the public sector.

Margaret Robbins is a software engineer with ten years of programming experience. She has spent the last three years at VideoTelecom, a manufacturer of multimedia conferencing systems. Her work focuses on making complex systems easier to use, and she has built several interfaces based on the direct-action graphical user interface model.

ClipBook Viewer Toolbar

Icon	Function
📖	Connect to another's ClipBook
📖	Disconnect from another's ClipBook
📄	Share a page from your ClipBook
📄	Stop sharing your ClipBook page
📋	Copy contents of page into Clipboard
📋	Paste Clipboard contents into a ClipBook page
✖	Delete a page from your ClipBook
🗒	Show ClipBook as a list
🖼	Show ClipBook as miniature pictures (Thumbnails)
🗔	Show a single page